CAMP MIMI

Leaving Legacies of Love, Experiences, and Faith for Children in Your Life

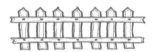

SIGNA BODISHBAUGH

Cover Design by Alex Bodishbaugh

Copyright © 2017 Signa Bodishbaugh

All rights reserved.

ISBN:-10:1548708674
ISBN-13:9781548708672

Dedicated to

Alex
Macy
Sophie
Caleb
Anna
Edie
Jake
Graham

our beloved BodishBabes

Other books by Signa Bodishbaugh

The Journey to Wholeness in Christ

Unterwegs zum neuen Menschen (German)

Op Weg Naar Heelheid In Christus (Dutch)

Putování za celistvostí v Kristu (Czech)

Illusions of Intimacy

Die große Illusion (German)

Intimiteit (Dutch)

Divine Conversations

Ich Will Dir Begegnen Und Mit Dir Reden (German)

Een Tas Gedroogde Shiitake Paddenstoelen (Dutch)

Camp Mimi (German)

CONTENTS

	Introduction	i
1	Manners	1
2	Around the World	17
3	The Tabernacle	39
4	Under the Sea	55
5	Journey to Israel	69
6	Heroes	101
7	Fearfully and Wonderfully Made	133
8	Camp Mimi Culinary School	173
9	Weather	221
10	BodishBabes in Bible Times	269
	Epilogue	311

Appendix
   Order for *Shabbat Shalom*
   Haggadah for Passover
   The Camp Mimi Song

Camp Mimi Eats

WHAT READERS ARE SAYING

Camp Mimi is a remarkably creative book by Signa Bodishaugh sharing ten very different summer camps with their grandchildren, where they imparted words and actions of life and truth. I particularly enjoyed the Camp Mimi where they 'took' their grandchildren to a different country each day, including Rwanda. Their Christ-centered faith shone through in unique ways that will inspire others seeking to impact children. Signa's many years in the healing ministry, with pioneers like Leanne Payne, shines through the entire *Mimi Camp* book. This is a book with practical wisdom on how to bring life, creativity, and healing to the children in one's life.

Rev. Dr. Ed Hird, Rector, St Simon's Church
North Vancouver, Canada
Author of Restoring Health: Body, Mind and Spirit

≈

What a pleasure it is to read, to savor, to reflect upon and, even to wonder how *Camp Mimi* could be adapted to other families. As a life-long learner, I appreciated the biblical scholarship coupled with relevant storytelling. The text of Scripture comes alive in the story of Signa's family camp(s).

As a grandfather, I was invited to consider how I/we might creatively impact our grandchildren in ways unique to our family but which could be used by the Holy Spirit in union with His creative activity in other families.

Thank you, Signa, once again, for sharing the goodness of the Kingdom of God with the greater Body of Christ.

Kevin and Laine Korver, Pastors, Third Reformed Church
Pella, Iowa USA

≈

This amazing book is full of creative lessons incorporating faith principles, life stories from the Bible, as well as personal experiences and practical activities to enthrall and engage your children in spirit, soul and body. It will help you to instruct, inspire and interact with the young ones. It will surely ignite your inventive skills. You yourself will become "like the owner of a house who brings out of the storeroom new treasures as well as old." (Matthew 13:52)

Moses and Cynthia Tay
7th Bishop of Singapore, 1st Archbishop of Province of Southeast Asia

≈

Signa did it again! Truly a book inspiring parents and grandparents to think about the relationship with their own (grand) children and the way they could learn and have fun together and at the same time invite the Lord into all their mutual undertakings in an honest and relaxed way.

Hans de Weerd Msc, BTh.
Teacher, Coach and Certified Pastoral Care Specialist, Founder of ConPas
The Netherlands

≈

This book is a treasure trove. Even more, a treasure chest for all those who work with children. Whether grandparents – such as the Bodishbaughs – whether parents, aunts and uncles, whether children, employees in the municipality, or educators and teachers. In *Camp Mimi* everyone can find spiritual inspiration, creative, child-friendly and loving ideas on how you can playfully convey knowledge and faith.

Signa and Conlee have prepared a spiritual heritage for their grandchildren in *Camp Mimi*. They now share it with us. What they have created is an inspiration for each person. Especially, in working with children, I recommend this spiritual treasure chest with all my heart.

Elke Werner
Consultant, Author, Leader of WINGS (Women in God's Service)
Germany (translated from German)

≈

As I read *Camp Mimi* amidst laughter, tears, and great delight, I found my own soul vicariously nourished and enlarged through Signa's shared legacy. More profoundly, I was deeply inspired to ponder and assess the unique things I'm passionate about. In doing so, I am now dreaming of intentional ways to engage my granddaughter and my future grandchildren; creating shared experiences that reinforce the precious and unique things I don't want lost from our heritage

This year we will grab our binoculars, boots, and journals and hold *our* first camp. The theme? Well….you'd have to show up for what Signa calls, "the big reveal" to discover.

Micki Ann Harris
Prayer Room and Spiritual Formation Director, Chattanooga House of Prayer
Chattanooga, Tennessee USA

≈

When Signa asked me to review *Camp Mimi*, I welcomed the opportunity. Having previously met the Bodishbaughs and received wonderful ministry at *The Journey to Wholeness* seminars, I was intrigued by the prospect of reading about how a couple like Signa and Conlee might engage their own grandchildren. Although I know of a few grandparents who do "camp" for their grandchildren, I have never heard of a couple who invested so much thought, prayer and preparation into an intentional week.

As Signa explains in the introduction, this is not a how-to manual. It is their story, filled with their experiences. The combination of content for the camps, the children's reactions, and some of the behind-the-scenes looks at their preparations do far more though than a simple how-to manual would. It gives a vision. Without a vision that something is possible, most often we won't attempt it.

Every grandparent or potential grandparent should read this book to ignite in their own heart a desire to bless their grandchildren. They have the same potential to hear from the Lord about how they can pass along a Godly heritage. Signa begins and ends by reminding you that you are unique. She doesn't share her story to tell you to do the same thing, or to feel guilty about doing something different. Instead, she seeks to inspire you to chart a course guided by prayer that will enable you to bless your own family in meaningful ways. I believe she has succeeded. May

many "camps" spring up around the land!
Rev. Mark Fesmire
Pastor, Grace Evangelical Free Church
Lynchburg, Virginia USA

≈

There is a deep desire in all of us to pass on our inheritance to the next generation, regardless if one has their own children. As a single woman, I was greatly interested in Signa's new book. *Camp Mimi* is full of creative ideas about how to share what God has entrusted to me. I already shared some of the stories with a small group and there was a great response.

Signa's style is very exciting, full of humor and wisdom. The pages are filled with much variety. There are stories from the Bible and from her own life, recipes for fine dining and quick snacking, and examples of the simplest things of life as well as the extravagant. I was very impressed by the ways Signa honored her grandchildren throughout the book, for example, by giving them full access to her china cabinet.

I have had the privilege to experience Signa as a captivating speaker and also the opportunity to visit with her and Conlee in their home on several occasions, always greatly enjoying their generous hospitality and fantastic cooking.

Camp Mimi encourages the reader to discover one's own treasures and make them available to others. Everyone is capable of sharing their blessings in unique ways to leave a legacy. I believe this book will light the fire in many people's hearts to do so.

Christiane Mack
President of Convita /NIS
Germany

≈

In amazement, I watched Signa over the years as she would run Camp Mimi!

The ideas she and Conlee incorporated were not only fun and creative but were foundational truths from God's Word. All her friends begged her to write a book about the experiences.

Last year I had enough participants for my own Camp Mimi. So I called Signa for help and fortunately she was able to send me the first three chapters of her book! Oh my! The kids are still talking about Camp Baldwin and asking for next summer's dates.

Signa has a recipe book for camp that is proven. Just season it to your own taste, add a heaping scoop of love, and *voila!* A life time of joyous memories are made!

Susan Baldwin
CEO, Woman's Resource Centers
Mobile, Alabama USA

≈

Families need grandparents! Each time we work together on a pastoral care conference, I am touched by Signa's enthusiasm, love, knowledge and in-depth walk with the Lord. The same enthusiasm and love vibrates in this book. She loves her grandchildren, she loves her husband, and above all, she passionately loves the

Lord Jesus. This book also breaths practicality. She is committed to good preparation, determination and effort. Year by year, the preparation of each camp seemed to become more elaborate and helpful in providing a week full of learning, adventures and fun.

This book also excels in family stories. Several of them were already known to me before, but I still love to read them because each story is authentic and displays Signa's positive approach even at unexpected and sometimes seemingly disappointing situations. One of them is the story of Signa and Conlee's trip to Puerto Peñasco in Mexico. This particular story especially gives a very precious and delicate view of her relationship with Conlee.

The book inspires me to think about my own still very young grandchildren. Although we live in different countries, and even on different continents, I feel very much connected with her approach and hope to use many ideas from this book and adapt them, together with my beloved husband, Hans, to my own family situation.

Annie de Weerd - van Leeuwen
Master Contextual Family Therapist, European Certified Individual and Family Therapist, Grief Therapist, and Supervisor at the University of Utrecht, Founder of ConPas
The Netherlands

≈

I would love to design a spiritually meaningful weekend — or a whole week of holidays – for my children, grandchildren, God children, children's group, etc. But how?

With this book Signa Bodishbaugh gives us a very inspiring collection of ideas and materials – an absolute treasure chest! It really makes one look forward to share times with one's future grandchildren! And, for a start, it doesn't have to be a full week.

Ursula Schmidt
Author of "Hörendes Gebet" and other books
Germany

≈

Camp Mimi! Every summer when Signa talked about preparing for Camp Mimi, I wanted to shrink and change my name to Bodishbaugh to join her happy camp. This book is not a "how to book" but rather a glimpse into the hearts of Loving Godly Grandparents giving their grandchildren the gift of legacy. You will enjoy their journey!

Nancy N. Gordon
Songwriter/Author/Speaker/Creator of Miss PattyCake, Mother's Heart Music
Fairhope, Alabama USA

≈

Signa Bodishbaugh has always had a special way of instilling faith, hope, and joy in all around her. When I learned she was planning to write the *Camp Mimi* book, I was thrilled. Over the years, as I had the opportunity to watch her lovingly prepare for the special week with her grandchildren and saw how much fun her grandchildren had, I often found myself wondering if I could try my hand at hosting a mini Camp Mimi of my own. After reading this book, I am looking forward to doing so.

Camp Mimi is a delightful and beautifully written book. I loved how the insightfully told Bible stories are meaningfully woven with Signa's family stories, and used as focal points in her Camp Mimi lessons and activities for her grandchildren. I also enjoyed reading about the practical rhythm for the Camp Mimi days and the loving tips she shares that helped things run smoothly.

Signa clearly shares how she filled their Camp Mimi week with lessons of truth, powerful stories, creative activities, fieldtrips, fun, and food in ways that engaged the hearts and minds of her grandchildren, filling them with a deep sense of their being loved by God and by their grandparents. Her book is a window into this part of her and Conlee's legacy of love for their grandchildren.

Signa's book encourages and inspires me to look for ways to creatively share my own faith, stories, and passions with the precious children and grandchildren in my life.

I highly recommend this book. I know each reader will be deeply blessed and encouraged, and in turn, will be inspired to share that blessing with the little ones God has put in their lives.

Thank you, Signa!
Judy Oschwald
W. C. Griggs Elementary School - Teacher of the Year 2016
Mobile, Alabama USA

INTRODUCTION

Dear Reader,

Before you begin reading my story about purposefully giving my most precious legacies to the children in my life, I want you to say to yourself,

"I am unique!"

No one else can tell your story like you can. The life lessons you have accumulated are rich and priceless, even the ones that hurt at the time. All of your experiences make you who you are today and no one can duplicate the uniqueness of *you*. Don't you think that makes it important to deliberately share with others the person you have become? Especially with those you love the most? And in particular, with those who are still impressionable and beginning to learn Godly values?

Camp Mimi is **NOT** a how-to book or a parenting book, nor do I offer lesson plans, many specific resources, or outlines. It **IS** a book to inspire! I want to inspire you to remember the life lessons that have made you the person you are today. While you read, pay attention to small, distant memories that pop up, seemingly insignificant details of your past experiences, and the stories that accompany both the most fun and the most poignant things you have done. What energizes you? What grabs your attention? Who are some of your favorite people and why? What are you passionate about?

Your responses will be varied, as mine are. That uniqueness celebrates our individuality that God imparts to each of us. Enjoy the opportunity to identify the various facets of your passions. You might be surprised!

All of your little memories and experiences add up to the unique life legacy you have to leave to someone. To whom are you going to leave it? It is not something you can include in a last will and testament. It is not something you can write in an autobiography. And yet, collectively, all of your experiences make you uniquely *you*. Who you are is too valuable to be forgotten one day. Make a plan to pass it on!

Camp Mimi is a fun, personal account of how I (called Mimi by my grandchildren) identified my favorite things and passions and then deliberately imparted them to the children in my life. My recipients just happened to be my grandchildren, whom we call the BodishBabes.

Above all else, the primary passion of my life is my faith, my relationship with Jesus Christ and my never-ending quest to grow in God's love. This colors all the rest. Everything we did at Camp Mimi was designed to reflect His abiding love. Therefore, the primary legacy my husband and I want to leave to our children and grandchildren is more than the impartation of their grandparents' personal interests; we want to leave them a legacy that is eternal.

Throughout the ten years my husband (Conlee to me and Papa to the children) and I hosted our summer Camp Mimi sessions, many friends wanted to bring their own grandchildren to participate with us. I chose to limit it exclusively to the BodishBabes, encouraging others to do something similar with their own family flavor. Many of them have done just that!

In Iowa, a grandmother started Camp Nana, beginning simply by sharing her love of gardening with her grandchildren, comparing it to the Biblical principle of sowing and reaping and the fruit of the Spirit.

In Michigan, grandparents transformed their annual extended family reunion to become Camp Baldwin (their last name). What had once been a time of free-falling activities on a lake, became structured and somewhat organized, involving heart-sharing conversations on various topics. They said it was the best reunion ever.

In Alabama, a friend, who is also known as Mimi to her grandchildren, began her own summer camp for them. Although she sees the children daily, their special Camp Mimi time was set apart for structured, themed projects, field trips, and Bible stories. They loved it!

Not restricted by having no children of her own, a single woman in the Netherlands, invites neighborhood children and children of friends into her home for "Time with Jetteke." She shares her love of God and the creative arts with them through numerous projects. They might spend a full day or even a week-end receiving her outpourings of attention and love through participating in the things that interest her most. When visiting in her home, we are always delighted at her childlike excitement as she shows us their latest projects. We have seen a dollhouse they constructed, paintings using several media, a small garden they designed, and a unique Medieval board game they made together.

It is not necessary to have special training in childhood education to do this. I don't have the training or the desire to teach children professionally. However, I am passionate about several subjects: God, the Bible, cooking, art, Hebrew, books, etc. I knew my children and grandchildren would not appreciate my passions by osmosis. Discovering Camp Mimi became a great vehicle for imparting what is in my heart

Don't think your plans have to be elaborate or complicated. Simple is good. The main goal should be your deliberate intention to lavish quality, uninterrupted attention on whomever God gives you to love.

Because God lavishes uninterrupted attention upon us, He has been my constant model. His extravagant outpourings of affection include rules, guidelines with flexibilities, plans, surprises, discipline, structure, joy, laughter, correction for wrong-doing, and incredible love. This describes Camp Mimi.

I hope that one day, when my grandchildren are grown with their own grandchildren, they will never have to say, "I wish I had known more about my Mimi, her life and her desires."

What are YOUR passions?

With whom are you going to share them?

Remember: *You are unique!*

Have fun!

Signa Bodishbaugh

CAMP MIMI ONE

MANNERS

"Guess what? I'm going to China this summer for a whole month!"

It was an exciting surprise to get such a phone call from our daughter-in-law, Margo. But the greater surprise came next.

"And, Mimi and Papa, would you please consider keeping Sophie for the month I'm gone?"

Sophie was five years old and the youngest of Matt's and Margo's three girls. It was easier to arrange care and activities for the two older girls, but Sophie was much too young to be taken somewhere every day while Matt was at work.

Of course, we said, "Yes!" but then wondered what in the world we would do with a female child for that length of time. Our three sons prepared us for the rough and tumble world of boys but we were totally ignorant about the long-term care, feeding, and entertainment for little girl interests and temperament. It was going to be a challenge.

Having grand-daughters was a wonder and a novelty to us, but we had always lived in another state and when we were together it was typically a whirlwind of activities for special occasions and holidays. We had no idea what *normal* looked like with a little girl in the house for as long as a month.

My husband was an only child and knew nothing about sisters. His initial contribution to the planning was, "You were a little girl. You should know what she'll like."

I reminded him that I, too, was an only child and, at my present age, could barely remember what I did when I was five. We were both convinced that we didn't want to park her in front of the TV all day. We had four months to figure it out, and in spite of our reservations, we were getting excited.

The good news was that we lived in a little cottage on Mobile Bay and had a pier and a boat. The bad news was that the water in the bay was not clean enough to swim in and we would only be able to use the boat on weekends when Conlee was home. The worst news was that July (the month she was to come) is unbearably hot outside in Mobile and we would need to do inside activities most of the time.

All of our brainstorming usually led down one path. *Wouldn't it be wonderful if we had a swimming pool?* But then practicality took over. A pool is expensive. There's a lot of upkeep. We would need a fence for protection. A child would need constant supervision. It was a big responsibility. It was a pipe dream.

As we entered June, only three weeks before Sophie was to come, the temperature was reaching 100+ degrees every day. One morning I sat fanning myself out on our back porch, looking longingly at the lawn, envisioning where a pool could be situated. On a whim, I took the phone book and looked in the yellow pages under "Swimming Pool Installation." *What could it hurt to just get an estimate?*

I started calling the list and got an answering machine each time, leaving my name and number. On the fifth call someone actually answered, "Bama Pools. This is Johnny."

Johnny turned out to be the owner who was working on a jobsite not too far from our house. He said he would come by after work, look at our location, and give me an estimate. As soon as I hung up, I thought, "What have I done?"

Johnny and I hit it off right away. He was a preacher in a small church on Sundays and installed pools during the week. He showed me pictures of some of his other installations and gave me a price far below what I expected. But I had to mention to him what I was sure would be the deal-breaker. "We must have the pool by July 4th!"

I couldn't believe his answer. "No problem. My equipment is not too far away. I can start here in two weeks and you'll be swimming three days from then."

Conlee also met with Johnny, loved his ideas, couldn't believe the reasonable price, and thought it was feasible for us to do it. Like me, however, he didn't expect that the equipment would actually be on the job in two weeks and finished in three days.

On the Fourth of July we were swimming in our pool with Matt, Margo, and our three grand-daughters! The next day they left Sophie with us and thus began the great adventure that became life-changing for our family.

Our time with Sophie was wonderful! She helped me cook. We taught her to swim, we painted, shopped, did our nails, styled hair, made paper dolls and designed their clothes, went to the library often, read tons of books, watched very little television, and laughed a lot. When we talked to Matt at night and Sophie told her daddy about all the fun things we were doing together each day he said, "Sophie, it's just like you've gone to camp – Camp Mimi." And so, the title was given. Little did we know it would evolve into an annual event for ten years and would become a Bodishbaugh family tradition!

Our oldest grandson, Caleb, is only three months younger than Sophie. The child of our youngest son, Ben, Caleb and his younger identical twin sisters and baby brother lived in Texas. Caleb and Sophie have always been almost like twins themselves, although they didn't get to see each other very often. When Caleb found out that Sophie was staying with Mimi and Papa for several weeks, he contrasted that with sharing his life with three younger siblings who demanded most of Mama's attention. He begged to come to Mobile, too. And so, it was decided that Caleb would come for a week to join Sophie.

Conlee and I began to brainstorm again as we prepared for Caleb's arrival. We couldn't just free-fall every day as we had been doing with Sophie. We knew we needed some plans and order in our daily activities with two five-year-olds to care for. We thought it would be fun to have a theme and, also, following Matt's idea, to call the whole week "Camp Mimi."

Conlee, Sophie and I worked on daily schedules, activities, and even surprises to enjoy when Caleb arrived. The whole "camp" idea took on a life of its own and provided a structure for us to have the opportunity to impart important values of ours to our grandchildren.

THE THEME

Conlee and I prayed a lot about what theme would be most appropriate for Sophie and Caleb to experience together that first summer. Our faith in God has always been the most important gift we have to share and we wanted to do it in an intentional and fun way. We also wanted to provide opportunities for the children to live out some of the principles that Jesus taught His disciples.

A scripture that kept coming to us was Luke 17:11-19. Conlee and I talked about it at length. It is the story of something that happened to Jesus as He walked along the border between Samaria and Galilee, on His way to

Jerusalem. In Jesus' time, the Samaria-Galilee border was a "no man's land" to Jews. Jews did not travel through Samaria because of old prejudices and a deep hatred for Samaritans. They took a much longer route to the east to get from Galilee to Jerusalem, just to avoid going through an area they considered unclean.

When Jesus arrived at this border, He was confronted by ten men who were lepers, plagued with a disease, perhaps not exactly what we think of as modern "leprosy," but a destructive skin infection that deemed them unclean from all of society.

For us, the lepers in Israel are the microcosmic example of how Jews at that time considered and treated all Samaritans. Jewish lepers could not live in villages, worship in the Temple, attend a synagogue, or have any semblance of a normal life. Their whole existence wasted away, just as the skin of their body rotted. Respecting the distance that was required when they approached other people, they yelled out to Jesus to take pity on them.

Jesus, always full of compassion, told them to go present themselves before the priest. The priest's examination and approval was the procedure the law required for one to re-enter society after such a skin disease was healed.

When they did what Jesus commanded, each one was healed! Their skin was renewed. Their status was changed. They were no longer outcasts. Each one was given a new life. This is the vibrant picture of each of us, rotting in our sins, calling out to Jesus, obeying Him, and receiving a whole new life!

In spite of such an amazing experience, only one of the ten who were healed returned to Jesus, praising God, throwing himself at His feet, filled with thanksgiving and gratitude. The ironic part of this story is that the one man who came back to Jesus in praise and thanksgiving was one of the despised Samaritans. He was the one whom every Jew would avoid. Yet, his heart was so filled with gratitude that he received more than a physical healing.

Jesus told him, "Rise up and go; your faith has made you *well (sozo* in Greek). This word *sozo* implies *saved, kept safe, rescued, restored to health*, and even *delivered from judgment*. This account shows us that gratitude to God brings many more blessings that what we know to ask for.

After Conlee and I read, discussed, and prayed about this account from Jesus' life and ministry, we each had lots of questions we shared with one another.

Are there people I avoid whom Jesus wants to help?
Are there people I don't like whom Jesus wants me to love?
Whom have I ignored?
Do I call out to Jesus for help?
Am I grateful for what He gives me?
Why is it important to say "thank you" to Him?

Is it enough to say the words or do I need a grateful attitude in my heart as well?

Why are good manners so important?

This early morning discussion between the two of us became the basis for choosing the theme of "Manners" for our first Camp Mimi. We wanted to impart to our BodishBabes that good manners are much more than just following a set of rules that parents and teachers give us. Manners show respect and give honor to others. They extend blessings to people. They open our own hearts to receive further blessings.

Our challenge was to present what God was showing us in a format that would be both exciting to five-year-olds and life-changing. A big order, but not impossible for our creative God!

RULES

I have to confess that I never attended a camp of any kind when I was a child. This was all new to me. I had no previous experiences or close observations about how a camp operated. Step by step we asked God to organize it for us. After our first year, a structure certainly evolved over time as more of the grandchildren came to join us and as they got older.

The primary thing I knew from the beginning was that we had to have rules and boundaries. God gives rules for our benefit. They are for our safety and protection and provide healthy parameters for us to freely explore what He provides. I once read about a study where pre-school children were divided into two groups during their outdoor play time. Each group had identical supervision, identical play equipment, and identical outdoor space. The only difference was that one group had a boundary fence around the perimeter of the playground and one did not. The children with the fence explored every inch of their playground. The children without the fence stayed huddled together near the play equipment in the center.

This simple example speaks volumes to me about how much I miss in life when I do not allow God's boundaries to be my protection. God provides His boundaries through all kinds of good authority in my life, both spiritual and secular.

Well-adjusted children are used to rules and have little trouble accepting them. The challenge is when you have very intelligent children who want to know the "whys" about everything. It's not enough for the authority figure to retort, "Because I said so!" It's important to have a reason for giving rules and also it's important to be consistent with your intention and enforcement of them.

Our primary intention was to avoid chaos and to have expectations for learning something new each day. The rules we listed for Sophie and Caleb were firm but light-hearted. After a while, when one of them got rebellious or slightly out of control, ignoring what we asked them to do, or even had the occasional "melt-down," Conlee and I would just ask, "Did you forget the #1 rule at Camp Mimi?" Their answer would be a resounding, "Mimi rules!"

Here is the set of rules we developed after a couple of years. Most of it is just practical. But each rule contributes to the formation of character and personal protection.

CAMP MIMI RULES

1. **MIMI RULES**

2. **POOL RULES**
   - No one under 11 allowed outside without an adult
   - No running around pool
   - Always wear sunscreen
   - Put all trash in trash can
   - Hang all towels and wet swim suits on porch rack

3. **HOUSE RULES**
   - Make up bed first thing
   - Put all dirty clothes in laundry room
   - Pick up, clean up, hang up

4. **TABLE RULES**
   - Daily teams help every day (including cooking, setting table and clean-up)
   - Respectful manners at all times
   - Leave table by permission only
   - Try (at least) one bite of everything

5. **FUN RULES**
   - Look out for your buddy
   - Share
   - Enjoy each activity, even if it's not your favorite
   - Be thankful for your family
   - Whiners go to bed / Grumps are tickled

Each year this set of rules was given out on the first day of Camp Mimi, read aloud by everyone, and placed in their three-ring binders which were filled up with teachings and activity sheets by the end of the week.

The Camp Mimi logo of the picket fence was chosen because that first year we had just put up a white picket fence with an arbor to surround the patio and kitchen garden leading to our front door. The logo illustrated seven of the vertical pickets, representing the seven BodishBabes we had at the time.[1] The horizontal supports represented Mimi and Papa. Although we didn't illustrate the arbor in the center, the children immediately got caught up in the symbolism and said that the arbor was Jesus. An appropriate meaning, since He is the Gate, the Door, the Center, the Way.

It's so exciting when little ones begin to think this way, connecting ordinary things of life to God! It only takes a tiny bit of encouragement for them to begin to look for Him in all they do.

THE ACTIVITIES

The first year of Camp Mimi we planned some simple activities that both Sophie and Caleb would enjoy. Swimming became a favorite. After her first week with us, Sophie was swimming the length of the pool, taking only one breath. She was also diving off the side into the deep end. When Caleb arrived, he had to catch up, of course. So each morning and after naps each afternoon,[2] we had swimming class. A little friendly competition does wonders to encourage practice and develop skills.

Knowing how vital it was for our grandchildren to know how to swim with a pool in the backyard, we made this a priority. Games, races, timed laps, prizes, cheering, and encouragement were not only fun in the pool, but by the end of the week they were both swimming like little fish.

Being in and out of the pool several times a day necessitated rules number two and three on our list. A clean beach towel for each child twice a day, thrown on the ground, or popsicle wrappers and sticks left poolside, or traipsing through the house dripping wet for showers and shampoos were all going to drive me batty. So, besides the safety rules, some practical housekeeping rules were put in place. We required them to take all showers and shampoos in the outdoor shower enclosure, which they loved. This was a large open-air, walk-in space with a latch on the door giving them privacy and plenty of hot water.

Later, when Camp Mimi grew in size, all the girls showered together, and then all the boys. We found it was necessary to keep track of which group went first each time, because alternating fairly became very important to them. Each child was assigned a hook on the wall identified as his/her very own to hang a towel and personal scrubby. The long shower shelf was well-stocked with fun princess body washes for the girls and super hero

---

[1] Graham Bodishbaugh, the eighth BodishBabe, was born in December, 2011.

[2] We continued this practice for many years, long after the children quit taking naps. We started calling them "rest times." They were primarily for Mimi's and Papa's benefit.

washes for the boys, along with plenty of the fruity smelling shampoos they loved.

Each activity required an emphasis on our theme, "Manners." Although children love to please and receive attention and rewards for their behavior, the reality is that their world is mostly all about ME. But we tried to reinforce the exterior evidence of *doing* things that show kindness and gratitude with an inner awareness of *being* a person who thinks of others more than oneself (or at least as much as oneself).

Each day we alternated teams to help plan, cook, and decorate the table for the evening meal. One day Sophie was the "head *sous chef,*" with Caleb serving as her assistant. The next day Caleb was in charge. All of this was done, of course, with my close supervision and direction. My goal was to have them try foods prepared in ways they had never eaten before. This was a huge challenge because at that time Caleb preferred only carbs, mainly bread. He enjoyed preparing other kinds of foods, just not eating them. The texture of food was a huge consideration for him. Amazingly, he was willing to give everything just one taste and it helped him tremendously to know exactly what went into every item on the table. He especially took great delight in presenting a different kind of bread each night.

One of the interesting discoveries we made about Caleb's pickiness with food was that there were certain combinations he just could not swallow. At age five, he didn't know how to articulate this in any other way than to say, "I hate this!" and refuse to eat it. But, in preparing "Sophie's Chicken *Spiedini*,"[3] one of her favorites, he realized why he "hated" it. He loved pounding the chicken breasts thin inside a plastic bag, spreading them with the wonderful savory mixture of olive oil, bread crumbs, garlic and seasonings, and layering on the prosciutto. But then he balked. When we took out the Swiss cheese slices and the Parmesan to layer on top, he had a visceral reaction.

"I hate cheese and meat together! I won't eat this!" Aha! The problem was exposed. All we had to do was let Caleb prepare his *Spiedini* without cheese and mark it clearly. Prepared his way, he ate most of it.

Always looking for meaningful segués into Bible lessons, we had a wonderful opportunity at supper that night to tell the story about the dietary restrictions that God gave the Israelites, especially the one about not combining meat and dairy.[4] I certainly do not know why this was one of God's rules for His people. From what I have read, even orthodox rabbis argue about why God instructed them to separate dairy and meat. But I do know that in each context where such a law was given, His people were

---

[3] Recipe included in the Appendix, "Camp Mimi Eats"

[4] Exodus 23:19, Exodus 34:26, Deuteronomy 14:21

admonished to obey Him and, above all, to *be holy because He is holy*.

Being *holy* meant that they were set apart, different and separate from all other people. The separation of ordinary things of life reminded them, and showed others, that they followed God's rules because they loved and trusted Him. There are some things in life that we don't fully understand. We just have to trust the one who protects us. And, in loving and respecting our protectors, we do what they ask us to do without rebelling. By being obedient, we are set apart for special blessings.

At the table that night, we began to name things we are asked to do by parents or others in authority that we don't understand. They were quick to respond.

Why can't I stay up as late as I want to?
Why can't I eat dessert first?
Why do I have to dress up for church?
Papa even voiced one of his own.
Why can't I drive as fast as I want to if there is no one else around?

The discussion around the dinner table that night proved to be one on manners that we never planned. This always proves to be a very important principle: When we make ourselves available to God and His instruction, He opens our eyes to see opportunities we could never imagine.

Manners around the table are, of course, a big deal in training children. In today's fast-paced family life, many children seldom get to experience sitting at table with the whole family, relaxing and enjoying a nicely presented meal, and learning to use proper utensils, etiquette, and mannerisms.

Instead of, "I want more potatoes," or "Give me the bread," we insisted on "May I please have more potatoes?" and "Will you please pass the bread?"

Instead of, "I hate this!" we encouraged them to say nicely, "No, thank you. It's not my favorite."

Instead of getting up and down with every whim, we insisted on "May I please be excused?"

Instead of wiping one's mouth and fingers on a shirt sleeve, we insisted on the proper use of napkins.

Instead of just woofing down whatever food is placed on the table, we insisted on taking time and savoring what someone else had prepared, and thanking the ones who had cooked and served.

Since the children had a big investment in the preparation of the food each night, they were much more aware of all that went into each platter and bowl before them. They took great pride in saying, "I chopped that! I mixed that! I decorated that plate!" They wanted each person around the table to admire and compliment their handiwork.

Realizing that there was no more important occasion to bring out the best china, crystal and linens than for my own grandchildren, we made a special effort each night to set the table beautifully. Caleb and Sophie alternately chose a theme for each evening meal and decorated accordingly. I let them have free reign over my linen closets, silver drawers, and china cabinet. Their choices were amazing! Mostly, they started with a color theme, gathering items from around the house to place in the center of the dining room table. Some were questionable to me, but meaningful to them.

Of course, Sophie had a "Pink Night," including hot pink feather boas down the center of the table with one of her favorite Barbies as the centerpiece in her finest pink ball gown. Conlee and Caleb kept their opinions to themselves because Caleb retaliated with a "Camo Night," with G.I. Joe figures, pewter plates, and bandanas for napkins.

One night they even imported sand from the beach, beach towels for a tablecloth, and flip-flops for a centerpiece. All of the tablescapes were spectacular.

These bursts of creativity caused us to want to linger a little longer after we had our dessert, because our special surroundings had too much care and meaning put into them to just abandon them immediately.

THE FIELD TRIP

After several days of learning about manners in all walks of life, it was time to take this show on the road! At the time, one of the very finest restaurants in Mobile was The Pillars.[5] Owned by Chef Matt and Regina Shipp, it offered upscale dining in a fine old mansion converted into a restaurant. Conlee and I belonged to a membership club they offered, where for a very reasonable amount of money, you received two three-course lunches, and two four-course dinners each month. This became our regular romantic date place for a couple of years. It reminded us that in the midst of busy lives, we needed to dress up, get out, and take special time for ourselves and our relationship on a regular basis. Having paid in advance for this great deal, we were highly motivated to take advantage of it.

We made reservations to take Sophie and Caleb to The Pillars for a late lunch one day. We thought that lunch would be better for children, less crowded at the restaurant, and take less time. So, dressing in our finest, we all had a date.

It was a great choice to go after the lunch crowd left because we were seated by ourselves in our favorite room of the mansion, the windowed conservatory with its stained glass windows, mosaic tiled floors and old-world charm.

We were welcomed and seated by the *maitre d'* and our waiter came

---

[5] The Pillars closed in 2010.

immediately to say hello. Because there were so few people in the restaurant, we took the time to explain to her about Camp Mimi, our studies on manners, and our reason for the field trip with our grandchildren to the restaurant.

Our waiter immediately got involved! Not only did she explain everything in great detail about the formal protocol of the restaurant for the children's benefit, Conlee and I learned a lot, too. She told us why we were met at the door and seated by a man called the *maitre d'*. His title is an abbreviated version of the French phrase *maitre d'hotel* which means "the master of the house." Instead of letting people just wander in and seat themselves, he takes reservations, welcomes each guest, decides where to seat the guests, and provides a sense of order and calm to an otherwise hectic environment. The *maitre d'* also supervises the wait staff and is responsible for the overall dining experience. Our waiter invited him to come back to our table to meet Caleb and Sophie and explained our mission to him with great delight. He was a bit formal, but very welcoming. Our waiter explained that each of the wait staff is referred to as a waiter, whether they are men or women.

When a young man, wearing a long white apron, came to our table to pour water, she explained his role of busser (or busboy) and why a welcoming goblet of water is served by him before the waiter takes other drink orders. Our busser also brought a silver basket filled with a variety of hot breads, as well as two little dishes of butter, one plain and one herbed.

She explained that the role of the busser is vital because he keeps everything looking neat, clean, orderly, and inviting, even though many people may eat at the same table during the day. He changes the linens and resets the table after each guest leaves, he provides the basics (bread and water) as a welcoming gesture, clears empty plates, refills water glasses, and removes all dirty dishes and linens from the table.

We noticed that he did not converse with us as she did. We asked her about this and she told us that the role of the busser is to remain invisible and to let each guest believe that order and neatness just happen without a big fuss or commotion. She also said that the waiters, too, are trained not to get into personal conversations with the guests, but yet are to be welcoming and friendly. They don't volunteer their names and they remain discreet as they serve and attend to the needs of the guests. This was certainly in sharp contrast to many restaurants where the waiter immediately says, "Hello, my name is _____ and I will be your server today." Sometimes the servers even wear their names on badges so that you will be sure to be on a first name basis with him/her. (Some will even tell you their life story as they serve).

Then our waiter took our drink orders and brought us menus, explaining the specials for the day. She asked if we had any questions about the items on the menu. We looked at the offerings, explained them to the children, and encouraged Caleb, the pickiest eater of the four of us, to ask anything he wanted about what was in the food preparation. She was very patient with him and even brought out Chef Matt to answer one of Caleb's questions. At first Caleb was embarrassed, but soon realized that the chef was very pleased to explain the ingredients to one of his guests. He even agreed to make some minor modifications to meet Caleb's preferences.

After she took our orders, our waiter removed the soup spoon from the far right of each place setting, since none of us had ordered soup. She also removed the wine glasses from the table. She asked the children to count all the knives, forks and spoons remaining at each place. They counted six. She told them not to be intimidated about the number or all the different shapes. Each one had a purpose which made sense, and you just had to remember to begin with the ones farthest away from the plate, eating from the "outside in." The forks were lined up on the left of the plate with a folded linen napkin beside them, and the knives and spoons were on the right.

"Let's begin," she said. "First, unfold your napkin and place it in your lap." Winking at the children, she whispered, "You wouldn't believe how many adults don't do that. We sometimes have to put their napkins in their laps for them." Giggling, they hurriedly put their napkins across their laps.

"Now, look inside the napkin that covers that little silver basket, take the kind of bread you want, and place it on your bread and butter plate. That's the little plate on your left. Then pass the basket around the table."

Very seriously, we all followed her instructions. The children were spellbound. They were learning far more from this kind woman in a formal setting than they ever would at home!

"Now, take your butter knife. That's the little one on the top of your bread and butter plate. Take a small amount of butter from one of the butter dishes and place it on your butter plate."

Both Caleb and Sophie chose the butter that didn't have the "green stuff" in it, and immediately started to spread it on their bread.

"The proper way is to place the butter on the plate first, then spread it as you eat, rather than buttering the whole piece at once."

Giggling again, they started over to do it her way.

"Once you have used your butter knife, rest it across the top of your bread plate."

She left us to enjoy our bread and our surroundings. Of course, we took pictures of each other and commented on the beautiful room, the fresh flowers on the table, and how nice our waiter was.

Soon, beautifully constructed salads on chilled plates were presented and set on top of our place plates. As she served the salads, our waiter once more went into her teacher/presenter, professional mode and she was a natural. She had our full attention. First, she explained that sometimes salads are served after a meal, and that if a guest prefers, they will, of course, bring it to them then. (I am one of those people who would much rather eat salad at the end of the meal). However, in most restaurants, especially American ones, a salad is served first while the entrée is being prepared in the kitchen.

"Now, which fork do you think you would use for the salad?" In unison, they responded, "The outside one!" She rewarded them with an exuberant, "Excellent! You may leave that fork on your salad plate when you're finished."

She immediately brought forth a huge pepper mill, asking if anyone would like freshly ground pepper on the salad. Conlee and I asked for some but the children declined. They were getting bolder now and as our waiter ground the pepper, Caleb asked, "Why do you do that since we have salt and pepper shakers on the table?"

"Great question!" she said. "It's really an old tradition from when spices were very expensive and kept in locked boxes and just brought out ceremoniously. But it also insures that the pepper the wait staff grinds at table is very fresh because we fill it with peppercorns every day."

To be truthful, the children didn't eat much of their salads, but they were respectful and there was not one comment like, "Yuck, I don't like this," or "I want something else!" They acted as grown-up as our waiter was treating them. They really got into this!

About the time Conlee and I finished our salads both children had to go to the restroom. They put their napkins on the table and returned just as the entrées were being served. Our waiter had one more lesson for them before they ate.

"If you leave the table before finishing your meal, place your napkin on the back of your chair. This tells your waiter that you are coming back. If you are leaving the restaurant, however, you leave the napkin on the table." We *all* learned something from that!

With our entrée plates replacing our place plates, all that was left was the dinner fork and the dessert fork on the left and the dinner knife and the teaspoon on the right. We had been training the children to ask questions and understand why manners are important. So, of course, the logical question was asked, again by Caleb, "Why is the fork on the left since so many people are right-handed?"

She explained that it has been fine dining tradition for more than 150 years to set the flatware in such a configuration. Originally, the right hand held the knife for cutting and the left hand held the fork. Then one's left hand, already holding the fork, would place the cut food in the mouth. Usually, it is only Americans who now change the fork back into the right hand to eat with it. In most other countries the left hand is still used for holding the fork throughout a meal. Both children agreed, "That makes more sense!"

"Is there anything else I can get for you?" asked our waiter.

"No, thank you," said Conlee, "it looks perfect. We'll just give thanks to God and then enjoy."

"Bon appétit!" she said, leaving us to join hands in prayer and thanksgiving before beginning our wonderful meal.

When it appeared that all of us had finished our entrées, our waiter returned to explain that the used dinner knife and fork were to be placed side by side inside the plate, signaling the waiter that you were ready to have your plate removed. She said that no one's plate would be removed until each person at the table was finished. That way no one would feel rushed.

Now there was only one fork left and the children knew what it was for – the icing on the cake, literally. Looking over the dessert menu and having everything explained to them, Caleb and Sophie couldn't decide which one to have. With a suggestion from our waiter, Chef Matt made them a sampler plate so they could try a little bit of all the most popular desserts on the menu. It was beautifully presented and they were definitely "happy campers."

That night we had a very simple supper since we had enjoyed a feast at lunch. But Caleb and Sophie wanted to re-create their fine dining experience and so, using a handout I gave them, the table was set with care and their manners were impeccable. (At least for that one night!)

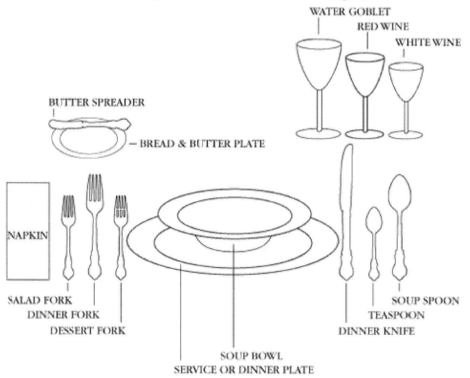

THE AWARDS

Children love to receive awards!

I remember many years ago when one of my elementary-aged sons (I won't say which one) was in a summer junior golf class. We moms were responsible for walking the course and keeping the scores for our own children. Our instructions were to make marks on a legal pad for each stroke our child took on each hole. At the end of the summer the scores were tallied and awards were given at a hamburger awards dinner. Unfortunately, my child's strokes filled up an entire legal pad! I was afraid he would be so disappointed when he did not receive an award of any kind.

Even so, our whole family set off for the awards night festivities. After all the first place, second place, third place, honorable mention, and other special trophies were awarded, my son was asked to come forward. He received "The Most Improved" trophy and he was thrilled! We still have that trophy which was proudly displayed in his room for many years. He had done his best!

We decided that Sophie and Caleb would receive small awards for *something* each night at dinner and that we would have an Awards Banquet on their last night. I found some lanyards left over from conference name badges and attached extra large safety pins on the ends. At craft stores I found very inexpensive packages of little charms depicting all sorts of animals, activities, Christian symbols, sports and others. Each night Conlee recounted some of the actions of each child that had been Christ-like that day and we gave them charms symbolizing what they had done to attach to their safety pins. He praised them for such things as telling someone "thank you," or waiting their turn instead of being pushy, or obeying Mimi and Papa.

They also received charms for swimming accomplishments, like swimming the length of the pool in one breath, or not running around the sides of the pool, or remembering to put on sunscreen without being told. Anything they did well deserved a charm and they were as proud of their necklaces as if they were Oscars. They kept them in a special bowl in the dining room and it became a ritual to put them on each night for dinner.

For our last night together, before their parents came, we planned our final awards ceremony. When asked what they wanted to eat, they both declared, "Steak!" So steak became the food of choice for each consecutive Last Night Awards Dinner. Traditions were being established. We recounted all we had done during the week, named our personal highlights, and laughed a lot. Conlee and I were asked to promise to have Camp Mimi again the following year.

THE ACTIVITIES

Karaoke was really popular that first summer and a special gift we bought for Camp Mimi was a kid's version of a karaoke machine, with a microphone on a stand, speakers, and even a foot pedal which turned on a recording of wild applause. We had a version of a "talent" show every night after dinner and ended with everyone bathed, in pajamas, and cuddled up to hear a book read aloud. That first summer we read *Linnets and Valerians*[6] by Elizabeth Goudge and assorted short stories by Hans Christian Andersen.[7]

Besides our outing to The Pillars, we took two other field trips during Camp Mimi and these were big hits. We drove over to Pensacola, Florida, one afternoon to go to the National Naval Aviation Museum. This is a place where kids can pretend to be jet pilots, climb into cockpits and "fly" with the Blue Angels. There is also a favorite mock-up of a little town that captures the essence of the 1940's and life in America during World War II. It is a fabulous museum – and it's free!

We also went to Bellingrath Gardens in Mobile. Here the children could walk for hours through meandering paths along the Fowl River, through a marsh, around a lake, amidst incredible plantings of flowers.

Both of these outings were enjoyed so much that they, too, became traditions, – the sacred, unchanging requirements for each Camp Mimi.

The first Camp Mimi was planned day by day, sometimes even hour by hour. It helped tremendously that Conlee took a week off from being a pastor to just be Papa. In subsequent years this became a priority for one of the weeks of his vacation time.

When parents came to claim their children that first year, we said our good-byes, thinking that this had been an awesome experience but not certain that it could ever be repeated.

A few months later, in keeping with our family custom of taking each six-year-old grandchild to Disney World the week after Thanksgiving, we took Caleb and Sophie. Sophie had just turned six and Caleb was about to have his sixth birthday, so we decided to take them together.

We had a wonderful time in the Magic Kingdom, but almost every day they talked most about what they would do next summer at Camp Mimi. By the time we got home it was settled. Camp Mimi would be held the next summer for any BodishBabe who could come.

As it turned out, all seven wanted to come! Game on!

---

[6] <u>Linnets and Valerians</u>, Elizabeth Goudge, Puffin Books, 1964.

[7] <u>Hans Christian Andersen, The Complete Fairy Tales and Stories</u>, translated from Danish by Erik Christian Haugaard, Anchor Books, 1974.

CAMP MIMI TWO

AROUND THE WORLD

I'm pretty realistic about the fickleness of children. They might be wildly enthusiastic about something one day and sort of ho-hum about it the next. Although the children had been excited about another Camp Mimi immediately afterwards, and even while at Disney World, Conlee and I still thought there was the possibility that it had been a once-in-a-lifetime event, albeit a great one. We were more than willing to do it again the next summer but we weren't going to push it.

However, at Christmas, among the cousins, it was talked up even more. Everyone was in. The parents had to plan some major choreography to arrange a week when they could get their children from Arkansas and Texas to Mobile, Alabama, and the older children already had full summer schedules. But Camp Mimi became a priority and a date was set for July.

Constantly, I was asked by the children on the phone or at visits, "Do you know the theme yet?" With seven BodishBabes coming for a week, I knew I had to be super-organized, well-prepared, and rested up. By Easter I was planning every detail of what we would do and getting more and more excited each day.

To heighten the suspense, we decided not to reveal the theme until the opening day. And we also declared that Camp Mimi would not officially begin until all the parents were gone. It was for BodishBabes only. This was their exclusive time.

As the parents brought children, spent the night before their long drives home, and then stayed for breakfast, lingering over their coffee, the children were so excited they could hardly stand it. The anticipation mounted. Every minute one of them would ask a parent, "Aren't you ready to leave yet?"

Finally, the parents drove home and we gathered around our large glass-top dining room table, now officially called The Camp Mimi Table. Interestingly, the places the children claimed that first morning became their permanent places for many years.

Conlee and Jake (barely one year old) anchored one end. Jake loved sitting above everyone else at the table in his high chair. I anchored the other end of the table with all of my outlines for the week. I had a large binder filled with lots of notes, hand-outs, schedules, menus, and project ideas.

On my left were Alex (14), Caleb (6), and Anna (4). On my right were Macy (12), Sophie (6), and Edie (4). Their faces all turned towards me, waiting for The Big Reveal.

Taking my time and milking the moment for all it was worth, I brought forth a tall candle in a glass jar. It was the kind you find on a grocery store aisle. I had printed two labels and glued them to the sides. On one side it read "Camp Mimi 2006." On the other side was printed our theme, "Around the World." As the oldest, Alex had the privilege of lighting the candle, declaring that Camp Mimi 2006 had officially begun. (Each year it became a major priority to be the one who lighted the theme candle in the mornings and blow it out after our lessons!)

Each child was given a three-ring binder with an insert on the front cover showing our official Camp Mimi logo, the theme and year, and his/her own picture. They were to use the notebooks to keep all their lessons and activity sheets organized and neatly stored. The first page given out was "Camp Mimi Rules" which everyone who could, read aloud.

I also gave each child a clear, plastic box, large enough to hold the notebook and other things they would collect during the week. This would help keep everything neat and out of sight when not being used. Our first assignment was to decorate their boxes to make them very personal. They were given peel-and-stick felt and plastic shapes and letters to be creative. Soon, it looked like an art class, everyone working hard on turning an ordinary plastic storage bin into a treasure chest.

With our craft project finished and admired by all, it was Snack Time. This proved to be one of the most popular times of the day. We tried to feed the children in a healthy way for each meal, but Snack Time threw away all the rules and we just went for junk food and candy. They loved it! Juice boxes and pouches were perfect for spill-proof drinks and a big bowl of assorted individual boxed or packaged cookies, candies or chips were the best way to make sure each child had something he/she liked.

Snack Time over, we settled down for our first lesson. Putting a big container of crayons and colored pencils in the center of the table, I explained that each day we would study a country that Papa and I had visited, or one we would like to visit. We would learn about each country's customs, foods, dress, and fun facts. We would be going "Around the World."

Our first lesson sheet showed the continents of the world. Alex taught us a rap she wrote for school to learn the seven continents.

North America, South America, Europe, too.
Africa, Asia, Australia, whew!
And don't forget Antarctica, the coldest of them all.
These are the seven continents. Now you know them, too!

We asked them to color North America green, South American red, Europe orange, Africa yellow, Asia purple, Australia dark blue, and Antarctica light blue. Coloring turned out to be one of their favorite activities for years. They would really concentrate on a lesson or a story if their hands were busy coloring a related picture.[8]

I bought polymer clays in various colors and we formed charms each day that would symbolize something about the country we would visit. These were easily modeled and then baked in the oven and painted. I also had some purchased charms to use if someone had a problem with their project. After our evening meal, Conlee awarded the charms to be put on their necklaces which we made out of braided yarn. They loved collecting these charms and looked forward to the presentations each evening. Conlee would call each child forward, one at a time, commending each one on Godly qualities he or she had exhibited that day. They kept their necklaces in their treasure boxes and wore them for dinner each night.

In planning a schedule, (definitely needed with seven children!) Conlee

---

[8] There are limitless free coloring pages available on the Internet. Just enter your subject with "Free coloring pages." I have found hundreds of these over the years, then printed and punched holes in the pages to fit in their notebooks.

and I decided that morning classes and projects were best followed up by swimming time and lunch outside by the pool while still in swimsuits. This definitely made clean-up much easier, both inside and outside. While I prepared simple lunches, Conlee supervised the pool. Alex and Macy organized games and contests, and everyone worked on teaching little Jake to swim underwater. We quickly got into a routine, loving the familiarity of it while knowing there would be surprises along the way.

Lunch was followed by outdoor showers and then rest-time. At least five of them would always fall asleep, but reading was permissible. I probably appreciated the rest-time more than anyone! After resting, unless we had a field trip, everyone was ready for another swim. Jake's playpen was put in the shade of a tree near the pool, and all the children joined him in it from time to time so that he never felt left out. His swimming skills improved every day and in just a few days he could swim underwater the width of the pool. Poolside popsicles became a favorite with everyone. It was easy to clean-up with the hose after drippy treats.

Back by popular demand, we also read fairy tales from Hans Christian Andersen before bedtime every night.

DAY 1 - RWANDA

They were excited each morning to see where in the world we would go for the day. On the first day we "visited" Rwanda because Conlee and I had been there recently. Although we didn't serve the children goat, which was considered a "special treat" served to us in Africa, we did show them how fish was served with rice and fruits.

They loved learning about the African custom of "wearing their babies on their backs" like the African women did. I showed them how I had been allowed to carry baby Iris Mugisha, the daughter of our friends Sam and Jackie, in Kigali. Jackie had instructed me on how to place a blanket on the bed, put Iris on the blanket, and then sit on the bed with her behind me. Then, leaning backwards towards Iris, I pulled all the ends of the blanket around me and tied it securely, top and bottom, in my front. I never quite felt secure enough to keep my hands free from holding her on, but Iris knew exactly what to do. As soon as I leaned back onto the bed, she wrapped her little legs and arms around me, ready for a ride. At Camp Mimi we practiced with dolls and blankets. Even the boys took a turn, although only the women in Africa carry the babies in this fashion.

One of the things Rwanda is famous for is being the home of the mountain gorillas. We "went on a safari" that night after studying the habitats of gorillas in the wild. We told the children that silverback gorillas live in families, called troups, of about 25-35 members with a leading male.

Alex took the lead as our safari guide while we all crawled through the house on our bellies, under obstacles representing the "bush," hoping to glimpse such a male gorilla leader. When I suggested that she take us near the front door as a likely spot to see a large male, she bravely led the group, now really engaged in our pretend safari. Being the oldest, Alex maturely assumed that my plan was for us to spot our large black Lab, Asher, on the front porch and that we would all pretend that he was the male leader of the gorilla troup.

What she didn't know was that Conlee had quietly dropped out of the safari, had donned a long black, hooded cape that covered him from head to foot, and was hiding behind a corner near the front door. When Alex led us forward he jumped up, roaring in his loudest voice, at his full height of six foot three inches. Alex screamed in fear; all the other children then screamed, and everyone was sure they had seen a real gorilla. As cruel as it may sound to scare children that way, that one event became a highlight. To this day, they talk about what fun it was to be scared by Papa the Mountain Gorilla.

I taught them the only words I knew in *Kinyarwandan*, the primary language spoken in Rwanda, along with French and English. *Imana Ishimwe!* means "Praise God!" When asked to speak anytime we were in Rwanda, such as to address a school group or a ladies' group, I could always say this with great enthusiasm. Each group always had the same hearty response, "Amen!"

I also learned the blessing, *Amahoro y'imana abane nawe*. "God's peace be with you."

And the important response, *Murakoze*, "Thank you."

One night, while in Kigali, a delightful young man, Onesimus Asümwe, taught us to sing this song: *Turanezerewe, turanezerewe, Ikitwasabye twakibonye, Turanezerewe*. It means "We are happy; we are happy. We've found what we prayed for. We are happy."

Reaching the extent of my very limited repertoire, we sang the little song and repeated the phrases I knew over and over. I'm sure our Rwandan brothers and sisters would not understand much of what we said, but we felt very international!

DAY 2 - GERMANY

The next day we "went to Germany." We played some German music for them, a bit of polka music and even some Wagner. For our German food, we tried soft pretzels for snacks and prepared both sausages (*Bratwurst*) and *Schnitzel mit Spätzle* [9] for dinner.

We told the children about the many castles we had seen in Germany, especially the one built by Mad King Ludwig of Bavaria at *Hohenschwangau*. Teaching them how to pronounce the name of this quaint little village in

---

[9] Recipe in Appendix "Camp Mimi Eats."

southern Germany was as challenging as trying to speak *Kinyarwandan*.

King Ludwig's true story is as interesting as any fairy tale. He became king of Bavaria in 1864, and owned many castles. He was a complicated and disturbed man who was fascinated with the dark side of Wagner (which is why we played a bit of his music for them). He yielded to every whim he had and designed and built a remarkable castle named *Schloss Neuschwanstein*, very near *Schloss Hohenschwangau*, which was built by his father, King Maximilian II. Interestingly, Ludwig never moved into his dream home.

Conlee and I toured both of these castles and we were impressed with the ornate details and extravagant excesses, especially in *Neuschwanstein*. This castle was the model used by Disney for Cinderella's castle in the Magic Kingdom.

While visiting Neuschwanstein, we stayed in a lovely inn at the bottom of the mountain where the view from our window was of the majestic edifice built high on the rocky peak. The castle was brightly lighted at night and was indeed magical to see. We went to sleep every night with the castle outside our window, brighter than the moon, transporting us to dream royal dreams. One night I awoke after midnight and realized the sky was dark. No moon, no castle, no light at all. My first reaction was, "The castle has disappeared!" Then, of course, I realized that the lights must go off automatically around midnight. To illustrate this experience, I wrote a children's story for them called *Schloss, the Mountain Castle*.[10] The children enjoyed having it read to them.

We "led them through the castle" with pictures, story, history lessons, coloring pages and activities. They became royalty in the castle of their own dreams. We dressed accordingly for dinner that night, raiding the costume box to become kings and queens, princes and princesses!

Bread, or *Brot*, being Caleb's favorite food, was served that night on an antique wooden plate I bought in Germany. Hand-carved around its edges are the words: *Gib uns unser täglich Brot,* 'Give us our daily bread." We all said the Lord's Prayer which includes this request of God.

I also showed them a hand-carved plaque I found in Germany that bears the scripture that Conlee and I consider our family motto: *Ich und mein Haus wollen dem Herrn dienen.* "As for me and my household, we will serve the Lord."[11]

After dinner, we tried to polka. It got very silly, but was lots of fun.

DAY 3 - MEXICO

"Going to Mexico" was much more familiar territory to the children since each one could already count in Spanish, mostly due to watching

---

[10] *Schloss the Mountain Castle*, Signa Bodishbaugh, unpublished.

[11] Joshua 24:15b

"Dora the Explorer" on TV. And, they all lived near some Hispanics, especially the BodishBabes from Texas. For our evening meal, they were expecting to prepare and eat tacos or burritos or enchiladas. However, we surprised them by making our own *tortillas*,[12] flattening them with a heavy cast iron tortilla press, cooking them, and serving them with *posole*,[13] a traditional Mexican pork dish, along with grilled shrimp. This wasn't something they could order at Taco Bell.

At our morning session, as they colored picture pages about Mexico, Conlee and I told them the story of renting a house for several days in *Puerto Peñasco* on the coast of Baja. With their hands busy, they fully engaged with the details of the story and put themselves into the adventure along with their Mimi and Papa, although none of them had been born at the time of our Mexican adventure.

Putting yourself in a family adventure and sensing your generational connection is the beauty of story-telling in families. This is a legacy that is often over-looked and neglected. Perhaps it is because it is hard for many children and adults to sit still and listen to the details which really make a good story. Or, perhaps a pattern of life develops that simply doesn't appreciate or allow for such luxury. It really is a luxury to explore the interesting experiences of other people. It's even better than reading good autobiographies or memoirs. The adventures don't have to be spectacular or thrilling. They may be quite ordinary or funny. The telling of one's story shares the person's character as well as personal facts.

God instilled the importance of telling family stories when He instructed His people to tell the Exodus story each year at Passover, to teach children the stories in Torah, and to share at every opportunity, as Paul did, your personal testimony of salvation. Story binds families together, whether it is the family of God or a nuclear family. Even among the team members of our "Journey to Wholeness in Christ" ministry, we always have a delightful time telling stories about past events that bound us together. They might be funny stories or stories declaring our awe of God and what He has done in our midst.

A proof of the value of family story-telling is that often our grandchildren will now ask for it. "Tell us a story, Mimi and Papa! Something real that you have done!" At Camp Mimi, we found that sitting around the table with coloring pages provided the perfect opportunity for such sharing. The stories they then shared about their own experiences were just as fascinating to us. We were able to hear stories about them that I don't think we would have ever known any other way.

---

[12] Recipe in Appendix, "Camp Mimi Eats"

[13] Ibid.

The Story of Our Mexican Adventure: Many years ago (like "back in The Olden Days" or "Once upon a time" in kid-speak), we lived in Fayetteville, Arkansas, and only had two sons, Rick and Matt, both in elementary school. Ben had not yet been born. One time their grandmother came to stay with them so that Conlee and I could go to a mechanical contractor's convention[14] in Phoenix, Arizona. It lasted for five days in a big hotel in the middle of the city. Afterwards, we planned to visit my aunt and uncle in nearby Paradise Valley, borrow a car from them, and drive down into Mexico for another five days for a holiday.

We had only visited border towns in Mexico before this trip and thought it would be fun to explore a totally different area south of the border. We wanted to go somewhere that was not too touristy. From friends of friends, we heard about an obscure place on the Baja coast in *Sonora*, a small village called *Puerto Peñasco*. The friends of our friends had rented a house there that they only described as "fabulous." We were given the phone number of the American woman who owned it. Her primary home was in Phoenix, and when we talked, she said she rented the hacienda often and that it was available for the time we requested, but that she would be in Europe during that time. While there, we would be entirely on our own.

She informed us that the house was fully equipped and we didn't need to bring anything. The main generator which supplied power to the row of American-owned beach houses was turned on every Thursday when the American homeowners from the Phoenix area arrived for the weekends. We definitely would have power by the time we arrived late on a Thursday. She assured us that there were many American homeowners at their beach homes every weekend and that they would be helpful if we had any problems, so it wouldn't be difficult that we did not speak Spanish..

We sent her a check for the rent and she sent us the key to the house with written directions. By the time we finished our convention in Phoenix, we were all set for our Mexican *vacacione*.

My aunt and uncle in Paradise Valley loaned us a large Chevrolet Suburban, their second car which had just been worked on and checked out by the auto repairman. We were assured that it was in great shape and would get us there safely and that my uncle had just filled it with gas that morning. So, early on a Thursday, we set off for a five hour drive into Mexico, with a good map and high expectations for an adventure. And an adventure it surely was!

All was well as Conlee drove and I navigated with an open map as large as a bed sheet. The terrain changed dramatically when we left Gila Bend,

---

[14] Before Conlee went to seminary and was pastor of a church, he owned a mechanical contracting firm. We participated in these annual conventions for many years.

Arizona. This was not the America we knew any longer! There were long, barren stretches of uninhabited desert as far as we could see. When we drove through Ajo, Arizona, there was an oasis of Airstream trailers gathered from all over North America. *Why did they all stop here? What do they know that we don't know?*

Then there was the border crossing, an experience that makes you *know* you are entering a foreign country. Asked many questions and showing the guards our destination on the map, we were finally waved through. Entering *Sonora*, we drove for miles and miles and miles without seeing anything more than a few cacti. Occasionally, there might be two or three adobe huts, some children playing beside the road, and a burro or two. That was all. It was desolate. These little places were not on our map. There was no traffic at all. We hoped and prayed our map and directions were accurate.

Suddenly, in the middle of the desert, with no sign of life around as far as we could see, our car engine sputtered and then just died.

(At this point, all the children put down their crayons and stared at us, startled. They were really getting into this story).

Conlee got out of the car and did the manly thing. He opened the hood and poked around inside. Plenty of water. Plenty of gas. We waited a few minutes. We prayed out loud. He started the engine again and it worked! Alleluia!

Driving along for several minutes, he kept trying to analyze the problem and figure out what happened. He thought of several possibilities, but then, grateful for a well-running vehicle again, we began to think of other things. Just about the time we were feeling secure once more, the engine did the same thing. Sputter. Sputter. Nothing.

Same routine. Same results. This time it took a bit longer after praying for the engine to start. We continued to pray as we drove and I started to think about *banditos*. Although we hadn't seen a car or truck for over an hour, I began to imagine that a band of robbers was going to appear in a cloud of dust on horses and take all we had, leaving us defenseless.

(This was when we had to reinforce the facts to the BodishBabes that this occurred *before* GPS, *before* cell phones, and *before* OnStar, all of which they take for granted).

Our car quit in the same way about five times during the drive through the *Sonoran* desert. Each time it took longer to start up again. It was a really scary trip. We quit analyzing the problem and truly prayed unceasingly. Finally, after many stops and starts, and hours longer than we planned, we saw water ahead. Hoping it was not a mirage, we realized we were near the Gulf of California and that *Puerto Peñasco* was just ahead. At last! We got into the town. We both began to praise God!

The town was much smaller than we realized it would be. Using the written directions from the owner, we began to navigate the dirt roads, many of which were unmarked. By now it was close to sunset, no one was out, and it seemed deserted. Driving south toward the coast, we eventually found the marked road for our rental house. We really wanted to arrive there before dark.

From a distance, we could see a long row of very nice homes on the beach. We had been told by the owner that these all belonged to Americans. Most of them were lovely hacienda-like homes with Spanish architecture, tiled-roofs and arched entries. They looked exactly like what we wanted to rent.

Only one of the houses stood out as very odd, a huge gleaming white monstrosity with a tall uneven protrusion on one side. From afar, it looked like the "Winged Victory of Samothrace,"[15] and I commented that it was the ugliest house I had ever seen. As we got closer, I said, "Oh, please, I hope that's not the one we rented!" But, unfortunately, it was.

By now it was nearly dark. It was tempting to watch the beautiful sunset over the Gulf of California but we felt we should get our things put inside and get situated. Our key unlocked a massive wooden front door in the center of a high adobe wall. We walked into the strangest house I have ever seen.

The front door opened into a central, tiled, open-air courtyard. Every room – kitchen, bathroom, and bedrooms – opened off the courtyard with not one door. There were no windows in the exterior wall, so to see the Gulf you had to go outside the courtyard. It was minimalist to the extreme.

The furniture, even the couches and the beds, was all white-washed adobe, built-in and curving around the walls. We felt like we had entered a very quirky modern museum of art with a Mexican flair. But, that was not the worst! About two inches of water covered the tile floors in the courtyard and every room!

Taking off our shoes, we walked into each of the rooms, flipping on wall switches, but all was dark. There was no power. *What happened to the promised generator?* Conlee took a flashlight from the Suburban and we decided to walk down the beach to find one of the many American homeowners as promised. But as far as we could see in any direction there was no power and there were no Americans. In fact, there was not a living soul anywhere.

With the help of the flashlight and the waning light outside, we found two candles in the meager kitchen and some matches in a jar. We got the car unloaded, found dry sheets and towels in a wardrobe, made up a bed, and checked for supplies in this "fully equipped" house. Other than the linens in a closed cabinet, there was nothing.

---

[15] The Winged Victory of Samothrace is a 2nd century BC sculpture of the Greek goddess Nike (Victory). It is on display in the Louvre in Paris.

Locking the house securely, we drove all along the road our house was on, but we did not see one car or light at any of the other beach houses. It looked like we had the long beach all to ourselves and no one had come on Thursday to turn on the generator as promised.

Heading back toward the little village of *Puerto Peñasco*, our plan was to stop the first person we saw to ask for help with the generator. We only spotted one person, an older man walking along the road. We stopped and attempted to explain our difficulty but there was no sign of his understanding. In fact, he seemed very anxious to move on from us.

Puerto Peñasco has always been a fishing village. Today, it is a popular tourist destination with many high rise condos and upscale restaurants. But, when we were there in the late 1970's, it had no tourism at all except for the few Americans from Arizona, who owned the nice homes on the beach. Most of the local population was crowded into a small area around the docks. The whole time we were there we did not meet one person who understood or spoke English. In this tiny fishing village, we were truly fish out of water.

We found a *cantina* near the docks, ordered shrimp by pointing to a picture, and it was delicious. All our attempts to ask anyone about our predicament were futile. So, taking some extra match books from the bowl near the cash register, we went camping with our two candles and a flashlight in our Winged Victory. At least we would have a dry bed!

The night was so quiet it was disconcerting. Carrying our flashlight, we walked around outside. The stars were breathtaking. There was no light anywhere to dim their brilliance. Conlee found some steps on the side of the house that led up to a rooftop terrace. Here there were lounge chairs, tables, and even an outdoor kitchen. We lay on the lounges, watching falling stars, comets, and other celestial attractions we don't often get to enjoy.

Occasionally a plane flying up the coast to Los Angeles would go over. It was our only awareness of other humans. Although it was breathtakingly beautiful, I was suddenly overcome with homesickness and a sense of longing to be anywhere but on this desolate beach with no communication with another human soul. To be honest, I was even afraid. All I could think was, *I don't want to be here*.

I was also worried that we would not be able to drive back to Phoenix in the badly behaved Suburban. We had no way to call anyone. No way to get the car fixed. We couldn't speak the language. We were isolated. Conlee held me in his arms and kept assuring me that in the morning light things would be different. But it was hard to shake the feeling of dread.

Then, he took the flashlight and said, "I'll be right back." Soon he returned to our rooftop with a small copy of *The Book of Common Prayer*[16]

---

16. *The Book of Common Prayer*, and Administration of the Sacraments and Other Rites and Ceremonies of

that we traveled with. He asked me to lie back and gaze at the wondrous sky and pray with him. He then led us in a most unusual prayer service that brought our focus away from our circumstances and upon God Himself.

> *Most loving Father, whose will it is for us to give thanks for all things, to fear nothing but the loss of You, and to cast all our cares on You who cares for us: Preserve us from faithless fears and worldly anxieties, that no clouds of this mortal life may hide from us the light of that love which is immortal, and which You have manifested to us in Your Son Jesus Christ our Lord; who lives and reigns with You, in the unity of the Holy Spirit, one God, now and forever. Amen.[17]*

> *Almighty and everlasting God, You made the universe with all its marvelous order, its atoms, worlds, and galaxies, and the infinite complexity of living creatures: Grant that, as we probe the mysteries of Your creation, we may come to know You more truly, and more surely fulfill our role in Your eternal purpose; in the name of Jesus Christ our Lord. Amen.[18]*

> *Be our light in the darkness, O Lord, and in Your great mercy defend us from all perils and dangers of this night; for the love of Your only Son, our Savior Jesus Christ. Amen.[19]*

We sat silently for a few minutes, more absorbed in the intense presence of God than the loneliness of the situation. He was with us!

Conlee then invited me to come over and share the flashlight with him as we read together Psalm 91.

> *He who dwells in the shelter of the Most High*
> *abides under the shadow of the Almighty.*
>
> *He shall say to the LORD,*
> *"You are my refuge and my stronghold,*
> *my God in whom I put my trust."*
>
> *He shall deliver you from the snare of the hunter*
> *and from the deadly pestilence.*
>
> *He shall cover you with His pinions,*

---

the Church, Oxford University Press, NY.

[17] *The Book of Common Prayer*, Collect for the Eighth Sunday after the Epiphany

[18] *The Book of Common Prayer*, Prayers and Thanksgivings, Prayer for Knowledge of God's Creation

[19] *The Book of Common Prayer*, Evening Prayer II, A Collect for Aid against Perils

and you shall find refuge under His wings;
His faithfulness shall be a shield and buckler.

You shall not be afraid of any terror by night,
nor of the arrow that flies by day;

Of the plague that stalks in the darkness,
nor of the sickness that lays waste at mid-day.

A thousand shall fall at your side
and ten thousand at your right hand, but it shall not come near you.

Your eyes have only to behold
to see the reward of the wicked.

Because you have made the LORD your refuge,
and the Most High your habitation,

There shall no evil happen to you,
neither shall any plague come near your dwelling.

For He shall give His angels charge over you,
to keep you in all your ways.

They shall bear you in their hands,
lest you dash your foot against a stone.

You shall tread upon the lion and adder;
you shall trample the young lion and the serpent under your feet.

Because he is bound to Me in love,
Therefore will I deliver him;
I will protect him, because he knows My Name.

He shall call upon Me, and I will answer him;
I am with him in trouble;
I will rescue him and bring him to honor

With long life will I satisfy him,
And show him My salvation.

By praying and invoking the Name of Jesus, *everything* changed for me. Fear was changed to awe and wonder. Instead of dread, I was filled with great expectation and an anticipation for what we would discover tomorrow. We went downstairs, waded to our bed, and slept peacefully in our Winged Victory.

In the morning we found that the water on the floors had drained off somehow during the night. All was dry inside. We discovered amazing coral reef tide pools right in front of our house. Left behind, as the tide went out, were sea creatures I had never seen before: starfish, unusual snails, slugs and crabs, octopi, sea urchins, and many fish we couldn't identify. Birds were everywhere, not the least bit disturbed in their fishing endeavors by our presence.

It was a magical morning as we walked hand in hand along the beach, as though we were the only two people in the world, blessed immensely and protected by God.

We had no electricity for three days, until one American homeowner came on Sunday afternoon and turned on the generator. However, we navigated the village quite well, discovering where to purchase more candles, bottled water, a fabulous bakery, and great seafood in the little *cantina* at the dock.

When we finished telling the story of our Great Mexican Adventure, we asked the children, "What lessons did you learn from this story?" Their answers were wonderful! And there was incredible variety among their insights.

"Stay at home."
"Don't listen to friends of friends."
"Always travel with extra batteries and candles."
"Learn to speak Spanish."
"Always pray."
"God provides."
"What did you eat at the bakery? I'm hungry."

DAY 4 - ITALY

Italy was a country that had always been on our "want-to-visit" list but we had never been there.[20] Since we had promised the BodishBabes that one of the countries we would "visit" would be on our wish list, this was our choice.

When I asked them what things they thought about being Italian, the #1 response was: pizza! Then followed spaghetti, and surprisingly, the Pope. So, it was a big surprise when I introduced them to: *Ta-da* – Michelangelo!

---

[20] For our 50th wedding anniversary, we were able to spend two delightful weeks in a villa in Tuscany. It far exceeded our expectations and we hope to return.

We had fun with coloring pages of some of his most famous masterpieces. While they were busy with their art, I told them stories about his life, his commissions, his genius and some of his greatest quotes. We learned that his full name was Michelangelo di Lodovico Buonarroti Simoni and that he was born in 1475, in a town called Caprese, in Tuscany. This immediately elicited a response from Alex, "I *love* Caprese Salad!" Right then I knew that we would have to make that for our Italian dinner.[21]

When Michelangelo was only thirteen years old, he went to live as an apprentice to a great painter to learn the art of *fresco*. This is the technique of applying paint pigments to fresh (*fresco*) wet lime plaster. The plaster and the paint then dry together.

Then he apprenticed as a sculptor, along with studying human anatomy to better portray the human body. Eventually moving from Florence (which he called home) to Rome, he began to receive many commissions for churches and wealthy patrons. Among his works that are well-known all over the world are his *Pieta, David, Madonna of the Stairs,* the Sistine Chapel ceiling, *Last Judgment,* and his *Moses.*

When we showed them a picture of his sculpture of *Moses,* of course the first question was, "Why does Moses have horns on his head?"

One of the Biblical translations of Exodus 34:29 says that Moses's "face was radiant because he had spoken with the Lord." Another says Moses had "rays of light" coming from his head. In Italian, the word for "rays" became translated "horns" and because of this mis-translation, for a time the depictions of Moses with horns became somewhat commonplace.

When looking at the immense blocks of marble he used to create his masterpieces, Michelangelo once said that he just chipped away everything that didn't look like the object of his creative imagination.

He was also the chief architect for St. Peter's Basilica at The Vatican.

As we studied his great works and talked about the Biblical significance of many of them, the children had coloring pages of many of these works as well as pictures of the master himself.

After our lessons were finished and after Snack Time, we adjourned outside to the pool-side table and out came watercolors, brushes and paper. We all became apprentices of the master.

"Just paint whatever has inspired you today."

There was instant artist's block for each of them. There are not many things more intimidating than a big blank sheet of paper and some paints. It's hard to know where to start.

"Close your eyes and just paint what God shows you in your imagination!"

Our results were not especially gallery-worthy, but they expressed some

---

[21] Recipe in the Appendix, "Camp Mimi Eats."

of the more beautiful images that God planted in our hearts with our limited abilities. We hung them on the sides of the deck to dry.

Just when they thought they were through with artistic endeavors for the day, we brought out into the yard an old leaky row-boat that had washed ashore on our property during a recent storm. I had wanted to save it because it was fairly small, had an interesting shape and I felt like I would know what to do with it one day. It had been resting on the side of the yard for such an occasion. It was about to be transformed.

We stripped all the children down to their undies and old throw-away t-shirts. Then we opened up dozens of small cans of acrylic paints in a variety of colors. Some were left-overs from past projects, others were purchased for a dollar or so at home improvement stores.[22] There were lots of cheap brushes and a water hose nearby. They were invited to decorate the boat anyway they wanted to.

Interestingly, the first thing they decided to do was to divide up the boat into sections so that each of them was responsible for a certain part. It ended up looking like a crazy quilt and was totally delightful. This was so much fun and extremely messy. Little Jake was covered in purple paint (his sole choice of color) from head to toe, more on his own body than on the boat. But on the hot day, the garden hose took care of the paint-smeared bodies and they were ready to jump in the pool and eat lunch outside.

Of course, supper had to be Grilled Pizza[23] to go along with our Caprese Salad! Together, we made the pizza dough. Making dough ourselves is a lot of fun and very easy for children to do. It's a little messy, which they love, and it's very hands-on. Besides, it tastes so much better than any ready-made pizza crust.

While the dough was resting we all joined in putting our favorite toppings in little bowls on a tray to take out by the grill. Their preferences were mostly cheese and sauce, but there were a few adventurous pepperoni, sausage, mushroom and even jalapeño takers. And of course, lots of *mozzarella* and *parmesano*. We rolled out small crusts for each person and everyone chose his/her own toppings. Papa grilled the individual pizzas outside and we ended our *al fresco* (they knew the meaning of this word, now!) Italian meal with a night swim with only the underwater pool lights, which makes an ordinary place seem magical.

Everyone went to bed early without any complaints!

DAY 5 - ISRAEL

By now the children were getting into the flow of changing countries

---

[22] Home improvement stores often have returned or mis-mixed cans of paint at very low prices.

[23] Recipe in the Appendix, "Camp Mimi Eats."

every day. They eagerly awoke asking, "Where are we going today?" We started our visit to Israel with a typical Israeli breakfast. They decided it wasn't their favorite but were good sports as we set out a buffet much like Conlee and I experienced every morning when in Israel.

We had hard-boiled eggs, sliced cucumber, tomato, cheeses, yogurt, nuts, breads, and fruit. There were several complaints such as, "This isn't breakfast food; it's lunch." Or, a couple argued, "No, it's a snack." But we persevered and our day in Israel began.

Since this was a Friday, we decided we would teach the children about *Shabbat*, the day of rest that God instructed His people to observe.[24] We planned to end our day by having a *Shabbat* meal at sunset.

Since our first trip to Israel, Conlee and I have often shared a *Shabbat* meal, whether alone or with guests around our dining table. What fun it was to pass along this tradition to our grandchildren! They love it so much now that any time they are with us on a Friday the first thing they ask is, "Can we do *Shabbat?*"

We talked about the ancient tradition of observing the Sabbath and how there were certain things that Jews have always done to make it very different from the other days of the week. For them, there is no mistaking this day from other days because it is set apart in so many ways. On this special day, which begins at sunset with the sight of the first star in the evening, there is no physical labor until about forty minutes after sunset, or the sighting of three stars the next evening.

For thousands of years, many debates and discussions have been held about what constitutes physical labor on *Shabbat*. It is an argument that can easily deter one from the purpose of the day of rest and the celebration of God's presence. Although no work occurs on the Sabbath, it is not necessarily a day of only prayer or even of only Biblical study. It is a day for God alone, to just enjoy His presence and take pleasure in Him and with family.

People who do not observe *Shabbat*, as instituted in the Ten Commandments, often think of it as a day to painfully endure, with many stifling and boring restrictions. Yet, for the Jew who honors God and observes *Shabbat* with a loving and thankful heart, it is eagerly anticipated all week long. This is a time when each family member can set aside all weekly concerns and concentrate on the joy of being a child of God. Many Jews such as Abraham Heschel, have called *Shabbat* a bride and its celebration like a wedding.[25] He says it is a day for praise, not for petitions.[26]

Because observant Jews do no work during *Shabbat*, it means that they

---

[24] Exodus 31:12-17

[25] *The Sabbath*, Abraham Joshua Heschel; Farrar, Straus and Giroux, NY, 1951, pg. 54.

[26] *Ibid*, page 30.

have to do many things in preparation before sunset. The house is cleaned, the table is set using one's best for the feast, the meal is prepared, and each person dresses up to celebrate.

We told the children what our dinner was going to look like, what we would do, and why we would do it. We were going to begin with the lighting of two candles by the mother of the family – me. The girls would assist. The two lights represent the two commandments that God gave concerning this special day: remember and observe.

We learned two Hebrew words. *Zakhor* means to remember something by recalling it as if you participated in it when it first occurred and then acting on it. *Shamor* means to obey God by observing His commandments. We talked about how in Hebrew the word "to hear" (*shema* from the same root) also means "to obey." If you hear what God says to you, then you *will* obey Him.

We talked about the days of Creation and how God declared the seventh day a day of rest and He blessed and sanctified it for all time. The children had coloring pages of all the days of Creation and then drew pictures of what it means to rest from all work, realizing that rest is not necessarily sleeping.

We read Deuteronomy 5:15 where Moses recalls the Ten Commandments to the Israelites. He says, "Remember that you were a slave in the land of Egypt, and the Lord your God brought you forth from there with a mighty hand and with an outstretched arm. Therefore the Lord your God commanded you to observe the Sabbath day."

I asked them why they thought Moses connected the observance of the Sabbath with slaves coming out of Egypt. It took a while for them to realize (with a few hints) that all the Israelites who walked freely on dry ground through the Red Sea had been slaves all their lives. Slaves had no days off. They worked all the time. As slaves, they would not be allowed to participate in God's declaration of *Shabbat* and His provision of a day of rest. But, once delivered, they were freed from slavery to obey God and enjoy His blessings.

In Exodus 9:1 God told Pharaoh through Moses, "Let My people go so that they may worship Me." It is a celebration of freedom.

This gave us a wonderful opportunity to tell the children how coming out of the slavery of sin and the world enables us to freely obey God and be blessed in so many ways.

We talked about the order or *siddur* for our *Shabbat* meal. I printed a simple program in a small booklet so that those who were able to read could follow along. There were opportunities for prayers and responses along the way. Symbolic actions would be performed. All of it pointed to something far beyond the ritual. Each part is geared to put us in touch with God and His love, leading us to Jesus, remembering and participating in all

He does for us.

They became really excited about the preparations and everyone had something to be responsible for.

The girls helped me make *Challah*,[27] the traditional braided egg bread. We needed two loaves and they were very excited to mix, knead, let rise, and twist it into the traditional shape. When done, these two loaves would form our centerpiece, flanked by the two *Shabbat* candles.

We also roasted two chickens and made rice pilaf, green beans and a vegetable salad. For dessert we made chocolate cake, always a favorite. We put two carafes on the table, one of wine and one of grape juice for the children. They immediately dubbed it to be the "kid's wine." This would be sipped from the *Kiddush* cup.

All was ready and we took special care preparing ourselves as well. The girls were given new sparkly scarves to wind around their heads and each wore a nice dress. Each boy was given a *yalmulke* (Yiddish) or *kippah* (Jewish), the skull cap traditionally worn by Jewish men and boys.

Conlee and the boys checked out the times for sunset and set our schedule. They also helped clean up our Camp Mimi table to make it ready to become a *Shabbat Shalom* table. On the table, they placed a pitcher for pouring water, a basin, and a towel.

When we were in Israel we purchased several small, clay oil lamps and we set one at each place on the table. They were filled with olive oil and fitted with a wick. We would allow the children to light the ones at their places after the two candles of remembrance and observance were ignited. What a great time to talk about Jesus being the light of the world!

Finally, all was ready and each place was set, along with a *Shabbat* booklet[28] to follow the order of celebration. Even young Jake, who couldn't read, followed along intently as though he could.

Papa began with the scripture readings and blessed the Lord. We told the children that when we bless God, it means that we acknowledge and give thanks for who He is and what He does. When He blesses us, He imparts His character (who He is) and gifts (what He does) upon us.

I invited the girls to stand and assist me in lighting the candles of *zakhor* and *shamor*. We symbolically waved the light toward the others around the table. Then the lighter was passed around to each one to ignite their individual oil lamps.

Conlee and I stood and he pronounced the blessing of being like Ephraim and Manashe[29] over each of our sons (who were not present) and over our grandsons. We walked around the table, asking each grandson to

---

[27] Recipe is in the Appendix, "Camp Mimi Eats."

[28] Included in the Appendix.

[29] Genesis 48:20

stand and we placed our hands on their heads, one at a time. Conlee prayed for each of them and blessed them in Jesus' Name. They beamed!

Then we did the same with the girls. I blessed them to be like the matriarchs, Sarah, Rebecca, Rachel and Leah. You could watch them soak up the blessing; it was evident on each face. Together, Conlee and I blessed them all with the priestly blessing: "The Lord bless you and keep you. The Lord make His face to shine upon you, and give you His *Shalom*."[30]

Conlee had practiced very diligently to be able to say this Aaronic blessing in Hebrew.

"Ye'varech'echa Adonay ve'yish'merecha.
Ya'ir Adonay panav eilecha viy-chuneka.
Yisa Adonay panav eilecha, ve'yasim lecha shalom."

I'm sure no Hebrew-speaking person would have recognized the words, but the children were duly impressed and hearing the Hebrew spoken gave a definite solemnity and awe to the occasion.

Each child was then given a small treat as a symbol of God's outpouring of love. One received a bubble-blower, another got a little wooden puzzle, another earrings, etc. These were not impressive items by themselves, but the meaning now far surpassed the value of the gift. They cherished them.

Then Conlee blessed me with a husband's blessing over his wife, reciting Proverbs 31:10-12. I received a small treat, too!

Next, he placed a towel over his arm, took a pitcher of water and a bowl, and went around the table to each person, pouring water over their hands and allowing them to use the towel. As he did this, he blessed God who cleanses us in many ways and blesses us with Living Water.[31] This is one of many symbolic acts at the *Shabbat* meal that points to our being set apart and equipped for God's purposes.

Then Conlee took the *Kiddush* cup, or the cup of wine, blessed God for providing the fruit of the vine, and passed it around the table for each one to take a small sip. As we did, he read the words of Jesus:

"I am the vine and you are the branches.
Those who stay united with Me, and I with them, are the ones who bear much fruit;
because apart from Me you can bear nothing.
This is how the Father is glorified – in your bearing much fruit.
This is how you will prove to be my disciples."[32]

---

[30] Numbers 6:24-26

[31] John 4:13, John 7:37-38

[32] John 15:5,8

He then poured grape juice into each of their wine glasses and asked them to wait to drink it until we had broken the bread. Very ceremoniously, he uncovered the two loaves of *Challah* bread we had made earlier. There are two loaves because they are symbolic of the double portion of Manna that God provided for *Shabbat* in the wilderness. He explained that bread is a symbol of the work of one's hands and sustenance. The girls affirmed that truth by interjecting, "Making *Challah* sure is a lot of work!" You could tell how proud they were of their offering to the meal.

Conlee blessed God for bringing forth food from the earth, broke one of the loaves in half and passed it around the table for each one to break off a piece. He explained that we do not use knives on the *Challah* because a knife too closely resembles an instrument of war and swords are to be beaten into plowshares. We all thanked God for the work we have been given to do, and the provisions we have because of the work of others. And we prayed for those who are without work and those who don't have enough to eat.

Then everyone raised glasses, clicked them together, and declared, *L'Hayim!* To Life!

Our meal was delicious. As we sat around the table by the light of candles and our little clay oil lamps I felt connected with an ancient form of worship that has always pointed to Jesus. I saw the results of this in the faces of our precious grandchildren. They reflected His glory.

After the meal, there were three more prayers with blessings. Everyone was invited to pray and each one did. First, we blessed God for providing the food and gave Him thanks. Second, we blessed God for our homes, both physically and spiritually, and for our eternal home. And third, we prayed for the peace (*Shalom*) of Jerusalem and the continued blessings of God for our future.

We ended by reciting together a Song of Ascents,[33] the same one that ancient worshipers sang as they climbed the steps of the Temple to worship God. Like them, we declared, "The Lord has done great things for us!"

As if the *Shabbat* meal were not enough, the next night we had our Camp Mimi celebration dinner. It had already been decided that we should end with a steak dinner each year and that is what we did. Those kids can eat steak! They are definitely carnivores. They planned the menu and it was delicious: small filets mignon, twice-baked potatoes, green beans, vegetable salad, rolls and the rest of our chocolate cake. Then we handed out awards and certificates to verify that they had completed "Around the World at Camp Mimi."

When their parents came to retrieve them the next day, everyone was

---

[33] Psalm 126

already talking about next year's Camp Mimi.

CAMP MIMI THREE

THE TABERNACLE

By January I already knew what this year's Camp Mimi theme would be. In fact, I kept "seeing" it in all sorts of ways. I often thought of my studies about the Tabernacle with Dr. Allen P. Ross at Trinity Seminary in Ambridge, Pennsylvania. He led us through the Tabernacle as a symbol of worship to God in his inspiring class, "Patterns of Worship." From the moment I finished that intense course, I was hooked. I wanted to share what I learned with someone and whom better than my own grandchildren!

I imagined what it would be like to help the BodishBabes explore each of the furnishings of the Tabernacle that God designed and instructed Moses to make. I wanted to show the children how each one points to Jesus in very graphic ways.

I even imagined that we might somehow "walk" through the Tabernacle as modern day pilgrims re-visiting an ancient site. Yet, I wanted them to experience this through the lens of faith, not just history.

Initially, what I didn't imagine was that we would actually "build" the Tabernacle to its exact dimensions in our own backyard! Or that God would demonstrate to all of us one of the most powerful truths in history!

When we began our opening traditions of The Big Reveal with the lighting of the Camp Mimi candle and the singing of The Camp Mimi Song[34] they wrote the year before, the announcement that we would study the Tabernacle was met with some confusion.

"What's a Tabernacle?"

"Huh?"

"What's that mean?"

They needed a picture painted for them to understand what God designed. Taking a long sheet of butcher paper and laying it down the center of the table, I took a thick black marker and roughly drew out a diagram of the rectangular tent that God told Moses to construct in the wilderness.

I explained that after the Israelites had come through the Red Sea which God miraculously parted for them, they were led into the desert and given instructions for living, both physically and spiritually. They were told to make a moveable "tent of meeting"[35] where God could have fellowship with them. Every part of the Tabernacle symbolized a step that all sinful people must take to approach a holy God. We were going to "walk those steps" and learn what God expected of us and what He wanted to give to us.

The actual Tent of Meeting would have fit in half of a football or soccer field. Its location was determined by God's pillar of cloud by day and pillar of fire by night. This indicated His presence and He was always the very center of the Israelite camp in the wilderness. Every time God instructed them to move, the Tabernacle was set up again the same way. If you convert cubits to feet, the Bible tells us that it measured 150 feet by 75 feet, which happened to be the exact dimensions of our lower lawn by the Bay. Not only were we going to learn about the Tabernacle on paper and in the Bible, on our last day we were going to physically lay it out so that we could literally walk through it.

There were twelve tribes of Israel, descending from the twelve sons of Jacob, whom God re-named Israel. We listed the names of the twelve sons: Reuben, Simeon, Levi, Judah, Dan, Naphtali, Gad, Asher, Issachar, Zebulun, Joseph, and Benjamin. Then we drew boxes on the butcher paper, positioning the camps of the tribes according to God's instructions found in Numbers Chapter Two.[36]

On the East were Issachar, Judah and Zebulun; on the South were Gad, Simeon and Reuben; on the West were Ephraim, Manasseh and Benjamin; and on the North were Naphtali, Asher, and Dan.

---

[34] *The Camp Mimi Song*, lyrics and melody by BodishBabes, unpublished. Lyrics found in Appendix.

[35] Exodus 25:1-2; 25:8-9

[36] This pattern corresponds perfectly to the plan for the New Jerusalem in Revelations 21:12-14.

CAMP MIMI

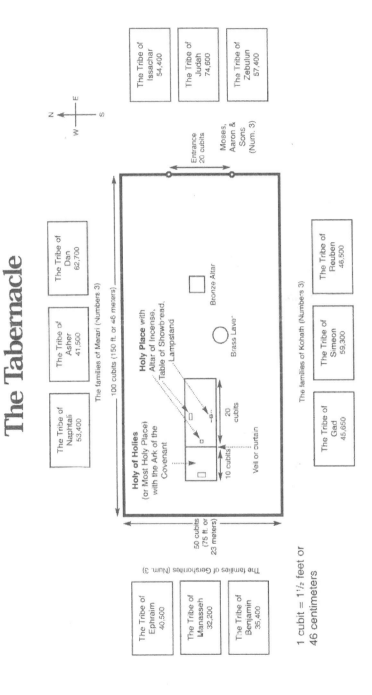

It didn't take long for the BodishBabes to notice a discrepancy.
Macy questioned, "Wait a minute. Something doesn't make sense."
"Yeah," said Alex. "What happened to Joseph and Levi?"

Great question! This became one of the wonderful Camp Mimi "rabbit trails" that lead to interesting discussions and life lessons.

Joseph was replaced by his two grandsons, Ephraim and Manasseh. Levi became a special, set-apart tribe of servants to the Lord. All of the priests came from the Levitical tribe. They were exempt from military duty. Their only responsibility was to serve the Lord. Although they were not numbered along with the other tribes, they camped in the center closest to the Tent of Meeting. It is also interesting to note that Judah, which means "praise" in Hebrew, is at the entrance to the Tent. We are to enter His courts with praise![37]

Each of us chose to "become" one of the tribes. The reasons behind everyone's choices were interesting and they put a lot of thought into it. Even our large, black Labrador, Asher, was given a tribe, after his namesake, of course. Papa was given the role of the high priest.

Alex was a tremendous help on the computer. She designed, printed and laminated a tri-fold passport for each child with a picture ID and a representation of the *ephod*, the breastplate worn by the high priest. This ornament contained jewels representing each of twelve tribes. She assigned each tribe a special color. The passports were placed in plastic sleeves on lanyards so that each child could wear his or her identification on this pilgrimage.

The BodishBabes love costumes, ornaments, and wearing anything special that symbolizes what we study. They were excited about locating their tribes on the butcher paper drawing and coloring them accordingly.

As a gift for our "high priest," we all worked together to make Papa a large cardboard *ephod* which we decorated with all the stones of the tribes. The high priest wore the reminders of the tribes over his heart. This was not at all difficult for Conlee to imagine because keeping his children and grandchildren in his heart is very natural as a father and grandfather. The wearing of the *ephod* demonstrates how God keeps each of us in His heart, wanting us to be as close to Him as possible and providing every opportunity for that to happen.

With tribes assigned, passports around our necks, the *ephod* over the heart of our high priest, and the diagram of the layout of the Tabernacle in the center of the table, we had Snack Time and I shared some facts about the Tabernacle.

The Tabernacle is discussed in fifty chapters of the Bible. The tent and its furnishings were made of very expensive materials such as gold, silver,

---

[37] Psalm 100:4

bronze, precious woods, rare fabrics, etc., all given as gifts by the Israelites.

A very intelligent question was asked by Caleb, "Where did former slaves get all those expensive things?"

This led us back to Exodus 12:35-36. When the Israelites were leaving Egypt and their slavery behind them, Moses instructed them to ask the Egyptians for articles of silver and gold and for clothing. The Lord gave them favor with the Egyptians and they were given everything they asked for. The Bible says, "They plundered the Egyptians."

To "plunder" literally means to take something by force from an enemy, such as the spoils of war. However, the Biblical account says that the Egyptians *willingly* gave the Israelites what they asked for. Why would they do that? The opinions around the table were varied.

"They wanted to get rid of the Israelites."

"They were afraid of what God would do to them if they didn't because they had experienced the plagues."

"God made them do it."

These were good ideas, perhaps truth in all of them.

"Plunder" became the word of the day after that discussion. There were lots of playful threats later among the children like, "I'm going to plunder you." And later, in the pool, they played "Plunder attack!"

The Israelites were so generous with their plundered treasures to build the Tabernacle that eventually Moses had to tell them to stop giving.[38] Their gifts of gold, silver and bronze were used to make exquisite vessels as furnishings. Their fabrics were used to make draperies and coverings. Some of the Israelites were accomplished craftsmen, having learned their trades working for Pharaoh. God used what they had done in their painful past for His glory.

We would become pilgrims on a journey through the Tabernacle.

THE BASIC LAYOUT OF THE TABERNACLE

Gathered around the large rectangle we had drawn on the butcher paper representing the whole Tabernacle, we now began to refine the details. The larger rectangle represented a seven foot high fence which formed a courtyard. It was covered with linen hangings held in place by pillars.

I drew a smaller rectangle within the larger one and told them that this was the Tabernacle proper, called the Holy Place. Inside the smaller rectangle was a square room called The Holy of Holies. Little Jake's response was, "I would be scared to go in there!" (His reaction – a holy awe – was appropriate).

The Holy Place was made of acacia wood overlaid with gold. On the

---

[38] Exodus 36:6

top were four layers of a curtain which formed a tent-like covering. The innermost layer was made of the finest linen and embroidered with cherubim (angels); the second layer was goat's hair; the third layer was red-dyed rams' skins; and the outermost layer was made of porpoise skins. These curtains were secured in the ground with stakes, loops and clasps.

Every detail of the interior is significant because each illustrates the way God says we are to approach Him, even today. For instance, there is only one entrance (no back door). You can't just go to Him anyway you choose. There is one gate and it is closely aligned with praise (Judah).

THE BRONZE ALTAR

When you entered through the one opening, the first thing you saw was the bronze altar. To help understand this, each BodishBabe was given a coloring sheet of the bronze altar, along with its dimensions: 7.5 feet long by 7.5 feet wide by 4.5 feet high. Papa took a measuring tape and they helped him block off these dimensions so they could see how large the altar was.

An altar was a place of death. The Hebrew root word for altar actually means a place of slaughter. It was on a raised mound of earth, higher than all the other furnishings in The Tabernacle. It was made of acacia wood and overlaid with bronze. Horns projected from each of the four corners and a bronze grating inside held the sacrificial animal. It was a place for burning animal sacrifices. This elicited lots of "Euwwww's" and "Gross!" comments around the table.

"So, why did animals have to die for someone to approach God?" I asked.

All of our children are animal lovers. Among them they had ten dogs and two cats. One of the most favorite Camp Mimi traditional field trips each summer became the animal rescue center where you can visit wounded wild animals that are being cared for. Are children too young to understand something as serious as killing an animal for God? I think not in this context. It was time to take a big breath and pray that God would speak through me.

Going all the way back to when Adam and Eve sinned and were ordered to leave Eden, it seemed there was no possible way back for people to have a close relationship with God like they originally had in the Garden.

Sin is a terrible thing and it has terrible consequences. This was far more than a "time-out" punishment so that they could then be re-admitted. This was permanent. Yet God wanted to have a close relationship with men and women, boys and girls. He longed to call them "son" and "daughter." As only God can, He made a way for this to happen.

Adam and Eve deserved to die for what they had done. But if they had died in their sin, there would be no more men and women to be the children of God. So, God said that something else could die in their place, a substitute to temporarily cover their sin. It wasn't the animal skins that covered sin, however. It was the *blood* that was shed. Blood is the only atonement for sin.

The Lord killed two animals and wrapped their skins around the naked Adam and the naked Eve, to symbolize the covering of sin in their souls by the covering of their nakedness on their bodies. Through this covering, they were able to once again have a relationship with God. It wasn't the same as living in Eden, but it was oh so much better than being without Him.

From that time on, God said that people could come close to Him by sacrificing an animal, remembering that although they deserved to die because of their sins, He would temporarily accept the animal's death as a substitute. A cruel thing? But sin against God is much worse! He said, "The life of a creature is in the blood, and I have given it to you to make atonement (exchange) for yourselves on the altar; it is the blood that makes atonement for one's life."[39]

This was a very sobering topic to talk about with children, but I didn't whitewash it at all and they took it very seriously. Even four-year-old Anna and Edie said, "Sin is bad!" "Really bad!"

In the Tabernacle, God showed the Israelites that as soon as they entered His courts they must be cleansed by the blood of an innocent animal. Each person coming to worship God was to bring an animal of some kind. Each animal had to be a male without any blemishes, scars, disease or defects. Each worshiper presented his offering to the priest who stood at the entrance. After an inspection of his animal, the worshiper laid his hand on his animal, identifying with the sacrifice about to be made, and cut the animal's throat. The priest took the blood and sprinkled it on the altar, burned the animal on the fire, and the worshiper was pronounced cleansed to continue to worship God.

We took turns reading about this in the Bible. "He (the worshiper) is to lay his hand on the head of the burnt offering, and it will be accepted on his behalf to make atonement for him."[40] "The law requires that nearly everything be cleansed with blood, and without the shedding of blood there is no forgiveness."[41]

We could tell that this was a pretty difficult concept for the children to comprehend but we persevered, believing that God would show us how to make it real to their young hearts. As you will see later, He really did!

---

[39] Leviticus 17:11

[40] Leviticus 1:4

[41] Hebrews 9:22

THE BRONZE LAVER

The next day we continued with a study of the next major furnishing of the Tabernacle, the laver. This was not a term the children knew so we had to explain about laver, washing, lavatory, etc. Being prompted often to "wash your hands before eating," they got the idea. It was a basin for washing one's hands and feet.

No size of the Tabernacle's laver is indicated in the Bible, but it must have been quite large to accommodate the usage it had. The priests alone used it to wash themselves for spiritual purification before entering the Holy Place and for physical cleansing after making the sacrifices. We read Exodus 30:17-21 and Exodus 38:8. As they worked on their coloring sheets of the laver, we talked about what it may have looked like as the sun shone brightly on the many faceted sides of the large basin, composed of the mirrors the women had given.

Great ideas and questions arose around the table:
"Did the Hebrew women get the mirrors from the Egyptians?"
"Was it made in a mirrored mosaic pattern?"
"Did the priests look at themselves as they washed?"
"Does God look at us and see what we see in a mirror or does He look at our hearts?"
"How often did they change the water in the laver?"
"Where did they get water in the desert?"
"Did they still have to take baths?"
"Did they use soap?"
"I'm thirsty!"

THE GOLDEN CANDLESTICK (LAMPSTAND)

After the priest finished his washing in the laver he passed through a veil into the Holy Place, a room containing three objects.

One was the golden candlestick on the north side. God was very specific when He told Moses how to have it constructed. It was to be of pure gold, hammered out of one piece, and formed with branches and cups shaped like almond flowers and buds. These cups were to hold the lamps to be filled daily with oil. The light was never to go out and a priest would make sure that it was always filled and the wicks always trimmed so it would burn brightly.

We looked at the small clay oil lamps we bought in Israel. The design is so simple that any of the children could have fashioned one out of modeling clay. Filled daily with olive oil, fitted with a simple wick, even a small lamp would burn brightly for several hours. Every home in the Bible had such a light source. With careful supervision we let the children fill their own lamps and set in the wicks, trimming them to about ¼" above the opening. Papa helped Jake assemble his and allowed him to help hold the lighter as we all lighted our lamps. Then we talked about the meaning of God's design.

God took something very simple like an oil lamp and told Moses to make a special, symbolic lampstand to hold seven oil lamps.

Why seven?
Why specially decorated?
Why did He have them decorate it with almond flowers?
What does this represent?

We read Numbers 17:8 and Jeremiah 1:11. Obviously, God likes the symbol of the almond tree!

During Snack Time, along with other treats, it seemed appropriate to have some almonds. It was a good time to talk about the interesting properties of an almond tree. We learned the Hebrew word for almond: *shaqed*. Its root word has a significant meaning for us: "to be watchful, alert, on the lookout, and sleepless." Now the whole idea of almonds and an ever-burning light and God's constant watchfulness over us made sense.

Of course, this discussion provoked other great questions:
"Why was the lampstand in the Holy Place?"
"What does light represent in a dark place?"
"What does John 12:46 say?"
"What does Acts 13:47 say?"

It was like a spiritual treasure hunt to find the answers and for over an hour they were intrigued.

Before bedtime we read Jesus' parable about the ten virgins in Matthew 25:1-13. It was the perfect story to act out as well as read because of the significance of the filled lamps. Caleb was the bridegroom, Jake was the groomsman, and the girls were the virgins with their lamps. Yes, it got pretty silly but the point was made. Be ready, watchful, on the lookout, and alert!

THE TABLE OF SHOWBREAD

The next morning we moved on in the Holy Place and studied the table holding the bread. The dimensions of this wooden table overlaid with pure gold are given in Exodus 25:23-30. It was 3 feet long by 1.5 feet wide by 2.25 feet high. That was fairly small and low, just large enough to hold golden plates with twelve loaves of bread, representing the twelve tribes of Israel.

The children worked on coloring pages while we talked about the table and how God said to construct it and what it would hold. Then we went for the "hands on" business of making bread. What could be simpler than taking flour and water (maybe adding salt and oil) and making it into dough and then cooking it on a hot surface?

How many kinds of flat bread are there? Every culture has its own and each is basic for daily life. There is pita (Greece, Lebanon), tortilla (Mexico), naan (Iran), chapatis and kulcha (India), focaccia (Italy), roti (India and Pakistan), bammy (Jamaica), bannock (Scotland), bazlama (Turkey), laobing (China), bolani (Afganistan), crisp bread (Scandanavia), crumpet and farl (England), flatkaka (Iceland), hallula (Chile), hardebrood (Germany), hubuz (North Africa), injera (Ethiopia), khanom bueang (Thailand, Cambodia), lavash (Armenia), lefse (Norway), malooga (Yemen), matzo (Israel), ngome (Mali), pane caarasau (Sardinia), pancake (America), papadum (India), tunnbrod (Sweden).

They were amazed at the number of versions of the same simple ingredients that every culture has made into a traditional staple. We were going to make a basic pita recipe [42] and stuff the pockets with our favorite ingredients for lunch. Yum!

We had a small island in our kitchen, barely large enough to get the children around. So it was important to assign a specific job to each child or they would be jostling for position and competing for each task. When I say specific, I mean as simple as: (1) get out the flour, (2) measure the flour, (3) add the salt, (4) stir the flour and salt together, etc. This takes longer and requires some preliminary preparations but it is well worth the effort when working with several children at the same time. Messy? Sure! But clean-up was easy and the results were spectacular. They loved seeing their pita pockets puff up like magic.

It also provided a great opportunity as we ate our pita sandwiches to talk about why Jesus called Himself the "Bread of Life."

THE ALTAR OF INCENSE

Also in the Holy Place was the wooden stand, overlaid with gold, where incense burned constantly. Its dimensions were only 1.5 by 1.5 and 3 feet high. When the children saw a table of similar size and stood next to it, imagining that they were the priest burning the incense, they determined that the men must have been very small in comparison to modern men. That is a good assumption.

Exodus 30:35-37 gives us God's special recipe for the incense that was to be burned on this altar. No other ingredients were to be used. It was an opportunity to obey God and enjoy His favor and presence. The only biblically required spice I had for the children to smell was an essential oil of frankincense and we passed it around for everyone to try it. There were mixed reactions.

---

[42] Recipe in the Appendix, "Camp Mimi Eats."

Exodus 30:7 says that the high priest, Aaron, burned the special incense every morning and every evening when he tended the lamps. As he did this, he prayed for the people. In Revelation 5:8 we are told that the prayers of all the saints are contained in golden bowls full of incense. Does that mean that our prayers to God are a sweet aroma to God? Does that mean that He keeps them stored in a special place in Heaven? What happens to your prayers after they are prayed? How important is each prayer to God?

We read that in Luke 1:5-13 the priest Zacharias was in the Holy Place tending to the holy incense, praying to God, when God sent an angel to him. The angel announced that he and his wife Elizabeth would have a son. This son would be John the Baptist. Our conclusion was that not only does God receive the prayers we pray, He responds to what we pray for!

We encouraged each one to ask God for something that was on their heart, something they knew that only God could do, and see that prayer, like incense, going up to God and being collected in His golden bowl. Then we thanked Him in advance for what He would do. Very solemnly each one closed their eyes and prayed. When a collective "Amen" was said, of course they were hungry again.

THE VEIL

Although one might not think of a curtain as a piece of furniture, the veil in the Tabernacle (and later in the Temple) was a very important item and as such was designed with intricate detail by God. In Exodus 26:31 we are given His precise instructions for how it was to be made. Woven of blue, purple and scarlet yarn and finely twisted linen, with cherubim worked into it, hung with gold hooks on four posts of acacia wood overlaid with gold and standing on four silver bases, it sectioned off the Most Holy Place from the Holy Place. This provided a barrier between God and man because God's presence was contained inside the Most Holy Place within the Ark of the Covenant. We were going to study the Ark next, but it was important to learn about the veil first.

It's hard to imagine the weight and design of such a curtain. We thought of theater curtains we had seen but modern ones are parted in the middle or raised and lowered by pulleys or ropes or electricity. The veil of the Tabernacle was of one piece with no separation in the middle. It was at least 15 feet wide. When the high priest, who only entered the Most Holy Place once a year, went in, he had to go around the side. No one could see through the veil and no other person, not even another priest, could enter. If he did, he would die.

When the Temple was constructed many years later, the veil was made exactly the same way. For millennia God's people needed a high priest to represent them before God. They could not approach God themselves.

The reason why the veil is so important is that when Jesus died on the

Cross, God split the veil from the top to the bottom, providing an opening for all believers to have access to the presence of God through the one, true High Priest, Jesus, the Messiah. We read about that event in Matthew 27:51. What a powerful symbol that is for us!

As the children colored their pages about the veil, using the colors that God specified, we talked about what it must have seemed like to the priests and Levites who were in the Temple when the veil was torn in half. What do you suppose they thought? Did they attempt to mend it? Did they take it down and make another one? Did they have any idea of what had just happened?

THE ARK OF THE COVENANT AND THE MERCY SEAT

Finally we got to the most important furnishing of all, the one everything had been leading to, the Mercy Seat. This was the entire focus of the whole Tabernacle. It was behind the veil, in the Most Holy Place, the place where God spoke to the high priest once a year. Exodus 25:10-22 tells us how it was constructed from wood and gold, then embellished with two golden cherubim facing one another on the cover. God said, "*Above* the cover (not *under* the cover) I will meet with you and give you all My commands for the Israelites." [43]

It wasn't "God in a box," but the Bible tells us it was His "footstool," a place where His presence was concentrated. King David had this vision from God when he said, "I had it in my heart to build a house as a place of rest for the ark of the covenant of the Lord, for the footstool of our God."[44] It was a place so holy that if one was not properly prepared he would immediately die in such intense holy presence. One can only think about such a place with awe and wonder.

Jake restated his earlier comment. "I told you that was a scary place!"

Once a year the high priest sprinkled blood from the sacrificial animal onto the Mercy Seat so that the people could receive forgiveness. God really wanted His people to be holy and to be close to Him. This was the only way people could have contact with God until He sent Jesus, the Messiah, into the world. Jesus is the high priest forever, and He leads us into God's presence.

A really great question was then asked by one of the children. "Is this why we pray in Jesus' name?" I am always amazed that just when you think children aren't paying attention, or are pestering a brother or sister or cousin, they receive a profound concept from the Lord.

---

[43] Exodus 25:22

[44] I Chronicles 28:2

THE HIGH PRIEST

Next to dressing up in a costume themselves, these children love to dress up someone else, especially Papa. So, with great care, and learning about each garment along the way, they dressed Conlee to be a high priest, showing how each part of his wardrobe pointed to Jesus. Exodus 29 gives great details about each garment and how they were to be made and worn.

First, they put a white robe on him, symbolizing purity. Then, over his head, they placed a tunic with bells and pomegranates alternating around the hem. We colored and cut out pomegranates to glue on, learning that a ripe pomegranate is said to contain 613 seeds, each one full of flavor and juice, representing the 613 laws that God gave to Moses. Pomegranates have long been a symbol of fruitfulness in Jewish culture. The bells provided a pleasing sound as he moved.

They placed the ephod they had made the first day around his neck, with each stone for the tribes resting over his heart. The children noticed right away that the same fabrics used for the ephod were also in the veil, gold, blue, purple and scarlet yarn of finely twisted linen. They were quick to make sure he knew where "their stone" was located so they would not be forgotten.

Then they wound a sash around his waist and a turban around his head. On the front of the turban, with a blue cord, they fastened a sign to represent the golden plate engraved with "Holy Unto the Lord."

These were very special clothes for the high priest for a special time with the Lord. Each garment represented an aspect of holiness to enter God's presence that the high priest did not wear all the time. In fact, he was told to cleanse himself and put them on before he entered the Most Holy Place and then afterwards to take them off and leave them there.[45] Since Jesus has become our High Priest, we can "wear holiness" all the time. He makes us holy so that we can enter God's presence.

THE FIELD TRIP

Field trips have always been a very important part of each Camp Mimi. Most of them are surprises, however some have become anticipated traditions, like the Naval Museum, the Wildlife Rescue Center and Bellingrath Gardens.

On the morning of our last day of Camp Mimi for the year we told the children we were taking them for a surprise field trip, somewhere they had never been. In spite of lots of begging to know and speculation among themselves, we put them all in the car and took off, Papa driving us all to a rather sketchy, industrial part of town. When we herded them all into the front door of Dewey's Machine Shop they were mystified. All they

---

[45] Leviticus 16:23

encountered inside was a grimy office, a maze of machines, lots of noise and people milling about everywhere working on all sorts of contraptions.

Dewey, the owner, met us at the nondescript entrance and led us inside through a heavy metal door into a back room. When the children all walked into the next room it was just like Alice through the looking glass or the children in England entering Narnia. We were transported into the Tabernacle! Yes, Dewey, the machine shop owner, had reconstructed the furnishings of the Tabernacle according to the specifications of the Bible and we were there!

In awe, we all walked past the high altar, to the laver, where we washed our hands. We proceeded into the Holy Place, saw the lighted *menorah* or lampstand, the table of showbread, and the altar of incense. Beyond the veil was the Most Holy Place where a life-sized mannequin of a high priest stood. Little Jake came and took my hand when he saw that.

The children delighted in pointing out each article that they had studied. Now it had come to life, thanks to Dewey and his lifetime vision. He most generously shared this experience with many people. Conlee and I had previously had some wonderful experiences in nights of worship in this space and it was always a time of entering into the intense presence of God, surrounded by Biblical symbols and truths.

Later, after lunch and a brief rest time, we all went out onto the lower lawn of our backyard. Conlee set out stakes in the ground measuring the exact dimensions of the Tabernacle, which the children gave to him according to their notebooks. With heavy string, they formed the "walls" around the courtyard, Holy Place, and Most Holy Place, exactly as the Bible said they were to be made. With boxes and improvised objects we set up all the furnishings. It had to be the hottest day of the year and we were all melting, but we worked hard to get it right.

Finally, it was time for us to become "worshipers" in the Tabernacle. Papa, as the high priest, instructed everyone to bring a sacrifice. It had to be a prized possession, an animal you loved and had cared for, without spot or blemish. They immediately chose Asher, our large black Labrador. They washed him, groomed him and had him brushed and shining to present before the Lord. The "priest" at the gate pronounced that he was suitable to be offered to God. Each child was beaming because their offering was acceptable.

Then the "priest" said they must take a knife and cut his throat. The horrified looks on their faces provided a picture I will never forget.

Not Asher! He's our pet! We love Asher! Jake even began to cry.

The "priest" said it was the only way to enter into God's presence and to receive forgiveness. The older children began to wail, "There must be another way!"

And then God provided the one *moment* that our whole week had been leading to. The "priest" said, "There is another way. God sent His only Son, Jesus, to die so you and Asher won't have to."

Really?
I love Jesus!
Jesus did that for us????
That's awesome!
I'm so glad we have Jesus![46]

---

[46] It took a while for each child to realize that it was not just Asher but *"I was pardoned when Jesus died on the Cross."* Each one has since asked Jesus to be Lord of their life and made a solid commitment to Him.

CAMP MIMI FOUR

UNDER THE SEA

By this fourth year I was much more organized prior to Camp Mimi. I printed daily planners with boxes to fill in each day for morning, afternoon, and evening activities, along with menus. This greatly tempered my tendency to "free-fall" and provided a much-needed structure as the children got older. Throughout the year, I accumulated little prizes for the ever popular Bingo games, awards, and treats. This became a priority every time I went shopping. Eventually I had a bag full in my closet.

I avoided going to the grocery store during Camp Mimi because meals were planned in advance and all the ingredients were purchased ahead of time in one big shopping excursion. Many of the meals were prepared ahead and frozen. Plus each night, I reviewed my planner and prepared for what we would do the next day. This was a huge help.

All the BodishBabes loved the water – like fish. Therefore, an "Under the Sea" theme was a no-brainer. They were old enough to do many things on the water; we lived on the water; they could accomplish some simple experiments and, because we always wanted to have our lessons be God-centered, we could learn about creation, the seas, the creatures of the seas, and how God's creative imagination produces infinite varieties of things for us to explore. But, I had to do my homework!

THE BIG REVEAL

When the Camp Mimi candle revealed our theme, there was not one negative or questioning comment. The boys "pumped air" and the girls collectively shouted, "Yes!" They were in from the beginning. Being under the sea was a favorite – from start to finish.

We sang the Camp Mimi song, lighted the candle, and decorated our boxes to fit the theme. This was all part of the now well-established tradition for the first day. Then I brought out a giant jigsaw puzzle of undersea creatures which covered the entire table. It had very large pieces, which even Jake could manage to fit into the proper spaces. We finished the puzzle and named all the creatures in no time.

THE HABITAT

Our first lesson was to learn about the environment that God made to support the life of sea creatures. Their coloring page was of the earth, divided into continents and oceans. They were asked to color all the oceans blue. In doing so they learned that oceans wrap around the globe and are divided into four main areas: Atlantic Ocean, Pacific Ocean, Indian Ocean, and Arctic Ocean. In fact our planet is sometimes called the "water planet" because seventy-one percent of its surface is covered by ocean.

We took turns reading Genesis 1:1–13 from *The Living Bible*. That set the stage for how it all began. Then, as they continued with other coloring sheets about oceans, we learned some fun facts about the sea.

- Ninety-seven percent of all water on Earth is in the oceans. Two percent is frozen.
- The Antarctic ice sheet is almost twice the size of the United States.
- The Pacific Ocean is the largest.
- The average depth of the sea is 12,200 feet.
- The deepest point measured is 36,198 feet in the Mariana Trench in the western Pacific.
- The ocean ridges form a great mountain range underwater, almost 40,000 miles long. It weaves through all the major oceans. It is the largest single feature on Earth.
- Ninety percent of all volcanic activity occurs in the oceans.
- Canada has the longest coastline of any country in the world.
- The volume of the earth's moon is the same as the volume of the Pacific Ocean.
- Although Mount Everest is the tallest mountain on Earth, the highest mountain in the sea is Mauna Kea, Hawaii. It rises 33,474 feet

from its base on the ocean floor. An inactive volcano, it's only 13,680 feet above sea level.
- The highest tides in the world are at the Bay of Fundy, which separates New Brunswick from Nova Scotia. At some times of the year the difference between high tide and low tide is 53'6", the equivalent of a five-story building.

The older children love these kinds of fun facts. The younger ones, reminded of Camp Rule #5c,[47] were content to color extra pages while we had a discussion with the older campers.

Since we were right on Mobile Bay and the children were familiar with high and low tides, I asked them how high they thought tides get on the bay. Their guesses ranged from one to ten feet. After we went outside to show them how high the water would have to be to get to even five feet; they decided their guesses weren't right.

Papa showed them how to read a tide table, how to find the closest location to our home, and how to tell when and how high the tides would be each day. We found that the highest tides during their visit would be a foot-and-a-half and learned when they would occur.

Then we asked them how high our house was above sea level. Again, there were some wild guesses. Since it was time to go outside for a while, Papa took them to a large tree on the street side of the house, where they found a marker at its base that they had never noticed before. It was the geological survey marker that showed that the elevation of the floor of our house was 17.4 feet above sea level. They were pleased to learn that the water had never been that high, even during hurricanes. The house had never flooded.

While we were outside, we went down to the beach, took off our shoes, and walked around to see what had washed up during the night. We found the very things that are most commonly found. (Another fun but sad fact is that the most frequently found items in beach clean-ups are pieces of plastic, plastic foam, plastic utensils, pieces of glass, and cigarette butts.) We found nothing of special interest that day. But while we were there, Conlee supervised the building of some sand castles while I went back to the house to make snacks to enjoy before a swim in the pool.

THE WATER CYCLE

---

[47] Enjoy every activity, even if it's not your favorite or too hard or too easy for you. Be patient. There is something for everyone.

It's a fun outside activity to construct a simple model of the cycle that water takes from the ocean to the atmosphere and down again. Oceans are always losing and gaining water in a never-ending process. Scientists call this the hydrologic cycle. Oceans lose water when the sun and wind lift tiny particles of moisture from their surface. These invisible particles of water vapor join up as water droplets to form clouds. Clouds shed rain or snow and most of it, about seventy-seven percent of all precipitation, falls directly back over the sea. Rain water and melted snow that fall on the land run into rivers flowing back into the sea. Therefore, the oceans never dry up.

On a table next to the pool I placed two half-gallon jars. I had the children fill one of the jars with about an inch and a half of water from the pool. I added a couple of drops of blue food coloring and a couple of drops of green to show that this represents the ocean. I had them put a rock in the middle of the jar to represent land. Some of the rock stuck up out of the water. Then, as they inverted the second jar over the first, Papa taped the two together tightly with some silver tape. We let it sit in the sun while they swam.

Of course, they all quickly forgot about the jar until it was time for lunch. When I brought out their sandwiches on trays and asked them to get out of the pool to eat, they noticed what had happened inside the glass. The colored water in the bottom of the jar had been heated by the sun. Some of the water received enough energy to evaporate into water vapor (particles of pure water too small to be seen). The water vapor rose in the warm air. When it came close to the cooler sides of the jar it cooled and condensed onto the sides. As more and more water vapor condensed onto the jar, droplets were formed big enough to precipitate down to the bottom.

Interestingly, the droplets on the sides of the jar were not blue-green. The larger food coloring particles were left behind in the "sea" just as salt and pollutants are left behind when water evaporates from the ocean. This pathway of water is called the water cycle.

We drank simulated "seawater" with lunch in the form of green Kool-Aid.

That night, since it was the Fourth of July, we decided to have a picnic on our beach with fireworks. We timed it so that we would be there at high tide.

SEA CRITTERS

Since the BodishBabes like fun facts, we started with some information about the creatures that God put into the waters (Genesis 1:20–21). We wanted to show them just how creative our God is! Each fact was accompanied by pictures and coloring sheets. The discussions were lively!

- The largest known animal ever to have lived on sea or land is the **blue whale**. An adult is more than 110 feet long and weighs almost 200 tons, more than the combined weight of 50 adult elephants. Its blood vessels are so broad that a full-grown trout can swim through them, and its heart is the size of a small car.
- The longest bony fish in the world is the **oarfish**. It has a snake-like body with a large red fin along its fifty-foot length. It has a horse-like face and blue gills.
- **Green turtles** can migrate more than 1,400 miles to lay their eggs. They can be five feet long and weigh up to 660 pounds. When sleeping, they can stay under water as long as two hours.
- The largest and fastest marine fish is the **bluefin tuna**. An adult may weigh 1,500 pounds and swim up to fifty-five miles an hour.
- **Penquins** "fly" underwater at speeds up to fifty-five miles per hour.
- A group of **herring** is called a "siege."
- A group of **jelly fish** is called a "smack."

PROJECT SEAHORSE

In the afternoon, after rest time, each child received eight coloring and fact sheets about seahorses. These are actually bony fish, despite their strange appearance. They are in the same family as the pipefish. There are approximately thirty-two species of seahorses, ranging from one inch to more than a foot long.

In the wild, seahorses eat live shrimp larvae and other small crustaceans. They have eyes that move independently of each other and this helps them spot food. They suck food up their bony snout as if it were a straw. They swallow their food whole because they do not have teeth. They have no true stomach so they eat large quantities of food to compensate for their fast rate of digestion. Most live from one to four years.

Seahorses are the only fish with prehensile tails, designed to grasp and hold onto sea grass, coral, or each other. To avoid being spotted by hungry fish or crabs, they can stay motionless by using their long, curly tails as anchors. When they do move, they swim upright very slowly.

Instead of scales, seahorses have semi-rigid rings of bony plates on them to provide protection from predators. Because of this, they don't move with a wave-like motion like most fish do. They fan their delicate fins to glide gracefully. They sort of look like an armored knight.

Their skin colors are vivid to blend with their colorful surroundings. The female seahorse produces eggs, but they are held inside the male's body in his pouch until they hatch. He is pregnant for about forty to fifty days. The seahorse is the only animal in which the father is pregnant.

After studying about seahorses, I brought out fabric "seahorse tails" I had made for the boys to wear. The tails had sashes we tied around their waists which allowed long colorful tails to fall to the floor behind them. I told the girls we would have a similar surprise for them the next day.

That night before bed, we read aloud *The Great Sea Serpent*[48] by Hans Christian Andersen.

PROJECT MERMAID

Bright and early the next morning the girls were more than ready to get into their project. The boys donned their seahorse tails and were ready to see if the girls' costumes would be as cool as theirs.

Again, beginning with fact sheets, picture pages and coloring sheets we attempted to answer the age old question: *Are mermaids real?*

- The word "mermaid" means a maid from the sea. It is a legendary sea creature with the head and torso of a human female and the tail of a fish. The male version of a mermaid is called a "merman."
- Various cultures around the world have similar legends about mermaids. I showed them an illustration from the Nuremburg Bible in 1483, which shows a mermaid and a mer-dog swimming near Noah's Ark.
- Mermaids were sometimes known as sirens. They sang to sailors and distracted them, causing them to walk off the ships' decks or wreck their ships. Some stories said they would squeeze the life out of drowning men while trying to rescue them. Others said they would take them to their underwater kingdoms.
- The first known account of mermaids appeared in Assyria around 1000 BC. A popular Greek legend related that Thessalonike, the sister of Alexander the Great, turned into a mermaid after she died.
- On the Isle of Man, a mermaid is called Ben-Varry. In Scandanavia, she is called Havfrue. In Ireland, she is called Merrow. In Cornwall, England, she is called Merrymaid. In Japan, she is called Ningyo. In Germany, along the Rhine River, she is called the Lorlei.
- The logo for Starbucks Coffee shows a twin-tailed mermaid wearing a crown under a star. This is based on the character, Starbuck, in Herman Melville's book, *Moby Dick*, who drank lots of coffee.
- Mermaids are said to be very vain, always looking into mirrors. They often fall in love with human men and will go to extreme lengths to woo the men, forgetting that humans cannot breathe underwater.

---

[48] *Hans Christian Andersen, The Complete Fairy Tales and Stories*, translated from the Danish by Erik Christian Haugaard, Anchor Books, Doubleday, 1974, pg. 1015.

- The images of mermaids are found on the official coat of arms of Warsaw, Poland, the city shield of Norfolk, Virginia, and the coat of arms of Hamilton, Bermuda.

Here are some interesting quotes from history:

- "This evening (June 15) one of our company, looking overboard, saw a mermaid, and, calling up some of the company to see her, one more of the crew came up, and by that time she was come close to the ship's side, looking earnestly on the men. A little after, the sea came and overturned her. From the navel upwards, her back and breasts were like a woman's, as they say that saw her; her body as big as one of us, her skin very white, and long hair hanging down behind, of colour black. In her going down they saw her tail, which was like the tail of a porpoise, speckled like a mackerel. Their names that saw her were Thomas Hilles and Robert Rayner."

    (Henry Hudson, 1625, English explorer, sailing near Norway)

- "We saw mermaids, but not as pretty as they are depicted, for somehow in the face they look like men."

    (Christopher Columbus, 1493, sailing near Haiti)

- "I saw a fish-tailed mermaid with round eyes, finely-shaped nose, well-formed ears and long green hair. By no means unattractive."

    (John Smith, 1614, rescued by Pocohontas)

While the children continued to color their pages, I read them the story of *Johnie Croy of Volyar and the Mermaid*, a folklore tale from the Orkney Islands. It's a bit of a dark story, but the children loved it.

"So, what do you think? Are mermaids real or not?"

The answers were unanimously, "No!" They loved the legends and the stories but didn't expect to ever see a real one. I gave them one possible explanation for how the legend began. We looked at coloring sheets and fact pages about Manatees.

THE MANATEE

The manatee is Florida's state marine mammal. Being a large marine mammal means that they breathe air, have hair, are warm-blooded, don't lay eggs, and give milk to their babies. Manatees come to the surface every three to four minutes to breathe air when awake. When sleeping, they stay on the bottom and only come to the surface every twenty minutes to take a breath.

They live in warmer waters. Their front flippers help them steer and even sometimes crawl through shallow water. They also use their front flippers to dig up plants to eat. They have a powerful, thick, paddle-like tail that helps propel them through water.

Even though their eyes are small and they have no outer ears, they can see and hear quite well. They resemble elephants because they have similar toenails and a big nose like a short elephant's trunk, which they use to pull food into their mouth.

They are herbivores and can eat up to 150 pounds of grass per day. They can live in either salt water or fresh water and reproduce every five years.

A full-grown manatee can be ten to twelve feet long and weigh up to 1,800 pounds. They live fifty to sixty years in the ocean. Because so many of them are injured by boats, they are considered an endangered species.

We spotted an injured one in Dog River, near our home on Mobile Bay. It had many scars on its back from boat propellers. We sometimes saw them in the bay as well, rolling and playing much like porpoises.

It is said that the legends of mermaids began when sailors saw manatees. Because they had been at sea so long, they thought they were women.

"What do you think?" I asked.

Their answers were consistent.

"The sailors couldn't have been that stupid."

"They sure were ugly women."

"They needed glasses."

We ended by giving the girls their mermaid tails. Similar to the boys' seahorse tails, they were made of fabric and tied at their waists, with long, beautiful, wavy tails that swept along the floor. Everyone modeled their costumes and I strongly suggested they not wear them in the pool.

That night we read *The Little Mermaid*[49] by Hans Christian Andersen.

PLAYTIME

Earlier in the summer, I found two items at a local discount store that were guaranteed to become BodishBabe favorites. I waited until the right time to bring them out for this year's theme.

One was a "slippy slide" which we set up on a gentle incline on the lawn near the bay. This became such a favorite that each afternoon they took turns sliding, cheering for one another, and filming videos of each other until we called an end to it or the antics got out of hand. For their safety, we had to insist on strict rules, such as sliding one at a time, no shoving, and only start down the slide when the person before you is walking away from his or her turn. Because of the hard use of the slippy slide it only lasted for one season. I was always on the lookout for another one at sales at the end of summer.

---

[49] *Hans Christian Andersen, The Complete Fairy Tales and Stories*, translated from the Danish by Erik Christian Haugaard, Anchor Books, Doubleday, 1974, pg. 57

Over the years, we found a variety of inflatable water slides. One had two side-by-side racing courses, one had a fort at the bottom with simulated fire, most had spray hoses along the sides, and one had a small pool at the bottom. Each one was more popular than any other outdoor toy, except perhaps, the inflatable island.

The island was an amazing find at a reduced bin in a discount store during the winter. This particular large box was extremely damaged and it was hard to see what I was buying, but I was willing to take a chance for five dollars! It turned out to be one of the best five-dollar purchases I ever made. It consisted of a huge inflatable island with a five-foot-tall inflatable palm tree, and a life boat with oars. Best of all, it was large enough for at least five children to play on at once. It filled nearly half of our pool! It was the perfect place for many imaginary excursions on hot afternoons for several years. To this day they still talk about that island!

UNUSUAL SEA CREATURES IN GOD'S CREATION

After learning about the manatee, we had a study session learning about another unusual sea creature called a **dugong**. Until I did the research, I had never heard of such a creature; neither had the children.

Smaller than a manatee, a dugong (which means "lady of the sea" in Malay) averages about 8.9 feet long and weighs about 660 pounds. Sometimes they are also called sea cows, sea pigs, and sea camels. There are groups numbering 10,000 near the Great Barrier Reef of Australia and in New Guinea. They also have been seen off the coast of Mozambique, Kenya, Tanzania, Malaysia, and Singapore, as well as in the Philippines, and in Egypt's Red Sea.

Their snouts are more tapered than manatees and they dig up grasses from the ocean floor. They may live fifty or more years and do not reproduce until around age eighteen.

An ancient creature, the sea cow is mentioned several times in the Bible (Exodus 25:5 and 26:14) and there is a 5,000-year-old painting of a dugong in Malaysia. Dugong hides may have been used in the outer hangings of the walls of the Tabernacle.

The other unusual creature we studied was the **giant squid.** This is a gargantuan invertebrate (creature without a backbone) that lives in very deep waters, about 2,000 feet under the sea, but swims even deeper. It can grow to forty-three feet long. It has a torso (mantle), eight arms, and two longer tentacles. The inside surfaces of the arms and tentacles are lined with hundreds of suction cups, one to two inches in diameter, each mounted on a stalk. Each cup is lined with sharp, finely serrated rings of sharp teeth. The rings attach themselves to its prey.

Whales have been found with suction marks on their skin where they had been attacked by a giant squid.

Only one other invertebrate is larger—the **colossal squid**. Bigger than a school bus, it can be twice as long as the giant squid. These squid are found in all the world's oceans.

A giant squid has three hearts. Two of them help the gills and one pumps blue blood, which actually is more clear than blue. The element in human blood (hemoglobin) that makes it red is absent from squid and octopi. Like other squid (calamari) and octopi, it contains dark black ink that it can release into the water to confuse its enemies.

In Norway, there are ancient stories about a sea monster called the **Kraken**, described as being as big as an island and having many arms. Sailors were on the lookout for him because he was said to be so large that he could wrap his arms around a ship and pull it under.

The Norwegian sailors who started the legend probably spotted a giant squid, which could have been larger than the sailing ships of their time. No doubt, the creatures were very frightening. And, it is possible that a giant squid could mistake a ship for an enemy sperm whale and attack the ship.

Caleb and Sophie immediately remembered riding Kraken, the giant roller coaster at SeaWorld, They had to relate every detail about their scary ride to the other children.

Dramatically, I read aloud to them the short sonnet by Alfred Lord Tennyson called *Kraken*. Written in 1830, some believe that this describes the ancient Leviathan in the Bible. It is also believed that the famous giant squid inspired Jules Verne in his book, *Twenty Thousand Leagues Under the Sea*, in 1870.

Most of the afternoon's swimming games involved one of the BodishBabes being Kraken and the others squealing and trying to get away. The floating island took a beating but held up!

FIELD TRIP

One morning we took an outing to Dauphin Island. This is a rather secluded beach about an hour from our house. Although we didn't see any unusual sea creatures, we did see a shark that had washed up on the beach and lots of sea birds. Afterwards we had a late lunch at the Fowl River marina where we ate great seafood and played an animated game of "courtroom"[50] for an hour, much to the delight of the waitress. No one ordered calamari!

---

[50] The BodishBabes made up this game and it was inspired by the huge, leather swivel chairs around the table at the restaurant. The children immediately thought that the chairs looked like they belonged in a courtroom. In their game, one child was the judge, one was the defendant on trial, and the rest were prosecutor, defense attorney, and jury. Sophie was the judge. Jake was on trial and was convicted for

Our other field trips were the customary Naval Air Museum in Pensacola and Bellingrath Gardens. They thought they were going for our annual "walk through the gardens and play hide and seek" which they enjoyed every year, but we had booked a special time for them at Dauphin Island Sea Lab's Estuarium. It is part aquarium and part science lesson, where experts allow guests to watch sea horses, feed stingrays, hold hermit crabs, and many other fun things.

Then we boarded the *Southern Belle*, a 150 passenger boat, for a lunch cruise on Fowl River. We didn't see many sea creatures, but we saw some osprey and herons looking for their lunch while we ate ours.

One afternoon we also took a boat ride in our small seventeen-foot boat. We went up Mobile Bay and into Dog River, hoping to have our own manatee sightings. Although we didn't see any manatees, we were stopped by the marine police who came speeding up alongside our boat with blue lights flashing and siren blaring. The BodishBabes were terrified!

The marine police were just checking to see if all our young passengers had lifejackets, a requirement on the water. Because each child was wearing one according to the law, the very nice policemen gave each of them a T-shirt that said "I was caught on Dog River wearing my life jacket!" A great souvenir of a great afternoon!

TREASURE HUNT

When Conlee and I brainstormed about fun under-the-sea adventures, our ideas progressed from sea to boats to pirate ships to pirates to booty to buried treasure to treasure maps. *Voila*! Our last afternoon adventure was determined. The children would discover a treasure map and hunt for buried treasure.

We began the morning by giving them lots of fun coloring sheets of little islands with palm trees, pirates, treasure chests, and maps. I read to them as they colored. Our stories were short accounts I had found online about real people finding real treasure, as well as some fictional accounts.

One of the stories told about a nine-year-old boy in Sweden who, along with his grandfather, uncovered two clay vessels containing more than 7,000 silver coins dating from around 1300 AD.

Another story told about a 34-year-old man in Wisconsin who found a rusted box on his farm while plowing. It contained 1,700 dollars worth of old currency.

I read them another account of three men in the late nineteenth century who tried to find a chest of gold left by the infamous Captain Kidd and his men on the Connecticut River's Clarke Island in Massachusetts.

---

stealing and wrecking a motorcycle. He was denied dessert for his punishment but the judge pardoned him because he said he was sorry.

Although they found an iron chest while digging in the mud late one night, it sank out of sight before they could retrieve it.

There are lots of legends about buried treasure and many of the treasures have actually been discovered. There are always just enough positive stories to encourage more attempts.

Evidently burying their booty was a popular way for pirates to safeguard their treasures. Often they left maps marking the spot.

There is a legend that near Poverty Island in Lake Michigan, a schooner transporting five chests of gold to be used by the Americans in their fight against the English, was wrecked. These chests would be worth about 400 million dollars today! Many people have attempted to find them, but none has been successful.

Another legend in Whitehall, New York, tells of a man named Robert Gordon who in 1775, left his home in New York, to go to Canada, to avoid the war. He put all his valuables in a strongbox and while on his journey to Canada, dropped it on the west shore marshes of the Haven. He made a map of the location of his strongbox but he never returned. In 1934, 159 years later, a person clearing up a swamp near the Haven brought up a metal box from the muck. He balanced the box on the debris but it then fell back into the water. Many people have since tried to relocate the box, but none has been successful. The stories of finding metal boxes which then disappear again are numerous!

Another longstanding legend tells of eleven boatloads of treasure, called the Great Treasures of Lima, that a pirate buried in a cave in 1822, on Cocos Island near Costa Rica. In fact, there are three other popular legends about buried treasure on Cocos Island! More than 450 expeditions have set out to locate these treasures and each has failed.

I told them about one of the most famous pirates in history, Edward "Blackbeard" Teach (also known as Edward Thatch). He was a notorious English pirate in the early 1700s, sailing around the West Indies and the newly-formed American colonies. His frightening appearance with a huge, full black beard gave him his nickname. He was said to light fuses under his hat, giving the impression that his beard was on fire, to intimidate enemies. His colorful history inspired many stories about pirates.

The interest of the children was piquing as we continued to talk about pirates and buried treasure. I just "casually" mentioned that Papa and I had "found" a map when we bought our house on the bay many years before. We "just wondered if it could be a treasure map." Of course they all wanted to see it!

Weeks before, Conlee and I had taken some parchment paper, drawn a crude map on it with an "X" to mark the spot, and rubbed dirt into it, wrinkled it, and even singed the edges. It looked fairly authentic, at least to our young adventurers.

We let them pore over the map for a while, discovering the bay, several large prominent trees on our property, how many steps to go from those trees, and where the "X" might be. It didn't take very long for them to be armed with shovels and spades, ready to find their fortune.

While I was chaperoning the treasure hunt, Conlee slipped away to don the costume of Blackbeard the Pirate! He tucked blousy pants into hunting boots, wore a loose-sleeved shirt and vest, attached his old ROTC Army saber to his belt, tied a bandana around his head, and put on a black fake beard. At his tall height, he looked pretty frightening.

When he came around the house, waving his saber in the air and yelling, "What are you doing with my map?" every child screamed and took off for safety. It didn't take long for the older ones to realize it was just Papa, but it took some coaxing for little Jake to become Blackbeard's first mate to help him uncover the buried treasure chest.

Finally, with a little help from "Blackbeard's memory," the children determined where the treasure was buried and began to dig. Fortunately, the sandy soil of our back lawn was an easy place to bury treasure and an easy place to dig it up. Although it was hot work and each took turns with the shovels, they hit pay dirt. At the first sound of metal hitting metal they got very excited and unearthed a large plastic garbage bag containing a metal treasure chest. Inside were gold-wrapped chocolate coins, small gifts for everyone and—*ta-da*—a new slippy slide! It was time for swimsuits and water!

AWARDS

We concluded our wonderful week "Under the Sea" with our traditional steak dinner preceded by everyone's all-time favorite appetizer, sautéed crab claws!

When Sophie was just a baby, she ate a pound of crab claws by herself!

I timed the Camp Mimi group once after bringing out two pounds of sautéed crab claws to have as appetizers by the pool. They attacked them like little piranhas and it took exactly nineteen seconds for them to eat the whole tray. With the current price of crab claws, that is a very special treat indeed!

Awards were given for the best camper in many categories and each one got a special prize. Their certificates were received with dramatic acceptance speeches and we finished the fourth annual Camp Mimi by reading aloud Hans Christian Andersen's *The Golden Treasure*.[51]

---

[51] *Hans Christian Andersen, The Complete Fairy Tales and Stories,* translated from the Danish by Erik Christian Haugaard, Anchor Books, Doubleday, 1974, pg. 832.

CAMP MIMI FIVE

JOURNEY TO ISRAEL

In early February of the fifth year of Camp Mimi, Conlee and I led a tour of about forty people to Israel. We had been several times before and this was our second time to organize a group to visit the Holy Land, receive excellent scholarly teaching from our local Shoresh[52] guides, and study the Bible on site.

I served for several years on the board of Shoresh International. (*Shoresh* means "roots" in Hebrew). The goal of this fine organization is to inform and educate Christians about our Hebrew heritage by visiting the land of the Bible and learning from scholars about the history and spiritual application of each landmark.

The main responsibility Conlee and I had as tour leaders was to recruit and organize the group, get them there and get them back home, and lead a relevant devotional at each site. It was always a wonderful experience.

It's hard for me to believe it now but the first time we went to Israel I didn't even want to go! Our first trip was a gift from a lovely couple in our church. Conlee called me one morning from his office at church and told me that Judge Champ and Emilee Lyons were giving us a wonderful trip and he would tell me all about it when he got home that night.

---

[52] Shoresh study tours. www.cmj-usa.org/content/shoresh-study-tours

All day I filled my imagination with thoughts and pictures of a Caribbean Island, relaxing in the sun, enjoying absolute rest and being pampered. That night, when he told me the gift was to find a tour going to Israel and join with them, I was actually disappointed. Going to Israel had never been on my radar and going on a tour with a random group of people we didn't know was definitely not my cup of tea.

But Conlee was already on it. He called Bishop Terry Kelshaw, an Anglican bishop friend from New Mexico. He knew that Terry had been to Israel numerous times and asked if he could recommend a good tour for us. It just happened that Terry was leading one himself in only a few weeks for some people in his diocese. We were welcome to join with them.

And so, I, reluctantly, flew to Israel with Conlee and about thirty-five strangers from New Mexico. Before the plane landed I was dreading the next two weeks. However, after only a couple of hours in the Land, I was praying and planning about how to come back! I am still extremely grateful to the Lyons for their generous gift!

I realized that reading about Israel (even from the Bible), hearing about it, or looking at someone's tour pictures just doesn't convey the spiritual pull that God provides when you actually walk the Land. Then it becomes a personal adventure and it can be life-changing. I am always ready to go back in a heartbeat.

Early in January, while praying about what to do for our fifth Camp Mimi in the coming summer, I wished we could take all the BodishBabes to Israel with us. Instead, I thought, *Why not bring Israel to them?*

One of the families going on the tour with us to Israel was the Holland family from Florida, Dan, Marcia, and their teenage son, Nate. I knew that Nate was a skilled videographer and video editor so I asked him if he would be willing to film Conlee and me speaking to the BodishBabes at each major stop on our tour. He graciously accepted and, at the conclusion of our tour, presented us with a most professionally-crafted DVD of our whole experience, with an episode on site for each day of Camp Mimi. So early in the year, it was decided that this would be our Camp Mimi theme for year five: *Journey to Israel!*

Our plan was to "take the BodishBabes to a different site in Israel" each morning via our DVD and then study about that place and what happened there in the Bible. Then, each night we would "celebrate one of the major Jewish feasts." This was quite an undertaking and took more preparation than any previous Camp Mimi. But the rewards were outstanding and far surpassed my expectations.

DAY 1 – THE LAND, BEGINNING WITH JAFFA AND ROSH HASHANAH

This year we had five BodishBabes. The two older girls were now so busy with their summer activities and athletic practices that they were not able to come.

For The Big Reveal (which unfortunately they initially mis-interpreted as an *actual* trip to Israel), instead of the candle revealing the theme, we all went in front of the big TV where we had cued up Nate's DVD. It began with loud, lively music (*Solution*),[53] showing time-lapse activity at our international gate at the Atlanta airport, then fading to a subdued scene of Mimi and Papa on the plane in the middle of the night, quietly telling them we were taking them with us to a place they had read about but never visited. We would be flying all night and would arrive early the next morning in the Holy Land, in Israel!

We paused the DVD at this point to let everyone settle in to see how our week would unfold. There was great expectation but tempered with lots of questions like, "Will there be any surprises? Will we go to the Naval Museum? Will we go to Bellingrath Gardens?" These children love family traditions! It was apparent that "going to Israel" had no personal reference point for them.

We adjourned to the table, lighted the Camp Mimi candle, read the rules together, sang the Camp Mimi song and decorated our boxes with sponges and acrylic paints. We then put together a large-piece jig-saw puzzle of the Land of Israel. This, plus some colorful maps, gave the children an idea of the small size of Israel as compared to other countries, and an idea of the topography. Mainly, I wanted them to see that the terrain changes drastically from left to right across the country (west to east): first there is water (the Mediterranean Sea), then the coastline, then the mountains, and, finally, the desert. We located the two large bodies of water inside the country, the Sea of Galilee (really a large, fresh-water lake) and the Dead Sea, both connected by the Jordan River.

They received coloring sheets of the Israeli flag and were directed to color them blue and white, matching the small Israeli flag we placed in the center of the table. We talked about the Star of David which is in the center of the flag. Although it does look like a star, in Hebrew it is known as the *Magen David*, "the shield of David." It is composed of two equilateral triangles. The flag also resembles the Jewish prayer shawl, the *tallit*, which we would study about later.

Our first stop in the Land of Israel was Joppa (*Jaffa*), so we went back to the DVD to continue where we left off. On the video it was now morning in Israel and Papa and I greeted them from our first stop.

---

[53] *Solution*, by Hillsong United

"Good morning, BodishBabes! Here we are in the center of the square of the ancient city of Jaffa. This is an important city in the Bible. Look around at the old buildings and listen to the sounds of the city coming awake this morning. Today we're going to study about two important people in the Bible who were here in Jaffa. We're going to walk down to the Mediterranean Sea in a few minutes and then read about a man named Jonah from the Old Testament who sailed on a ship from this very port. He was trying to go to Tarshish, all the way across the sea. Then we'll read in the New Testament about Peter, who had a remarkable experience here in Jaffa. So come with us and look around the port, and some of Jaffa's quaint streets."

Nate spliced together many wonderful scenes of the ancient city for the children to see, the sea wall, old fishermen sitting on the wall, the house of Simon the Tanner where Peter stayed, the bell tower of St. Peter's church, ancient buildings and houses, all with the background of modern Tel Aviv looming up right next door. We definitely were in another land!

After handing out coloring sheets, I read them the story of Jonah. They knew the general story, but not so many of the details. They answered some questions written on their coloring sheets as they listened to the story and busied their hands with crayons.

"What did the Lord want Jonah to do? What did Jonah do instead?"
"Why didn't he want to go to Nineveh?"
"What happened when Jonah got on a ship going in the opposite direction?"
"What was Jonah doing during the storm?"
"What did the captain of the ship tell the sailors to do?"
"Was Jonah afraid? What did he do?"
"What did the sailors do when the captain told them to throw Jonah overboard?"
"What did Jonah tell them to do with him instead?"
"Was the big fish waiting for Jonah?"
"Did the Lord tell the fish to swallow Jonah?"
"Jonah prayed to be delivered. How did the Lord answer his prayer?"
"What did Jonah tell the shepherds who found him?"
"The Lord again told Jonah to go to Nineveh. What did Jonah do this time?"
"What did Jonah say to the people in Nineveh?"
"Did they believe what Jonah told them?"
"When the people turned to the Lord, how did Jonah feel about it?"

Our memory verse for the day was Psalm 119:17, which one version translates, *"I will obey Your word!"*[54] How hard it was for Jonah to learn that verse!

Our snacks included gummy fish, which seemed appropriate after

---

[54] New Living Translation

reading about the big fish that swallowed Jonah. While they continued to color lots of relevant pictures, we talked about the people from Nineveh who finally repented.

"Do we have people in our lives we dislike the same way Jonah disliked the Ninevites?"

This question prompted a lively discussion with unexpected honesty.

Thanks to Jonah's obedience, the Ninevites were able to experience God's mercy and forgiveness.

After a fun afternoon of swimming, playing "Jonah and the Big Fish" in the pool, and slippy-sliding, we were ready for our second tour stop of the day, so after lunch and rest time it was back to the DVD. With the lyrics of *Over and Over Again*,[55] we went up the coast of Israel, to Caesarea, the city Herod the Great dedicated to Caesar Augustus. On the big screen they watched us at the seashore of the Mediterranean where I picked up some shells for them (which I gave them later), pointed out some of the ancient steps leading from the port, the aquaduct which brought fresh water down from Mt. Carmel, and the amphitheater where Paul was imprisoned and spoke with Festus (Acts 25).

It was in Caesarea that the Roman centurion, Cornelius, received a message from God to have the man of God (Peter) brought from the house of Simon the tanner in Jaffa to speak to him.[56] This led to the first non-Jew believing in Jesus as his Messiah and becoming a Christian. Again, our verse for the day *("I will obey Your word!")* was very important.

We announced that that night we would study and celebrate the first of our Jewish festivals: *Rosh HaShana*, the Jewish New Year. Instead of having separate lessons for our celebrations, we incorporated learning about the Feast Days right along with the feasting. We attempted to teach some traditions associated with each celebration, pointing the children to the Biblical references, and having some fun. In no way did we want to make the experiences seem less solemn or less meaningful than faithful Jews traditionally observe these holy days, but we wanted to provide a bit of the essence of each one and allow the children to become somewhat familiar with them. So, we did our best!

Rosh HaShana means "head of the year" in Hebrew. However this name is not used in the Bible, but rather *Yom HaZikkaron*, the day of remembrance, or *Yom Teruah*, the day of the sounding of the *shofar*. It is a call to "Wake up and repent!"

During dinner we read about this holy day in Leviticus 23:24-25. In the center of the table we placed the large *shofar* (ram's horn) we brought home

---

[55] *Over and Over Again*, Tree63.

[56] Acts 10.

from our first trip to Israel. Everyone took turns blowing it and we all agreed it is harder than it looks. Our best attempts sounded like a moose in great pain.

As we ate our meal, we told them the story of almost having our *shofar* confiscated in our stop-over, Amsterdam, when we were returning home from Israel.

A customs official at the Amsterdam immigration control was convinced that we were bringing the horn of an endangered species into The Netherlands.[57] He insisted that we leave it there in order to board the plane to Atlanta. We, in turn, politely refused to turn it over to him and insisted on seeing his supervisor. The supervisor was on a coffee break and was paged on the phone numerous times to make a decision. Meanwhile passengers boarding the plane were passing ahead of us, observing us holding our "suspect *shofar*" and being questioned by the authority. They could overhear our conversation with the customs control officer.

Many of the boarding passengers stopped to comment to the customs official, "Oh, that's not endangered; that's a religious item." "That's a ram's horn." "That's common in Israel." Some even strongly encouraged the official to allow us to bring it aboard.

All of the pressure to relent only caused him to become very stubborn. However, we became just as insistent. Finally, he became much more than stubborn; his face turned bright red and he was really angry. We were still held to one side, waiting for his supervisor to answer his page.

Finally, everyone had boarded but the two of us and the departure time had already been delayed for over five minutes while they were waiting for the missing supervisor to respond about our situation. The pilot was more than ready to go and we could hear his impatient pleas on the mobile device the Dutch official was holding. The pilot was telling him that if he had no authority to hold us, he had to let us board. Finally, the angry customs officer thrust our passports at us and told us to get on the plane with our *shofar*. His parting words to us actually were, "You can go but I'll get you next time!"

Since we were the last ones to board the plane, we were very obvious getting to our seats. Many of the people onboard cheered to see that we did not have to leave our souvenir. A few people even offered to blow it for us but we decided not to push our luck with the airline personnel.

At our meal we practiced saying the common greeting for *Rosh HaShanah*, "*Shana Tova!*" It means "Good Year!" A popular observance is to

---

[57] In retrospect, I wondered why he wouldn't want us to take it out of his country since we were leaving within minutes for the United States. But after several overseas flights, one learns not to question custom officials.

eat apple slices dipped in honey to symbolize having a sweet and fruitful year. This, along with some grilled pineapple, was our dessert after dinner and it was messy but very tasty.

While eating dessert, I taught them about the practice of *Tashlikh*. It is not a practice from the Bible but is a long-standing Jewish tradition, and it certainly emphasizes a biblical principle.

You go to a place where there is running water and empty your pockets of everything in them to symbolize casting off your sins and seeing them float away in the current. Most people fill their pockets with bread crumbs[58] or small stones to "cast into the sea." The tradition comes from Micah 7:18-19, which we read aloud.

"Where is another God like You,
Who pardons the guilt of the remnant,
Overlooking the sins of His special people?
You will not stay angry with Your people forever,
Because You delight in showing unfailing love.
Once again You will have compassion on us.
You will trample our sins under Your feet
And throw them into the depths of the ocean!"[59]

To illustrate this tradition, we all took several strips of paper and pencils. We wrote each sin we wanted to confess and to ask God to forgive on individual strips of paper, folded them tightly and we put them in our pockets. Then, right at sunset, we went down to the bay, read the passage from Micah once again, and *"cast our sins into the depths of the ocean."*

Each of us was especially solemn as we did this. We watched the waves take our "sins" out farther and farther until we could no longer see them. Then Papa laid his hands on each child and prayed, "Know that according to God's Word, when you confess your sins, He is faithful and just and will forgive you and cleanse you from all your wrong-doing."[60]

What a wonderful way to end our first day in Israel!

DAY 2 – THE GALILEE AND SUKKOT

As soon as the children were up, while still in their pajamas, we gathered before the TV to watch Day 2 in Israel. They watched Conlee and me standing at the seashore with mountains behind us and dark clouds in the sky. It was a very windy day and my hair was blowing all over the place. Also, it was softly raining and, unlike the day before when we were warm

---

[58] This tradition also relates to Ecclesiastes 11:1. It illustrates that you reap what you sow.
[59] NLT
[60] 1 John 1:9

on the Mediterranean and trying to keep the sun out of our eyes, today we were obviously cold and wearing rain jackets. This is typical weather when traveling in Israel.

"Good morning, Sophie, Anna, Edie, Caleb and Jake! We're here at the Sea of Galilee, at the very place where Jesus came after His crucifixion and sat on the shore and cooked breakfast for His friends. They had been out all night fishing on this big lake and hadn't caught one fish. That was unusual because His friends were professional fishermen. They were discouraged and heading towards shore when they smelled a charcoal fire and saw a man tending to it. He told them if they wanted to catch fish to throw their net on the other side. They did and caught 153 fish! They knew then that the man was the Lord! Jesus was risen from the dead!

"Peter was so excited that he jumped in the water and waded to the shore to get to Jesus. Then, Jesus invited them to come share His breakfast of fish. Their fish was probably tilapia, which they call St. Peter's fish here in Israel. Let's have some for breakfast this morning, just like Jesus and the disciples did right here at the Sea of Galilee!"

Then Nate's video panned to show the rocky shore and the church built on the site of the breakfast event. While the children got dressed and made their beds, I cooked tilapia for breakfast. They didn't like it very much but they were good sports. All of them agreed that even if it wasn't their favorite for breakfast, they wouldn't have told Jesus if He cooked it for them, so they didn't complain to Mimi.

Our first coloring sheets and Bible story for the day were about "The Boy who Shared His Lunch of Bread and Fish."[61] I read it to them from a children's Bible and they enjoyed commenting about it while they busied their hands with coloring. It didn't take long before they began to wonder, *Are we having a fish theme today? Fish for breakfast; fish for lunch?*

Our memory verse for the day was *Give thanks to the Lord for He is good; His love endures forever!*[62] We reinforced this many times during the day as Papa or I would say to them at various times, "Give thanks to the Lord for He is good." They would quickly respond, "His love endures forever!"

After the Bible story and coloring, it was back to the DVD and this time we were in one of the Jesus boats on the large lake known as the Sea of Galilee.

In 1986, there was a severe drought in Israel and the waters of the lake receded to the extent that two fishermen discovered the exposed remains of

---

[61] John 6:5-13

[62] Psalm 118:29

a first-century boat. The men were amateur archaeologists and knew how to carefully extract the boat from the mud and quickly submerge it in a chemical bath to preserve it.

Conlee and I first saw the boat in a big warehouse shortly after it was discovered and today it is displayed in a museum in Tiberias. Based on radiocarbon testing, the boat has been dated to between 50 BC and 50 AD, so it would be comparable to the boats that Peter, James and John fished from and the ones Jesus sailed on when crossing the Galilee.

It is 27 feet long, 7.5 feet wide, and 4.3 feet high. Because of the smaller size of men 2,000 years ago, it is believed that such a boat could have held a helmsman, four rowers, and up to 15 additional persons.

Today, there are larger boats built on this model that take passengers for an hour-long ride on the Sea of Galilee. After a wonderful lunch of tilapia at a little outdoor seaside restaurant in Tiberias, our tour group boarded one of these boats to head out to the middle of the Sea.

The gulls were flying around, the waters were still and it was cloudy and misty, but very peaceful that afternoon. As we reached the half-way point, we asked our captain to stop the engines and Conlee led us in a very solemn and meaningful communion service. The video for Camp Mimi captured the holy awe on everyone's face as they received the bread and wine. They sat in silence gazing at the surroundings and realizing where they were and how they were taking in the same Body and Blood of Jesus who once sailed these same waters. For many in the tour group it was the highlight of the whole trip.

After the video, we took the children down to the pier, got into our small boat with a basket of pita bread and a flask of grape juice, and went out on the Bay of the Holy Spirit (the original name of Mobile Bay) which is about the same size as the Sea of Galilee.

Conlee then led our BodishBabes in a very simple communion service. We passed the bread and the wine to each one and were all reminded that He is always with us in a very special way. As He instructed, we did this *in remembrance of Him.*[63]

They begged to fish, too, while we were on the bay, but that seemed like a formidable task with five children in a seventeen-foot boat! So, we lazily cruised around for a few minutes and headed back to the pool.

Late that afternoon, after swimming and rest time, we gathered around the table with more coloring pages that showed children decorating homemade shelters with leaves, branches and fruit. That night we were going to celebrate *Sukkot* or the Feast of Tabernacles! We also gave them lots of pictures of fruit to color and cut out, which they then strung

---

[63] 1 Corinthians 11:23-26

together like Christmas chains. We were going to use them to decorate our very own shelter.

Sukkot is another festival about *remembering*. We remember the time when the Israelites lived in very temporary dwellings in the wilderness for forty years. So, today, observant Jews follow the custom of building a temporary shelter outside, decorating it with branches and fruit, and living in it for eight days, remembering their forefathers who relied entirely on God to supply their needs.

The eight day Feast of Tabernacles was one of the three feasts Jews were encouraged to celebrate in Jerusalem at the Temple. When Jesus attended one *Sukkot* (which means "tabernacles" or "shelters"), it is written: *On the last and greatest day of the Feast, Jesus stood and said in a loud voice, "If anyone is thirsty, let him come to Me and drink. Whoever believes in Me, as the Scripture has said, streams of living water will flow from within him."* [64]

There is a very poignant reason why Jesus made His statement about living water on this particular occasion. Traditionally, every day during *Sukkot* the high priest carried water from the Pool of Siloam in the City of David, up the pilgrim road to the Temple and poured it around the perimeter of the Temple. This was called "the water-drawing ceremony," *Simchat Beit HaShorievah*, and was a time of great joy and celebration. The waters poured out were called "the waters of salvation," referring to Isaiah 12:3, *And you shall draw water in joy from the springs of salvation.*

People sang, shouted, danced, played musical instruments, and demonstrated their delight. Whoever witnessed the joy that accompanied the pouring of the water was believed to draw happiness for his soul and salvation from the travails of life. The Mishnah[65] states, *He who has not seen the rejoicing at the Place of the Water-Drawing has never seen rejoicing in his life.* No doubt it got a bit wild and disorderly at times.

Now we can understand why Jesus had to shout in a *loud voice* in order to be heard in the crowd and why He gave a new perspective to the demonstrations of pouring out ordinary water. He wanted to pour out something extraordinary into each of them if they would just come to Him!

We had a small pergola outside our kitchen door that had been there when we bought the house many years before. At one time it had an observation deck on top. However, we had removed the deck and planted jasmine vines to grow over it. It was the ideal place to have our *Sukkot* celebration. The thick vines with yellow and white fragrant flowers formed a canopy and the children decorated it even further with their paper chains of fruit and added branches. They brought in outdoor benches and a small table, pillows, lanterns and candles. What they created was beautiful and

---

[64] John 7:37-38 NIV

[65] A compilation by subject of Torah commentary.

they had a great time doing it!

Supper in our "tabernacle" was simple but delicious. Grilled beef and chicken ka-bobs with a couple of dipping sauces were always popular, plus it could be eaten with our hands.

After dinner we all went with Papa to the bay. He took a large pitcher which he filled with bay water and we brought it back to our *sukkah*. Very solemnly he poured it around the edges and we watched it soak into the sandy soil. Almost immediately, it was as though nothing had happened. It must have been the same in sandy Jerusalem.

What an opportunity to teach that "worldly refreshment" is like that. It doesn't last very long at all. But what Jesus offers us lasts forever! Out came the iPod, on came the music, and the singing and dancing began. We had our own celebration under the stars and the shelter of our *sukkah!*

DAY 3 - JERUSALEM AND PASSOVER

Beginning our Camp Mimi day after breakfast and early morning chores, we went right to the DVD to see where we were traveling in Israel.

There I was, standing in the central plaza area of the Jewish quarter of the old city of Jerusalem. It was about noon; it was loud and crowded, music was playing, and people were milling around everywhere. In the background you could see teen-agers in military uniforms standing around, flirting with one another, dancing to music and carrying machine guns.

Little boys wore their *kippahs* on their heads, many with long forelocks, holding their *abba's* hand; men were attired in long black dress coats and wide-brimmed hats, the tassels from their *talits* flying as they briskly walked.

Women in scarves and brightly colored sweaters carried packages. Activity was everywhere.

Good morning, BodishBabes! Here we are in the center of the Jewish Quarter in the old city of Jerusalem. Look how busy it is! Our group has just been in the Shoreshim Gift Shop here on this corner and we listened to the owner, an orthodox Jewish man named Moshe, explain his faith. Today, we'll talk to you about some of the things he shared with us, especially, about the word Shalom. *We just came out on the street and bought some dried fruit from a vendor and we all shared it with one another. It's a more popular treat here than candy. And we're getting ready to walk to a little restaurant to eat Jewish pizza for lunch. Doesn't that sound good? Would you like to have pizza today? We'll do just that! Now, look around at what people are doing and look at the contrasts between this old city and the newer Jerusalem.* Shalom!

With the background music of *Divine Romance*,[66] Nate's camera panned the square and effectively caught the energy of the crowd. It seemed that

---

[66] *Divine Romance*, by Phil Wickham

everyone was moving, dancing to music, or animatedly engaged in conversations. There was nothing stagnant about this noon-time crowd.

Into the scene of the local area he spliced scenes of life just outside the walls of the old city. Here was the picture of modern life as in any large city. There were crowded sidewalks, four-lane major streets with bumper to bumper traffic, impatient drivers, and large multi-story buildings, while in the background stood the ancient walls and our spiritual history.

Nate also captured the constant motion at the Western Wall, with throngs of people coming to pray at noon, men on the left and women on the right. A portable divider separated the two. The movements of the Jewish men, bobbing back and forth to pray the *Amidah*,[67] caught our attention right away. Their forms of dress varied strikingly. Some men were dressed in formal attire with coats and ties, some were in long robes of varying styles, and others more casual. All had covered heads. The women were more subdued, many sitting in folding chairs with hands and foreheads touching the wall. Some prayed aloud softly from prayer books, others prayed silently, some wept. It is a holy place for many reasons.

The Wall (or the Wailing Wall) is a relatively small segment of the walls which surrounded the Temple Mount on the western side, considered to be the closest remaining wall to the former Temple. It was built around 19 BC by Herod the Great.

It has been a site for Jewish prayer for centuries and you can sense the accumulation of prayer to God when you approach the stones. Into tiny crevices of the Herodian stones people place small pieces of paper with prayers written on them. I wrote the names of each of the BodishBabes and tucked them into such a crevice as I prayed for each one. I showed them a picture of their names contained by this ancient monument.

We learned the respectful tradition at the Wall of never turning your back on it, even as you leave. When people finish their prayers, they back out until they reach the barriers.

Since the BodishBabes had just observed some of the dress of the Israeli men and women, we began our morning by bringing out our beautiful *talit* or prayer shawl. Papa demonstrated how each man respectfully placed it on his head to pray, how it was intricately knotted and that each knot was significant, and how the *tzitzit* or fringes were the most important part of the shawl.

We also gave each of the boys a *kippah* or cap and they wanted to wear them all day. The girls received colorful Israeli scarves which they wound around their heads. We all decided that we definitely would wear them for dinner.

---

[67] Originally eighteen, now nineteen prayers said three times daily by observant Jews, the *Amidah* is part of the Jewish prayer liturgy or *siddur*.

We practiced using the greeting *Shalom!* as a blessing the way Jesus used it. *Shalom* has many meanings and when you pronounce *Shalom* to someone you are blessing them in a multitude of ways. You are blessing them with peace, a sense of well-being, good health, prosperity, safety, security and completeness, among other things. No wonder Jesus pronounced *Shalom* to people so often!

I told them a little more about our conversation with Moshe, the owner of the *Shoreshim* Gift Shop. Moshe believes he has a calling to promote reconciliation between Jews and Christians. He and his brother own and operate a very successful and lovely gift shop where he uses every opportunity to speak candidly with tourists.

As was his custom for tour groups, he put a "Closed" sign on his door for about an hour, brought out many little stools for us to sit on, and told us about his faith, inviting us to ask him any questions at all about Judaism.

My question was, "As Christians, we are encouraged to pray for the peace of Jerusalem according to Psalm 122:6. How do you, as a Jew, pray for Jerusalem?"

His answer was quite astonishing to all of us. "I'm afraid that more Christians pray for the peace of Jerusalem than Jews do. However, you probably pray for a cessation of strife and unrest politically and militarily according to the latest news reports. You must understand the Hebrew word you translate "peace." *Shalom* means much more than political and military peace. It is a condition of the heart. When the psalmist says to pray for *Shalom* in Jerusalem, he is saying to pray that every person will be whole so that the whole nation might reflect the glory of God."

When I told the BodishBabes this, they said, "We just learned that! But only Jesus can bring *Shalom* and they don't believe He is the Lord!"

Ah … I love it when they find their own way to a fundamental truth without being hammered over the head with doctrine. This led to a great discussion about how Jesus, the Messiah, is called the Prince of Peace or *Shalom* because He is the only one who can bring it to our hearts. I think at that moment they were zealous enough to preach it!

Making preparations for a Passover meal can take a good amount of time, however our meal was more last minute organization than actual cooking since I had done a lot of the work in the days before Camp Mimi began. Conlee supervised some outdoor activities while I organized the kitchen for the festive meal we would have that night. I never dreamed the Lord would surprise us with much more than I had planned!

It seemed appropriate to eat reclining as Jesus and His disciples would have done, so I placed pillows on the floor around our large square living room coffee table and set the table for our Passover meal. In the center I placed the traditional Seder Plate with a lamb bone (*zeroah*), parsley representing hyssop (*karpas*), a small bowl of salt water, bitter herbs (*moror*), hardboiled egg (*beytza*), and a mixture of fruit, nuts and applesauce (*haroset*). I put two candles on the table, along with a bottle of wine and a carafe of grape juice. There was also a plate holding three *matzot* (the simple flatbread called *matzah*), wrapped in a white napkin. Each would have special significance during the meal.

SEDER MEAL

Seder Plate with Matzot

Wine and Grape Juice

Hummus and Olives

Mesclan Salad with zucchini, tomato and Parmesan cheese, with olive oil vinaigrette

Chicken and rice casserole with fried-onion rings
Fresh green beans with toasted almonds

Chocolate-Orange Tart

Although this seems like a complicated menu to prepare in a short amount of time, some careful preparations a week or so *before* Camp Mimi greatly helped for this meal and for most of the others. I am grateful for my old catering days which helped me make constructive lists and organize preparations in a systemized way. A good freezer helped too!

The casserole and dessert were both made and frozen ahead and only had to be thawed in time. The salad mostly came from a bag with added fresh veggies and tossed at the last minute with a simple homemade vinaigrette I always have in the refrigerator. The green beans were already washed and snapped to be quickly sautéed with the almonds and a little chicken broth. Everything else was purchased already prepared. It really just took some assembly time while the children were outside. I let them help with the final arrangements of the Seder table. The casserole was put in the oven and the green beans were warming on a low fire. We were ready to begin!

Every Jewish family has some of its own unique customs, themes, special plates, and ceremonies for a Seder meal. These are wonderful and meaningful, but not necessary. However, some requirements are essential. We focused on these "essentials," explaining them along the way.

The children got cleaned up, dressed, and put out the plates, silverware, and wine glasses for me. They were excited about entering into an ancient annual event that Jews have been observing for more than 3,500 years and that Jesus re-symbolized over 2,000 years ago. It all involves *remembering* and *observing*.

After everyone was seated at our Seder table, I gave each of them a small printed *Haggadah*, the Jewish text that sets the order of the Passover.[68] I explained that most of the components of our meal were the same as the Passover Meal that we call The Last Supper, which Jesus shared with His disciples.

Papa turned out all the lights and I stood to light the two candles. As at a *Shabbat* observance, this is traditionally the mother's privilege and I asked all the girls to stand and help me. One candle is called *zakhor*, which means "to remember." What were we remembering? The story of Passover in the Bible from Exodus 12, which we would read in a few moments.

The second candle is called *shamor*, which means "to observe or obey." Therefore, we lit both candles to remember what God did and to obey what He commands. Then I symbolically fanned the light of "remembrance" and "obedience" to the whole family, praying this prayer, first in Hebrew, then in English: *Blessed are You, O Lord our God, King of the universe, Who has set us apart by His Word and in Whose Name we light the festival lights.*

Because they expected to begin our meal after this initial prayer, they were surprised when Papa stood and asked them to fill their wine glasses with a small amount of the fruit of the vine. The children all poured some grape juice and Papa and I poured wine into our glasses. This was the first of four cups that we had during our meal. This first one is called the "Cup of Blessing." *Blessed are You, O Lord our God, King of the universe Who creates the fruit of the vine.*

Then Papa draped a towel over his arm and took a pitcher of water and a basin. He went to each child, inviting us to wash our hands over the bowl as he poured water over them, and then to dry them on his towel. He prayed a prayer of cleansing their hearts as well as their hands.

After all hands were washed, Conlee then said that, like Jesus did with His disciples, he also would wash their feet. There were lots of giggles at first but they quickly removed their shoes and reverently waited their turns. Then they wanted to wash each others' feet. I could see already that this was going to be a long night. As they quietly washed feet, I read aloud Psalm 24:3-6.

After that, it seemed wise to wash our hands once more in the bathroom with soap before eating. Children have the amazing capacity to go in and out of the moment much easier than adults. So the break was welcomed and well-placed.

---

[68] The abbreviated *Haggadah* we tailored for Camp Mimi is in the Appendix.

When we gathered once more at the table we passed the Seder Plate we had prepared earlier. Each one was asked to take a sprig of the parsley, called the *Karpas*, and dip it into the salt water and taste it. As they did, Papa prayed, *Blessed are You, O Lord our God, King of the universe who creates the fruit of the earth.* The parsley reminds us of the hyssop branches that the Israelites used to paint the blood of the first Passover lambs on the doorways of their houses. The saltiness reminds us of their tears because Pharaoh made them work very hard in Egypt, as slaves and commanded them to kill their baby boys. We asked them to take turns reading verses in the Bible that explain Passover.[69]

Then we moved to a most important part of the Seder, the breaking of the *Matzah*. Unlike *Challah*, it is made without yeast to remember that the Israelites in Egypt had no time to let the bread rise before their last meal in bondage. God wanted them ready to leave at his command. Otherwise, they would miss the blessing and their deliverance.

Papa opened the napkin containing three *Matzot*, ceremoniously took out the middle *Matzah*, held it high and broke it. Even the youngest one present caught the vision: *This is like Communion!*

Papa took one of the broken pieces of the middle *Matzah* and wrapped it in the napkin and hid it while everyone closed their eyes. This hidden piece is called the *Afikomen* which means "that which comes after," or "dessert." Then he passed the remaining *Matzot* around the table and everyone took some.

Next, we let the youngest one present ask the four important questions that have been asked for hundreds of generations. The questions are the means to tell the ancient story (the *Magid*), explaining the meaning of Passover to future generations.

1. ***On all other nights we eat bread or matzah. On this night why do we eat only Matzah?*** They already knew the answer to this one!
2. ***On all other nights we eat all kinds of vegetables. On this night why do we eat only bitter herbs?*** Once again we passed the Seder plate and each one spread a very small amount of the *Moror* (I used horseradish) onto a bite of *Matzah*. This bitter taste reminds us of how terrible life was for the Israelites when they were slaves in Egypt.
3. ***On all other nights we do not dip our vegetables. On this night why do we dip them?*** On Passover it is the custom to dip the vegetables twice. Once in the salt water reminds us of the tears, and again in the *Haroset* which is sweet. This reminds us that

---

[69] We read Exodus 12:1-14, 17, 21-42, 50-51.

even in slavery, we can have hope in God. The *Haroset* is like the mortar between the bricks the Israelites made in Egypt. Everyone took two small pieces of *Matzot* and made a little sandwich of it with the *Haroset*, like setting bricks. They all agreed that they liked this much better than the *Moror*.

4. **On all other nights we sit at table. On this night why do we recline at table?** To recline at table means to sit comfortably, as free people. The Israelites ate the first Passover standing, still slaves, and ready to leave their slavery at a moment's notice. But today we have been freed from slavery and sin's punishment by the Lamb of God so that we can recline and enjoy our meal.

Papa briefly recounted the whole story and explained why we were reliving the experience of God's people in a dramatic, traditional way.

Then he invited them to pour the second cup of wine. This one is called the Cup of Judgment (or Cup of Plagues). This was probably their favorite part to that point because they really got enthusiastic about their participation.

He told them the story of God sending ten plagues on the Egyptians to force Pharaoh to let the Israelites leave Egypt. When each plague was mentioned, the children were encouraged to dip a finger into their wine (juice) and place the drop on their empty, white dinner plate, yelling out the name of the plague. *Blood! Frogs! Lice! Locusts! Disease on cattle! Boils on skin! Hail! Flies! Darkness! Death of firstborn!* By now, their plates were dotted with reminders of each plague. It was a vivid symbol of God's judgment.

Very appropriately, next we called their attention to the *Zeroah*, on the Seder Plate. Here was the reminder of what saved those who believed in God from the destruction of the plagues and the judgment of God: the blood of the Passover Lamb! It pointed to Jesus, the Lamb of God, giving His life to take the punishment we deserve for our sins.

Then we sliced the *Beytza*, the egg that symbolizes new life. Each one took a taste.

It was time to pour the third cup, the Cup of Redemption (or Cup of Deliverance). As we raised our glasses, clinked them together, we toasted life – New Life – *l'Hayim!* We celebrate our own deliverance from sin and death!

They did this with great joy, making sure each one got the blessing of Life through the toasts.

Finally, it was time for us to enjoy our feast. They were really hungry by now. The hummus, olives, and *Matzot* were not exactly what they had in mind for dinner. I brought out the salad from the refrigerator, the casserole from the oven, and the vegetable, placing the serving bowls in the middle of the table so we could eat family style. Afterwards, we also enjoyed our chocolate tart and they were surprised to learn that there was still more –

the *Afikomen*.

A very spirited hunt took place looking for the hidden piece of *matzah*. The one who found it was able to redeem it for a prize. This was the time when God surprised all of us.

Papa explained that the *Afikomen* was the piece of *Matzah* that Jesus broke at the Last Supper when He said, *This is My Body given for you; do this in remembrance of Me.* It is has been hidden; it is revealed; it is redeemed!

Papa prayed the ancient prayer: *Blessed are You, O Lord our God, King of the universe, Who brings forth bread from the earth.* Then he suggested that we each break off a piece of the *afikomen*, and give it to the one next to us, saying, "This is the Body of Christ. Do this in remembrance of Him."

He also asked us to pour the fourth cup of wine, the Cup of Praise, and he prayed, *Blessed are You, O Lord our God, King of the universe Who creates the fruit of the vine.*

When Jesus took this final cup at the Last Supper, He added, *This cup is the new covenant in My Blood, which is poured out for you.* We asked the children to pass the cup to one another saying, "This is the Blood of the Lamb, poured out for you."

As we began our Holy Communion service, I turned on my iPod to a song I had recently discovered, *In Remembrance of Me,*[70] by Cheri Keaggy. So that they could sing along after they received the bread and wine, I gave each of them a sheet with the following words of the song and a picture of Jesus and His disciples sharing the Passover meal.

> *This is My Body given for you.*
> *This is the cup that holds the Blood of the New Covenant.*
> *This is forgiveness, simple and true.*
> *This is the way that I have made for you.*
> *Before you eat, before you drink,*
> *Take a long look inside, and tell Me what you see.*
> *He said, "Do this in remembrance of Me."*
> *This is the Bread of Life broken for you.*
> *This is the cup that holds the wine of the New Covenant.*
> *This is the love of Christ poured out anew.*
> *This is the Son of God who died for you.*
> *I will remember the Cross that You bore for me.*
> *I will remember the crown that You wore for me.*
> *I will remember the reason You suffered and died.*

Each one reverently took the bread and the cup and slowly began to sing along with the recording. And then, totally un-orchestrated by us, the

---

[70] *In Remembrance of Me*, words and music by Cheri Keaggy.

Spirit of God fell upon us all and we all began to weep. First the children, then me, and then Conlee. It was too holy to speak; we could only respond to His presence. In His presence there was forgiveness and there was blessing. It was a most unusual Passover meal; one not just remembered, but one experienced!

When we could finally speak, we completed our Passover liturgy with the antiphonal responses to Papa's leading us in Psalm 136. And we ended our celebration[71] with the ancient declaration to one another: *Next year in Jerusalem!*

Perhaps it will be the New Jerusalem?

DAY 4 – MOUNT OF OLIVES AND PURIM

The children knew we would be going to Pensacola for our traditional visit to the Naval Air Museum in the afternoon so we got an early start on our breakfast, clean-up, and the beginning of our day watching the DVD from Israel. It showed Papa and me standing in front of some huge gnarly trees with silvery green leaves and there was a lot of noise in the background. You could hear people talking and moving around, busses stopping and starting, and you could tell we were in a place with a lot of activity.

We were standing on the Mount of Olives. It was a beautiful day and should have been a quiet, retreat-like place to go outside of the city of Jerusalem and away from the busyness of life to think and pray about important things. But this remaining section of an ancient olive grove is a very popular place because people from around the world want to see where Jesus and His disciples retreated, where He prayed all night until He sweated blood, and where He was betrayed by one of His friends. This is the Garden of Gethsemane.

The word *Gethsemane* comes from an Aramaic word meaning "oil press." Besides being a garden of olive trees, it probably was a place where olives were harvested for their oil. And, it most likely belonged to a friend of Jesus.

Tour busses bring throngs of people to this site every day. A large church, the Church of All Nations (or Basilica of the Agony), is situated next to the remaining olive grove. Fortunately, more than a quarter of an

---

[71] There are many elements of a traditional Passover that we purposefully omitted from our observance for the sake of time and for the reality of the attention span of the children. A traditional Jewish Seder has fifteen steps and takes at least four hours or longer. We did not observe the tedious cleansing of the home and burning the *chametz* (representing sin) which tradition demands. We did not pour the additional Cup of Blessing for Elijah or send a child to the door to see if he had appeared. Since Jesus, the Messiah, has already come, we felt this would be a bit confusing for the children at this time. And, at the end, we did not sing the full group of psalms traditionally sung to complete the full *Hallel*.

acre of olive trees is preserved in its original state. At least nine of the trees are nearly a thousand years old. The root stock may be older than this. It is possible that some of the trees you can see date back to the first century!

If you can find an unobstructed view away from the tourists and the traffic, you can look from the Garden, across the Kidron Valley, beyond the Temple Mount, and see the site of the Church of the Holy Sepulcher, the place where Jesus was crucified. Was Jesus gazing in this same direction when He prayed there that night after the Passover meal? Perhaps.

My Father, if it is possible, may this cup be taken from Me. Yet not as I will, but as You will.[72]

My Father, if it is not possible for this cup to be taken away unless I drink it, may Your will be done.[73]

After the BodishBabes left the TV and adjourned to our Camp Mimi table for our morning lesson, I read to them the most important writings we have about the Garden of Gethsemane. They all had their Bibles so they took turns reading from Matthew 26:36-46, Luke 22:39-46 and Mark 14:32-42.

I asked them if they had ever prayed for anything as seriously as Jesus prayed in the Garden. They all said, "Yes!" Their immediate and emphatic answers surprised me. But then I realized that whatever situation is your biggest concern, at that moment it is the only one you focus on. It will consume you until God either resolves it or something larger takes its place.

For Jesus, it was crucifixion and everything that implied: the agony coupled with the eternal effects for all mankind. Problems for nine-year-olds might seem trivial to an adult, but they can consume the child just the same. The most important element of any problem is: *What are you going to do about it?* Jesus prayed to the Father with all His might! *Do we?*

On the DVD, as Conlee and I showed the children around the Mount of Olives, down into the Kidron Valley, and across to the Eastern Gate of the Old City, *An Audience of One*[74] played appropriately. After our lesson, I played that song for them on my iPod and also gave them the lyrics to read while they listened.

> *I come on my knees to lay down before You*
> *Bringing all that I am, longing only to know You*
> *Seeking Your face and not only Your hand*
> *I find You embracing me just as I am*
>
> *And I lift these songs to You and You alone*

---

[72] Matthew 26:39 NIV

[73] Matthew 26:42 NIV

[74] *An Audience of One*, Big Daddy Weave

As I sing to You, in my praises make Your home

To my audience of one, You are Father and You are Son
As your Spirit flows free, let it find within me
A heart that beats to praise You

And now just to know You more has become my great reward
To see Your kingdom come and Your will be done
I only desire to be Yours, Lord

So what could I bring to honor Your majesty
What song could I sing that would move the heart of royalty

And all that I have is the life that You've given me
So Lord let me live for You, my song with humility

And Lord, as the love song of my life is played
I have one desire, to bring glory to Your name

This not only is a great song to listen to, but it is a great prayer to offer to God. It is reminiscent of what Jesus prayed in the Garden of Gethsemane.

Next it was time to study about olives! The children's preferences for olives were mixed. Those who like salty, savory tastes better than sweet flavors, loved olives. The rest of them tolerated tiny tastes of the choices I had in a bowl. I offered them a variety of what I could find in our local grocery store, the best ones coming from the deli counter selections rather than those in jars.

They loved it when I told them that Papa and I had been married for several years before he discovered that olives did not grow stuffed with a pimiento! He got lots of teasing for that. *Papa!!!!!*

We looked at lots of pictures of olive trees, the fruit on them, people picking the olives, and ancient and new olive presses. While they colored their olive tree pages, Papa told them about the ancient olive presses we saw in Israel and how they worked.

Some were operated by donkeys pulling a heavy round stone around and around in a stone trough over the olives, crushing them until the oil began to run freely into the trough.

The olive seeds contain oil as well as the flesh, so all is collected in large round doughnut-shaped baskets and hung to filter the oil, then to be poured into vats or jars. The first oil to filter through the basket is called "extra-virgin." (In Bible times this was the first fruit, given to God to be used in worship and to anoint kings). Then weights were put on the baskets to extract more oil. The second and third pressings were used for food, lighting, fuel, soaps, and medicinal purposes. Even the last residue of pulp and crushed seeds would be fed to the animals. Nothing from the olive was wasted.

I let them taste a tiny bit of some olive oils I had. We tasted varieties from Italy, Spain, Uruguay, California and Israel. They all agreed that each had a different and unique flavor.

Then I showed them some small Christmas ornaments that were hand-carved from olive wood. These are very popular in gift shops throughout Israel and we had purchased ours in Bethlehem. Each child got to choose one to take home.

We also brought out the small, crudely-made clay oil lamps meant to burn olive oil that we had purchased in Nazareth previously. Less than one shekel apiece, they were identical to the ancient ones used in Bible times. We showed them how to fit a wick in the small opening and pour some olive oil into the larger opening. In a small home in Israel that had only tiny, high windows and very little outside light coming in, one or two of these on niches in the wall would provide a lot of light. We planned to use ours for our dinner table that night.

It was time for us to spend the afternoon at the Naval Air Museum and return home for our next Jewish Feast, which was still a surprise to the children. On the way to Pensacola, I taught them our memory verse for the day, *You are here for such a time as this.*[75] They didn't quite understand what this meant for them but I assured them that it would make sense that night.

After a fun afternoon, coming home to rest and getting cleaned up, I told them we were going to celebrate *Purim*. Not one of the children had heard of it, so we began by reading the story of Esther from a children's Bible, keeping the story short and simple. This story is the basis for one of the most fun celebrations for children in Israel. They dress up and act out the ancient story to remember the time when all the Jews in ancient Persia were saved from extermination in one day.

Conlee and I were in Jerusalem once in early spring and saw children in the streets everywhere in costume. Little girls were dressed like queens and brides. Little boys wore fake beards and long robes. There was a lot of excitement in the air. We had no idea what was happening until a friend explained *Purim* to us.

Purim means "lots." It refers to the book of Esther and the lottery

---

[75] Esther 4:14

which Haman, the villain, used to determine the day when all Jews in Persia would die.[76] Although the name of God is not mentioned once in the whole book, God plays the most important role in the story. He had other plans and saved His people from destruction through very unusual circumstances. Esther, the heroine of the story, learned she was "born for such a time as this."[77]

Today, when the story is read or told as part of the *Purim* celebration, every time the name of the villain, Haman, is spoken, everyone yells, boos, hisses and stomps their feet.

In the story you have quite a cast of characters: King Ahasuerus of Persia, Queen Vashti, Mordecai, Esther, and Haman. It so happened that with five BodishBabes we could have a play and each one would have a starring role! So, after dinner, out came make-shift costumes and wigs for our impromptu production of "For Such a Time As This." Each of the children is a natural ham and the evening got pretty silly and we had a great time, making the story unforgettable.

DAY 5 – MASADA AND HANUKKAH

The story of Masada is not in the Bible and few Christians outside of Israel know much about it unless they study Jewish history. But most tour groups in Israel include a trip to the southern end of the Dead Sea in the desert to visit this impressive fortress.

After Jerusalem, Masada is said to be the most popular site for tourists. It is something to see at least once because of its historical value and the incredible views, but spiritually, it is not a highlight for me in Israel. However, we decided that the BodishBabes would find it interesting so we spent a morning talking about it and learning some history. The boys loved it! The girls, like me, not so much. (Remember Camp Mimi Rule #5c!)

Masada is probably the Israeli equivalent to the Alamo or a Revolutionary War or Civil War battleground in America. High on a large plateau overlooking the Dead Sea, it soars 1500 feet over the desert. The view is breathtaking in all directions, although besides the Dead Sea, there is absolutely nothing to see but rocks and sand. Today, you can climb to the top via the old Roman ramp, or by a Snake Path up the side, or take a ten-minute ride on a cable car. Conlee has made the climb a few times. I always take the cable car.

Masada was established as the "winter home and fortress" for Herod the Great, a true madman and eccentric who ruled Israel during its Roman period. He recognized the strategic importance of its location as a fortress from his enemies but also designed it as a magnificent getaway for himself

---

[76] Esther 3:7

[77] Esther 4:14

and his family. He maintained well-stocked storehouses, cisterns, Roman baths, and a luxurious three-level palace, all enclosed by a casemate wall.

Our morning DVD viewing began by showing me standing on a high precipice, surrounded as far as you could see by desert in every direction. My straw hat and sunglasses shaded my eyes and the scarf around my neck was being whipped by the wind.

Good morning, BodishBabes. I'm at a really interesting place we're going to talk about today. It's called Masada, which means "fortress." Look how high I am! Way up on top of this huge rock in the middle of the desert! It's where King Herod had a palace. We'll show you some pictures of what it looked like when he built it, talk about the amazing amount of slave labor that it took to construct, and the movie-like drama that took place here in the first century.

The camera then shifted to our local tour guide telling us about the heavy ballista stones which the Romans catapulted from the base of the rock to the top. What a feat! Those stones are heavy!

Then I walked the children through some of the many structures left standing in what was once a whole city on top of Masada. We could see houses with stone foundations still intact and remains of mosaics on partial walls, a synagogue, a huge cistern, Roman-style baths, barracks for soldiers and storerooms for supplies to withstand a siege for up to ten years, and, of course, the king's personal palace, which alone covers more than an acre of the mountain top.

Can you imagine living up here with this view, up and away from the rest of the world? You'll be amazed to learn how long the king who built this actually lived here.

The truth is, he *never* lived in this amazing palace. He and his family retreated there once for a military refuge, but it was never used as their residence, even for holidays.

To Jews, the real interest in Masada is the story of a group of Jewish rebels' resistance to their enemy and oppressor, Rome, which happened over 74 years after King Herod's death. The story comes alive in the celebration of *Hanukkah*, which we were going to celebrate that night.

The children had never heard of *Hanukkah* so we needed a bit of explanation in the form of a history lesson. As usual, they all listened better when their hands were busy, so we had lots of coloring pages about Masada and Hanukkah for them.

Hanukkah or *Chanukah* is the Hebrew term for "rededication." It is an eight day celebration and remembrance of a time when there was a great Jewish military victory, after which God provided the miracle of enough holy oil for the lamp stand in the Temple to last for eight days.

In order to understand the power of *Hanukkah*, (and the subsequent significance of Masada) one has to understand the heart of a Jewish zealot. There are two outstanding stories of incredible courage and faith that go together, although they happened at different times in Jewish history.

First, about 164 years before Jesus was born, the Syrians conquered Israel, and commanded that the one true God could no longer be worshiped and that other gods would take His place. They brought a statue of the Greek god, Zeus, into the holy Temple and commanded that pigs be sacrificed to him. The Jews were outraged but felt like there was nothing they could do because their lives were threatened.

However, there was one Jewish family who rebelled against the evil reign. The father of the family was named Mattathias and he had five grown sons. Mattathias said, "How could I not worship God? He is the one who made me. He is the ruler of heaven and earth. How could I not sing to Him and pray to Him and celebrate His holy days? We will not stop worshiping Him!"

This brave family hid in the hills near their village and fought the army of the Syrian leader. Soon, other Jews were inspired to join with them, forming an army they called the Maccabees. They fought for their freedom because they believed that God would help them win and they fought for the right to worship Him.

God did help them; He fought for them, and they won! God inspired them to set traps for the enemy and even though the Syrians had a much larger army, the Maccabees knew the territory so well that they were able to organize successful surprise attacks.

After the Syrian army was defeated, the first priority of the Maccabees, led by Judah, one of Mattathias' five sons, was to clean up the Temple in Jerusalem which had been profaned and to re-dedicate it to God.

They washed and scrubbed everything and removed all the traces of Greek symbols and idols that had been placed there. However, when they were ready to re-dedicate it to God, they could not find any of the special blessed oil that God required for fuel for the lamp stand in the holy place.

They searched everywhere and finally found one very small jar of the holy oil hidden away. They knew it was God's commandment that the holy light never be extinguished, but they also knew, realistically, that they only had enough oil for the lamp stand to burn for one day.

In faith, they lighted the lamp stand with the only oil they had, prayed, and the miracle occurred! That tiny bit of oil lasted for eight days! This gave them just enough time to prepare additional oil according to God's specifications and to fulfill God's will.

This lesson alone led to a great discussion among the BodishBabes about giving God the last of our resources to see how He will provide and even multiply them beyond our imaginations. They recalled the boy who gave away His lunch of five loaves and two fish which Jesus used to feed thousands. They talked about how Jesus took water and made wine for a wedding celebration, and how He even took a dead body (Lazarus) and made him come to life. He does this in many ways in our own lives when we allow Him to!

But, back to our history lesson! Although the Maccabees were very brave and successful against the Syrians, eventually the Romans conquered the Syrians and thus began another reign of tyranny against the Jews.

Once more, small pockets of Jews revolted against the enemy – this time in opposition to the tyranny of Roman rule, which began in 66 AD.

These revolts, at the grass-roots level, spread across Judea. The Jews revolted, not only because they did not want foreigners ruling over them but also, they were once again subjected to the desecration of everything they held most sacred and dear.

The Romans crushed the small Jewish rebellions, one after the other, until finally, under the leadership of the Roman leaders, Vespasian and Titus, additional troops were brought from Rome. This culminated in the total destruction of everything in Jerusalem, including the Temple, in 70 AD.

Again, the indomitable Jewish spirit that armies could not defeat rose up in the hearts of a group of 967 Zealots[78] who barricaded themselves on top of Masada. Their courageous act inspired Jews across the country to rebel and the Romans had to put a stop to it.

In 72 A.D., Roman legions besieged the fortress and built a wall studded with small forts all around the plateau. As the months passed, the Romans constructed a huge earthen ramp to bring their siege engines into play. They forced thousands of Jewish slaves to do their work. To stop the building of the ramp, the Zealots at Masada would have to kill their fellow Jews who labored below.

Finally, the ramp was completed and the Romans broke through the walls and stormed the fortress. To their amazement, they discovered that the Zealots had burned all their belongings and killed themselves the night before rather than become prisoners of the hated Romans. Only two Jewish women and five children survived the siege because they hid in a cistern. Captured by the Romans, they later told their story to Josephus, the Jewish historian who later defected to Rome.

The ballista stones we saw on the plateau were ones the Romans had catapulted into the fortress. One of the potshards found on the site bore the name of the leader of the Zealots, Eleazar ben Ya'ir. Perhaps this was one of the lots they cast on the night before the Romans breeched the wall,

---

[78] The Zealots were a political movement in the first century committed to overthrow the Roman rule in Israel.

to discover the lot that would determine who would kill the last survivors before turning the sword on himself.

The story remains such a vivid example of courage and patriotism that today all military inductees into the IDF take their oaths on the top of Masada. It is also a popular place for *bar mitzvah* and *bat mitzvah* ceremonies and we have seen both while visiting the site.

When we showed the children pictures of large groups of military youth receiving their induction orders at Masada, they remembered the teenagers we had filmed in the Jewish quarter of the Old City two days before. They were fascinated that the soldiers were acting like any other young people gathered on a break in a public place. They were laughing with one another, dancing around to music, boys flirting with girls, girls putting on lipstick and fixing their hair, and all having fun. The one thing that was different was that they were all in the dark, olive green Israeli Army uniforms and they were carrying machine guns. And they were everywhere! Their presence in Jerusalem is intentional and it is undeniable.

Every Israeli citizen over eighteen is obligated to serve in the Israeli Defense Forces (IDF). The IDF was founded in 1948 when the State of Israel was established. Although the requirements and obligatory times for service are complicated, based on family situation, health, and special talents, no one is exempt from registration. Most nineteen-year-olds serve for at least a year before entering higher education.

While we had our morning snacks, we had a lively discussion about the time when Papa was in the U.S. Army. They were surprised to hear that when we were young, every young man in America was obligated to serve for at least two years in the military. You either went to ROTC to train to be an officer, you enlisted in the branch of your choice, or you were drafted. There were few exemptions. We found old pictures of Papa in his Army uniform as a Second and First Lieutenant and his buzz-cut hair. They loved looking at them.

Then, of course, they wanted to hear "war stories." Papa always has some funny ones because he served as a Battery Commander for an Artillery unit based in the Everglades swamp in southern Florida during the Cuban Missile Crisis. There were some characters in that swamp!

Each of the children received dog tags with a scripture verse on them and the boys immediately wanted to wear something camo. It was a morning of serendipity but the children needed that mid-week and it was lots of fun.

Our scripture verse for the day was *"I desire to do Your will, O my God!"*[79] We talked about some of the things we might not want to do, unless we wanted to please God more than ourselves. Is God's will always something

---

[79] Psalm 40:8a

we would choose if we had our own way? What happens if we ignore what God wants? What happens if we obey Him anyway? Everyone had good examples, totally appropriate to their ages.

Of course we had to have pizza for lunch. They had been promised this all the way from Jerusalem two days before and we hadn't done it yet! I told them that I had eaten pizza with hummus, eggplant, and avocado in Israel. I also had been served pizza with egg and banana. For some reason no one wanted to try that!

The children really like to make their own pizzas because each one can be incredibly picky. Making pizza dough and putting out favorite toppings might sound formidable but it's so easy.[80] While they went out for a swim I made the dough in the mixer and let it rest for a few minutes while I assembled the toppings. This group doesn't require too many unusual ingredients so I kept it simple with pepperoni slices, grated mozzarella, parmesan, and cheddar, jarred pizza sauce, and left-over chicken in bowls. Now, if it was for me, I would have loved sautéed onions and bell peppers, olives, artichokes, and mushrooms. But that gets more complicated, they wouldn't have touched it, and it wasn't my turn to choose.

Conlee fired up the gas grill on the deck and invited them to come, one at a time, dripping from the pool, to choose ingredients and help him cook their personal pizza on the grill. Sure, it was messy, but between the dogs eating the left-overs and the hose washing it down, it was a quick outside clean-up. Not exactly Israeli style, but fun.

After rest time, we took our traditional Bellingrath Gardens field trip. Their favorite way to see the beautiful gardens is to separate boys and girls, each group getting walkie-talkies. Going off on their own, they explore all the trails and different sections around the lake and on the walk-way through the marsh.

We always try to go when there are not going to be too many people there. They were hot, tired, and thirsty afterwards, so we enjoyed cold drinks and ice cream in the Bellingrath café.

When we got home it was time to make our preparations for *Hanukkah*. The children got cleaned up and dressed for dinner. The cooking team helped me in the kitchen, while the theme team decorated the table according to my instructions.

We brought out a small *menorah* or lamp stand to show them the eight candles, including the "servant" candle in the center, which is used to light the others.

During *Hanukkah* one additional candle is lighted each night until the

---

[80] Recipe in Appendix in "Camp Mimi Eats."

whole *menorah* is ablaze. This is to remind the people of God's miracle. Our little *menorah* became the centerpiece of our *Hanukkah* dinner table that night and they lighted it respectfully and reverently. The boys wore their army camo, scripture dog tags, and *kippahs*. They were "ready to battle the Syrians and the Romans."

The girls wore their new colorful scarves and their scripture dog tags.

Papa read the appropriate prayers from a Jewish *siddur* or prayer book and we recounted and thanked God for all the miracles in our lives.

We also introduced some *Hanukkah* traditions that have developed over the years. One of them is eating *latkes*[81] or potato pancakes with apple sauce. I'm not sure why this has become a tradition; there are many explanations. But one thing is required: they must be fried in oil. That part makes sense at least; this feast is all about oil. *Latkes* are delicious and everyone loved them. The other culinary tradition for *Hanukkah* is eating *Sufganiyot* or jelly doughnuts without the hole, also fried in oil. They made a great dessert.

After dinner we sat on the floor around the living room coffee table and played *Dreidel*. The children had played this in school so they were familiar with the game and wanted to play for hours. We played with Bingo chips which they redeemed for small prizes at the end of the night. The wooden four-sided top (*dreidel*) with Hebrew letters on each side is spun and you must respond to whatever letter comes up.

Nun (נ) means you do nothing. *Gimmel* (ג) means you take everything in the pot. *Heh* (ה) means you take half of the pot, or if there is an odd number you take half plus one. *Shin* (ש) means you put one chip in the pot.

I was surprised at how much they loved this game. You could see why it has become a long-standing tradition for children!

DAY 6 – THE HOLY SEPULCHRE AND JERUSALEM

This was our last day in Israel and the last day for this year's Camp Mimi. Our final day is always bitter-sweet for each of us, for different reasons. Conlee and I are tired, but hate to have our little family go their separate ways. The children want to get back to their friends at home, but are nostalgic about ending their special time with us. It helps to have certain traditions to bring closure to the week and declare it's over.

Certainly, celebrating *Shabbat* with the traditional steak dinner on this final Friday night and having our awards ceremony accomplishes that closure quite well.

I'm always amazed at how drastically their behaviors change after Camp Mimi is declared officially ended for the year. They hurry back to their electronic devices which have basically been ignored, and they begin to text

---

[81] Recipe in Appendix in "Camp Mimi Eats."

friends and talk about plans for what they will be doing when they return home. Because we have observed this happening each year, it became apparent that there is a special spiritual dimension to what we do. It's as if God seals us in a little cocoon of Presence for a time and when we leave it, we go back to what we considered normal.

We began our last Camp Mimi morning with the final installment from our DVD.

Good morning, BodishBabes! I'm here in Jerusalem in a place where there are large crowds of people all wanting to enter the door right behind me. Look at all the people and all the different styles of clothing they are wearing. Listen to all the different languages they are speaking! They're here because they want to see the place where Jesus was crucified and where He was put in a tomb. This building is composed of many churches built on top of that site and it's called The Church of the Holy Sepulchre. It was completed in 335 A.D. We're going inside in just a minute to see the rock where they put up the Cross and the tomb where they probably laid His body. Remember, the good news is: He rose from the dead three days later! So come on ... let's look inside.

The camera followed us walking into the huge church along with many noisy people who all grew very quiet upon entry. There is a holy atmosphere inside despite the many distracting religious adornments that have accumulated through centuries of adoration at this site.

We first encountered a large pink marble slab, scarred and pockmarked, which many believe is the stone on which Jesus' body was laid for anointing and wrapping before He was placed in a borrowed tomb. Many modern pilgrims, following an ancient custom, bring anointing oil and rub it into the stone. On the day we visited, there were dozens of people kneeling and praying there.

A shallow trough along the edges caught the overflow of oil poured out and several people filled little bottles with the anointing oil. The perfumed air from the various oils was a bit overwhelming. I rubbed my hands along the surface of the stone and the lingering aroma of the anointing oil was with me far into the night. I wondered if Jesus, on the Cross, could still smell the expensive spikenard that Mary rubbed into His feet only a few days before He was crucified? He told the critics of her gift that it was a loving preparation for His burial.

Next, on the DVD, we walked with a large group into a church built over the traditional site of the rock where the Cross was placed. Surrounded by ornate and opulent hanging lamps, crosses, crucifixes, statuary and burning candles, each person reverently crawled under the altar to peer through a glass in the floor that showed the crevice in the rock beneath.

Honestly, there wasn't much to see for all the adornments, and there were lots of distractions. However, I was reminded of how many pilgrims have worshiped on this site for centuries. And how, without the churches built over the holy sites, they would have been lost for us today.

I think this is why the Garden Tomb, just outside the Old City, is more popular with many Christians than the traditional site of the crucifixion and burial. The Garden Tomb is a tranquil, quiet, devotional, park-like setting with trees and flowers. In this peaceful place it is perhaps easier to imagine the tomb of Jesus in a garden setting. However, at the time of Jesus, the Church of the Holy Sepulchre was also outside the then-existing walls of the city and its site was most likely a tranquil garden.

Inside the immense enclosure known as the Church of the Holy Sepulchre, not only are there numerous churches represented (Eastern Orthodox, Roman Catholic, Armenian, Byzantine, Alexandrian, East Syrian), there also are many caves and other tomb enclosures one can explore. It takes some imagination to overlook the large edifice built over everything, but one can still sense the rocky hillside of Golgotha, the caves that provided tombs, and the garden surrounding them.

In our final scene on the DVD, we were atop the roof of Christ Church, near the Jaffa Gate in the Old City. The view is spectacular and offers a panorama of much of Jerusalem, ancient and modern. With permission from our friend, the Rev. David Pileggi, rector of Christ Church, we climbed ladders and roof-tops to get to this amazing vantage point.

Immediately below us is a maze of houses, shops, mosques, synagogues, and churches, one right upon the other, most with large TV antennae or satellite dishes. Children play on flat roofs, washing hangs out to dry, music is loud, people are shouting, and singing is heard.

A little further out to the east is the Temple Mount, the site where Abraham took Isaac, intending to sacrifice him to the Lord before the lamb was substituted. It is the site where many sacrifices for forgiveness of sin were later offered until the Lamb of God became the everlasting sacrifice. Today it is also known as the site of the Dome of the Rock and the al-Aqsa Mosque.

Beyond it is the Kidron Valley. Then, looking up the terrain above the valley, you can see the entire hillside covered with the tombs of Jews, crowned at the top with the Mount of Olives. Further to the north is the large Hadassah Hospital on the hill, and then, modern Jerusalem with six-lane roads spreads out as far as the eye can see.

To the west, immediately across the street from us, is the massive structure of the Tower of David and the ancient site of Herod's palace.

At one time, this whole area within our sight was considered the center of the world by some. It is still an important place over which wars have raged and for which many people lost their lives. It is a place to remember and honor.

After breakfast, we studied the city of Jerusalem at the Camp Mimi table. Showing the children some maps of the city, both old and new, we were able to see how the ancient walls have been expanded and gates to the city added over scores of centuries. Coloring pages helped focus their attention as we read about the many places where Jesus was taken after His arrest before His crucifixion. Pointing them out on the map helped the accounts come to life.

Surprisingly, what the children were most interested in from the video was the anointing marble block, the anointing oil, and the customs for burial. We explained Biblical *anointing* as we understand it; that it is the rubbing in of oil until it becomes one with the recipient. Kings, priests, holy vessels, and sick people were anointed in the Bible.

When the oil was infused with prayers, the process of anointing then infused the recipient with the power of the same prayers.

Anointing for burial served other purposes as well. For instance, myrrh (the typical burial oil) has a drying and preservative quality that keeps the body from decaying rapidly.

Papa brought out a small vial of olive oil that had been blessed for anointing. He rubbed some into the forehead of each child, making the sign of the Cross, and prayed a special prayer for each one. They soaked up the prayers as much as their skin soaked in the oil.

After lunch, swimming, and rest time, we began to prepare for our closing dinner, which would be *Shabbat* this year. The girls helped me mix together *Challah* dough so it could rise for a couple of hours. The boys marinated the steaks and prepared the baked potatoes in foil. Chocolate mousse in individual ramekins was brought out of the freezer to thaw for our dessert. All that was needed was to toss a salad at the last minute.

At the conclusion of our *Shabbat* meal and awards ceremony with certificates, we all were tired and happy. Stories abounded about which part of Israel was each one's favorite and it was especially poignant to end our evening with the traditional toast to life, *L'Hayim!*

CAMP MIMI SIX

HEROES

    My inspiration for the sixth annual Camp Mimi theme came from hearing the children argue at Christmas about which superheroes had the most impressive powers. Conlee and I also had just given a talk at a "Journey" conference about the heroes children emulate today.

    A hundred years ago, a child's heroes were from the Bible or classic literature. Today, heroes are primarily from television, sports, and movies. Most of the modern heroes lack a lot in the godly character department.

    And so, the inspiration came: *What if we instill an excitement about godly heroes that surpasses the fads of today?*

    Ask any kid to list the essential elements of superheroes, and the first answer usually is their "superpowers." However, overwhelmingly, the cape is second on the essentials list! So, in the spring I started making each child a special superhero cape. I found shiny, sparkly, very tacky, cheap material in bright colors on the bargain tables of local fabric stores. A simple pattern made from newspaper provided a template.

    Making the capes was mostly cutting the shape out of fabric, with no elaborate sewing required. Velcro closures around the neckline kept them on safely. A craft store provided a variety of squeeze-on puffy paints and glitter that I used to emblazon each cape with a "Superman" style logo, substituting each child's first name initial in the center. They turned out gaudy, colorful, cheap, and *perfect!*

    I also chose five Bible heroes and planned lessons around each one. To further demonstrate the Bible stories about our heroes, I searched the internet and found short cartoons about each of the heroes, just to make it more interesting. I also found DVDs of animated Bible stories in a dollar bin in a local discount store. The quality wasn't so great, but the basic stories were presented in a succinct, fun way.

My thought was that since they enjoyed beginning each morning the previous year with a video snippet about a place in Israel that became our topic for the day, we would do the same with the daily animated Bible hero. After that, I just needed to plan activities to correspond with each story.

And, of course, I had to plan menus! As the children grew older each year, they certainly ate more – and more often. Snacks had to be present in abundance to do whatever it took to prevent grumpy, hungry campers.

The trusted menu planner I had been using for a few years was a lifesaver, because each morning I could just look at the appropriate day's space and know what meals were already prepared, labeled, and in the freezer.

It's hard – impossible really – to be the camp director and the cook at the same time. I needed all the help I could get!

It had became a custom for me to collect little "prizes" all year long, separating them into "boy bags" and "girl bags." That way, when Camp Mimi launched again, I had an ample supply of Bingo and other game prizes, awards, and special *Shabbat* treats stowed in my closet. Sometimes, as I reached in a bag to give away a prize, I was as surprised as the recipient, because I may have bought it a year earlier. Doing things for prizes makes everything more fun!

This year, Sophie came three weeks early because of a scheduling conflict with her parents and because she wanted to. We were glad to have her, of course, but it made it more difficult to get all the details ready before the opening day of Camp Mimi. We didn't want to spoil any surprises for her, so Papa entertained her with various activities while I finished many of the last-minute preparations.

My walk-in closet was definitely *off limits!* That space became Mission Control for anything to do with Camp Mimi. In addition to my preparations and Sophie's visit, I was leading a two-day conference in a church in a neighboring town! Sophie attended all of it with us, and even sang with the praise team. By the time Camp Mimi started, she was more than ready and I was more than a bit disorganized.

When the rest of the children arrived on our first day and the parents were gone, the BodishBabes were beside themselves to know the theme.

They knew the drill. Each one was in place around the Camp Mimi table, ready for The Big Reveal. We prayed, sang the Camp Mimi Song, read through the Camp Mimi Rules, brought out the candle, and chose one of them to light it. (They remembered exactly who held that honor for the past five years and demanded the privilege be shared!).

This year when the candle revealed "HEROES" they squealed in delight. *Yes! I'm Spider Man! I'm Captain America! I'm Wonder Woman! No, I am!*

I quickly explained that we would be studying some heroes from the Bible, some modern heroes, and that they, too, would become heroes as they took on qualities that Holy Spirit gave them. They had to think about that for a few minutes but they were willing.

We decorated our boxes as treasure chests to hold our "super powers." The decorations became more ornate each year as their artistic gifts developed. Instead of being content with felt stick-on shapes, they now requested paints, hot glue guns, trims, and assorted embellishments. Each one was unique and personalized!

Then they were given their notebooks, ready to be filled. On the front cover, along with their name and picture was a cartoon logo of a super hero, cape flowing, with the word, HEROES. Under it was a six-fold definition I asked them to read aloud and discuss.

HERO
A champion
A distinguished person
A brave person
A great person
A person of exceptional quality
A person who is admired

Then I asked them some questions using this definition of a hero. *Do you know anyone who meets these standards? Who in the Bible? Who your age? Who in the news?*

The answers and discussion ranged from God, Jesus, Daddy, Brandon (a boy in school), the president, football and baseball players, Papa, and the Pope. They were amazingly focused and thoughtful.

Then we went to the TV to watch the animated Bible story to reveal the first day's biblical hero.

DANIEL

The short cartoons were great segués into the biblical stories. They sparked the children's imaginations and re-introduced them to the characters we planned to study. The children then were given their first-day cover sheets to place in their notebooks. These were pictures of Daniel standing in the lions' den, not cowed or afraid, but confident in his God who would save him from danger.

We had some word search and crossword puzzles about the lions' den and the fiery furnace, as well as some pages to color. While they were busy with these, I read a simplified version of these two accounts of courage from the book of Daniel.

Then we had a test! Yes, there were groans and moans, but there was the great incentive of prizes to give them momentum.

The test was a "fill-in-the-blanks" page with choices of words at the bottom. It was easy enough for everyone to accomplish. Here are some examples:

King _____ was having a big _____.
A _____ appeared and _____ on the wall.
_____ told the king the meaning of the words.
He said, "Your _____ is about to end and it is being _____."
Daniel prayed to God ____ times a day.
Why was Daniel put in the den of lions?
How was Daniel saved from the lions?

Even though our children were very competitive, they were willing to help one another with answers since they were told that there were prizes for each one who got a perfect score. Everyone got a prize!

Now that they had seen the short animated version about Daniel, heard a condensed version of the book read from a children's Bible, completed some word puzzles about the facts of his life, and even mastered a little test, it was definitely time for a snack break.

It seemed appropriate that we eat something healthy, similar to what Daniel chose to eat instead of the rich food prepared by the Babylonian king's chef. We had a plate of carrot and celery sticks and broccoli florets along with ranch dressing dip and bowls of nuts and sunflower seeds. For drinks they had fruit juices.

They liked it more than I thought they might but asked if there would be junk food snacks tomorrow. After snacks, we got out several coloring sheets about Daniel's life and let them choose which ones they wanted to work on while I gave them a spiritual application of the story.

Daniel is a larger than life hero in the Bible. His story is one of extreme courage and faith. His name in Hebrew means "God is my judge." We talked about living your life with that truth above all else. If you are always aware that God's approval is far more important than any person's approval, will you do things differently? The consensus was a resounding *YES!* This led us to talk about what our names mean and how we live into that meaning.

Caleb spoke up instantly, "My name means 'dog' and I love dogs!" He was pleased to learn that *Caleb* also means "wholehearted."

Sophie knew that her name means "wisdom." Edie knew that her name, *Eden*, was from the Garden. Anna knew that her name means "grace," which is also her middle name.

That left Jake. "What about me?" He beamed when he was told that Jacob is a Biblical name which means "one who overcomes." They were very sympathetic when Conlee and I told them that our own given names from family ancestors have no biblical basis or inherent meaning. However, we told them we were sure that one day God would give us new names that would glorify Him.

This rabbit trail about names came to an end, although the intense coloring never ceased. We continued with our lesson about Daniel.

Daniel had every excuse to identify himself as a pathetic victim and to compromise his values. He was raised in a noble, faithful household in Judah in Israel, but when he was a youth, he was captured and taken as a prisoner in exile to Babylon.

Babylon was a center of idolatry and one of the most evil cities in the world. Daniel was thrown into a culture which was obsessed with pagan practices and the worship of idol gods. This is interesting, because God told the prophets that the reason why He allowed the Babylonians to take the Jews captive was because they had given themselves over to idolatry in Israel and had forgotten God's commands about how to live holy lives. In a way, He gave them over to their baser desires.

What was it about Daniel and his three companions that kept God's holiness alive in their hearts in the midst of such idolatry in both Israel and Babylon? Even when everyone around them was behaving in ungodly ways, these four young men respected and honored the God of Israel. They had obviously been well-trained by their parents to respect God and to love Him with all their heart, soul, mind and strength.

This nobility of soul and upbringing caused the four youths to come to the attention of the king of Babylon. He selected them to receive special educational training for three years, along with the royal household.

They were given Babylonian names. Instead of being called "God is my judge," Daniel was re-named Belteshazzar, which means "Bel protects me." Bel was one of the main Babylonian gods, whom God forbids one to worship. Daniel never assumed the identity that the king of Babylon wanted to give him. Instead, he always lived into his true identity that God had placed upon him.

The king ordered the four youths to eat food from the royal kitchens, believing the extravagant offerings of meat and wine would keep them healthy. However, according to Jewish law, Daniel and the other young men were forbidden to eat such things the way they were prepared in Babylon.

Again, Daniel's name and character, "God is my judge," were more important than what the king of Babylon commanded. They bargained with the steward of the young trainees. "Let us eat what we think best for ten days and see if we are not as healthy as the others."

The steward agreed and allowed the four Israelites to eat healthy vegetables and a diet of seeds, nuts and fruit. In ten days they were even stronger and healthier than the other youths in the training program. To this day, their kind of diet is known as a "Daniel Fast" to promote healthy digestion.

Because of their faithfulness to God, the four youths received favor in many ways. They excelled in their studies of Chaldean literature and leadership, and Daniel also excelled in an understanding of dreams and visions. He became one of Israel's great prophets, hearing from God and seeing what God showed him about future times.

The action-packed stories about Daniel are what get children's attention. They love the dramatic telling of being thrown into a fiery furnace for refusing to worship the king. The rescue scene, where the Holy One is with them in the furnace to keep them from being destroyed, is exciting and awe-inspiring.

The scene where Daniel is thrown into a lions' den is frightening and also encouraging. It shows us that God's power can protect us from the most certain dangers.

Yet, what I wanted the children to see was how this remarkable kind of faith and courage had been formed in Daniel's soul. It started when he was a child. Small, repeated acts of obedience to please God rather than man led to big, dramatic events that still inspire us today.

Are you ever tempted to do something that other kids are doing, when you know it is not right?
What were the consequences when you disobeyed your parents or God?
How can you grow stronger in your faith in God?

The responses were varied and sincere. Everyone admitted to being tempted to do wrong – at school, with friends, with parents. They all agreed it was easier if you had a friend who would stand with you when you stood against everyone else. They thought it was a gift from God that Daniel had three good friends who encouraged him to be faithful to God.

Papa prayed for each one to be strong in the Lord and to live into the name that had been placed upon them: Wholehearted, Wise, Full of Grace, Fruitful as the Garden, and Overcomer. Then he prayed that each of them would be a friend and have friends who stood with each other in serving God rather than other people. It was a great first morning and definitely time for swimming.

After rest time, we talked about some hometown heroes who protect us. The first group we chose were **sailors**. An unlikely choice, perhaps, but it worked with our planned activity for the late afternoon.

There were several connections to sailors for our family. My father and Conlee's father were in the Navy for a short time and so was our son, Matt, Sophie's dad. Also, we lived on the water and we had a small boat.

Recently, there had been an incident in the bay that the children had heard about. A sudden storm came up while several sailboats were out and three of them capsized, leaving several people missing. The Coast Guard was out immediately, searching all night. Coast Guard cutters navigated up and down the bay, following the currents. Helicopters with powerful searchlights hovered overhead. Most, but not all, of the missing people were rescued. When the children arrived, the community was still talking about this tragedy.

We talked about the many ways sailors risk their lives to protect ours. Occasionally, we saw a stranded boat out in the bay or heard their horn or whistle blowing. We always got in our own boat to assist them. People who live on the water are always aware of the dangers and are ready to help others in times of need or trouble.

We showed them pictures of Sophie's dad and their great-grandfathers, whom they never met, in their Navy uniforms. Then we adjourned outside to re-paint the infamous little boat that had washed up on our beach years before.

It was now becoming a tradition to paint this little vessel every year. The procedure was much more organized and much less messy than it had been the first time we did it. This time the whole design looked like a psychedelic nightmare! But they were proud of it and messy enough to require a hosing down before jumping in the pool.

After dinner that night they received their first day's rewards. They were presented with their capes, the trademark of all superheroes. As they let Papa place their personalized capes around their shoulders, their whole countenance and demeanor changed. They stood taller; they assumed heroic poses; they lifted their heads, looking into the future; they raised an arm in salute to their followers.

This provided the perfect photo-op, so we all adjourned outside to get the heroic shots. As they were photographed individually, they each announced their particular super powers. Caleb assumed the title of BIG C, with the ability to grow and shrink. Eden had the power to grow plants. Anna had the power to fly and run fast. Sophie had wisdom. And Jake was strong. They collectively named themselves **The Fantastic Five**!

DAVID

As the BodishBabes got older, it became apparent that they loved crossword puzzles and word search pages more and more. The intensity with which they tackled these was astounding! Jake and Papa worked as a team and it was obvious that little Jake was extremely attentive to the stories because when Papa asked him the questions, he got most of them right. It became unbelievably quiet as everyone tried to finish first. Although each one got a prize for finishing, they seemed to have an inbred competitive spirit.

After our breakfast, chores, and a short animated presentation on the life of David, the shepherd king, we returned to the table where they donned their super capes. The children were given divider pages for their notebooks which depicted the young David, standing over the slain Goliath, with the giant's sword lifted high. It was a hero's pose for sure!

I read them a very condensed version of this exciting part of David's story so that they could then begin their crossword puzzles and word search pages about the details.

Goliath was a nine-foot-tall soldier from Gath. He bragged that he could beat any Israelite soldier who would fight him. But all the Israelite soldiers were afraid to confront him.

David was a young shepherd boy who believed in God. He said, "The Lord who delivered me from the paw of the lion and from the paw of the bear will deliver me from the hand of this Philistine." David took his sling and five smooth stones from the brook. Then he went to fight Goliath.

King Saul wanted to put his heavy armor and helmet on David. He also tried to give David a big sword, but David said he could not wear them. He knew that his strength and protection came from God.

Goliath cursed the boy coming out to fight with him. David said to the Philistine, "You come against me with sword and spear and javelin; but I come against you in the name of the Lord Almighty, the God of the armies of Israel, whom you have defied."

David threw a stone with his sling at Goliath. It hit Goliath in the forehead and the giant fell face down. Then David took the giant's own sword and killed him.

David believed in God, and God helped him win over the giant.[82]

While busy hands colored pages about the life of David, we began our studies. Like studying Daniel, we focused on the heroic character of David being formed from his youth.

He developed the characteristics of a hero through the most ordinary tasks of his large Bethlehem family of eight sons, headed by their father,

---

[82] Excerpts from 1 Samuel 16 and 17

Jesse. David was the youngest. His willing obedience determined the many heroic actions he would perform as he matured. He didn't just wake up one morning, hear about a bully of a giant in the land who wanted to destroy the Israelites, and volunteer to take him down.

His training, both physically and spiritually, came through being obedient to family responsibilities. He spent his youth tending sheep, a rugged training ground – not for the weak of heart and body. This meant that he spent a lot of time alone, learning to hear God's voice, even as the sheep learned to recognize David's. He sang to them, perhaps praising God through music on his homemade harp. He was compassionate to their needs.

He protected sheep from danger, so he had to be strong and courageous. When he encountered predators that wanted to attack his flock, he killed them. He must have spent hours gathering stones from the creek beds and practicing hitting targets with his sling shot. His aim was perfected over time, taking down wild animals and keeping his flock safe.

Occasionally, he even wrestled sheep out of the mouths of bears and lions and killed the predators with his bare hands. All of these experiences made David physically strong, mentally tough, and spiritually sensitive.

This was a combination that pleased God because He sent the prophet Samuel to Bethlehem to anoint the future king of Israel. Samuel went to Jesse's home and asked to see his sons so that the Lord could confirm which one should be anointed with the power of God to become king.

Of course, Jesse brought out his older sons first, all large and handsome, strong and impressive. But God did not speak to the prophet about any of them. Samuel asked if Jesse had any more sons and he was told about the youngest, David, out in the fields with his sheep. They brought him in and the Lord told Samuel, "This is the one."

The Lord said to Samuel, *"The Lord does not look at the things man looks at. Man looks at the outward appearance, but the Lord looks at the heart."*[83]

Samuel had anointing oil that symbolized the outpouring of Holy Spirit power upon David. Samuel took the oil and rubbed it into David's head while his whole family witnessed this surprising act. In that moment the power of the Lord came upon David and set him apart for a ministry he did not yet understand.

The anointing came in a moment, but many years would pass before he would actually become king and fulfill the Lord's calling. None of those years was wasted, however. Each experience proved to be important for the formation of the next king of Israel.

.

---

[83] 1 Samuel 16:7

Meanwhile, David went back to the ordinary responsibilities of being Jesse's youngest son, the shepherd boy. It may have been a relief to escape to the fields from the tensions of the family because the other sons became jealous of the attention lavished upon their baby brother.

Later, David's oldest brother, Eliab, became angry with David, accused him of shirking his duties and said, "I know how conceited you are and how wicked your heart is!"[84] This shows us that not everyone understands God's calling on another person. Sometimes there are false accusations for being different.

Sometimes there is persecution, bullying, or criticism. This, too, can form godly character when we choose to obey God rather than worry about what others think about us. Each BodishBabe had a great and personal example of being criticized by friends for doing what they knew to be right.

On the day of the fateful and fatal demise of Goliath, David was in the field with his sheep, performing his most ordinary tasks. His father, Jesse, asked him to take food to his three oldest brothers and their commander who were fighting in the army of Israel, against the Philistines.

He traveled to the battle site and arrived just as the war cry sounded. Troops on both sides took their positions for battle. He located his brothers and was greeting them when the giant Philistine, Goliath, stepped forward, shouting and cursing at the Israelites. The Israelites cowered in fear.

David was incensed that such a barbarian would defy the armies of the Living God! And on the spot, he volunteered to fight for God when no one else would.

At first the king of Israel, Saul, decked David out in the royal armor of heavy metal, a bronze helmet and a large sword. But David wasn't used to such weight and he took it all off.

Instead, he reached for his familiar sling in his shepherd's bag, and gathered five stones from the stream. Armed with the physical weapons of a shepherd boy, yet with the power of the Almighty God, he approached Goliath.

The giant ridiculed, laughed, cursed, and defied David. But David ran towards the enemy, took one stone from his shepherd's bag and aimed it from his sling. It hit the mark, right in the center of Goliath's forehead, the most vulnerable exposed part of his body. It knocked the giant unconscious and David then killed the enemy of Israel.

We had a great discussion about what kind of things prepared David for this important battle. *When David practiced with his sling in the pastures, did he*

---

[84] 1 Samuel 17:28

know he was practicing for such a confrontation, or did he just do it because he wanted to get better at throwing a sling? Or did he do it for fun? How does God use the things that seem so natural to us for His purposes?

After Snack Time, we had a short study about biblical slings. The children were surprised to learn that they were not at all what they supposed. Slings were not toys, but were considered instruments of war by some ancient cultures. Ancient hand slings generally were made of a single long strip of leather or woven wool, with a central pocket for the stone. The longer the sling, the greater its range.

Some of the slings with a long range were about three feet long. An accomplished slinger could accurately sling his stone about one quarter of a mile away. When the stone left the sling, it could easily travel as fast as sixty miles per hour.

The motion for slinging is much like a softball pitch, one wind-up and a fast underhand pitch. The best stones are smooth, round shapes, somewhere between a tennis ball and billiard ball size. These can best be found in stream beds, washed smooth by running water.

Of course, they all wanted to make one and practice. I may be a sport about many things, but I am not crazy! No way was I going to give five children stones and slings and hope for the best. We distracted them from the slings with swimming and lunch by the pool.

Our afternoon lesson about a hometown hero was focused on the **police officer**. Everyone had a story about a policeman coming to their school to speak to them. They were impressed with all the gear they wore and always asked the popular question, "Is your gun loaded?"

If we knew anyone at the local police station, we would have arranged a field trip and the children would have loved it. However, the art of serendipity took over and we had an interesting and unplanned discussion.

The girls wanted to know if women were police officers, too. They said they had never seen a woman in uniform. Of course, I said yes, but had to go to the internet when they asked questions like, "How many women? What do they do when bad guys attack them? Do they have to be really big women?"

We found out that only about fifteen percent of all police officers are women, yet most of them are very well respected in their field. None of them was described as larger than an average woman. Many of them are very small and petite. One woman said that the biggest weapon she carried is her mouth. She said her ability to "talk down" someone who is very agitated is invaluable. When a show of force is not working, her "mom voice" can be extremely effective.

We asked the children if they would feel more comfortable going to a man or a woman police officer for help. Interestingly, they all said a man. Perhaps that's because they are used to the stereotype. None of the girls wanted to go into law enforcement.

Some of the facts about preparing to be a police officer were interesting to discuss. Every police cadet (student) has to at least complete high school. They study many different subjects at police academies, including physical fitness, self-defense, firearms operations, first aid, hostage negotiation, traffic control, high-speed driving skills, conflict resolution tactics and crowd management. They also learn about civil rights, how to question suspects, and other aspects of law and criminal justice.

I asked them, "What is the most important part of a police officer's uniform to look for?" I thought they would say the police badge to identify the office, and I had police badges to give each one to wear. However, they all said, "A gun!"

Fortunately, I also had plastic water pistols for each one, too! So, back to the pool we adjourned to play a rousing game of cops and robbers.

Our evening was a fun game night with many rounds of Bingo and competitive jig-saw puzzle contests with boys against girls. Of course, we awarded lots of little prizes which made it all more fun.

JOSEPH

By the third day the children were familiar with our routine. They quickly made their beds, dressed, ate breakfast in the kitchen, brushed their teeth, and seated themselves in the living room in front of the TV, capes on and ready for the animated introduction to our next Bible hero.

We watched the life of Joseph. It was a brief overview of the most exciting parts of the adventures of the young, mistreated Israelite who became the second most important authority in Egypt.

In the little video the scenes that got the most attention were the jail scene, and the reunion of Joseph with his brothers. However, like the lessons with our other two heroes, Daniel and David, I wanted to focus on Joseph's youth and the godly character instilled in him before any of his big adventures began. They were handed their coloring sheets of events of Joseph's life and we started the lesson.

The story opens in Genesis 37, when Joseph is seventeen years old, and runs to the end of Genesis, when he dies. Joseph was a shepherd boy, like young David, tending his family's flocks. He was the eleventh son in his family, born when his father, Jacob (whom God re-named Israel), was very old. Because of this, he was daddy's favorite. One of the things that best illustrates the way Jacob treated Joseph differently is that he made a special richly-decorated coat for him to wear. Evidently, it was so ornate and colorful that it was noticed everywhere he went. His brothers were jealous of their father's attention and in their hearts they hated their little brother. Their feelings were so strong that they wouldn't ever say a kind word to him.

John tells us that when we harbor hatred in our hearts it is very closely related to murder. *"Anyone who hates his brother is a murderer, and you know that no murderer has eternal life in him."*[85] We can see the truth of this statement played out in the story of Joseph and the hatred his brothers had for him.

How would you feel if all your brothers and sisters hated you?
Would you be mean to them in return?
Would you find comfort in the gifts you had or things you do best?
Would you forgive them?
Would you tell your parents?
Would you act like you are more special than your siblings?
Would you ignore them?

The discussion was varied around the table. A lot of blame was placed on Jacob the father for playing favorites. It was noted that these Bible families had a lot of sons; there were eight in David's family and twelve in Joseph's. They wondered why the oldest son was not the favorite. They wanted to know why the mother wasn't mentioned. Sometimes their comments were disjointed but I love it when they pay attention to details and ask questions. This is a wonderful way to learn to study scripture.

Joseph tended to handle his difficult situation by exercising the special talents he had. Primarily, we are told that he had a special ability to receive dreams from God and to interpret their meanings. The first account of this is a dream he had about him and his brothers. In his dream they were all binding together sheaves of wheat in the field when his sheaf stood up and the other sheaves gathered around him and bowed down to it. The problem arose when he told his brothers what he dreamed and they hated him all the more.

The children were astonished.

"Why would he tell them that?"

"Didn't he know they wouldn't like it?"

They were even more astonished when we read that he did it again. Joseph had another dream about the sun and moon and eleven stars bowing down to him. This time he told his father as well as his brothers. His brothers were even more angry and jealous, but his father, Jacob,

---

[85] 1 John 3:15

remembered the dream.

The next scene shows Joseph obeying his father to check on the brothers who were working some distance away tending the family's flocks. His siblings spotted him coming and the hatred in their hearts turned to thoughts and plans of murder. They decided to kill him and throw his body into a cistern, and then tell their father that a wild animal devoured him.

The oldest brother, Reuben, talked the others out of actually killing him, but instead convinced them to throw him alive into an empty cistern. Reuben secretly planned to take Joseph back to their father later. They took off his ornate coat, threw him into the hole, and then sat down to eat their meal.

While they were eating, a traveling caravan of spice traders heading to Egypt came near. The brothers decided to sell Joseph to the traders for twenty shekels of silver, to cover his coat in the blood of a goat, and to tell their father that his youngest son had been killed by a wild animal.

This is the kind of family behavior that would warrant calling in social services and law enforcement today and probably would result in minor children being removed from the home. The BodishBabes were astonished that such a thing would happen to a "Bible family."

Because their discussions about this story got so animated and lengthy, I quickly told them the highlights of the rest of Joseph's life in Egypt, the imprisonment, the temptation, the rise to power with Pharaoh, and the ultimate reconciliation with his family after a famine in Israel.

The children couldn't get past the fact that all the time Joseph was growing up he had to be aware that his own brothers hated him enough to kill him. *Why would Joseph forgive his brothers? Why wouldn't he treat them the same way they treated him? They didn't deserve to be treated so well.*

And then I read them what Joseph said to his brothers after they were finally repentant. *"You intended to harm me, but God intended it for good to accomplish what is now being done, the saving of many lives."*[86]

How hard it is for us to see things through God's eyes when people close to us hurt us so deeply! I am so thankful that none of these children have ever been hurt in such a way as Joseph was, but they will face pain and rejection in their lives. It is part of our human condition. We prayed for them that whatever happens to them in the future, that they will keep their focus on God and His plans for them, and not on the evil in other people's hearts.

We also prayed that whatever special gifts and talents God has given them will not be ignored or neglected. We asked God to use them for His glory.

---

[86] Genesis 50:20

We reminded the children that the same gift of dream interpretation that got Joseph in trouble when he was a boy, was then used by God to save his life and prepare his future when he was an adult. He learned to use his gifts wisely and to give God the glory.

Even when he was tested numerous times and tempted by others to compromise his values, he remained true to the faith his father, Jacob, had instilled in him. The rewards of this faithfulness provided the establishment of the large numbers of Hebrews in Egypt.

This was a pretty heavy lesson for one morning and the BodishBabes definitely were ready for a lunch break and some afternoon fun. We took them to the Environmental Studies Center after rest time, a popular field trip that is always fun and educational. This 600-acre site serves as an outdoor classroom for Mobile County Public Schools. It has a carnivorous plant bog, a twenty-acre lake, forests and nature trails. Live animal exhibits, classrooms, laboratories, natural history displays, and a planetarium round out the center.

Their favorite part is visiting the wild animals that are being rehabilitated for release. Each year more than 700 injured, diseased, or orphaned wild animals are brought there for care. Wildlife that are permanently damaged become pets that visitors can see each time. They especially loved the three-legged goat and the injured deer.

The day we were there, a police officer was giving a safety talk with the assistance of a beautiful trained cockatoo. The children were fascinated and he showed each of them how to hold the bird and command her to do tricks. She would duck and roll over when you yelled, "Fire!"

They were quick to tell the policeman, "We studied about police yesterday!"

Of course, he asked, "What did you learn?"

Our favorite answer was from one of our girls, "You need to hire more women."

By the time we got home from the animal preserve, all of us were very hot, tired, thirsty and needing a rest. Since it was late in the afternoon, I decided to scrap the "hometown hero" lesson for the day, let them head straight for the pool, and have an early supper.

Being flexible is vital!

After supper we played several games including Extreme Borders, Create the Band, and Bingo. There were lots of prizes in various forms of little animals, - charms, figurines, pictures, erasers, earrings, etc. It was a fitting end to our afternoon.

SAMSON

I began to wish I had made the hero capes a bit more substantial, because they were getting a workout! Jake even slept in his a couple of nights. However, they were serving their purpose and the children didn't mind fraying edges or some missing glitter.

Our little superheroes were excited to learn that Samson was the subject of the morning DVD. A couple of them didn't know who he was, but when Caleb began to flex his muscles to try to look like the Incredible Hulk, Jake followed suit. This looked fun!

After much posturing and acting silly, we finally settled at the Camp Mimi table with subject sheet pictures of Samson pushing down the pillars of the pagan temple. They each got several coloring sheets to work on as I began to relate the fascinating story that starts in Judges 13.

The beginning of Samson's story is one that is duplicated several times in scripture. A married couple is childless and one or both of them prays to God. Sometimes an angel appears and announces that God has heard their prayer and that they will have a child. Often the angel brings prophetic words about the child to be born.

Briefly, we mentioned this happening to Abraham's wife, Sarah, who gave birth to Isaac; Isaac's wife, Rebekah, who gave birth to Jacob and Esau; Jacob's wife, Rachel, who gave birth to Joseph and Benjamin; Elkanah's wife, Hannah, who gave birth to the prophet Samuel; and Zechariah and his wife, Elizabeth, who gave birth to John the Baptist.

The only woman whom we are told remained childless in scripture was David's wife, Michal. She remained barren because she ridiculed and criticized a genuine expression of worship to God from her husband and others. The dryness of her soul was reflected in her body.

Finally, we told them about Manoah and his wife, an Israelite couple who prayed for a child. The angel of the Lord appeared to her and said, *"You are sterile and childless, but you are going to conceive and have a son."*

The angel then gave her several specific instructions about how to raise the son she would conceive. The child's diet was always to remain pure according to the Law, with no fermented drink; he was never to cut his hair; and he would be set apart from birth as a Nazarite.

Numbers 6 tells us a lot about what it meant to be a Nazarite. This is a totally different word than being a Nazarene, which indicates that someone is from the town of Nazareth – like Jesus. The word *Nazarite* indicates a separation for God's purposes.

Some people were told to be Nazarites from birth (Samuel, Samson and John the Baptist). Others took the vow of being a Nazarite for a limited period of time as an act of devotion to God. The vow, which could be made by either men or women, consisted of three main components:

1. For the *diet*, one could not eat or drink anything fermented or anything having to do with grapes, – neither juice, wine, raisins, grape seeds nor grape skins.
2. For the *appearance*, one could not cut his or her hair.
3. For one's *actions*, one could never go near or touch a dead body for any reason.

Manoah's wife gave birth to a son and they named him Samson. They faithfully raised him to be a Nazarite, beginning with his mother also obeying the Nazarite vows as soon as she knew she would have a child.

God blessed the boy and he was filled with the Spirit of God. The anointing of the Spirit became apparent through his physical strength.

Again, as with Daniel, David, and Joseph, the way this child was raised contributed greatly to the heroic character that developed throughout his life. Mistakes were made. At times, values were compromised, but ultimately their lives glorified God as they lived out their callings.

When he was of marriageable age, Samson desired to marry a Philistine woman. This was an odd choice because the Philistines and the Israelites were enemies. In fact, the Philistines had conquered the Israelites years before and ruled over them. While he was on his way to meet with the Philistine woman, Samson encountered a lion roaring toward him and he tore the lion apart with his bare hands, as easily as he might kill a young goat.

Later, when he went back to marry her, he saw the carcass of the lion he had killed previously. Inside the lion's carcass was a bee hive filled with honey. He took enough of the honey to eat on the way and also some to take to his parents as well. However, he never told anyone where the honey came from.

Later at his wedding celebration, Samson told his wedding guests a riddle. *"If you can give me the answer within the seven days of the wedding feast, I will give you each a set of linen garments and a set of clothes. If you can't tell me the answer, you must each give me a linen garment and a set of clothes."*[87]

Here was his riddle for them to solve: *"Out of the eater, something to eat; out of the strong, something sweet."*[88]

Of course, the children shouted out, "Honey from a lion!" But then they realized they already knew the story. They agreed it would be impossible to guess the answer if you didn't already know the facts. No one would think of such a thing

---

[87] Judges 14:12-13

[88] Judges 14:14

At Samson's seven-day wedding feast, the guests guessed for three days without coming close to the answer. On the fourth day, they threatened Samson's new wife. *"Coax your husband into explaining the riddle for us, or we will burn you and your father's household to death. Did you invite us here to rob us?"*[89]

The responses from the children were consistent, "Those weren't very nice friends!" They couldn't wait to hear what happened next.

For the rest of the week, Samson's new wife cried and begged him to give her the answer to the riddle. Every day she cajoled him and pleaded.

Finally, on the last day of the celebration he was so tired of her pressure that he told her the story. Of course, she immediately told their guests.

Because they "guessed" the answer, Samson owed each of them new clothing. But his response was not very godly. He went to the Philistine town where the guests were from and robbed enough people to provide clothing for his guests. His behavior was so bad that he lost his wife, who left him for one of his friends. It was not a very good ending to a wedding celebration!

But, things only got worse. When Samson found out that his wife had left, he became even more angry and did something very cruel. He went to his wife's Philistine hometown, caught three hundred foxes, and tied them tail to tail in pairs. Then he fastened a torch to every pair of tails, lit the torches and let the foxes loose in the harvested grain sheaves and in the vineyards and olive groves, destroying all the crops.

This is the kind of action that would send a person to jail and therapy today. The Philistines found out who had done this and took revenge. They went to his wife's family home and burned her family to death.

Of course, then Samson wanted further revenge.

This kind of cruelty and anger never ends. When it gets out of control, the viciousness escalates and innocent bystanders always get hurt. Soon, more than 3,000 men were involved, fighting army to army, the Israelites against the Philistines.

Israelites from Judah, went to Samson to admonish him for the rebellion he had started. They had no choice but to tie him up and hand him over to the Philistines. They tied him tightly with two new ropes and sent him to their camp. However, when he approached the Philistines and heard them shouting at him as if to kill him, the Spirit came upon him in strength once again. He broke through the ropes, picked up a jawbone of a dead donkey lying on the ground, and with it, struck down a thousand men.

After this, Samson was regarded as a leader or judge in Israel for the next twenty years. However, the Philistines never forgot what he had done

---

[89] Judges 14:15

to them and they were waiting for a time when they could take revenge. By exercising his supernatural strength, he escaped from several schemes to take him down. Once, in the central Philistine city of Gaza, he even tore off the doors of the city gate, and carried them to the top of a hill.

His undoing came, however, when he loved another Philistine woman, Delilah. She was promised a lot of money by the Philistine rulers if she could lure him to reveal the secret of his strength. She begged and begged him to tell her and he continually lied to her.

First, he told her that if he were tied up with seven fresh bowstrings that had not yet been dried, he could not escape. But when she did so while he was sleeping, he awoke and snapped them easily.

Then he told her that if he were tied up with new ropes that had never been used, he could not escape. Again, while he slept, she had him tied in this way, but he awoke and snapped the ropes as if they were threads.

Then he told her that if she wove the seven braids of his long hair into the fabric on the loom and tightened it with the pin, he could not escape. She did so, but when he awoke, he pulled up the pin and the loom with the fabric and escaped.

She continued to nag him and complain that he didn't love her by keeping his secret, until finally he told her the truth, *"No razor has ever been used on my head, because I have been a Nazarite since birth. If my head were shaved, my strength would leave me, and I would become as weak as any other man."*[90]

She immediately told the Philistine rulers who shaved his head while he slept. His Nazarite vow was broken and his strength left. The Philistines captured him and gouged his eyes out. They took the blind Samson to a prison cell in Gaza and left him there for a long time working as a slave grinding grain. During this time his hair grew long and he began to live into his Nazarite vow again.

The Philistines, thinking that they had permanently subdued Samson's powers, brought him out for public display during one of their pagan festivals which honored their god, Dagon. The blind Israelite was placed between the pillars of the great temple to this unholy god. The Philistine rulers and several thousand citizens were present to see the once mighty Israelite whom they believed had been overcome by the powers of their god.

As they shouted and celebrated, Samson prayed to the One True God. *"O Sovereign Lord, remember me. O God, please strengthen me just once more, and let me with one blow get revenge on the Philistines for my two eyes ... Let me die with the Philistines!"*

Then Samson reached out to brace his hands between two pillars of the pagan temple and pushed with all his might. His strength returned and

---

[90] Judges 16:17

he destroyed the temple and all those who were in it. The scripture says, *"Thus he killed many more when he died than while he lived."* [91]

The children were shocked at the ending of the story. Their responses were animated. "That's not a very godly story." "Samson wasn't a very good example. Why is he a hero?" "He did some pretty terrible things to be considered a hero."

I admitted that there was a lot of truth in what they said. I had to ask them some questions to make sense of this man's life and the reason why he is still considered a hero to Israel.

"What was Samson's calling from God?"

At first glance it seemed to be a calling to be physically strong, but, "For what purpose?"

After a lot of discussion, the children finally found a reason that satisfied them for having Samson as a hero. We found it in Judges 14:4.

His parents did not know that this (his marrying the Philistine woman) *was from the Lord, who was seeking an occasion to confront the Philistines; for at that time they were ruling over Israel.*

The Lord prepared Samson from birth to confront His enemies who worshiped a pagan god, Dagon. Even Samson's parents did not fully understand the path that their son followed. The man of God's choosing wasn't perfect, but after making many serious mistakes, at the end, he turned his heart to God and served Him with his life. Even in his blindness and weakness, Samson fulfilled God's calling.

The best response to our extended discussion was this: "It saves a lot of trouble for everyone to just obey God without all the drama." (I think someone had been hearing, "Don't be such a drama queen!").

Our hometown hero for the afternoon was the **firefighter**. Although a trip to a fire station would have been fun, all of the children had done this in school and even had pictures of themselves in a fire truck. Instead, we opted for our annual trip to Bellingrath Gardens. We had our brief lesson about firefighter heroes in the car on the way there.

"What makes a person a hero?"

The consensus was that a hero is brave.

A hero risks his own life to save others.

A hero cannot be a coward when facing danger.

A hero has skills that most people don't have.

A hero has power that gives him authority.

These are all excellent answers. Then we applied them to firefighters.

---

[91] Judges 16:30

Most of the applications came from personal stories Papa and I told them. They got so interested that we sat in the cool car in the parking lot of Bellingrath Gardens for about half an hour relating adventures concerning fires.

When my oldest child, Rick, was a toddler, we visited my parents' home in another city. They babysat Rick while Conlee and I went to an afternoon movie. On the way back to their house, we saw numerous fire trucks passing us, lights and sirens blaring, going in the same direction we were.

"I wonder if it's on our street?" "I wonder if it's our house?"

You always think such things, but it turned out we were right! My parents' street was blocked off, and we could see three fire trucks and a large crowd of people. We pulled up in a neighbor's yard and I jumped out, running to the blazing house where I knew my child and my parents were. It was a panic like I had never experienced!

Police listened to me, held me back, and calmly told me that my family was across the street and they were all fine. Meeting up with them was a relief, and then we watched the amazing teamwork of the firefighters who contained the fire to the destroyed attached garage and saved the house.

There was a lot of smoke and water damage, but it was not as devastating as it could have been. Rick was delighted with the whole adventure, pointing to the fire trucks and saying "Fire!" over and over.

When Conlee and I were dating, we returned to our university town late on a Sunday afternoon, going the back way through little country towns. As we approached the outskirts of Prairie Grove, Arkansas, we saw a huge column of smoke. We took a detour to see what was on fire.

Unfortunately, it was a house on fire and flames were shooting out of the roof. The volunteer fire department had not yet arrived and the elderly couple who lived there was in the front yard, confused and frightened.

Conlee jumped out of the car and ran into the house, pulling out all the furniture he could manage. Within a few minutes, some neighbors came and helped him.

At last a few of the volunteer fire fighters began to show up in their trucks and cars. They had difficulty finding a water hose and hooking it up. Mostly they watered all the outside walls and grasses around the house to keep the fire from spreading.

By this time, Conlee and the neighboring men had almost emptied the house and had all the family's belongings away from the house on the front lawn. An odd assortment of sofa, chairs, tables, drawers, beds, and a TV, was scattered around. I stayed with the couple, keeping them as calm as possible.

The house was totally destroyed along with everything that was left inside. The couple kept thanking Conlee over and over. "We wouldn't have anything at all if you hadn't brought it out! Thank you, thank you, thank you!"

By then, some of their family arrived to take care of them and sort through their belongings. In my eyes, and now in the eyes of his grandchildren, Conlee was a hometown hero!

Another story, this one funny, was about Alex, our oldest grandchild. When she was four years old, she visited us by herself in Mobile, for a couple of weeks. While she was there, we saw a fire a few houses down from us on our street.

Conlee had read in the paper about the family who owned the house. They wanted to tear it down to the foundation to rebuild a new home on the site. The costs for demolition were so expensive that they sought other ways to get rid of the old structure.

They donated their empty house to the Mobile Fire Department to use for a training course for firefighters. In return, they got their house demolished for free and got a charitable tax write-off as well. The fire department set a controlled fire to the house and trained their rookie firefighters how to contain the fire and protect the surrounding property.

We took Alex down the street to watch the whole procedure. She saw many fire trucks, the commotion of firemen setting fires, and watched others putting fires out. She didn't say much but she was fascinated. It really was quite a show!

We didn't realize what Alex internalized until some days later, while driving, we saw a fire truck going past with sirens and lights.

Alex panicked. "Oh, no! The firemen are going to set someone's house on fire!" It took several years to get that false impression of firefighters out of her mind.

That night as a special treat, we took the children to the Dog River to eat at the River Shack. It really is just a shack but, being only two minutes from our house, it was our neighborhood "restaurant" with lots of rustic character and live music. The children love it because it's super casual, you eat under a covered pavilion out of plastic baskets, and you watch the boats and fishermen only a few steps away. They consumed crab claws and hush puppies like they were starving!

Just as we were getting ready to leave, a strong wind began to blow and before we could get to the car we all got drenched from a hard, sudden rain.

In the short time it took us to get home it had subsided, - typical of a coastal rain shower. However, as soon as we started down our driveway we saw that devastation had hit our property. The long driveway had to be cleared of fallen limbs and debris before we could approach the house, yard furniture was turned over, and when we got to the bay side of the house it looked like a tornado had touched down.

Large tree limbs were in the pool, a thick cover of leaves was everywhere, umbrellas were tossed around the yard, pool toys were long gone, and the children went crazy. We turned on spotlights and began some cleanup as best we could. We were extremely thankful that the damage was minimal and we were only left with a colossal mess.

ABRAHAM

Early the next morning, as soon as everyone got up, there was excitement. While I prepared breakfast, everyone else helped with clean-up outside. The sound of the chain saw cutting up limbs, leaf blower, and shouts of "I found something!" permeated the quiet summer morning.

By the time breakfast was ready, they all had pitched together and had done a great job of getting the yard back to being usable.

They also were excited because they knew this was the day we were going to the Naval Air Museum in Pensacola. The anticipation was high because we had been several times before and they knew what to expect from this favorite activity. But first, we watched a video and had our morning lesson about Abraham, our Bible hero for the day.

Capes on, coloring sheets about the life of Abraham in hand, the children listened to excerpts from Genesis 12-22 about the adventures of his life. Then we gave them lots of pages of crossword puzzles, word searches, fill-in-the-blanks, and word scrambles that all pertained to stories about Abraham. The intensity with which they approached these challenges was amazing.

This was our first Bible hero to study that didn't give us any background about his childhood. All we know is that he lived his early years in Ur, a city not too far from Babylon.

Like Babylon, Ur was thoroughly pagan, wealthy, and beautiful. The citizens of Ur worshiped the moon and participated in despicable rites such as human sacrifice.

This doesn't seem like a good environment in which to hear God speak, but God's voice is more powerful than all the puny, pagan gods. Abram (his original name) heard God say, "Leave Ur and everything you know and follow Me."

Hebrews 11:8 says, *By faith, Abraham obeyed when he was called to go out to a place he would later receive as an inheritance, and he went out without understanding where he was going.*[92]

---

[92] Net Bible

"Would you do that?"

My question went unanswered for a few minutes as they continued coloring. Just when I thought they weren't paying attention, one said, "How did he know it was God?" This led to a great discussion about how we hear God's voice.

"Have you ever heard God speak?"

Edie was the first one to answer. "I didn't hear God speak but I saw Jesus once."

Of course, we were all anxious to hear her story. She had been on her way to school one day and saw a man standing alongside the road, near some trees. She knew it was Jesus. She described to us what He was wearing and the expression on His face.

She didn't hear him say anything but the way He looked at her made such a lasting impression that she couldn't forget how she felt inside after this experience. No one else in the car at the time had seen Him but it didn't matter. She had an encounter that was especially designed for her. It may take years before she understands why she saw Him, but it was indelibly imprinted upon her soul.

We talked about Abram, living in Ur, perhaps going about his normal activities just as Edie had been. Even if no one else heard God speak, Abram did and it changed his life.

"Do you think it is heroic to follow God when no one else around you is interested?"

This question got some quick responses from the older children. They were already the victims of peer pressure and the cult of "I don't want to be different."

It seems from a detailed reading of Genesis 11:27-12:9 that the migration out of Ur was in phases over several years. First, we're told about Terah, the patriarch of the family with his three sons, Abram, Nahor and Haran.

This was a good time to use some simple paper dolls of people in biblical dress representing the family structure because, to be honest, Abram's family tree is a bit convoluted and surpasses the cast of a complicated soap opera.

With the names of each character written on the front, the children could move the people around a map of the ancient Middle East that we laid out in the center of the table.

We identified Terah (the father), his three sons (Abram, Nahor and Haran), Haran's son (Lot), Abram's wife (Sarai, who is also his half-sister), and Nahor's wife (Milcah, who is also his niece). We aren't told anything about Haran's wife. You need a score card, don't you?

Conlee and I told the children about how in 1980 (the olden days), we heard God's voice to us in the midst of our normal life. With three sons, a prosperous business, a lovely home and a promising future, we heard God say, "Leave all this and prepare yourself for full-time ministry. Go to seminary and become a pastor!" I was studying the life of Abraham that year at Bible Study Fellowship and the similarities were astounding.

Together, Conlee and I pored over the details of this heroic patriarch's life and, at the same time experienced the day-by-day revelations of our own adventure.

Our move was in phases over several years just as Abram's was. It is very unusual to hear God speak one day and have everything in place to see His will accomplished the next. It is much more likely to have the word/vision/command take root in your heart and then, over time, see the details come to pass.

For us, it took three years of preparation to meet with discernment groups, pray, sell our business, sell our house, apply and be accepted at a seminary, and actually move to another state to attend. Then there were three years of intense study, another move for an internship, until we finally arrived at the place of God's choosing – eight years after the initial call!

To go through such difficult and laborious steps you have to be very sure you have heard God. Someone once said to Conlee, "It must have taken such courage to leave everything behind and follow God's call."

Conlee's response was profound. "It would have taken more courage (or stupidity) not to follow God. I would always know I missed a divine opportunity and the fulfillment of God's blessings."

There have been no regrets for either of us!

We had such a fun afternoon at the Naval Air Museum. Imaginations worked overtime as the children sat in cockpits of real fighter planes and moved all the controls, lost in their own heroic adventures.

Pilots became our hometown heroes for the day. Lots of stories were shared on the ride home, including every detail about how Papa had soloed in a small plane when he was only sixteen years old.

After supper we had fun making origami airplanes and sailing them around the house. Everyone received a light-up necklace and we went outside for games of tag and hide and seek in the dark. It was a full day and an early bedtime.

ELISHA

The last day of Camp Mimi is always bittersweet. We're all tired but happy and reluctant to say goodbye to the sweet community we've built during the week. Because it was Friday, we planned a *Shabbat* meal that night. It would include our traditional steak dinner, our awards ceremony and the now-familiar ritual of celebrating the ancient Jewish weekly feast day. We had a lot to do on our last day.

Before we began our morning study, the girls helped me make *Challah*[93] dough. It rose while we had our lesson.

Sophie had now been with us for nearly a month. Before Camp Mimi week started, she had been a part of the weekend conference on discipleship that I led in a nearby community. The focus of the weekend had been an intense study of Elijah and his disciple, Elisha. The stories of these two biblical heroes were new to Sophie and afterwards she said over and over, "Their names sound alike. I keep getting Elisha and Elijah mixed up. It's very confusing."

Knowing I needed to greatly simplify the details, I decided to tell the BodishBabes the story of Elisha and use some modern day examples to paint the picture of what it means to become a disciple. Our last lesson was designed to show that becoming a disciple is becoming a hero.

When we gathered at the table I brought out some pottery I had made in an art class a few years before. There were assorted pieces of *raku*, a kind of stoneware that is formed with clay, painted, buried in burning ash or sawdust, fired for several hours and then rapidly cooled. The result reveals surprising colors and details as the oxidation works with the clay. One never knows what the finished product will look like and it is hard to predict a satisfactory result. Many of the fired pieces break in the fire and few are works of beauty. It is a challenge to say the least.

After I explained the process of making *raku*, and while they passed around the pieces I had formed, I told them the story of Ange Sabin Peter, an American artist who became fascinated with the art form of *raku*. She tried and tried to get artistic results and was frustrated with her efforts.

She heard about a well-known Japanese *raku* potter named Masaaki Shibata. He lived in Tokoname, Japan, which had been a pottery center for over a thousand years. This area was famous for its unusual clay and the techniques that potters like Shibata had developed.

Ange contacted the Japanese artist and received permission to apprentice with him for six months. Her excitement mounted as she anticipated going to Japan, taking classes, working alongside the master, and learning his secrets.

However, what Ange experienced was not at all what she expected. The only thing he taught her was this: "You cannot separate life from work. The way you do the most insignificant activity in your daily life will reflect in your work."

She literally became Shibata's servant. She lived with the family and ate her meals with them, but other than that, she waited on them hand and

---

[93] Recipe in Appendix, "Camp Mimi Eats."

foot. She was never allowed to sit at his potter's wheel, work with his clay, or form a piece of pottery from clay. Instead, she dug clay from the rice fields, gathered ash from the forest, cleaned up his mess, and did menial tasks.

Shibata seldom spoke to his young apprentice and mostly ignored her presence. He did not even acknowledge her when she departed after six months, frustrated and angry.

His wife gave these parting words to Ange when she left for home.

"When you came to us you were like a fully grown tree with big branches. We had to cut those branches for something new to be able to grow."

Ange's disappointed response was, "All I felt was the cutting."

When Ange returned home she went into her potter's studio to resume her previous activities making pottery the way she always had. She felt she would be very rusty, having been absent from the potter's wheel for so many months.

Yet, what she began to produce was magnificent, better than anything she could have imagined. Every piece she removed from the fire was exquisite, like nothing she had ever made. She realized that without her being aware, the influence of the master had transformed her life and her art – because she had immersed her life in his life.

While the children drew pictures of clay pots they could imagine making, I told them another story about Dennis, a young man we met while staying at a *SchlossHotel* on the Neckar River in Germany.

Dennis was a modern day apprentice in an old world tradition. We first met him when he waited on us in the elegant dining room of the castle.

When we arrived at this romantic destination there was snow and ice on the ground and we were the only guests. We got to choose any room we wanted and we chose the honeymoon suite, even though we had been married for decades. It was a good choice. We were treated as royalty, with true European dignity and every concern for our comfort.

Although Dennis remained anonymous to us for the first few days, he amazingly seemed to do everything. Besides being the most efficient waiter, we observed him arranging flowers, supervising the housekeepers, and answering the phone at reception. He seemed to be everywhere and yet most inconspicuous.

In a writing mode at the time, on the third day of our visit I asked him if I could interview him for a story I was writing. Of course he looked very surprised but did not give me the typical European refusal, "It is not possible." Instead, he said he would have to receive permission from *Frau*, the owner of the castle and his supervisor. The next morning as he served us our breakfast, he quietly said he would arrange afternoon coffee and cake for us in a little private dining room to meet with us. *Frau* had given permission, probably because we were the only guests in the castle.

We arrived at the appointed time and he seated us at a small, elegant table, beautifully set with fresh flowers, lovely china, tea sandwiches and little cakes. He poured coffee from a silver pot, passed us cream and sugar and then stood at attention.

We invited him to please sit and join us so that we could have a conversation. It was obvious that he was uncomfortable at first but it didn't take long for him to noticeably relax and enjoy an unusual break from his duties and the chance to talk about himself.

I asked him lots of questions about how he came to work at this remote, yet elegant place, what his duties entailed and what he planned to do in the future. His story was so intriguing that I planned to include the details in a children's novel.

Dennis grew up in a rural region of northern Germany, the youngest of many children. His parents apprenticed him to a hotelier to learn a trade so that he would be able to make a living beyond what the family farm could offer.

This meant that he left home for a minimum of three years to live as a servant for the owner of the *SchlossHotel*. He received no pay but he was given room and board and uniforms. He worked every day with no vacation time. He did as he was meticulously instructed in the arts of cleaning, setting a beautiful table, flower arranging, serving food, selecting wines, maintaining guest rooms, supervising housekeeping, keeping financial records, and dealing with vendors and service people. And on and on and on.

Yet, while submitting to the rigorous discipline, he was learning every nuance of a trade that would someday be greatly beneficial to him.

When we asked him what he saw in his future, he did not hesitate to answer, "Oh, I will manage a grand hotel!" He knew the benefits of his devoted discipleship to a master in the craft of hotel management. For him, it was worth the sacrifice.

We talked with the children about the differences between what Dennis did and the more modern approach to learn a craft. *Would Dennis learn more in his three years of apprenticeship or more studying hotel management in a university setting, hearing lectures, learning techniques, and only gaining experience after graduation?* This was a very adult conversation and they had some great insights and questions.

"What did he do for fun?"

"He would have to really love what he did."

"If he couldn't afford to go to a university to study, he would have to work on his farm."

"Did he have friends?
" How old was he?"
"What kind of cake did you eat?"

After Snack Time we turned our attention to our hero of the day, Elisha ben Shaphat, a farm boy much like Dennis. Elisha's story is found in 1 Kings and 2 Kings. It is a graphic and beautiful example of what it means to be a disciple. His story begins with the life of the great prophet Elijah, the man of fire and miracles who also learned to hear God in the still, small voice of the Spirit within.

The prophet Elijah heard God say to "pass the mantle" of his anointing and gifting to the young man, Elisha ben Shaphat. Elijah found the young man plowing with oxen in the field of his family farm.[94] He approached him in the field and literally threw his cloak around him. This symbol spoke to the heart of the young farmer. Something in him awakened and he was ignited to leave all he knew to follow the call of God.

At first he was tempted to follow the customs of tradition. He told the prophet that he would like to say goodbye to his parents in a proper manner and then he would follow God's call. Elijah's response to this is interesting. *What have I done to you? Go back!*

What did Elijah see happening if Elisha, the farmer, went back to his parents for a farewell dinner? Was his heart still with the farm and family or with the call of God? Where was his identity?

The mention of turning back to say goodbye to his family and Elijah's response must mean more than a simple farewell. It implies that Elisha must choose which master he will serve: God's call or the demands and desires of his family?

Elisha did go back, but not to have the farewell, painful scene of explaining why he must leave and what he was being called to do. He went back and did a most remarkable thing to prove to Elijah, God, and himself that he was sold out for God's calling on his life. He slaughtered the oxen he had used for plowing and burned the wooden plows for firewood to cook the meat and provide a farewell banquet for the people of his family.

Now everyone knew there was no turning back for the young man; his bridges were burned.

This story is very reminiscent of the story Jesus told about a rich synagogue ruler who was struggling to find contentment in God's will.[95]

Jesus told him to sell everything he had to follow Him. Why did he tell him this? He didn't tell everyone who had wealth to sell their possessions.

---

[94] I Kings 19:19-21

[95] Matthew 19:21

Jesus saw the man's heart and knew he had a struggle with serving two masters, God and mammon. He knew the man had to make a choice.

Elisha chose to follow God. It obviously was not an easy decision but he did it with his whole heart. He left no back door to return if he failed with God. There was no Plan B. What a picture of complete trust!

Elisha did what Ange Sabin Peter did in Japan, what Dennis did in Germany, and what each disciple of Jesus did in ancient Israel. He left everything behind to follow his master.

He lived with him; traveled with him; imitated his life-style and habits; watched his reactions to life; and immersed himself in the life-style and teachings of the one he followed. His choice made him a different person in every way. After a time of discipleship/apprenticeship he developed the same characteristics as the one he served.

Eventually we see that Elisha became so close to his master, Elijah, that when Elijah was going to die, Elisha was ready to go with him. *As surely as the Lord lives, and as you live, I will not leave you.*[96]

Other prophets told him that he had to let go of Elijah, but Elisha couldn't even think about such a thing. Their lives were too entwined. As God led Elijah to the Jordan River, Elisha never left his side. He was allowed to participate in Elijah's last miracle, the parting of the Jordan River so that the two of them could cross over together. Then Elijah asked his disciple, *What can I do for you before I am taken from you?*[97]

Elisha had a big, bold request: *Let me inherit a double portion of your spirit.*[98]

Elijah told him that this was a difficult thing. What did he mean by difficult? Difficult for him to give? Or difficult for Elisha to receive?

Elijah was willing to give the double portion to Elisha, but demanded this requirement: *If you keep your eyes on me, it will be yours.*[99]

I asked the children, "What is the anointing we receive when we fix our eyes on Jesus, our Master?"

They all stopped their coloring and looked at me with big eyes. Although no one offered an answer, I could tell they were seriously pondering this question. "Let me read you a scripture and see if you can find a connection."

Jesus said, *I tell you the truth, anyone who has faith in Me* (keeps their eyes on Me) *will do what I have been doing. He will do even greater things than these, because I am going to the Father.*[100]

---

[96] 2 Kings 2:2
[97] 2 Kings 2:9a
[98] 2 Kings 2:9b
[99] 2 Kings 2:10

There were lots of "Wows!" "That's the same thing!"

Elisha fixed his eyes on Elijah through the amazing scene that unfolded before him. A chariot and horses of fire came from heaven, enclosed Elijah, and whisked him off in a whirlwind back up to heaven. Surely Elisha saw it but couldn't believe it!

His first response was to mourn the loss of the man who had become a father to him. But immediately, the same miracles that Elijah had done began to happen through Elisha, the disciple, after his master had gone. He parted the waters of the Jordan; he healed polluted water; he made water come forth out of desert ground; he multiplied oil; he raised a dead boy to life; he made poisonous food healthy; he fed one hundred men with twenty loaves of bread, leaving left-overs; he healed a Syrian military officer of leprosy; he caused iron to float in water so that an ax head (a means of livelihood for a prophet) could be recovered from the water; he prayed that God would open eyes to see the unseen, and that enemies would be made blind. And many more miracles were recorded.

Like the examples of Ange Sabin Peter and Dennis the apprentice, Elisha demonstrates for us the courage and determination it takes to be a true disciple. His goal was not only to *learn* from the master but to be *transformed* by the master.

The conversation around the table quickly turned to *Star Wars*, and the disciples of the Jedi Master. That was fine with me because they were recognizing the principle. They went from only thinking about disciples as the twelve men Jesus trained, to seeing disciples in many areas of life. The important question is always, *What master will you serve?* The obvious conclusion is that whatever master you serve will transform you into that image!

The children put a lot of thought into decorating the table for our *Shabbat* meal and awards' ceremony. They used the *raku* pottery from our morning lesson, some *Star Wars* figures, a Jedi light saber, and pictures of Superman, Spiderman, and Wonder Woman. To an outsider, it was a strange combination of symbols, but for us, it recalled the highlights of our week.

There was a fitting majesty in the demeanor of each caped child receiving an award that night, and striking the pose of a hero in the making.

---

[100] John 14:12

CAMP MIMI SEVEN

FEARFULLY AND WONDERFULLY MADE

When the children arrived for their seventh annual Camp Mimi, the excitement was at a fever pitch. The Fabulous Five could hardly wait for the big reveal and repeatedly begged me to give them hints. Anna especially hated surprises and wanted to know every detail before anyone else. She almost made herself sick trying to find out the theme.

Finally, the parents were gone and the BodishBabes were all in their places around the table. We sang the Camp Mimi song and they were more than ready for me to bring out the candle which had the name of the theme on the side.

"What does that mean? 'Fearfully and Wonderfully Made?' It doesn't make sense!"

Their reactions were expected because I was pretty sure they were not familiar with Psalm139, the scripture that inspired the theme. I gave them the first pages to insert in their notebooks which were copies of this entire psalm with their own picture at the top. The psalm describes how personally the Lord planned for and designed each of us, how intimately He knows us, and how we can never distance ourselves from His presence.

In bright red letters, verses 13-14 were highlighted:

For You created my inmost being;
You knit me together in my mother's womb.
I praise You because **I am fearfully and wonderfully made***;*

Your works are wonderful, I know that full well.

I explained that we were going to study the miracles contained within five systems of the human body, learning that we are uniquely put together by a loving God and that every part of our body is amazingly detailed and crafted by Him. This elicited some fairly negative responses like, "Ugh!" "We don't have to look at blood, do we?" "That's disgusting."

The tide turned immediately, however, when I told them that our week would be like a mini medical school for Camp Mimi.

Of course, each junior medical student needs a uniform. I presented them each with a bright blue set of medical scrubs monogrammed with "Camp Mimi" on the pocket of the shirt. Now they were interested! A costume of any kind makes all the difference in the world to a child. It gives them a sense of importance and purpose and changes their whole perspective towards learning.

They loved these scrubs so much that they put them on first thing every morning and didn't want to take them off except to swim, which is when they were laundered each day. The uniform totally changed their outlooks on the subject of the human body, a theme that began with disappointment but actually turned out to be one of their favorites.

DAY 1 – BONES

After they decorated their boxes with their names and personal embellishments, we settled down with coloring sheets about the human body, labeling various major organs. While they were busy with this, I shared some basic facts about our bodies.

- *The adult body is made up of 100 trillion cells, 206 bones, 600 muscles, and 22 internal organs.*

I had them write these numbers in their notebooks. We got a little sidetracked learning how to write 100 trillion with all the zeros, but it made an impression about how many cells are in the body.

- *The systems of the human body include:*
    1. *Circulatory System (heart, blood, vessels)*
    2. *Respiratory System (nose, trachea, lungs)*
    3. *Immune System (many types of protein, cells, organs, tissues)*
    4. *Skeletal System (bones)*
    5. *Excretory System (lungs, large intestine, kidneys)*
    6. *Urinary System (bladder, kidneys)*
    7. *Muscular System (muscles)*
    8. *Endocrine System (glands)*
    9. *Digestive System (mouth, esophagus, stomach, intestines)*
    10. *Nervous System (brain, spinal cord, nerves)*
    11. *Reproductive System (male and female reproductive organs)*

This was a long list but they were impressed with how many different parts of the body there are to study.

"We aren't going to study ALL of those, are we?" I assured them that we would only focus on one part each day and not come close to learning even the basics of what there is to know on each subject. This is why most doctors attend medical school for eight years before they are qualified to practice medicine.

- *Each square inch of the human body has about 19 million skin cells.*

I had them take markers to draw one inch squares on their arms to see the size of an area that contains this many skin cells.

- *Every hour about 1 billion cells in the human body must be replaced.*

By the time we would eat our snacks that morning, a billion of their cells would have been replaced without their knowing it.

- *The average human head has about 100,000 hairs.*

Edie asked, "Is it true that God knows how many hairs we have?"

We looked up the Scripture that tells us this. In Luke 12:7, Jesus says, "Indeed, the very hairs of your head are all numbered. Don't be afraid; you are worth more than many sparrows." It was unanimous that God has infinite patience because, with all the full heads of long hair in this group around our table it would take a very long time to count each one.

- *The circulatory system of arteries, veins, and capillaries is about 60,000 miles long.*

To give them an idea of how long this is, I gave them sheets of paper with a map of the United States. I had them mark Seattle, Washington. They all knew this was where their Uncle Rick, Aunt Lisa, and cousin Graham lived, although at that time none of them had been there.

Then I had them mark Key West, Florida. This is the southernmost point of the continental United States. These two cities are about 3,500 miles apart. They drew lines from one point to the other. I told them they would have to do this 17 times to measure the length of the pathways of our blood.

- *The heart beats more than 2.5 billion times in an average lifetime.*

We passed a stethoscope around the table so that they could listen to their own hearts and the heart of the one to their right.

- *The human heart creates enough pressure when it pumps out to the body to squirt blood 30 feet.*

Papa walked about 30 feet from the table to show them this distance. This elicited a lot of play-acting, pretending to bombard Papa with make-believe squirt guns.

- *It takes about 20 seconds for a red blood cell to circle the whole body.*

I set a stopwatch to have them imagine one red blood cell moving through the whole body in record time.

- *There are about 9,000 taste buds on the surface of the tongue, in the throat, and on the roof of the mouth.*

Just to have some fun with taste buds, I set out some salty pretzel sticks, sweet gum drops, and sour pickles. The more adventurous ones tried all three in one bite.

- *The strongest muscle in the body is the tongue.*

You don't even want to know what this looked like!

- *You blink more than 10 million times a year.*

We tried counting how many times we could make ourselves blink in 30 seconds.

- *Your brain weighs about three pounds.*

I let each one pick up a half gallon carton of milk which weighs the same as the brain.

- *Only 10 percent of the population is left-handed.*

Edie and Anna are both left-handed. They told us some interesting stories about teachers who tried to force them to use their right hands.

- *One fourth of the bones in your body are in your feet.*

Most of the feet under our large, glass-topped table were bare, so we had some fun demonstrations of feet-wiggling to show what bones made possible.

- *The most sensitive finger on the human hand is the index finger.*

There was a whole lot of touching going on.

- *Children tend to grow faster in the spring.*

"Why do you think this happens?" Their answers were as accurate as any scientists' best guesses.

"We get more exercise."

"We stay outside more."

"We start using parts of our body that have been lazy all winter."

We all remembered that when Jake first came to Camp Mimi he could easily walk under the glass-topped table where we had our lessons. He often looked up at us from underneath and Conlee and I had to work hard to avoid the adorable distractions.

The next year he forgot he couldn't walk under the table and constantly hit his forehead on the corners. To avoid bumps and bruises, we put a large padded quilt on the table top.

- *More men are color-blind than women.*

We had to explain that a color-blind person doesn't see in black and white, but that they confuse some colors.

- *More people have brown eyes than any other color.*

This wasn't true for our campers. There were far more blue eyes around our table. Only Sophie had brown eyes.

"Do you think any person could have imagined or designed such a complex structure?"

Their responses were brilliant: "It's like God created the first computer!" "No, God *was* the first computer!"

For children growing up in our technical age, the human body must indeed seem like a very sophisticated computer. And like using computers, we take our body's perfection for granted until one of its systems malfunctions due to unwise care or a virus.

It was time to narrow our discussion to the system of the body we would study our first day – the skeletal system.

Earlier in the year I found the most amazing learning tool – a three-foot-high model of the human body. It stood erect on a stand and was made entirely of sturdy plastic, containing removable organs, bones and skin covering.

They immediately gave him a name: Skelly. He took center stage in the middle of our table and was assembled and disassembled several times a day. It was easier for them to learn about anatomy and biology from Skelly than to think about it more personally.

They were fascinated when I told them that when they were born they each had about 300 bones, but that some of these bones slowly began to fuse together to become the 206 bones that adults have. Some of the bones in a baby are made of a soft, flexible material called *cartilage*, which eventually hardens into strong bones, helped by calcium.

Sophie immediately told everyone about the surgery she had when she was two months old. She knew the story well because she heard it frequently. She was born with a condition called *craniosynostosis*. We all practiced saying this long word. *Cra-ni-o-syn-o-sto-sis*.

The skull of a newborn is comprised of several sections or plates (called *sutures*), held together by soft cartilage. This allows room for the skull to expand to accommodate the rapid growth spurt of the brain in the first few months. The largest of these sutures is on the top of the baby's head, an area of soft cartilage called the *fontanelle*. Normally, this soft spot hardens over many months while the brain grows and the skull is gradually fused together.

However, when Sophie was born, her skull had already fused into hard, solid bone. Within about two or three weeks after her birth this was evidenced by a slightly misshapen head with a bulge where the soft spot should be and a bulge on her forehead. As her brain grew, there was no space to contain it. Without surgery, serious brain damage would occur, along with many possible physical side-effects.

Once a diagnosis was made of her condition, her parents located an expert in this field and the surgeon set the earliest date possible for her operation.

Conlee and I traveled with the family to a great facility at the University of Missouri Medical Center in Columbia, Missouri, for Sophie's surgery. A portion of the top of her skull was surgically separated along the normal suture lines. This allowed her brain to grow normally without restrictions.

After her surgery, she was fitted with a plastic, perforated helmet to allow the proper reshaping, protection, and healing of her skull. She wore these cute little helmets for a year. Each Christmas it is still one of the prized family ornaments that they put on their tree in thanksgiving for Sophie.

Everyone around the table stopped what they were doing to feel the top of Sophie's head. There was only the tiniest bump to serve as a reminder of the miracle she experienced. There were lots of, "Oooo, you had your head cut open?" and "Did it hurt?" Although she confessed she didn't remember any of it, she was definitely the heroine of the Camp Mimi table as we talked about bones for the rest of the morning.

Because the children always love to hear family stories, Papa and I told them about the night before Sophie's surgery. It was my birthday and we were in an unfamiliar city with Matt, Margo, and baby Sophie. Everyone was concerned about the surgery that would take place very early the next morning, but they wanted to take me out to dinner for a bit of a birthday celebration.

Matt and Conlee asked the receptionist at our hotel to recommend a nice place for a special dinner. She didn't hesitate to recommend a steak house that wasn't too far away and she made a reservation for us. We were going to make it an early evening and hoped it wouldn't be too crowded.

However, when we arrived there was a sizeable crowd waiting to be seated. Having a reservation didn't seem to make any difference. Margo's "mama anxieties" were working overtime and little Sophie internalized it all, becoming very fussy and restless. Nothing seemed to soothe her. I suggested several times that we leave and find some takeout for our hotel rooms. But everyone was determined to have a proper birthday dinner.

When the waiter took our order for steaks, we were told something we had never heard in a restaurant before. "It will be five dollars extra if we cook your steak for you." We all burst out laughing, releasing the growing anxieties and picturing the waiter bringing us raw meat to eat.

We weren't too far off the mark with our imaginations. We began to notice other tables being served big platters of raw steaks. The guests took them to a huge fire pit in the middle of the room and stood in the blazing heat, cooking their own steaks. Conlee and Matt looked at each other and said in unison, "We'll pay the five dollars. Please cook our steaks medium rare."

The tension was broken and the steaks were delicious, although none of us had much of an appetite. During the meal we all took turns walking Sophie in the lobby to comfort her. It was not a very relaxing evening but I was blessed by my family's thoughtfulness and I felt loved.

We opted to skip dessert and return to the hotel. When we paid our bill at the entrance we noticed a sign on the desk: "If it is your birthday you eat free." We all laughed at this unexpected birthday gift and as I produced my driver's license to prove my birthday, a man came to the desk to do the same thing. He was ninety-five and insisted that his family take his picture with me on our common birthday. He said he came every year to eat a free steak on his birthday and he loved getting to cook it himself!

We still talk about that being one of the most unusual birthdays I ever celebrated.

After we exhausted the subject of Sophie's surgery, we took turns feeling the *spine* of each person. Each spine has 26 bones called *vertebrae*, shaped like rings. Everyone tried to count the bumps. You could easily see the thinnest kids' spines, even through their shirts. The spine protects the spinal cord, the bundle of nerves that sends signals from the brain to the rest of the body.

It also supports the head and neck, anchors the ribs in place, and bears the weight of the body, giving us the ability to walk, run, dance and skip.

We took a snack break (because no one considered pretzels, gum drops and pickles a real snack) and tried some physical activities.

Cartwheels, somersaults, and handstands demonstrated the work of the skeletal system which supports the stress we put on our bodies just by having fun. I explained that there are also disks made of cartilage between each vertebra that act as shock absorbers to cushion the bones from pressure and twisting.

After our break and exercise we all felt our *ribs*, the 12 pairs of bones that are attached at the back of the spine, some directly to other bone and some attached with cartilage. The ribs protect our lungs and heart, providing a cage around them.

Then we examined our *fingers, hands,* and *arms*. We learned that each of these bones is wider at the ends where they meet another bone. This gives them extra strength. The most flexible area is the wrist, made up of eight small bones. Everyone flapped their wrists, twisting and turning to show the amazing ways we can manipulate this small portion of the body. The center of the hand has five separate bones and each finger has three bones. The thumb has two. Because of this unique structure, we can grasp things, write, pick up objects, and throw a ball. Amazing!

With every example, we dissected Skelly, seeing what these bones look like with no skin or muscle surrounding them.

The *pelvis* is the large, bowl-shaped structure that supports the spine, and protects the digestive system, parts of the urinary system, and parts of the reproductive system. The pelvis supports the legs. This is the work horse of the bones, holding up our weight and allowing us to stand, walk and run.

Finally, we talked about the moving *joints*, the places where bones meet. Some joints move and some don't. They are a little bit like hinges on a door. I opened the door to the back porch, right next to our table. It only moved so far, met resistance, and then stopped. It only moved one way.
Our joints are like that, too. Like door hinges, they need to be lubricated to move freely and the lubricant our bodies manufacture is called *synovial fluid*. Without it, we will have pain and stiffness. We might even crack, pop and groan, like rusty hinges on a door.

Ligaments, like strong rubber bands, hold bones together at the joints. We finished our study of bones with each one receiving a large page showing all the major bones of the human body, disassembled and out of order, to be cut out and glued together on a poster to compose a large skeleton. In their blue scrubs, working hard on the intricacies of the skeletal system, this group did indeed look like a mini version of an orthopedic classroom.

"Do you see why the Word of God says we are fearfully and wonderfully made?"
I explained that "fearful" here doesn't mean to be afraid of your body, but it means to be in awe and wonder of it, experiencing something so complex that we can barely understand it.

After our swim, lunch, playtime, and rest time, we had Q&A time around the table. I gave them illustrated pages for each question and each one received a large hand mirror with a handle. There's something about a child and a mirror that just invites making funny or scary faces, so we took a little time to get that out of their systems.
The first question was, "What is that dewdrop thing in the back of your mouth?"
The illustration on the page was of a girl, mouth open wide, revealing the *uvula*. No one at the table had ever heard that word. But now they were all staring into their mirrors, mouths wide open, trying to speak at the same time. It was comical.
Doing my homework in preparation for Camp Mimi, I learned as

much as the children on many of these subjects. This was one of them. I found that the *uvula*, made of connective tissue containing glands, has several purposes. First, it assists in swallowing. Along with the soft palate, it keeps food and drink from entering the nasal cavity. It also produces large amounts of saliva to keep the throat lubricated. And, finally, it helps us produce certain sounds known as "uvular consonants."

In French, Hebrew, German and Dutch, for instance, there are some common sounds, like pronouncing "g" and "ch" that are very difficult for some of us to learn. It involves the use of the *uvula* and making it vibrate.

We all practiced with the word "*Challah*" because they love to make it for *Shabbat*. I told them about a Dutch man named Gert and a Dutch woman named Gea, both translators for us at conferences we led in Holland. It took me a long time to learn how to correctly pronounce the "G" sound in their names. Again, we tried and there were lots of disgusting sounds and spitting at the same time because they were working their *uvulas* overtime.

If you manually stimulate the *uvula*, the gag reflex is initiated. It is a way to induce vomiting. We didn't try this.

If the *uvula* becomes swollen, it can contribute to snoring and sleep apnea. Of course there were lots of exaggerated snores around the table.

The word *uvula* is interesting because in Latin it means "little grape." The mirrors were used once more to see if, indeed, it looked like a grape.

While they were looking in their mouths, I asked them to look for their *tonsils*. A little harder to spot than the *uvula*, but they were all successful. They are easiest to see in children because they atrophy as we grow older. These tissue growths are helpful to the immune system, defending us from ingested or inhaled foreign matter.

They were interested to learn that I had my *tonsils* removed surgically when I was seven years old. I remember getting to eat all the ice cream I wanted. Immediately, everyone wanted ice cream! Oh, the power of suggestion! We had choices of vanilla, chocolate, and rocky road. Some had all three.

In addition to our daily lessons, Conlee and I found several simple experiments on the internet that we could do with the children each afternoon to demonstrate our lessons. Our first experiment involving bones would take about three days to complete so we began it the first night after a dinner of fried chicken, a family favorite.

We carefully washed the left-over chicken leg bones and put each one in a jar, adding two cups of water to one jar and two cups of vinegar to the other. We would look at them again later in the week.

Vinegar, which is acidic, dissolves calcium in the chicken bone. The bone in the water retains its calcium. The experiment is to show how bones need calcium to stay strong. Without calcium, they become weak and cannot support the body.

We talked about how eating certain foods will keep our calcium levels high. Everyone agreed that they liked calcium-forming foods such as milk and dairy products, broccoli, green leafy vegetables and almonds.

This was a fun time, exploring parts of the body that none of them knew anything about. We agreed once more: We are fearfully and wonderfully made!

DAY 2 - MUSCLES

The next morning everyone was up early, dressed in their scrubs, beds made, hair and teeth brushed, ready to begin another fun day. After breakfast they were immediately in their places around the table, notebooks open and already taking Skelly apart, trying to guess which part of the body we would study that day.

When they received their pages on muscles, there was a lot of posturing, imitating weight lifters and muscular super heroes. The pictures on their first page showed several views of the human body without skin, revealing the extensive muscular system that covers the internal organs and bones. We all agreed that everyone looks a lot better with skin on!

I also showed them a picture of a man who was so over-developed muscularly that he looked freakish. Our muscles are part of our being fearfully and wonderfully made, but you can obviously distort the beauty of the human body if you engage in extreme weight lifting and take illegal steroids to alter muscles.

While they colored pages of people doing tasks that require strong muscles, I gave them a little lesson on this amazing system of the body.

There are more than 600 muscles in the human body. They do everything from pumping blood throughout the body to helping lift a heavy backpack. I asked them how much they thought their school backpacks weigh and was surprised to learn that they were required to weigh them before bringing them to school.

Some of them weighed as much as 40 pounds! This has to be hard on young backs. They are only allowed to pull packs on wheels if they have a verified disability. This is to avoid tripping other students with many wheeled pull-alongs in the hallways. Think crowded airports!

The muscles are made of a type of elastic tissue, sort of like the material in a rubber band. There may be tens of thousands of these elastic fibers in each muscle.

Within the body, there are three kinds of muscles: *smooth, cardiac,* and *skeletal.*

Smooth muscles, sometimes called involuntary muscles, are in layers, one behind the other. We don't control smooth muscles because our brain and body tell them what to do without our thinking about it. We can't make food digest. The smooth muscles that control digestion contract (tighten up) and then relax, allowing what we eat to move through the body.

If you are really sick and need to throw up, the smooth muscles of the stomach push food back up so that it comes through the esophagus and out of the mouth.

Smooth muscles in the bladder allow you to hold in urine until you can get to the bathroom. Then they contract to push the urine out. Babies' bladder muscles are not strong enough to do this so they have to wear diapers until they mature. Of course children the age of our campers (between six and eleven) love bathroom humor, so this elicited lots of stories about little Jake, whom they could all recall wearing diapers and having accidents not too many years before. He took it in stride, the way the youngest in a family learns to do.

Also, when a woman gives birth, the smooth muscles of her uterus or womb contract to push the baby out of her body.

There are smooth muscles in your eyes that keep your sight focused.

The heart is also made of smooth muscle, but because of its special function it is known as a cardiac muscle. It is very thick and is strong enough to contract and pump blood out and then relax to let blood back in after it has been circulated through the whole body. They immediately remembered that their hearts could pump 30 feet to hit where Papa stood the day before.

The muscles that you think of making you strong are called the skeletal muscles. They are striped in appearance because they are striated, meaning light and dark. These are the voluntary muscles, the ones you can control. You make your leg muscles kick the soccer ball. You make your body do a cartwheel.

These muscles are held in place attached to bone by tendons. Some of the biggest and most powerful muscles are in the back, near the spine. They support our body weight and allow us to stand upright and tall. They also give us the power to lift heavy objects and push things.

Taking our hand mirrors out of our boxes, we all looked at what our facial muscles could do. Some of these muscles are only attached to skin so we can manipulate them easily into smiles, frowns, chewing, sticking out the tongue, and pouting. Everyone tried it all!

I asked the children if they ever had growing pains. All of them raised their hands. These pains normally occur when kids are between the ages of three-five and/or eight-twelve. Our campers fit right in this range. They all agreed that they usually had pains in their legs at night, either in the front of their thighs, in their calves, or behind their knees. Usually they occurred in both legs at the same time.

These growing pains only occur in the muscles. It may be because children overwork their muscles during the day with all their activities, or it may be that the muscles are stretching as they grow and irritating surrounding nerves. Several things can help alleviate the pain: massage, getting up to walk around, stretching the muscles, or using a heating pad.

Now that we knew something about muscles, we worked on word search sheets, fill-in-the-blanks sheets, and crossword puzzles on the subject. These activities kept them busy while I prepared some snacks.

During snack time, the conversation turned to one of their favorite subjects: food. This year they were much more interested in what foods they would be served, what they would be cooking, and how they would decorate the table for the evening meal. As Caleb matured, he became more adventurous in eating proteins and other foods besides carbs. This made it a lot more fun for him to participate in cooking.

Jake, the earliest riser, loved to be the first one into the kitchen every morning, to look at the daily teams posted on the chalkboard, to see who he was partnered with for the day and whether they were cooks, servers, or decorators. And he delighted in waking up everyone else to tell them what their daily job assignment would be and who would be their partner for the day.

I divided them into different teams every day, alternating which pairs worked together so that everyone had the opportunity to spend quality time with someone different. This took out the competitive factor between the older ones and the younger ones or the boys against the girls. We wanted each of them to experience working as a team with one another.

As the children got older and more creative, the complexities of the menus and the table decors at night took on new proportions. They would begin to plan early in the morning, scouring the house for props and ingredients. As usual, I gave them free reign to use whatever they chose. I only required that they respect the value of things and put everything back in its proper place. They never once abused the privilege and through their eyes and efforts, beauty filled our home.

Sophie wanted to know which night she could cook her favorite, *Chicken Spiedini*. There were requests for grilled pizza, waffles, and of course, steak.

Although I let them think I was spontaneously preparing their moment-by-moment requests, the fact was that the menus were planned in great detail weeks before they arrived. Each day's breakfast, lunch, snacks, and dinner were on my Camp Mimi menu planner, all of the ingredients had been purchased, and many dishes were already prepared and frozen.

My goal was to never go to the grocery store during Camp Mimi. We were very nearly able to do this, thanks to a large freezer in our storeroom.

One of their annual favorites was fried biscuits for breakfast. This couldn't have been easier to prepare and, although it isn't very healthy, it was such fun to do together, that we ignored the nutrition facts. We used canned biscuits, the kind you whack on the table to open. Because they went through three cans at a time, everyone got a turn at the whacking until the cans popped open. It was a bit like a *piñata* party. With table knives, they cut each biscuit into fourths and I put them into the deep fryer basket until they were golden and puffy, turning them a few times.

Then came the fun part, which fit in well with our medical theme. They took food injectors, filled them with a mixture of melted butter and honey, and injected each golden hot biscuit until the goodness oozed out. They ate as fast as I could cook them!

Other favorites that year were:
- hot dogs baked in crescent rolls, dipped in their favorite condiments of ketchup, mustard, or a combination of both
- fish tacos
- chicken fried steak
- roasted broccoli with ranch dressing dip
- pork tenderloin and hash brown quiche
- chopped salads served in jars
- chocolate cake
- make-your-own ice cream sundaes with various toppings of sauces and sprinkles
- crème brulée, which they each got to torch
- and, of course, steak

Our afternoon experiment showed how the muscles and the brain work together. We observed their reflexes and recorded the time it took for each child's brain to process and act on a verbal command.

Papa held a yardstick upright a few feet off the ground, just high enough for each child to hold out their arm and loosely touch the bottom of the stick with their fingers and thumb. Then they closed their eyes.

When Papa said, "Go!," he released the yardstick and the child was supposed to close his fist and catch the stick as quickly as possible. Then Papa measured how many inches the stick fell before the child caught it.

He recorded their efforts by measuring time and distance to see how long it took for each child's brain to react to the command, send the message to their muscles, and catch the stick.

To be more accurate, we did it several times. We found that it was much easier and faster, when eyes were open, and after they knew what to expect.

For the evening meal tablescape, Caleb and Sophie revisited the measuring theme by using brown craft paper as a tablecloth, drawing graphs on it, marking precisely where each plate and glass would be set, and a centerpiece of yardsticks, measuring tapes, rulers, pencils, with the invitation to measure everything you saw and write it on the paper. It was a fun time at dinner and totally unexpected.

DAY 3 -- CELLS

The next day our morning introductory page on cells was a picture that looked like a raw egg, cracked open on a plate. Four parts of the "egg" were labeled: *nucleus, cytoplasm, mitochondria,* and *membrane.*

Each child was given a fresh egg and a little plate so that they could crack open their egg to look at a macrocosmic example of a human cell. A couple of the children needed extra eggs and clean plates because they ended up with broken yolks. Fortunately, we had backyard chickens which gave us an ample supply. All of the untouched raw eggs were collected in a bowl to scramble for a quiche later.

After an examination of their eggs, comparing the yolk to the cell's nucleus, the white to the cytoplasm and the nearly invisible film that held it together as the membrane, they were given a coloring page of a large cell and asked to color code each part.

The mitochondria, free-floating in each cell, keep the cell full of energy.

As they worked with their crayons, I explained that cells group together to make skin, bones, and blood. Inside the nucleus or center, is DNA, which stands for deoxyribonucleic acid.

Our DNA determines the color of our hair, eyes, and skin. DNA also affects the way we look and act. DNA is the genetic coding that decides if we will be male or female, or if a bird embryo will be a robin or a blue jay. It determines and reads every detail of our makeup.

They each received a sheet of paper with the outline of a head and I asked them to draw themselves, showing what their own DNA revealed, – their hair, skin, and eye color, and something about their temperament.

Edie and Anna are identical twins and you would think their pictures would be similar, but they perceived themselves quite differently from one other. Although the girls are hard to tell apart physically, from birth their parents have deliberately referred to them by their given names or as "the girls," never calling them "the twins." Also, they have never been dressed alike. Perhaps this is why their personalities and perceptions are so distinct.

Sometimes it seemed that the children were so absorbed in their coloring projects or their own thoughts that they were not paying attention to the lessons. I was surprised when they mentioned some of our information in later conversations. A few times that day I heard two of them telling the others that they couldn't help the way they acted because it was in their DNA!

That afternoon they received their Q&A sheets. The first question for the day was, "Why is my eye color blue, brown or green?"

On the page were inserts of large, up close pictures of human eyes showing several different colors. To fill in the blanks on the page, they had to answer: "My mother's eye color is _____." My father's eye color is _____." My eye color is _____."

Again, their hand mirrors were brought out and a very studious inspection of eyes was conducted. The predominant eye color around our table was blue, followed by brown.

The next Q&A question was, "What is the black circle in my eye?"

We learned that the purpose of the eye's pupil is to allow light to enter the eye. We looked closely at each other's eyes after being exposed to the bright light of a little flashlight, and after being closed for several seconds. The size of the pupils was noticeably different.

Then we had pages showing the different parts of the eye. How intricate and delicate this one part of the body is! We saw diagrams of the muscles that open, close, focus, and dilate the eye. They completed a page with fill-in-the-blanks about the complex parts, identifying the lens, pupil, eyelid, retina, iris, cornea, optic nerve and muscles.

It was time for another Q&A page. "Why don't my eyelashes grow?"

I showed them a fake picture of a girl whose eyelashes grew as long as her hair. It was pretty silly and they all decided that God knew what He was doing when He kept eyelashes short. They are only used to filter foreign matter from entering the eye. They also perform the same function as whiskers do for cats and dogs, warning them of approaching danger. For humans, touching them triggers a blinking action or closing the eye.

The children were extremely interested in learning and talking about themselves! So, we pressed on with some further questions about genetics. This was directly related to our study on cells and the way traits are passed on in a family. I gave each one a chart to fill in pertinent data about themselves. They delighted in sharing this information with everyone around the table.

- What color hair do you have?
- Do you get freckles on your face?
- Do you have cheek dimples when you smile?
- Are your earlobes attached or do the ends hang free?
- Can you roll your tongue up into a tube?

- Are you double-jointed? If so, in what part of your body?

I asked them to answer the same questions about their parents and their siblings, too. All of this information would be helpful to understand their genetic makeup.

After lots of fun examining freckles and earlobes, and then demonstrating tongue tricks or double-jointed thumbs and elbows, I told them that they have two copies of each gene that makes up their physical structure and abilities. They receive one from each parent.

For instance, if both of their parents can roll their tongues, they will probably be able to do so, too. If only one parent can do this, one of their genes will be dominant and one will be dormant. They will be able to roll the tongue if they inherited the dominant gene.

What if only one sister in the family is redheaded? She may have inherited a gene from a long-ago relative whose red-haired gene stayed dormant while being passed on.

We had lots of rabbit trails with this discussion but their stories and opinions were priceless. Conlee and I laughed and applauded their ingenuity and vulnerability with great pleasure.

Our experiment for the afternoon once again utilized the large supply of eggs our hens produced. For this lesson we had to have several hard-boiled eggs (which I had cooked, cooled and peeled during rest time). Each child received a peeled egg and an empty, glass juice bottle that I had saved.

We asked them to put each egg on top of the bottle to see if it would fall inside. No way! It's impossible to get the egg into the bottle in one piece.

Then Papa took kitchen matches, lit two of them, quickly dropped them into a bottle, placed the egg on top of the bottle, waited a few seconds, and amazingly, we all watched the egg drop into the bottle. Of course, there was a chorus of, "I want to do it!"

Papa went around the table with matches until each child had a bottle with an egg inside. Then it was time to tell them how it works. When you drop matches inside the bottle, the air in the bottle heats up. Heated air expands and some of it comes out of the bottle. When the match flames burn out, the air inside the bottle cools and contracts. The egg on top of the bottle creates a seal. The pressure inside the bottle is now less than the pressure outside the bottle, and the egg is forced into the bottle.

To get the egg out of the bottle, you can heat the bottle or blow into it. The increased air pressure will force the egg back out.

We did this several times and then thought it wise to feed the eggs to the dogs, not to make egg salad. We had happy dogs.

We had one more experiment that night after the table had been cleared, the dishes washed, and the kitchen cleaned up. We had chopped fresh spinach for our jarred salads for dinner and I kept some out for this interesting lesson. We were going to extract DNA from spinach.

We gathered around the kitchen island to have make-your-own ice cream sundaes with lots of toppings. We conducted our experiment on the adjacent kitchen counter. Preparing and eating ice cream while timing the results for our DNA tests kept everyone interested and made studying science lots of fun.

For this experiment we needed several things lined up on the counter: rubbing alcohol, a blender, a timer, a half cup of our left-over fresh spinach, liquid dish washing soap, meat tenderizer, a strainer, cold water, salt, and a glass measuring cup. The children had the list of supplies and gathered them while I put out the ice cream fixings.

Before they got into the dessert, we went down our check list with everyone contributing. They poured 1 cup cold water, ¼ teaspoon salt, and the ½ cup spinach into the blender and let it run until it was like soup.

Then we poured the "soup" through the strainer into the glass measuring cup. We added 2 tablespoons of the dish washing liquid and set the timer for ten minutes. While we waited it was time for ice cream!

Before the second round of ice cream sundaes, we checked our spinach mixture. We added a pinch of the meat tenderizer and stirred it slowly. When it was combined, they measured the volume very carefully and added exactly that same amount of rubbing alcohol. Then we set the timer for three minutes.

After three minutes, our mixture looked entirely different. There was a white, cobwebby substance present in the murky liquid. The strands we saw were the DNA! We had broken down the spinach to its simplest cellular structure and the soap helped the process. The alcohol made the strands adhere to each other.

To be honest, the children enjoyed the process of setting up the experiment, adding and mixing ingredients, and eating ice cream more than they were impressed with the results. However, it was a fun time and we easily accomplished our objective.

DAY 4 - BLOOD

This was the day they all dreaded. Yes, we actually were going to study blood! They had various reactions when they saw their subject sheets, which were splattered with pictures of blood, arteries, red and white blood cells and platelets. I encouraged them to see the subject through the lens of our theme: I am fearfully and wonderfully made!

While their hands were busy with coloring pages of the human heart and pictures of Jesus healing people, I introduced our study of blood with a lesson on divine healing and the biblical concept that "life is in the blood."[101]

They were very attentive to stories about how God has always been considered the Healer of His people and how seriously God commanded His people to respect blood. They were not to have any associations with death or the shedding of blood, except for the blood of the sacrificial animals which substituted for their sins. Jesus referred to the final cup of blessing at the Last Supper (the Passover Meal) as, *"My Blood of the New Covenant for the forgiveness of sins."*[102]

I read Exodus 15:26 to them. *If you listen carefully to the Lord your God and do what is right in His eyes, if you pay attention to His commandments and keep all His decrees, I will not bring on you any of the diseases I brought on the Egyptians, for I am the Lord, who heals you.*

They remembered from the Passover Meal teachings about the diseases that God sent to the Egyptians when they rebelled against Him. It was their favorite part of the traditional liturgy, shouting out the plagues and, with each one, dipping their finger into the wine to make a dot on the clean white plate. I told them that each drop of wine signified blood which was shed in some way to indicate an absence of life. We recounted the ten plagues and they shouted out the names with gusto: water turned to blood, frogs, lice, flies, livestock diseases, boils, hail, locusts, darkness, and death of the firstborn.

The above passage from Exodus, the foundation verse which biblically establishes Yahweh as Healer, tells us that when we take God's word seriously and obey Him, He acts as our Restorer and the One who makes us whole. In Hebrew, one of God's names is *rp'* (*rapha*), which means "the one who draws near, who brings together, who makes whole, who mends, who restores, who heals."

When God speaks of life, He always speaks of healthy life. When we proclaim *L'Hayim!* (to life!), we are speaking of being strong and healthy in every way. This is a favorite toast at meals with the children. They love to clink glasses and shout this blessing to everyone around the table.

Jesus spoke about coming to bring us *abundant life.*[103] He also demonstrated how divine life is restored in sick people. Sometimes He did it in unusual ways.

Once He put His fingers into a deaf man's ears. Once He spat and touched a mute man's tongue.[104] Once He spat on a blind man's eyes, and placed His hands on blind eyes.[105] He made mud in the dust with His saliva and put it on a blind man's eyes.[106] In each case, health was restored.

---

[101] Leviticus 17:11

[102] Matthew 26:28

[103] John 10:10

[104] Mark 7:31-35

[105] Mark 8:22-25

"Ooooooo!"

"That's disgusting!"

"Even if it was Jesus, I wouldn't want someone's spit on me."

"Or mud either!"

Their reactions to the unconventional ways Jesus sometimes healed were not unusual. Adults may not be as vocal, but probably have thought the same things. I, too, was puzzled for many years until one day I came across some ancient rabbinical writings on the subject of healing. They were written before the first century. By the time of Jesus, these traditions were esteemed and easily recognized by both Jews and gentiles.

Rabbinic tradition stated that the spittle of the first born son of a father has healing properties. Jesus was the first born son of His Father.

Caleb immediately asked if any of us wanted him to spit on them! As the first born son of his father, Ben, Caleb took this lesson to heart. No one took him up on his offer.

In the Bible, health is thought of as the expected, normal condition of humankind who is in right relationship with God. There is no glory in sickness. During the Temple period, anyone who was ill, afflicted, or who had come in contact with blood (associated with death after it leaves the body, not life) could not participate in corporate worship. It was expected that they would go to the Lord to be healed and cleansed.

All of us can worship and glorify God in the ways we respond to any illness, but we are not to glorify the suffering itself. If disease comes to us as a result of sin or disobedience, it is assumed that confession and repentance will release the body to receive healing. We often see this today.

If disease comes from other sources, it is assumed that the Lord is still the Healer. We are to ask Him.

In His love, and the wonderful way He made us, God gave our bodies the ability to heal themselves. This is called the *immune system*. The breakdown of the immune system usually results in premature death.

Whenever circumstances compromise our God-given immune system, we then turn to the Lord, asking Him to bring it back into His divine order. Jesus declared and demonstrated that healing is a part of the inheritance of all the people of God. In nearly every book of the Bible, there are confirmations of healing from God.

Healing prayers for the sick became the heritage of the early believers. *Is any one of you sick? He should call the elders of the church to pray over him and anoint him with oil in the name of the Lord. And the prayer offered in faith will make the sick person well; the Lord will raise him up. If he has sinned he will be forgiven. Therefore confess your sins to each other and pray for each other so that you may be healed. The*

---

[106] John 9:1, 6-7

prayer of a righteous man is powerful and effective. (James 5:14-16).

Papa brought out his oil stock, a lovely little round silver box that is fitted on a ring to wear on your finger. In it is a ball of oil-soaked cotton, the oil having been blessed especially for healing purposes.

"Would you like to be anointed for healing?" Although none of them was sick, they all responded affirmatively, because, like the cotton, they like to soak up all the blessings they can.

Conlee went around the table, anointing each forehead with the sign of the Cross and praying very personal prayers for each one. Every crayon and colored pencil was laid aside, with full attention placed on the praying. Each one was transformed by a holy presence.

Afterwards, while we had our snacks, we could still sense the lingering effects of the anointing prayers. Surely it was because we gave glory to God and shared biblical testimonies of God's healing power and His desire for us to be whole.

After Snack Time we had lots of fun activity sheets to complete. One of them was a huge human heart, showing veins and arteries attached. Their assignment was to color the arteries (marked #1) red and the veins (marked #2) blue. This was a simple task but was made relevant as I explained to them that blood vessels are hollow tubes that carry blood all over the body.

In the human body there are three kinds of vessels: *arteries*, *veins* and *capillaries*. In the human heart there are arteries and veins. Arteries carry blood away from the heart and veins carry blood toward the heart.

Capillaries connect the arteries to the veins throughout the body. By hearing, seeing and coloring, the children were able to capture the concept and thought it was "cool."

They even made the connection themselves that the heart is like a pump. We gave them lots of accolades for this conclusion, and I explained that it is really like two pumps. The right side receives blood from the body and pumps it to the lungs. The left side does the exact opposite. It receives blood from the lungs and pumps it out to the body.

We also had word search pages and crossword puzzles about the cardiovascular system and how it works. On another page was a picture of a large, divided heart. I instructed them how to color in the different parts.

There are four different areas called *chambers*, two on each side of the heart, one on top and one on the bottom. The two on top are called *atria* (single *atrium*) and the two on the bottom are called *ventricles*. The atria fill with the blood returning to the heart from the body and lungs. The ventricles squirt out the blood to the body and lungs.

"And it will squirt 30 feet!" They remembered and shouted the fact in unison!

They also labeled the thick wall of muscle that runs down the middle of the heart, separating the left and right sides. This is called the *septum*. I showed them how the atria and ventricles work together as a team, the atria filling with blood and dumping it into the ventricles. Then the ventricles squeeze together, pumping the blood out of the heart. While the ventricles are squeezing, the atria are refilling and getting ready for the next contraction.

We brought back the stethoscope so they could listen to this amazing procedure. It made much more sense now that they knew what was happening. "Wow!" The whole process is called *circulation*.

We demonstrated another way to see how our hearts were working. We found our pulse points on our wrists and used a stop watch set at one minute to count how many times we felt the beat. This measures how many times the heart contracts in a minute. It is much slower when resting than when active. We tried it both ways and they wrote their results on the heart page.

After all of this concentrated attention on a very mature subject, it was definitely time to give our hearts some physical workouts. I was ready for a break, too, because I was definitely attempting to convey information that was not terribly familiar to me. But we all learned some new things and had a lot of fun doing so.

After lunch and a rest, we continued to exercise our hearts by walking and running through Bellingrath Gardens, until we all collapsed over ice cream in the Garden's café.

For dinner that night, Edie and Jake decorated the table and – you guessed it! Their theme was hearts all the way. We had valentine night.

They drew, colored, and cut out hundreds of hearts and scattered them everywhere. Surrounded by red napkins, red candles, and the paper cutouts, we felt very festive.

They knew there was still "experiment time" after dinner. Sophie was the most skeptical about each experiment working, and teased Papa quite a bit about "doing one more experiment that he didn't know how to do." It was all good-natured and we persevered.

First, it was time to look at our two jars of chicken bones we had submerged in water and in vinegar first night. When they pulled the bones out, they were surprised to see that the one in water remained the same as when they put it in the jar. But, the bone submerged in vinegar for three days was like rubber. They bent it back and forth and, although it looked the same, it felt totally different. This was because the vinegar had drawn calcium out of the bone, keeping it from being strong and dense. Sophie had to admit, "Ok, so this one worked. Good job, Papa!"

Our experiment about blood worked, too, much to everyone's surprise.

We made "plasma soup." I had planned for this to double as dessert but the concept was a bit too weird for everyone's taste, so we substituted dessert with chocolate cake, which looked nothing like blood.

I shared the facts and Papa did the logistics. I told them that *plasma* composes 55% of our blood and is 90 % water. It carries dissolved nutrients like glucose, protein and hormones to all the parts of the body. It also picks up waste to be cleaned or filtered.

We lined up our ingredients on the counter so that each one could take part in making artificial plasma. We took a clear glass bowl and poured in white corn syrup a little more than half way up, representing the 55% of plasma in our blood.

Red blood cells comprise 44% of our blood. They contain *hemoglobin* and carry oxygen around the body. The cells only live about three months, so we have to keep making new ones. They are produced in the marrow of bones.

The children poured red hot candies less than half way up to represent the red blood cells.

White blood cells make up .5% of our blood and they are larger than red blood cells. They fight infections. A few white jelly beans were added to the mix to represent the white blood cells.

Platelets account for .5% of our blood and they help the blood to clot when we get a cut. We added a few candy sprinkles to the bowl to represent the platelets.

Then they stirred it all together to see the representation of the life source of our blood. It's no wonder that none of them wanted to give it a taste! In fact the consensus was that no one wanted to eat red hots or white jelly beans again. They agreed that sprinkles were still okay on ice cream.

However, the visual concept was made and Sophie gave Papa a "C" for trying.

Before reading a bedtime story, they received two more Q&A pages. The first was, "Why does my blood look blue when it is in my body?"

They saw a picture of an older person's hand, whose veins were more apparent, with a prominent network of blue veins. Papa's veins were the most pronounced of any of ours, so each one examined Papa's hands, feeling the protrusion of large veins.

"Does it hurt?"

"You have blue blood!"

I made the statement, "Blood is never blue!"

"But Papa's is!" they retorted.

So we had a mini lesson. Even when blood is oxygen deprived, it is never blue, only a darker red. The reason it looks blue under the skin is because of the way light is absorbed into the blood and reflected from the skin. It is an optical perception.

The veins are not blue either. They are just the only blood vessels we can observe under the skin. If we could see arteries, they would appear the same way. Everyone agreed that Papa didn't need to bleed to prove the point.

The second Q&A page was, "Why do I get scabs?"

There was a picture on the page of a girl with a skinned knee.

The medical name for a scab is *eschar*. The kid name is *boo-boo*. Immediately, each one had a story or a show-and-tell about their personal boo-boos, with all the gory details. This took a while.

Each one testified that their cut or scrape formed a hard covering called a scab and did not continue to bleed forever.

We now knew that the sprinkles in our plasma soup represented a part of our blood called platelets that cause it to clot and get hard so that we won't lose all our blood. While this happens, the white jelly beans (white blood cells) come to the rescue to fight infection, and the red hot candies (red blood cells) work to keep oxygen flowing around the boo-boo.

They knew the drill now and together, everyone declared with enthusiasm, "I am fearfully and wonderfully made!"

DAY 5 - THE BRAIN

Today's subject was the most popular of the week. From the time it was announced, the children were enthusiastic about studying the "mother board" of the body, as the computer-savvy generation put it.

We looked at pictures of nine stages of the human brain growing inside the embryo in a mother's body, at three weeks from conception to the time of birth. The growth rate and development is phenomenal.

The human brain is the most complex thing in the world. It only takes up 2 % of our body, only uses 20 % of our oxygen supply, and only 30 % of our body's energy, but it does the most work.

We had several coloring sheets of the brain with all its many crevices, compartments, and convoluted pathways. The children were extremely creative in their color coding of the different areas. While they were coloring, I talked to them about *memory*, one of the functions of the multi-talented brain.

I asked them what they were doing last year on the Fourth of July. They had vivid memories of where they were, who they were with, and what fireworks they liked best.

"How do you know that since it happened almost a year ago?"

They were quick with, "I remember!"

When an event happens, when we learn something, or when we meet someone, the brain determines whether that information needs to be saved.

If the brain judges the information important, it places it in its memory files. We learned a big word: *hippocampus*. This is the part of the brain that processes memories. This is what makes it possible to remember what you did last year on the Fourth of July.

The part that allows you to access that stored memory is called the *cerebral cortex*. Located in the *cerebrum*, the largest part of the brain, it is sometimes called the "gray matter." It also controls more complex functions like language and processing information. You need this part of the brain to solve math problems, figure out a video game, and draw a picture.

As we all know, in spite of the extremely complex "mother board" within our body, our memory isn't always perfect. Everyone around the table gave examples of learning something at school and then not being able to remember it for a test. The frustration was universal.

As we grow older, we joke about having a "senior moment," when we can't recall something we know really well. Often, the lost memory will pop up at an unexpected time. Memories are accessed slower with age.

There are some diseases like *Alzheimer's* in which deposits are built up in the brain. The deposits inhibit the proper connections with nerve cells so that memories cannot be recalled.

When someone has a *stroke*, blood doesn't get to all the parts of the brain. Among other things, this also can affect one's memory.

At any age, an injury to the head and brain can cause trouble with your memory. Often a person will recover from the injury but have to learn simple things all over again, like how to talk, how to tie shoes, or how to pick up a fork to eat.

Amnesia is the name for a condition when you can't remember things that happened recently or maybe can't remember anything about your past life. This is a popular plot in novels, movies and soap operas. People with amnesia usually get better slowly.

The most common cause is a traumatic brain injury, usually from a severe hit to the head. If you've ever seen a football player knocked out on the field, you'll see the team doctor asking the injured player some basic questions.

"Where are you?"

"What team do you play for?"

"What day is it?"

If the player doesn't know the correct answer, it could be the first sign of a brain injury.

Abusing alcohol and using harmful drugs can also cause the brain to malfunction and alter chemicals in the brain which make memories harder to recall or even cause hallucinations.

Doctors can take pictures of the brain and skull to determine the severity of head injuries. This picture is called a CT scan.

We asked the children how they could protect their brains in practical ways. Wearing protective helmets while biking or skateboarding, as well as always wearing a seatbelt in the car, were unanimous answers.

They were not so sure about eating certain foods to nourish the brain, so we talked about some specifics. Caffeine stimulates the brain for a short time, but too much in the system can make you jittery. Eating something sweet can also enhance your memory for a short time because sugar stimulates the brain. (This fact got fist pumps and a chorus of "Oh, yeah!").

Eating breakfast will give your brain a head start to remembering all the information you need to accumulate each day. Foods like fish, nuts, chocolate, avocados and blueberries (probably not all together) also help the brain work efficiently.

Taking a multi-vitamin is a good idea as well.

Doing challenging tasks like crossword puzzles, solving complex problems, and staying active, keeps the brain working, stimulated and healthy.

They agreed that their brains were overly stimulated with all the puzzles they were doing and the facts they were learning at Camp Mimi.

Our Q&A page for the day was, "Why does your foot fall asleep?"

Everyone had an example of this happening, sometimes after sitting in one position for too long or while sleeping.

A foot, leg, or hand could feel odd and very heavy and feel like pins and needles were sticking in it when you tried to move it.

While preparing this lesson, I learned that the explanation is not that you've cut off the blood supply to your foot, which is what most people think. Instead, it is because of a temporary compression of nerves in that area. The nerves can't send messages back to the brain normally, so for the moment, the connection is cut off and you don't feel anything. It's like when someone cuts off a telephone conversation before you're ready. Your brain is saying "hello," but your foot is not able to answer.

When you stand up or uncross your legs the nerves are no longer compressed and the feeling soon comes back. As it does, the sensation of the nerves reconnecting is tingly and perhaps a bit painful.

The nervous system controls everything we do involuntarily, like breathing, walking, thinking, and feeling. The whole system is made up of the brain, the spinal cord, and all the nerves in the body.

A good way to describe how it works is this: the brain is the control center, the spinal cord is the major highway to and from the brain, and the nerves carry messages to and from the body, so the brain can interpret them and take action.

On the diagram of the brain we labeled the *cerebellum*, the small but powerful part of the brain that controls balance, coordination and movement. It is located in the back of the brain, down low, near the spinal cord. This enables you to kick a ball, walk, run, swim, stand on your head and balance on one foot.

We located the *brain stem*, another very small but important part. It connects the brain to the spinal cord which runs down the neck and back. It is in charge of all the functions we need to stay alive, like breathing air, digesting food, and circulating blood. It controls the muscles that make these functions operate without our being aware of it.

The *pituitary gland* is even smaller; it's only pea-sized. It is at the base of the brain and, although it looks insignificant, it has a hugely important role producing and releasing hormones. These hormones help keep many bodily functions we take for granted in healthy working order. They help us grow up to be men and women; they determine how tall we will be; they keep our metabolism going so we can digest food and get nutrition from it; they assist in reproduction; and they help the kidneys function properly, among other things.

We located the *hypothalamus* on the diagram of the brain. We weren't going to study the *endocrine system* and the *nervous system* separately but I mentioned them briefly so the children would continue to discover the complexity of the body. Just knowing these systems exist and that they function in harmony with all the other systems is another proof of how intricate our amazing body really is.

The *hypothalamus* links the endocrine and nervous systems together. It is located above the pituitary and is slightly larger, maybe the size of an almond. Its many jobs include being an inner thermostat, keeping the body temperature about 98.6 degrees (F).

I brought out a thermometer that fits inside the ear to take everyone's temperature. They were all in the normal range. We now knew to thank our inner hypothalamus. It was working!

Everyone had stories about having a fever, when their body temperature got too hot working overtime to fight off an infection. We know that if we stay in the sun too long we get hot and our bodies sweat. If we get too cold, our bodies shiver. Both of these physical reactions to temperature are attempts by the hypothalamus to get our inner temperature back to normal.

We also shared stories about when we were the hottest and the coldest. When our son Ben (the father of Caleb, Anna, Edie, and Jake) was a boy, we lived through a terrible ice storm without any power for two weeks. It was cold beyond anything we had experienced. Fortunately, we had a wood stove and a fireplace. Papa's job all day long was to chop firewood for us and for many of the elderly people on our street. When the power was finally restored, we bought t-shirts that said, "We survived the Sewanee Ice

Storm!"

On the day that Caleb and Sophie were baptized, we held an afternoon celebration BBQ for a large group of people on the lawn at our bay cottage in Mobile. People who attended still recall it being the hottest day in Mobile they could remember. One of our guests was our dear friend, Archbishop Henry Orombi, visiting us from Uganda. He said that although he had lived in Africa all his life, he had never been as hot as he was that day.

Other jobs of the small *hypothalamus* are controlling heart rate and blood pressure, fluid and electrolyte balance, including thirst, appetite and body weight, and sleep cycles.

It didn't take much suggestion talking about thirst and appetite for everyone to agree it was Snack Time!

After snacks, it seemed appropriate to imprint the complex lesson about the brain and all its hidden parts with some fun activities finding hidden objects. We had some complicated treasure hunts with obscure clues and hints they had to figure out and locate. One of these yielded new swim goggles for everyone at the end of the trail.

Another hunt yielded the prize of a three-foot-long puzzle of the human body. It had two sides, one of the skeletal system, and the other of the internal organs. For the rest of Camp Mimi they put the large pieces together dozens of times.

Treasure hunts are such fun and they remembered a previous Camp Mimi quest when Papa dressed like a scary pirate. They were all on the lookout for a repeat performance, but evidently the pirate had retired.

Sophie and Anna were our table team for supper. They closed themselves up in my office for more than an hour, preparing the complicated format for our evening meal. First, we had a treasure hunt with progressive clues to find our silverware. Then we had to guess riddles to receive our plates. When we were all sitting around the table with our earned plates and found silverware, we were informed that each dish would only be brought to the table if someone could answer some trivia they had found on the Internet. For instance, one question was, "Which author has written the most books?"

The answer was Phillip Parker, but none of us knew it. No food.

"Which president of the United States had the most children?"

None of us knew that either. It was John Tyler who had fifteen children. Again, no food.

It became apparent that this creative way to showcase the workings of the brain and our knowledge was definitely going to ruin a nice, warm meal. So, we put a stop to the questioning and delayed it for after-dinner entertainment.

We let the girls ask a few more of their impossible-to-answer questions and then diverted the children with more Q&A pages while we were still around the table having dessert.

"Why do humans cry?" I gave them a picture page of several people crying, from babies to adult women with mascara running down their faces, to President George Bush on 9/11. I asked the children, "Why do *you* cry?" Their answers were typical.

"When I'm hurt."

"When I'm sad."

"When someone hurts my feelings."

"When I'm embarrassed."

I explained that there are many factors involved in human tears. All of the ones they mentioned are valid. But crying also helps a mother and her newborn baby bond together in a healthy way. When the baby cries, the mother comes and comforts or feeds. Babies who seldom or never cry have little attachment to their mothers.

Crying is an involuntary response to emotion, triggered by the brain. It may release certain hormones, along with toxins and stress from the body. That's why sometimes people are told, "Go ahead and cry. You'll feel better." It works.

Although some animals shed tears, such as apes, camels, and elephants, theirs is not an emotional response. Only humans continue to cry into adulthood.

We have tears contained in and released from tear ducts in our eyes. The salty liquid lubricates and protects our eyes from dust and other particles. Interestingly, research shows that the chemical composition is different in emotional tears versus those that are shed from irritants in the eye or from cutting an onion.

The next question was, "What is my ear made of?" On the Q&A page was a small insert of a very complicated schematic of the human ear, with other pictures of various shapes and sizes of ears. They were asked to draw the ear of the two people beside them and compare them.

The part of the ear that we see is made of cartilage. This is why an ear can be pierced and not bleed very much. The girls around the table all had pierced ears and they testified that it didn't hurt too much, just a quick sting.

There are very few nerves running through the ear lobe, so the pain is minimal, unless one of the piercings becomes infected. The girls all agreed that taking care of newly pierced ears was not fun and required a lot of discipline to avoid the dreaded infection.

The intricate ways in which the ear channels sound to the brain were beyond our scope for Camp Mimi. However, everyone could attest to having ear aches at times and recalled how painful they were. There are so many pathways, tubes, canals and nerves within the ear that the smallest infection can be potentially dangerous to our hearing, so care must be taken. Ear infections usually require a trip to the doctor.

It was definitely time to allow our brains to rest with a good night's sleep. I was always more than ready for bedtime.

DAY 6 – DIGESTION

Most children in elementary and middle school (our campers this year) delight in making various bodily noises, most of them having to do with the digestive system. Therefore, this day's subject was perfect for them.

Although they each received a subject page showing a detailed diagram of the human digestive system, our best illustration was inside Skelly. After we removed his plastic skin, plastic muscles, and plastic bones, we located a plastic digestive system, consisting of the esophagus, stomach, liver, gall bladder, pancreas, large and small intestines, and the appendix. Each part was connected to its neighbor, so taking it apart for examination and then reassembling it was like working on a complicated puzzle. But we tried!

While the children colored pictures of the intricate workings of the digestive system, I led them on a travelogue of the breakfast they ate that morning.

Before they took the first bite of scrambled eggs, bacon and biscuits with strawberry jam, milk and orange juice, their digestive systems were already at work. When they smelled the bacon cooking, *saliva* began to form in their mouths. This is an involuntary reaction to smelling something you love to eat. And all these children love bacon!

Saliva breaks down the chemicals in food a bit, which helps make things like bacon softer and easier to swallow. While chewing the bacon, the tongue helps out, pushing the food around while the teeth grind it up. When you're ready to swallow, the tongue pushes tiny bits of mushy food toward the back of the throat and into the opening of the *esophagus*, the second part of the digestive tract.

The esophagus is like a stretchy pipe about 10 inches long. It moves food from the back of the throat to the stomach. But also at the back of the throat is the *trachea* or windpipe, which allows air to come in and out of the body. When you swallow a bit of food or liquid, a special flap called the *epiglottis* comes down over the opening of the windpipe so food will only go into the esophagus and not into the windpipe.

Everyone had a story about "food going down the wrong way." When this happens you get choked, you cough, you may throw up, or, in extreme cases, someone may be needed to assist you to get free from the obstruction. This is because the epiglottis didn't flop down in time to cover the windpipe.

Papa and I told them about a dinner party we attended one time at the home of a surgeon and his wife. About eight people were seated around the elegant table eating a delicious steak dinner when one of the guests got choked on a bite of meat.

She made a strange little choking sound, trying to cough unsuccessfully. She had a fearful look on her face and our host, the doctor, responded immediately. He asked her if she could breathe. She shook her head, "No!" He went behind her chair, placed his hands around her abdomen and gave a sudden, upward squeeze. This is called the Heimlich Maneuver. The action usually dislodges whatever is stuck and it projects the morsel up the windpipe and out of the mouth. However, this time it didn't work.

He tried it a second time, again unsuccessfully. She was beginning to panic, thrashing her arms around wildly. In one motion, he picked her up, told his wife to clear the kitchen island, carried his guest to the makeshift operating table, picked up a filet knife from the counter, told his wife to pour vodka over the knife, and poised it over the terrified guest, holding her head back to expose her neck. He was prepared to do a *tracheotomy*, surgically opening her windpipe to save her life.

As all the other guests gathered around this bizarre scene, the woman saw the filet knife coming toward her throat and desperately attempted to scream, releasing the lodged piece of steak. Emergency surgery averted! It was a most unusual dinner party, to say the least.

We babysat Sophie once when she was a baby in a high chair. She was nibbling on a baby cracker and got choked in exactly the same way the dinner guest did. Instinctively, I jerked her out of the highchair, turned her upside down, squeezed her abdomen tightly and out came the culprit, flying across the room. Her older sisters who hadn't seen her choking were terrified at my actions. But Sophie was too astonished to cry; she just wanted another cracker.

Caleb had a story about how he swallowed some milk the wrong way one time and got choked and it came out his nose. A rather disgusting image, but perfectly illustrating the way the esophagus, epiglottis and trachea are all supposed to work in conjunction as part of the digestive system.

Once the breakfast bacon is chewed, swallowed, and goes down the esophagus, it travels to the *stomach*. It doesn't just drop into the stomach but is slowly squeezed in a wavy motion by the muscles of the esophagus. This may take two to three minutes for it to reach the stomach.

We looked at Skelly's stomach to illustrate. It is a stretchy sack shaped somewhat like the letter "J". It has three important jobs. It stores the food we swallow. It breaks down solid food into a liquidy mixture, thanks to strong stomach muscles and the release of gastric juices. These juices come from the walls of the stomach and help kill bacteria as well as liquefy the solid matter. Finally, the stomach slowly empties the liquefied food into the small intestine.

"Uh oh, I can see where this is going!" Caleb declared.

"Are we going to talk about poop?" Jake asked hopefully.

Now, they were really attentive.

The *small intestine* really isn't all that small. It is a long tube about 1.5-2 inches wide and is about 22 feet long in an adult. It is packed tightly inside the body, underneath the stomach. We looked at Skelly's small intestine and they thought it looked a lot like the garden hose we have that coils up on itself when not filled with water.

While the liquefied food is inside the small intestine, it is being broken down even more. Three other organs assist in this process. The helpers are the *pancreas*, the *liver*, and the *gallbladder*. Each one sends different kinds of juices to the small intestine, allowing the body to absorb the nutrients that are contained in the food.

The juices from the pancreas help the body digest fats and protein. The liver juices are called *bile*. They help absorb fats into the bloodstream. The gallbladder is like a warehouse for the bile, storing it until the body needs it.

Food may spend up to four hours inside the small intestine, becoming a thin, watery mixture. This is time well spent because the bacon, eggs, biscuits, and milk have passed their nutrients from the intestine into the blood, bringing nourishment to the body.

The nutrient rich blood goes directly to the liver which acts as a refinery. If there are any harmful substances or wastes, the liver gets rid of them. The wastes that are not turned into more bile are pushed on into the *large intestine*.

The large intestine is much fatter, about 3-4 inches in diameter. If stretched out, it measures about 5 feet long. This is almost the last stop on the breakfast train.

The last step is to get the remainder of the waste out of the body. It is pushed through the part of the large intestine called the *colon*. Here the body has its final chance to absorb the water and any minerals into the blood. As water is removed from the waste product, what's left gets more and more solid as it keeps moving along and finally leaves the body as … ?

"Poop!" everyone shouted in unison.

We can help our digestive systems by drinking lots of water and eating a healthy diet with food rich in fiber. These include fruit, vegetables and whole grains. This makes it much easier for food to pass through our body.

They worked on some fun word search pages about the digestive system while I prepared some snacks for their own digestive systems.

Then I asked them if they ever ordered liver and onions in a restaurant. There was a chorus of "Yucks!" around the table. We located Skelly's *liver* and noted that it was nestled under the ribcage. It is the largest solid organ in the body. The liver of an adult is about the size of a football.

We already learned that the liver makes an important digestive juice called bile. However, the liver is also vital to clean the blood of toxins. Some toxins are naturally produced when protein is broken down. Other toxins come from food and drink that is harmful to the body.

The liver also helps the body use carbohydrates which are found in lots of foods such as bread, fruit, and milk.

"Bread and milk are my favorites," declared Caleb. (As if we didn't know!).

"Then, Caleb, your liver works hard to break down those carbs into a type of sugar called *glucose*. This is the main source of fuel for our cells. The glucose stored in the liver is called *glycogen*."

We all practiced saying this new word. I gave them a quick oral quiz on the other new digestive words we learned that morning. With everyone helping, they were able to answer them all.

I took them to the kitchen to show them a raw chicken liver. For most of them, this was the most disgusting thing we had ever done at Camp Mimi. I thought Sophie was going to faint.

The rest of them touched it but Sophie actually had to leave the room. We all discovered that Sophie would never be able to work in a butcher shop. She has an aversion to raw meat, although she is definitely a medium-rare steak lover.

One of their favorite bodily noises to make is burping. They were great about saying, "Excuse me," with an involuntary burp, but most of them seemed adept at the voluntary kind.

"We're going to *talk* about burping, not do it!" I cautioned. A few escaped anyway.

Sometimes called a belch, it is nothing but gas. When we eat or drink we swallow air as well. The air we breathe contains gasses, such as nitrogen.

When these gasses are swallowed, they need to get out. That's what burping does. Extra gasses in the stomach are forced back up through the esophagus and out of the mouth. When you drink carbonated drinks with lots of extra gas, you burp more. Carbon dioxide gas is what makes the drinks fizzy.

Sometimes eating or drinking too fast causes burping because it brings extra air into the stomach. Drinking through a straw can do this as well.

It's funny that when little babies burp, everyone cheers.

"What a good burp!"
But when you get older, everyone complains.
"What do you say?"

"Alright, we have to talk about it because it's part of the same process: gas from the other end."
"Farts!" they all exclaimed.
"Do not demonstrate!" I commanded.
Also called flatulence, this occurs because of small amounts of gasses that travel through the digestive system with the food we eat. Certain foods like beans, onions, and fried foods release more gas than others when they break down in the body. When these gasses, such as tiny amounts of hydrogen, carbon dioxide, and methane, combine with hydrogen sulfide in the large intestine, it has a bad smell.

If you have a lot of gas while eating ice cream, yogurt or milk, your body may be having a hard time digesting the natural sugar, called *lactose*, found in dairy products. If this happens, children should tell their parents.

We hadn't yet mentioned how we get rid of the liquid wastes from our body through the urinary system. We looked at Skelly again to find the organs that comprise this system. We found the *kidneys* where urine is formed, the *ureter*, or tubes that carry urine to the bladder, the *bladder* where urine is stored, and the *urethra*, the opening from which urine is passed out of the body.

We even had a word search puzzle about urination. During this discussion, there were several bathroom breaks due to the power of suggestion.

We learned that we have two kidneys and that we have to have one to survive. Conlee and I know several people who have received kidney transplants from a living family member. This has saved them from endless infections and being on severe maintenance medications, including *dialysis*, an artificial way to provide the function of removing waste and excess water from the kidneys.

We showed them kidney beans, showing the approximate shape of our own kidneys. In the adult body, each kidney is about 5 inches long and 3 inches wide. It looks somewhat like our computer mouse.

To locate them on your body, put your hands on your hips and slide your hands up until you can feel your ribs. Then, put your thumbs on your back and you will know this is about where your kidneys are located.

Healthy kidneys filter the blood as often as 400 times a day! They also balance the volume of fluids and minerals in the body.

We feel thirsty when our brain tells us to get more water into our body. If we don't get fluid, the brain tells the kidneys to hold on to some fluids.

When we get enough, the brain tells the kidneys to let go in the form of urine.

Sometimes urine is darker than normal. This is because there is more waste being filtered out of the blood than water. If you exercise or sweat a lot, the urine has less water and appears darker. If you drink lots of fluids, the extra fluid comes out in the urine and it appears lighter and clearer.

We were friends with a woman who had a very serious kidney disease. She had received transplants and still her new kidneys were failing. She attended a class I was teaching about all the many Jewish prayers that are included in the Jewish prayer book. I mentioned that there was even one thanking God for being able to eliminate toxins from the body by going to the bathroom. Everyone in the group laughed, but our friend gave a poignant personal testimony.

She told us that it is so easy to take such a bodily function for granted until it ceases. She said that she thanked God every time she was able to eliminate in the *fearful and wonderful* way God made our body to perform. It put being able to pee in a totally different perspective.

We were going to celebrate *Shabbat* that night so we didn't have a field trip that afternoon. We had already been to several of our favorite places that week, the Naval Air Museum, Bellingrath Gardens, and the animal preserve. These stops had become requisite.

Instead, we spent the afternoon in the pool or on the slippy slide. It was a hot day and playing in the water was refreshing. In between games outside the girls helped me make *Challah* and then returned to play while the dough rose. They loved having some ownership in the traditional *Shabbat* bread.

After a delightful meal and all the traditions associated with the celebration, we all helped to clean up the kitchen and had one last experiment. Yes, they guessed it: we were going to make poop!

I gave the children the list of ingredients they needed and they lined them up on the kitchen counter.

Two pieces of bread (leftover *Challah*), a can of spaghetti in sauce, a clear mixing bowl, a potato masher, artificial saliva (water and detergent), a blender, artificial stomach juices (vinegar), artificial bile (3 drops food coloring), an old nylon stocking, and a white plate. When everything was gathered, they followed my instructions.

- To simulate putting the food into the mouth, put the canned spaghetti and sauce into the bowl. Add saliva. Use the masher like teeth.
- To simulate the food going into the stomach, pour the mashed food into the blender and add the vinegar. Blend.
- To simulate getting the food ready to go into the small intestine,

add food coloring and stir with a spoon.
- To simulate the food going through the intestines, hold the stocking and pour the "stuff" in, squeeze, letting the liquids run through the sides.
- Finally, to simulate having the waste come out of the body, cut a small hole in the end of the stocking and squeeze solid bits through the bottom onto the plate.

As you can imagine, everyone took a turn squeezing and there were many varied comments flavored with lots of "Oooooos!" and "Disgusting!" and "Gross!" They all declared they would never eat canned spaghetti again, which is a great vow as far as I am concerned.

It was our most successful and memorable experiment and is still a topic of discussion years later.

DAY 7 – SKIN

Yes, you may have noticed that Camp Mimi lasted for seven full days this year, unlike our normal schedule of five. This had to do with parents' plans and their schedules to pick up the children. Conlee and I had learned from experience that it was much easier to keep on with the Camp Mimi schedule, including two extra days, than to "free-fall" without the structure and discipline. And so we kept moving.

The longer our little community stayed intact, the stronger we became. We developed an ease with which we related to one another; competitions ceased; laughter came easier; hurt feelings were soothed quicker. We saw the children help one another more readily and heard lots of encouragement for each other without any critical, biting accusations.

Of course, there was the occasional whining and pouting over not getting one's way, but the Camp Mimi rule of being lovingly sent to bed for a period of time always solved the problem and soothed the hurt feelings because no one wanted to miss out on the fun for very long.

To finish strong on how fearfully and wonderfully we are made, I asked them this question, "What is the body's biggest organ?" There were lots of guesses: the liver, the heart, the brain, etc. But no one guessed the right answer: *skin*!

We don't usually think of skin as an organ but indeed it is a very important one, covering and protecting everything inside the body.

Without skin, people's muscles, bones and organs would be hanging out all over the place. We only had to look at Skelly with his plastic skin removed to get the idea. It's not a very pretty image.

I gave the children several different coloring sheets of outlines of the human body. They could give them whatever skin colors and details they chose while I related some facts about the skin.

Besides covering other organs, the skin helps keep the body at the proper temperature and also allows us to have the sense of touch.

We looked at some intricate diagrams of the different layers of skin, beginning with the outermost layer called the *epidermis*. This is the part we can see. At the bottom of this layer, new cells are forming all the time, slowly moving to the surface. This trip takes about 2-4 weeks. As newer cells move up, the older cells near the surface die and rise to the top. Most of what we see on our skin is actually dead skin cells. They are tough and strong enough to protect the body. Eventually they flake off so that newer cells can come to the surface, continuing the never-ending process.

Every minute we lose 30,000-40,000 dead skin cells from the surface of the skin. That's almost 9 pounds of cells every year!

A small part of the epidermis contains a substance called *melanin*. This is what gives skin its color. The darker your skin, the more melanin you have. When you go out into the sun, the epidermis cells make extra melanin to protect the skin from getting burned by the sun's ultraviolet rays. If you spend a lot of time in the sun you will be very tan.

Melanin doesn't protect the skin from all the damage, however. We need to wear sunscreen and protective clothing. Doing this when you are young will help protect your skin from getting skin cancer when you get older.

The next layer under the epidermis is called the *dermis*. This is the section that contains nerve endings, blood vessels, oil glands, and sweat glands. It also contains *collagen* and *elastin*, which are tough and stretchy.

The *nerve endings* give us our sense of touch. They send messages to the brain to let us know if we are touching a soft kitten's fur or rough sandpaper, even if our eyes are closed. This is for our protection as much as for our enjoyment. If we touch something hot, the nerve endings in the dermis respond immediately, warning us to take our hand away quickly. It all happens so fast we don't have time to think about it.

The dermis is also full of tiny blood vessels. They continually bring oxygen and nutrients to the cells and take away the waste.

The *oil glands* are located in this section as well, keeping the skin lubricated and protected, and making the skin waterproof. Without these oils, the skin would become soggy, absorbing too much water. The lips of humans are covered with very thin skin. This is why you can see the blood vessels which are very close to the surface. They give our lips their red or dark pink appearance.

The third and bottom layer of the skin is called the *subcutaneous* layer. This is mostly composed of fat and it helps the body stay warm and absorb shocks. If you bang into something or have a hard fall, the subcutaneous layer keeps the skin bound to all the tissues underneath it.

This layer is also where hair begins to grow. Each hair on the body begins out of a tiny tube in the skin called a *follicle*. Its roots are bound in this bottom layer of skin and as they grow, the hairs come up through the dermis and epidermis. Every part of adult human skin has hair follicles except for the lips, the palms of the hands and the soles of the feet. There are more hair follicles on some parts than others, and on some people more than others. We all had to examine our exposed body parts to compare how much hair we had in relation to everyone else.

The normal body temperature is 98.6 degrees Fahrenheit (37 degrees Celsius). This is the proper temperature to keep the cells healthy. If you run a lot on a hot day, you need to release some of the body's heat. The *hypothalamus* in the brain signals the blood vessels in the dermis to release some of the body's stored up heat. This is why you might get a red face.

Sweat glands swing into action as well to cool the body. As the sweat evaporates (changes from liquid to vapor), you cool down.

If you stay outside in the winter for so long that your body loses heat, you might get tiny bumps on the skin's surface. This is evidence that the blood vessels are narrowing as much as possible to keep the warm blood away from the surface of the skin. Kids call these *goosebumps*, but the medical name is the *pilomotor reflex*. The reflex makes tiny muscles pull on the skin hairs so that they stand up very straight.

Skin needs to be kept clean and healthy. That's why we use soap and water, cover cuts and scrapes, and use sunscreen.

We had some fun word search puzzles, finding the new words we had just learned and trying to remember where they are.

We finished our study by looking at our finger prints. I gave each of them a sheet with all our names and a blank square under each name. Papa helped us carefully press our index fingers onto a black stamp pad and then gently press and roll the finger into the square with our name on it.

We also stamped our finger prints on each other's pages so we could compare the varieties. Finger prints are left on surfaces we touch because of the oil glands that leave impressions through the ridges of the skin of the fingers.

Finger print analysis has led to many crimes being solved because no two finger prints are alike, and they cannot be altered throughout one's life.

I told them that my finger prints are on file with the police in The Netherlands.

"Mimi! *What did you do?*"

They insisted I tell the story.

A few years before, Conlee and I led a "Journey" conference at a Christian conference center in the heart of The Netherlands. We had been there many times and knew it well. Conlee had to leave for the States before the conference ended due to some prior commitments, so I was finishing the last three days by myself.

We had a two room apartment on the ground floor of the dormitory at the conference center. The apartment had a small locked anteroom that you entered from the hallway. From that enclosure, a door opened into a little sitting room with a bedroom and bath.

Conlee left for the airport early one morning and I taught two sessions. At noon, I finished my lunch before the rest of the group in the dining room and left early to return to my room to look over some notes before the afternoon sessions. The whole dormitory appeared to be empty during the lunch hour.

When I unlocked the anteroom to our apartment, I heard a loud noise and the sound of breaking glass. I barely opened the door into the sitting room when I spied a man crawling out the window. A quick glance showed me that the room was in shambles. Glass was all over the floor. Drawers were emptied and chairs were overturned. I left immediately, ran back to the dining room, and reported the incident to the conference organizer.

He alerted the conference center staff and they called the police. While we waited, we cautiously entered the apartment, accompanied by the staff.

It was such a mess inside that I wanted to sort it out to see if anything had been stolen, but they insisted we not touch anything until the police arrived.

That was wise because the police wanted to dust everything for fingerprints. Of course, they had to take mine so that I could be eliminated from the suspects. It did little good, however, because the police concluded the investigation with this "sage" word of advice, "Unfortunately, these things just happen."

The conference center staff seemed very worried that I would blame them, so they graciously moved all my sorted-out belongings to a third floor room, and compensated me with a basket of fruit and some terry cloth slippers monogrammed with the name of the center. I didn't need any reminders of the incident so I left the slippers in the room when I left.

Interestingly, the next year we were leading another conference in the same place. We were in a newly renovated building that year since the center was under new management. Unbelievably, again, on the first day, someone broke into our room using an electronic key card and stole nearly everything we had that was of value. The police investigated again, remembered the other burglary, and issued the same statement, "This just happens."

That was the last time we held a conference in that place.

Everyone had a fun afternoon swimming while I prepared our celebration steak dinner and the presentations of certificates and awards.

Each child got to choose a different large book about the physiology of the human body. These were reference books I bought months before and used for much of the information I shared with them. Most of them were large illustrated books so they would be good reminders of all our lessons.

During and after dinner we all shared lots of memories of past awards' dinners and fun stories of the activities of years before.

With our dessert, we were entertained by one of their favorite things to do: we watched home videos of past years of Camp Mimi.

It is always fun to see how much they have grown each year. Surprisingly, many of the same activities they have been doing for years are still their favorites today.

CAMP MIMI EIGHT

CAMP MIMI CULINARY SCHOOL

    This year, Conlee and I had five campers, ages six to twelve. They were old enough to tackle more complicated "hands-on" activities and to venture out a bit more than our normal field trip destinations such as Bellingrath Gardens, the Naval Air Museum, and the Animal Preserve. We knew we would enjoy these outings, too, but the BodishBabes were in for some surprises.

    The children arrived on a Friday and were scheduled to be with us until the following Saturday, when we would drive to Destin, Florida, to meet up with their parents and all have a week's holiday at a large rented beach house. Destin was only two hours away from our Mobile, Alabama, home and we were going to make the beach trip a part of our Camp Mimi plans.

    We were able to have our first Camp Mimi meal a *Shabbat* celebration. As soon as their parents left, the children were excited to head to the kitchen to make *Challah* and to prepare the *Shabbat* table in the dining room, since this is always one of their favorites. They knew where everything was: the candles, the pitcher and bowl for washing hands, the special towel, the booklets, and the wine glasses. Everyone helped to make it beautiful and meaningful.

They were a bit disappointed that we wouldn't have The Big Reveal for the theme until the next morning, but they got so involved in all the preparations that they managed to contain their curiosities. There was an abundance of enthusiasm, joy and excitement as we gathered around the table once again to celebrate God's presence and our family.

The next morning, everyone was up early, dressed, and ready for another big adventure. After breakfast we gathered around the Camp Mimi table, ready to resume our now firmly established routine. We sang The Camp Mimi Song, recited The Camp Mimi Rules, and brought out The Camp Mimi Candle which was labeled, "Camp Mimi Culinary School."

The chorus of voices immediately questioned, "What's *culinary*?" Caleb and Sophie, both twelve, guessed right away.

"It's cooking school!"

"Do we get to cook?"

The best part for them, of course, was the presentation of the appropriate costumes. On an equal par with past costumes of sea horse and mermaid tails, hero capes, and medical scrubs, they were more than delighted with their very own white chef's coats with blue monograms on each pocket that read, "Camp Mimi Culinary School." Fortunately, each one fit perfectly and Papa and I had our own as well. We looked very official and "chefy" sitting around the table.

I told the children that we were going to study at least two different topics every day. We would look at the importance of food in the Bible and we would learn some techniques about classic cuisine and food preparation.

In addition, we were going to "open our own restaurant" and learn what it takes to do so. The official "opening" would be when all the family gathered at the beach house. Their parents and older siblings would be our first (and only) guests.

They were ready to roll!

DAY 1 – FOOD IN THE BIBLE AND ITALIAN CUCINA

Before we began our lesson, I showed the children the detailed Camp Mimi Menu Planner that I used every year to designate the daily teams and what foods would be served for each meal. I showed them some planners from the last few years to give them an idea of how much preparation had gone into each week's meals.

Edie voiced their collective astonishment, "You didn't just think this stuff up at the last minute?"

Caleb looked at the past years' menus, remembering which foods he liked and which "were not his favorite." We always insisted that they never say, "I hate this." Instead, they learned to say, "That's not my favorite."

Sophie made certain her favorite Chicken *Spiedini* was served every year. She had a great deal of pride of ownership in this dish.

Anna asked if they could make biscuits every morning. That girl surely can put away homemade biscuits – or any other kind, for that matter. Preferably with lots of butter and strawberry jam.

Jake was already raising his hand high in the air, asking if he could crack the eggs, his favorite culinary activity.

While their comments were being voiced all at once, I realized that they had no idea what it took to plan meals, make shopping lists, buy groceries, bring them home, prepare recipes, and store food safely. Children tend to think it just happens magically and then they eat it. We would be learning a lot this year! I hoped their moms and dads would appreciate it.

The evening meals for each day were already planned and I had the details written in the boxes.

Saturday:	*Pasta Bolognese, Chopped Salad, French Bread, Chocolate Mousse*
Sunday:	*Field Trip*
Monday:	*Roasted Chicken, Vegetables, Salad, Eve's Apple Crumble*
Tuesday:	*Grilled Pizza, Manna Cookies*
Wednesday:	*Red Lentil Stew, Chicken Spiedini, Green Beans, Lemon Ice Box Pie*
Thursday:	*Seder Plate, Chicken and Rice Casserole, Broccoli, Challah, Chocolate Cake*
Friday:	*Steak, Challah, Twice-Baked Potatoes, Salad, Ice Cream Sundaes*

Together, we would all plan our breakfasts and lunches and they would help me shop for the ingredients and participate in meal preparation.

Excitedly, they filled in the blank areas with foods they all decided they wanted to eat such as French Toast, BEB (bacon, eggs, biscuits), cereals, waffles, pancakes, fried biscuits, cinnamon rolls, Sophie's Chicken *Spiedini*, sandwiches, and their all-time favorite, sautéed Crab Claws. It was a good start.

We moved on to the Bible lesson! They had their own Bibles with them so we started with a "fill-in-the-blanks" page which required them to look up verses to find the answers. I learned quickly to appoint a different person to read each answer since the competitive spirit took over and each child wanted to be the first one to find the verse, leaving the younger ones frustrated. Now that we had established some camaraderie around the table, we proceeded.

- *What is the first mention of food in the Bible? Look at Genesis 2:9.*

We talked about some of the good food that grows on trees. Besides the obvious fruits such as apples, pears, oranges, lemons, limes and grapefruit, we included pomegranates, kumquats, avocados, olives, peaches, coconuts, cherries, figs, and nuts.

- *There are many examples of families bonding and celebrating with a meal.*
On the page there were pictures of families gathered around *Shabbat* and Thanksgiving tables. We looked up the references and wrote descriptions of the following examples: *Job 1:4-5, 2 Kings 4:8-10, Genesis 18:1-8, John 12:1-3, Revelation 19:6-9.*

- *There also are examples of refusing to eat with someone because they are considered to be the enemy.*
We looked at *Genesis 43:31-34, 1 Samuel 20:34, Luke 15:25-28.*

- *God shows how He can heal problems with enemies so completely that they can even eat together in peace.*
We looked at *Psalm 23:5.* "You prepare a table before me in the presence of my enemies." We tried to picture God preparing a beautiful table filled with our favorite foods and then inviting us, along with our worst enemy, to sit together to eat. How would we respond to such an invitation?

- *Sometimes miracles happen as people begin to share a meal together.* There was a picture of a dog and cat sharing a meal from the same bowl. We looked at *Luke 24:28-35, Matthew 14:13-21,* and *Matthew 26:26-29.*

To further illustrate Psalm 23 and the idea of miracles at mealtime, Papa told them the true story of a very special Christmas Eve during the midst of World War I. In 1914, the Germans and the British were engaged in a fierce battle in France in an area called the Western Front. The fighting to take land and overcome the enemy was horrendous and the frozen, snowy ground was littered with dead bodies from both sides.

The opposing troops took a brief respite in their miserable trenches as night approached, both sides aware that it was Christmas Eve. Although the respective watchmen from both sides remained in place, the soldiers independently decided to wait until dawn to continue the bombardments on one another.

Many preserved letters from the battlefield testify to the miracle that occurred near midnight. During the temporary ceasefire, the Germans began to sing one of their Christmas carols, very softly. Then the British sang, "O Come All Ye Faithful." The Germans, recognizing the tune, joined with them in singing, "*Adeste Fideles.*"

Two opposing nations sang the same carol in different languages at midnight, under a full moon, on Christmas Eve, in the middle of a battlefield!

The Germans slowly raised lanterns out of their trenches and began to shout Christmas greetings to the British. *Frohe Weihnachten!*

Cautiously, the British troops poked their heads out to see if it was a trick. One or two soldiers from each side bravely left their trenches and approached their enemies. Soon the trenches were empty as German and British soldiers exchanged greetings and small gifts with one another.

They shook hands, showed pictures of wives, girlfriends, parents and children to their enemies, and then even shared food and drink.

Letters written home from the battlefield confirm that their gifts to one another consisted of chocolates, cigarettes, cigars, barrels of beer, bottles of brandy, personal belongings such as pocket knives and handkerchiefs, and warm Christmas greetings.

They allowed one another to gather their dead comrades from each side and assisted each other in digging graves. For a brief time, a few of them kicked around a make-shift ball and played a spontaneous, unorganized, moonlight game of *futball*.

The story of the Christmas miracle and the spontaneous battlefield meal that was shared by enemies has been told around the world. It is a testament to the power of God's love to melt the hardest hearts when Jesus is remembered and honored.

Although the miracle of "peace on earth, good will towards men" was temporary, lasting only a few hours, it did happen! It is possible!

The Christmas Eve truce did not occur along all of the Western Front, but for a small group of war-weary soldiers who responded with hearts ablaze with the memory of the birth of Christ, it was life-changing.

The impression of their experience inspired a poem written about the event, published around 1918.[107] Papa read it to us.

In Flanders on the Christmas morn
The trenched foemen lay,
The German and the Briton born,
And it was Christmas Day.

The red sun rose on fields accursed,
The gray fog fled away;
But neither cared to fire the first,
For it was Christmas Day!

---

[107] A Carol from Flanders, Frederick Niven, (1878-1944), Public Domain

They called from each to each across
The hideous disarray,
For terrible has been their loss:
"Oh, this is Christmas Day!"

Their rifles all they set aside,
One impulse to obey;
'Twas just the men on either side,
Just men – and Christmas Day.

They dug the graves for all their dead
And over them did pray:
And Englishmen and Germans said,
"How strange a Christmas Day!"

Between the trenches then they met,
Shook hands, and e'en did play
At games on which their hearts were set
On happy Christmas Day.

Not all the emperors and kings,
Financiers and they
Who rule us could prevent these things –
For it was Christmas Day.

O ye who read this truthful rhyme
From Flanders, kneel and say,
"God speed the time when every day
Shall be as Christmas Day."

Caleb, always fascinated with history, asked, "Is this really true?" The reality of such a miracle is validated for us by letters written from the battlefield, souvenirs obtained that magical night and preserved as family keepsakes, and a few photographs taken under the bright moon.

- *Can you think of any people you know who would not want to sit at the same table together to share a meal?*

Initially the children only thought of interactions between students in their school cafeterias. This is normal because their worlds were still very contained, and they had relevant illustrations. However, we tried to broaden their scope a bit, suggesting ethnic groups, warring nations, and people of different religions.

- *How do you think Jesus would use you to heal any of these divisions?*

At their ages, the children had no idea how they would be peacemakers on a global level. We assured them that whatever efforts they put into sharing something as personal as a meal with someone now would set godly character traits into them for reaching beyond their present borders someday.

And so, they came up with certain people they could make an effort to sit with during lunch at school instead of automatically sitting with their closest friends. They also thought of people they wanted to invite to their homes but had not done so because of the influence of other friends. These were all honest and vulnerable solutions and we prayed that God would strengthen the desires in their hearts so that they could carry out their missions.

"Why are meals so important in our relationships?" I asked. "Why not bond over sports or going to movies together?"

They had no idea but were willing to learn.

For centuries, families, tribes, and cultures have bonded around the table. Conversely, people who are unfriendly to each other do not want to eat together. There are several examples of this in the Scriptures. We looked at some of them. It helped that the children were getting familiar with a few examples by working on their fill-in-the-blanks pages.

Job 1:4-5 shows us the ancient celebration of reunion by sharing a meal at a banquet.

2 Kings 4:8 tells us that sharing a meal with a traveler or stranger was an ancient custom and was expected.

The virtue of hospitality is reinforced in Genesis 18:2, when Abraham and Sarah prepared a meal for strangers who were actually angels.

Jesus told parables that emphasized the tradition of some of these customs. One story told of a persistent neighbor who awakened his whole village at midnight, insisting to borrow bread to feed a traveling guest.[108]

In the parable of the prodigal son,[109] Jesus related how the father wanted to bring harmony to his family by having a celebratory meal. Perhaps this is a preview of the Great Wedding Feast for believers that will take place at the end of time.[110]

Jesus shared meals with His friends Mary, Martha, and Lazarus whenever He was in their village of Bethany.[111] Around the table they formed trust, community and a sense of family.

---

[108] Luke 11:5-8

[109] Luke 15:11-32

[110] Revelation 19

[111] John 12:1-3

The Passover Meal (Last Supper) demonstrated God's love on many levels. Jesus broke bread with an enemy (Judas) and also reinterpreted the ancient symbols of the meal to prophesy His coming kingdom.

After His crucifixion, Jesus shared a meal with fellow travelers in Emmaus, breaking bread and revealing His true identity, alive and risen from the dead.[112]

We also see in Scripture that one's refusal to eat with someone is a sign of enmity. The refusal demonstrates a lack of trust, community and sense of family. In Genesis 43:22 the Egyptians would not eat at the same table with the Hebrews. This was an ethnic discrimination.

By contrast, Jesus, a Jew, ignored the long-standing Jewish discrimination against Samaritans when He accepted a drink of water from a Samaritan woman.[113] Over something as simple as sharing a cup of water from a well, Jesus and the sinful woman bonded in a healing, life-changing miracle of her soul.

I once sat on the rock ledge of that very same ancient well. I pulled up a rope from its depths, until I was holding a crude pottery cup filled with cool water. Part of my common sense told me that the water could be polluted, the cup full of germs, and the experience should be theoretical, not experiential. However, knowing I would regret missing this once-in-a-lifetime opportunity, I took a sip of the water.

It tasted rusty and pretty bad. But in the act of sipping, I was transported to the first century, hearing Jesus say, "If you drink the water I give you, you will never thirst again."[114]

His "living water" provides a never-ending meal that fills us beyond imagination, quenching our thirsts for the things of the world!

There is also the Biblical example of Jonathan leaving the table of his father, King Saul, because of anger.[115] It is impossible to sit at table with people to share a meal when anger towards someone around the table is your primary emotion.

The older son in the parable of the prodigal son refused to sit at table with his younger brother whom he resented. He chose not to attend the lavish party his father hosted for their family.[116]

All of these stories paint vivid pictures of the ancient, and still present, tradition of sharing meals and the deeper aspects of hospitality. I was moved by the children's rapt attention and innocent acceptance of being at

---

[112] Luke 24:13-35

[113] John 4:9

[114] John 4:14

[115] 1 Samuel 20:34

[116] Luke 15:28-30

table as a loving, bonding time with family and guests. They were accustomed to everyone holding hands and praying in thanksgiving after being seated. That was the only way they had experienced sharing meals.

Although I didn't tell my story to the children at the time, I was painfully reminded of the fact that when I was their age, my experiences with family meals were far different.

Growing up in a dysfunctional family, mealtimes were painful, not loving or comforting. Motivated by tradition at holidays such as Christmas or Thanksgiving, our extended family usually gathered at my grandparents' home for a big meal. Yet, because of the distrust among many of the adults, their lack of genuine communication during the rest of the year, and their dishonesty with one another, what should have been celebrations turned into disasters.

Every year there were arguments, tears, someone leaving the table in anger, and frequently, explosions of bottled up frustrations. Lavish meals which took hours to prepare were often left untouched, to be taken home to separate households. Instead of looking forward to such holidays, I dreaded them.

How I had yearned all my life for a family who knew how to really celebrate and love one another unconditionally! To see the fruit of those desires around our Camp Mimi table filled me with inexpressible joy!

I realized that Conlee and I had established priorities in our family when our children were very young. Our family always shared a meal together at least once a day, prayed together, talked about our activities, and provided a venue for honest concerns. There were few subjects that were off-limits for discussion, as long as it was done appropriately. We celebrated special occasions and events, no matter how small, and acknowledged victories and accomplishments. We never allowed name-calling or accusations, and we laughed a lot.

Our deliberate intentions imprinted traditions on our children who considered it only normal to incorporate them into their own families. We were now seeing the third generation bearing the same fruit. I was overwhelmed to realize that when Jesus establishes His values in our hearts, we are empowered to change the next generations just by focusing on the simplest goals and making them a priority.

All of this talk about meals and food soon had everyone thinking about Snack Time. While they enjoyed their choices of cookies and juices, I assembled some items in the kitchen for our first hands-on culinary adventure. We were going to learn two French terms, *mise en place* and *mirepoix*, and practice some techniques.

When they finished their snacks, I called them into the kitchen to wash their hands for their first culinary assignment, which was to prepare our evening meal. Since none of them remembered what was on the menu for that night, they raced back to the Camp Mimi table to look at The Meal Planner. Jake was the fastest and he ran back into the kitchen waving the paper and trying to pronounce the name of our *entrée*. He got "pasta" right, but stumbled over "*Bolognese.*"

"Americans say, *bo-lo-nays*. But let's pronounce it the Italian way: *bo-lo-nyaaa-zay.*"

After a few choruses of singing the new word, Edie asked, "What is it?"

"*Bolognese* means 'according to the style of making it in Bologna, Italy.' In Italian, our recipe is called *Ragu alla Bolognese*. It means 'sauce in the Bolognese style.'"

It is a mild red sauce, without as many herbs as are in the more southern Italian or Sicilian sauces. It contains no rosemary, basil or oregano, which we consider typical Italian herbs.

The earliest written recipe for Bolognese sauce comes from the late 18th century. Traditionally, it is tomato-based with meat and is delicious served over any pasta. We were going to serve it over home-made *pappardelle*, a wider pasta that can absorb more sauce.

We all gathered around the kitchen island, looking at The Menu Planner. They saw that each evening meal was divided into three categories: *entrée*, vegetables and dessert. Assorted breads were included as well, since they all loved this addition.

I told them that only we Americans refer to the main course as the *entrée*. This is the category listed on most American restaurant menus showing the most substantial items served. However, in all other parts of the world, the *entrée* is considered the first course, or what we call the appetizer. In some countries, like Great Britain, it is called the starter.

The French word *entrée* means "entrance" and the term has been adopted into cuisines around the world. It indicates the course that serves as an entrance to the main part of the meal. It is at least half the size of the main course.

Some American restaurants offer a smaller version of a main course as an appetizer. Often, if I'm not very hungry, I'll order an appetizer for my meal instead of a regular-sized portion. I suggested that if they ever tried to order from a kids' menu but didn't want the usual fare of chicken tenders or macaroni and cheese, to look at the appetizer category on the regular menu.

"But why are American menus different from everybody else?" Anna wanted to know.

The best answer I had was that in America in the nineteenth century, many long-standing culinary traditions changed. Meals were simplified in most households and the whole meal was either presented on one's plate, or served family style on the table. The number of courses for a traditional meal was greatly reduced.

"Could we have an appetizer tonight?" Caleb begged.

"Yes!" they all chorused.

"Crab claws!" "Crab claws!" "Crab claws!" The chant took on an intensity.

"Pleeeeez!"

Around the table they all folded their hands in petition. This was beginning to look as if their demands were not met, we might have a small rebellion on our hands.

On the spot I had to change our afternoon's agenda, since I had not purchased crab claws. An impromptu field trip was in the making.

We had gotten very side-tracked and hadn't prepared anything yet, so to start again, I sent everyone back for another hand-washing. They had been touching many things, including the dog, since the last trip to the sink.

At last, I brought out a baking tray filled with the ingredients for our *Bolognese* sauce, which we would make first because it required the longest time to cook. On the tray were carrots, onion, celery, garlic cloves, sage leaves, bay leaf, bacon, canned tomatoes, white wine, an almost-thawed chuck roast, and milk. The recipe we used was a combination of two of the most popular ones by well-respected chefs and cookbook authors, Marcella Hazan and Alice Waters.

Our cooking school was going to dissect some of the more tedious recipes so that each child would understand the process and have all the ingredients ready to use.

Before I handed each of them a printed recipe, I explained that what they saw on the tray was the beginning of a *mise en place*. It is a French term which literally means "put in place." For us, it meant getting everything ready and prepped before we actually began to cook. This takes time but makes certain we will have a properly prepared dish. There were a few things we had to do before our *mise en place* was complete.

Papa brought the large KitchenAid mixer to the island and put on the meat grinder attachment. We were going to grind our own meat for this sauce with the recommended 80/20 ratio of meat to fat.

While he set it up, I handed out the recipes, one for each child. They were printed on sturdy card stock and encased in plastic sleeves. Every step of the process of making the sauce was broken down into individual tasks and one child was assigned to accomplish each step. It looked more like a script for a play than a recipe,[117] but it insured that no one was left out and each could anticipate what to do next. This system worked great with no

---

[117] See Appendix, "Camp Mimi Eats."

competition and a minimum of confusion.

First, the chilled meat was cut into medium sized chunks, fed through the meat grinder, and placed in a bowl. Knowing Sophie's aversion to raw meat, this was not her assigned task, for which she was grateful. Jake and Celeb gleefully fed the meat grinder, pushing the plunger inside to get every morsel to come through transformed. They finished it by grinding a few crackers to clean the blades.

Then we talked about *mirepoix* (meer-pwa), the French word for a basic mixture of finely chopped onion, celery, and carrot. This would form the flavor base for our sauce.

Every distinctive culture has its own version of *mirepoix*. In Italy, with the addition of garlic and fennel, the mixture is called *battuto*, and when cooked becomes *soffritto*. In Spain, it's *sofrito* and in Germany, *suppengrun*, which includes celeriac and leeks. In Cajun cooking, chopped celery, green pepper and onion is known as *the holy trinity*. Almost every culture in the world has a common flavor base to start traditional recipes.

The size of the *mirepoix* is determined by the recipe. For a long-cooking stew, the chunks are larger. For a sauce to go on pasta, as we were preparing, a finely diced mixture was ideal. Instead of giving the children knives to chop with, however, I purchased two small, electric food choppers at a discount store. Together, they cost less than $10. This way, they could pulse the blade to get a small dice without making *mirepoix* mush.

We wanted to retain the texture of the vegetables, but have them diced very small. For the most part, they were successful with this, although we did have to start with fresh onions a few times since they contain so much water.

Because everyone had a part in this venture, they took pride in what they put together. There was a lot of collaboration and the results made the whole house smell fabulous. We left our sauce to "lazily simmer"[118] for a few hours on the stove. This gave us time to clean up the kitchen and head outside for a casual lunch in swim suits around the pool.

While they swam, I tossed all the chefs' jackets into the washing machine. They were dotted with sauce, demonstrating the efforts put into our dinner. I wanted to get them clean to wear on our afternoon field trip after rest time.

Our first culinary field trip was to MudBugs, a local seafood store. The name implies the Louisiana bayou description of the freshwater crustaceans also known as crayfish, crawfish, crawdads, and freshwater lobsters.

MudBugs is always a busy place, especially when mudbugs are in season. People will stand in line for nearly an hour, having taken a number

---

[118] Marcella Hazan's description of the cooking process

to be called up to place their order. The afternoon we went it wasn't too busy, but there were enough people there to take interests in who we were in our brilliant white chef jackets and to start conversations. Everyone wanted to know what we were doing. When we explained our mission to get crab claws, there were as many suggestions about how to prepare them as there were customers.

Waiting for our turn, we showed the children all the different fish on ice. They were much more interested in the cleaned fillets than in the whole fish. The staring eyes got to them in a way that made them more repulsive than appealing. MudBugs is an extremely clean and neat fish store, but you can still definitely tell where you are. The children had such a reaction to the smell that they couldn't get out fast enough once we made our purchase.

A pound of crab claws is expensive and this group could eat two pounds easily. They were amazed at how much they cost. Here was a valuable lesson. When you purchase your ingredients yourself, you appreciate much more the value of what you're eating. I timed the children once the year before when I set out a pound of crab claws and they were gone in exactly 19 seconds!

I knew that when they ate the ones they selected and prepared, they would savor them much more slowly and enjoy them more.

Back home, we checked on our simmering sauce and tasted it for the correct seasonings. It was delicious!

Then we prepared the crab claws. We all prefer them sautéed rather than battered and fried, although they are good both ways. A family story everyone loves to tell about Sophie happened when she was about one year old. The whole family had gone out to eat at The Wharf House, a nearby seafood restaurant. We were seated at a table on the water-side porch.

Conlee and I took Caleb inside for a few minutes. Sophie's parents were talking to each other and not paying attention to the server who set a pound of fried crab claws on the table within reach of Sophie, seated in her high chair. The appetizer had been ordered for the whole table to enjoy.

When Conlee and I returned to the table, Sophie had eaten every one of the crab claws, without anyone noticing. Thus began a tradition.

The recipe for making sautéed crab claws is fun and totally unstructured. You just put a stick of butter into a big cast iron skillet with all the savory seasonings you like, the spicier the better. Crab claws are purchased already steamed so all you do is heat them slowly, letting them absorb lots of flavor.

Edie and Anna raided my pantry, collecting their favorite savory condiments. Sophie melted the butter. Jake and Caleb added several healthy shakes of hot sauce, Worcestershire sauce, steak sauce, soy sauce, Cajun spice, and Sriracha sauce. We also threw in sprinklings of salt and pepper.

I'm not sure what else ended up in the skillet, but when everything was sizzling, in went the two pounds of crab claws which we stirred gently. Oh, my! The aroma was amazing!

After thoroughly heating everything, we poured the crab claws out onto a big platter with all the juices and took them outside to eat around the pool. A loaf of French bread on the side to dip into the sauce made it perfect and very messy.

We had our appetizer several hours before dinner because we had one other hands-on project to complete. We were going to make pasta! Making pasta is such a fun project for kids. It's easy and comes out perfect every time. Homemade pasta[119] is in a totally different category than any dried pasta from the store. And once it's made, it cooks instantly.

We started by giving each child another scripted recipe.

Anna measured out approximately three cups of flour onto a pile in the middle of the island. It looked somewhat like a volcano.

Sophie added salt and made an indentation in the middle.

Jake cracked three eggs into the volcano, and Edie and Caleb added a few splashes of extra virgin olive oil and a couple teaspoons of water.

Then I demonstrated how to scramble the eggs with a fork, incorporating flour from the edges along the way.

Soon, we forgot the fork and everyone had a turn mixing and kneading the pasta dough with their hands. If it was too wet, we added a bit more flour. If too dry, a splash of water. Soon it was just right.

It's almost magical when the mixture forms into a smooth ball, looking and feeling like the proverbial "baby's bottom." This, of course, elicited lots of suggestions that Jake, the baby of the family, show us what it should look like. Instead, we used our imaginations.

When we had a smooth ball of dough, we covered it with a damp towel and let it take a nap for about 30 minutes or more. This gives the gluten time to develop so that it will be smooth and elastic. Otherwise it will crumble and fall apart when you try to roll it out.

Their next favorite thing about making pasta, after getting their hands in the dough, was using the hand-cranked pasta machine to roll out the dough after its nap. So, about an hour later, we all reassembled around the kitchen island to become pasta makers. Everyone had clean hands and chef's jackets and we were ready for the last steps before our dinner.

The girls divided our well-rested pasta ball into five pieces and each child flattened a portion with their hands. Jake asked to be first cranking the machine. Caleb changed the settings on the machine for him, after each rolling, going from #1(the thickest) to #8 (the thinnest).

Working with lots of flour, each portion was inserted into the opening

---

[119] See recipe in Appendix, "Camp Mimi Eats."

of the machine and Jake began to crank with all his might. He made it look much harder than it really is. Everyone else took a turn as well.

Our reward was long sheets of very thin, very perfect dough. Then we took a knife and cut the sheets into strips about one inch wide. This is the typical size for *pappardelle*. The word comes from *pappare* which means "gobble up" in Italian.

Each strip was hung over the rungs of a collapsible wooden clothes rack we set up in the kitchen, the very one we used to hang up our wet towels outside by the pool.

We let our pasta air dry on the rack for about ten minutes before cooking it, although it wasn't required. It could dry overnight or even be cooked immediately. The cooking time would vary, depending on how fresh it was.

Into a large stock pot of boiling water, Sophie carefully poured in a big handful of sea salt. I put our beautiful pasta into the boiling salted water, stirred it well, and let it cook for about three minutes.

Along with a small amount of the pasta water, I mixed the cooked, drained *pappardelle* with our *Bolognese* sauce and it was a masterpiece. We all agreed! All it needed was a sprinkling of freshly grated Parmesan cheese, which Jake volunteered to do, and some bits of fresh basil leaves, which Anna volunteered to pick from the kitchen garden.

Proudly, each one helped carry the large platter of pasta, a bowl of chopped salad, and a wooden board with hot bread to the table.

With prayers, clinking of glasses, and greetings of *Buon Appetito!* we thoroughly enjoyed our feast. Our individual efforts in the preparation made it the most special pasta dish we had ever eaten together. The dogs had no leftovers that night.

DAY 2 – CHURCH AND NAVAL AVIATION MUSEUM

The second day of Camp Mimi was on a Sunday. Our schedule was slightly different this year since the children came two days early. Going to church and out to lunch afterward would take up the whole morning, so we decided to postpone our Camp Mimi lessons for one day and spend the whole afternoon in Pensacola at the Naval Air Museum.

We did talk about how food was presented in many ways in the museum. We noticed several examples of dried and canned foods used by the military during wartime. We were amazed at the odd dehydrated food that early astronauts used while in space. We walked through models of canteens set up for military personnel on Pacific islands during World War II, commenting on the menus crudely written on chalkboards. And we saw the little mockup of a 1940's grocery store, looking at what kind of limited items were available, what ration coupons were, and how very little food cost.

There is a fun restaurant in the museum called the Cubi Bar Café where we ate an early supper. While eating, we were surrounded by a replica of the NAS Cubi Point Officers' Club in the Philippines. When the original notorious Officers' Club closed in 1992, the whole interior and all the memorabilia were reassembled as a working restaurant in the museum. It is an entertaining and educational place to eat.

The original Cubi Point O Club had quite a reputation among naval officers for many years as a traditional, rowdy place for R&R. Besides the fantastic food and drinks, some of the games that were regularly played were notorious, often involving physical injury. They included competitions in the rolling bar chairs and simulated cockpits, propelled by air pressure.

Many an officer had tales of broken bones and other injuries that occurred while on recreational leave in the Philippines.

The children had fun pretending they were in the Navy and living in the generation of their great-grandfathers, both of whom had been Naval officers. Neither of the great-grandfathers had ever been to Cubi Point, however.

We had gone non-stop all day and before we made it back home that night most of them were asleep in the back seats of the mini-van.

Tomorrow, we would resume our Camp Mimi schedule.

DAY 3 – FORBIDDEN FRUIT AND EVE'S APPLE CRUMBLE

When they settled in around the Camp Mimi table, eagerly anticipating the morning lesson, I handed them several coloring sheets illustrating the Garden of Eden and the temptation of Adam and Eve. There was an assortment of drawings of the first man and woman picking fruit, surrounded by lush vegetation. And there were pictures of the snake in the garden, and of the woman picking from the one tree God told her to avoid.

The boys immediately took the snake pictures and the girls began to color beautiful flowers and gardens.

Edie proudly reminded everyone that she was named after the Garden of Eden. Her full name is Eden Paige Bodishbaugh, named for both the Garden and her mother. This immediately took us on a detour as everyone wanted to give their full name and tell what it means. (They had done this before but didn't seem to remember). They were all familiar with the meanings of their names since it was something their parents had impressed upon them.

Caleb Benjamin Bodishbaugh, named for his father, means dog, strong and courageous, and son of my right hand.

Anna Grace Bodishbaugh means favor and full of grace.

Jacob Adrian Bodishbaugh, named for his father and great-grandfather, means overcomer.

And Sophia Conlee Bodishbaugh, named for her father and grandfather, means wisdom.

With that subject exhausted, we got back to coloring and I shared with them a very simplified version of Genesis 1-3.

God created the heavens and the earth, the stars, moon, sun, and planets. The whole universe with all its galaxies was created by God. It is too immense for us to comprehend.

In the midst of all the immensity, God created something much more intimate, an environment perfect for a human. The human being would be the crown of everything else He created. Into this special environment which was a beautiful garden, He placed a man and named him Adam, which means "red soil."

Adam was made of the dust of the earth, but he became a living soul when God breathed His own breath into him. Everything Adam needed to enjoy a perfect life was placed in the garden by God. There was delicious food growing on trees and plants, animals to keep him company, and beauty everywhere.

But God saw that Adam needed a companion who was like him, yet different, one who would complement him. So, God created a woman and her name was Eve, which means "life."

At this point, Caleb, intently coloring, interrupted, "I thought *L'Hayim* meant "life." He was referring to our toast at meal times, "To life!" I explained that the Hebrew words for Eve and life are from the same root word, *haya*, and complimented him on being very observant. We all raised imaginary glasses in a raucous toast, "*L'Hayim!*"

God gave Adam and Eve a job to do: they were to take care of the garden and the animals. God provided everything they needed to have a perfect life. It was intended to be their forever home. The only restriction God gave them was for their own protection. And that one restriction was about their meals.

He told Adam, "You may eat everything you see, *except* for the fruit on that one tree in the middle of the Garden. If you eat from that you will die. Its fruit gives knowledge of good and evil."

Adam and Eve already experienced everything that was good. But God wanted to protect them from evil which always leads to death.

We don't know how long Adam and Eve lived in harmony with one another and with God in the Garden before Eve had an encounter with a talking snake. She didn't seem surprised to hear it talk so maybe all the animals could talk at that time. But what this particular creature said was a deadly lie. He told her that God didn't really mean what He said.

The serpent told Eve that the one restriction God gave them about what she and Adam could eat was a silly thing and that it wouldn't really hurt to eat that fruit. The snake said that God only forbade them because He didn't want to share His wisdom and He didn't want them to be like Him.

The talking snake must have sounded convincing because soon Eve began to question what God had told Adam. She looked at the forbidden fruit and it looked beautiful, as beautiful as all the other fruit she was allowed to eat.

The more she looked at it, the more she wanted to find out what it tasted like. Soon, she wanted the fruit more than she wanted to obey God. She picked the fruit, tasted it and gave some to Adam who ate it, too.

Although it may have tasted good at first, it soon gave her a sick feeling. Something was wrong, terribly wrong. She felt different and so did Adam. Instead of being happy and confident and feeling loved by God, which was all they had ever known, they both began to feel afraid and uncovered by His protection. It was so frightening that they tried to hide themselves in bushes but God knew where they were.

They blamed one another for what happened, and although they loved each other dearly, they were never as close as they had once been.

God was so sad to see the results of their disobedience. He had to banish them from the beautiful Garden, so that they would not eat from the tree of Life and have to live in fear and sin forever.

Out in the unprotected world, they had to learn to live the hard way, working hard to survive, discovering how God wanted to properly cover their sin, and how they could reestablish a loving relationship with Him.

The children's responses to the story were typical for their ages.

"That's so sad!"

"Why would they do that?"

"I wouldn't listen to a snake!"

"I hate snakes!"

After they expressed their indignation about what Adam and Eve did, I asked, "Have you ever listened to someone who told you to do something that you knew was wrong? Something your parents told you not to do? Something you knew would not please God?" I waited while they pondered this.

"Well," Jake started tentatively, "sometimes my friend tells me to lie about some things and says no one will ever know."

"Isn't that what happened to Eve?" I asked.

From here the discussion became very animated. We heard stories of everything from "getting away with it but feeling guilty" to "getting caught and being punished." It turned into a half hour of true confessions.

Papa, who realized some of the stories were becoming "I can top your confession," was able to redirect the discussion by saying, "No matter what you have done in the past or even this morning, you can tell God, bring it to the light, and receive His forgiveness. Only then will you be cleansed from the effects of your sin."

He asked them to close their eyes and silently tell God what they had done that was wrong. Then he asked them to lift their hands in a gesture of surrender and receptivity to take in God's forgiveness, letting it wash over them like a cleansing shower. Finally, he led us all in a prayer of thanksgiving. It was one of the most refreshing and freeing lessons we had ever had.

After Snack Time, we talked about the different kinds of fruit that people believed to be The Forbidden Fruit. Like many, the children had heard and assumed it was an apple. This theory has been so widespread that the enlarged larynx in a man's throat is referred to as his Adam's apple, suggesting that the forbidden fruit got stuck when he tried to swallow it.

Perhaps the apple illustration is commonly used because when the Bible was translated into Latin the word "evil" was translated as *malum* which also means "apple."

The Bible doesn't tell us what the specific fruit was. That has led to lots of speculation and it has been going on forever. Many other ideas include figs, pears, pomegranates, tamarinds, mushrooms, grapes, grapefruit, and even wheat berries. Each theory has complicated explanations of why it must be correct.

However, all the speculation in the world about what kind of fruit they ate leads us astray from the fact that they disobeyed God and lost the covering of glory they were intended to wear. Ever since, mankind has been attempting to cover themselves.

We used our information about this event, which is called "The Fall" in the Bible, to work on a word search page. It became very quiet as each child seriously tackled the jumble of letters to find words such as "promise," "afraid," "serpent," "knowledge," and "shame."

After lunch, rest time, and swimming activities, we donned our clean chef's jackets for another field trip. This time we went to Fresh Market, an upscale grocery store that carries a variety of foods that you may not find in most supermarkets.

Each child was given a small notebook and a pen. Their assignment was to find the fruit section and choose a variety of apples, weighing out at least 1½ pounds total. They would be used for our dessert that night. We were going to make "Eve's Apple Crumble" and any extras would be for snacking.

I asked them to write down the different names of the apples they selected, with a description of each one. The labels in the store helped immensely and they chose about six varieties, much more than what we needed, but a good selection. When we got home we would cut into them and taste for sweetness, firmness, and tartness, recording their opinions about each variety in their notebooks.

Also, they were each instructed to find one thing in the store they had never eaten before, preferably something they never heard of. I cautioned them to be very considerate of other shoppers and not run around. Because they were wearing their chef's coats, they were aware of the attentions of others and were very well-behaved.

They gathered such things as Irish cheese, brightly colored rainbow carrots, Mexican chocolate discs, Italian *biscotti*, and apple wood-smoked, peppered bacon. Great choices!

We met at the meat counter to purchase organic chickens for our dinner. Our little group in our crisp, white jackets, soon drew a crowd observing our interactions with the butcher who was very pleased to help us.

The children were used to seeing pre-cut chicken pieces in Styrofoam trays, wrapped in plastic. The butcher explained to us the difference between purchasing just any chicken and a whole chicken that is labeled "USDA (United States Department of Agriculture) Organic."

There are so many different labels that it can be confusing. "Organic" means that the chicken ate a vegetarian diet with no genetically modified ingredients (GMOs), and no toxic pesticides or antibiotics.

"Hormone Free" is another label, although no chickens sold in American markets are allowed to contain hormones.

Then you have the option of buying "Cage Free" and "Free Range" chicken, however the amount of space the chicken had outside a cage is never specified or required to be noted.

The most misleading and non-informative label is "All Natural." It basically means that it is chicken and not some other meat.

The children's point of reference and their gold standard for all this chicken talk were our backyard chickens. Knowing what we fed them, the children were certain that our chickens could be labeled "Organic," "Cage Free," "Free Range," and "Natural" – the best of everything. However, we would never eat our own chickens because we named each one. They were our pets as well as egg producers.

We selected two organic hens suitable for roasting and watched the butcher weigh and wrap each one and tie them with string, as carefully as birthday gifts.

Their next assignment before heading home was to find a small jar of orange marmalade. It would be used in our dessert recipe that night. By now they were learning to navigate a grocery store, realizing there was an order to the arrangements of items. Then it was on to check-out where we gave everyone a bag to carry to the van.

"Whew! That was exhausting!" Jake exclaimed as we got into the car. I reminded him that someone did that for every meal he ate at home. It was something he never considered before.

We had a lot of cooking to do when we got home and they were inspired after their shopping trip.

First, we all got clean hands and started on our chicken.[120] Again, each child was given a scripted, printed recipe, insuring that each one had a significant part in the preparations.

Following the script, Jake opened the gift-wrapped chickens in the sink and washed them thoroughly. He was happy to do this and Sophie was extremely grateful because she didn't have to touch raw meat.

Anna zested two lemons and Sophie very carefully (with tongs) placed the cut lemon halves inside the chickens with generous sprinklings of salt and pepper.

Edie picked fresh thyme and rosemary from the herb garden and stuffed it in with the lemon.

Caleb tied up the chickens' legs and wings with kitchen twine. It was an interesting looking truss but it did the job.

Sophie used her salt and pepper again on the outside of the chickens.

Then Edie and Anna got messy with rubbing olive oil all over the chickens.

We put them in a large roasting pan into a preheated 375 degree oven for about an hour. We checked them with a meat thermometer, wanting it to register 160 degrees in the thickest part of the thighs.

Then, removing the pan from the oven, we covered the chickens with foil so they could rest, knowing the internal temperature would rise at least five more degrees, a safe temperature to eat chicken.

Meanwhile, Anna mixed together soft butter and the lemon zest to spread over the hot, cooked chicken before we served it.

Oh, my! The house smelled so good while the chickens roasted!

Everyone was hungry so we taste-tested our apples. The BodishBabes got the notebooks they used in the grocery store and tried to match the varieties of apples with the notes they took about their appearance. All of us were stumped on some of them.

I had an old-fashioned apple peeler that I attached to the kitchen island countertop. They took turns cranking the handle and watching long spirals of apple peel come off, along with removing the core. Sometimes the old ways are best – and a lot more fun.

We tasted and chose the firmest apples for our dessert, Eve's Apple Crumble,[121] again following a scripted recipe. Papa cut the apples into slices and the pieces that weren't eaten were placed in a saucepan by Jake, who also buttered a pie plate.

Anna, now quite adept with the microplane zester, zested one orange

---

[120] See recipe in Camp Mimi Eats, Appendix

[121] Ibid.

and then squeezed its juice through a sieve into the sliced apples.

Edie added some of the orange marmalade we purchased at the store along with a bit of cinnamon. She stirred it all together and declared it smelled like cinnamon rolls.

We cooked the apples gently on a low heat until they began to soften. It didn't take very long. As I held the hot pan, Jake carefully spooned the mixture into his buttered pie plate.

Caleb sifted flour into a mixing bowl and Anna added her orange zest. Sophie measured four tablespoons of soft butter into the flour mixture and smushed it with her fingers until it looked like fine bread crumbs. She had no trouble touching pastry, only meat.

Everyone wanted a turn mixing with their hands so Edie added oats and mixed, Anna added brown sugar and mixed, and Jake just mixed.

Caleb sprinkled the mixture evenly over the apples. Sophie dotted it all with extra butter and into the oven it went. It was set to bake during dinner for about thirty minutes until the topping was golden brown. Then we would serve it warm with vanilla ice cream for our dessert.

We all decided that the aromas wafting through the house of roasting chicken and baking apple crumble were the best in the whole world, except maybe for chocolate.

Their efforts and the enticing smells from the kitchen did not disappoint when we gathered around the table for our meal.

DAY 4 – MANNA FROM HEAVEN AND PIZZA

We started our morning's lesson with the story from Exodus 16. While their hands were busy with coloring pages of Israelites in the wilderness collecting the bread that God sent from heaven, the children listened attentively to this story of God's provision. Like all Bible stories, it has a lesson for us today.

Being delivered from Egypt through a series of miracles, the Israelites were not exempt from going through trials and hardships as they learned to live in God's freedom. For generations their ancestors had served as slaves.

After generations of slavery, a people's attitudes toward life become immature and often irrational. Slavery is a terrible thing to inflict upon a human soul. It diminishes the grandeur God intended.

This is why every account of the newly freed people following Moses' leadership into the wilderness shows them grumbling, murmuring, and complaining about first one thing and then another. Their memories of what God had just done for them seemed short and distorted. God had to put them through a "training school" to learn that He would provide everything they needed if they would put their trust in Him.

Caleb interrupted, "That's just like what He did with Adam and Eve in the Garden!"

Exactly! We were very impressed with his comparison, because it really is the same lesson, and one we all go through on a daily basis.

In our story, the thirsty Israelites have just been led to springs of water in the desert, but now they are hungry. Instead of asking God to provide food for them the same way He provided water, they complained to Moses, even to the point of wishing they had died in Egypt where they mistakenly remembered having plenty of food.

Like them, we all tend to distort truth when we are in distress. We see their memories about their past and attitudes toward their present situations terribly warped.

God told Moses how He was going to provide food for the large number of people each day and it was certainly a plan they would never have imagined. He was going to send down bread from heaven like rain.

Every morning they were to go out from their tents into the desert to collect enough bread to feed them for a day. Every sixth day they were to gather twice as much as they needed so there would be enough for *Shabbat*, their day of rest. If they hoarded any, attempting to keep the bread overnight until morning, it would spoil, smell bad, and be full of maggots.

"What's a maggot?" Jake asked.

We looked it up to be sure and found that maggots are the larvae of flies. They remembered that flies were one of the plagues in Egypt so this could not be good and was a vivid reminder of God's power.

God told the Israelites that His method of providing food for them was to see whether or not they would follow His instructions by trusting Him completely. Otherwise they would die.

Again, Caleb piped up, "Just like in the Garden!"

The bread from heaven came in the form of thin, white flakes that covered the desert ground. Every morning they would discover a new fresh layer of food to eat during the day. At first they did not know what it was.

The Hebrew word for "What is it?" is *manhu*. Thus the miracle food became known as *manna* by the people. It tasted like wafers made with honey. Evidently, it was the perfect nourishment because as long as the people trusted God and only ate His provision, they never got sick.

God also sent quail for a period of time when the people complained about not having meat. However, the diet of quail made them sick. They learned the hard way that manna was a perfect diet for them. God provided it for the forty years the people were in the wilderness.

"Do you remember that when Adam and Eve were expelled from the Garden that God told them they would have to work really hard to survive?" They all answered, "Yes."

"Why do you think they didn't have to work hard in the wilderness?"

Their answers were interesting and thoughtful.

"He delivered them."

"He was training them for their future."

"He wanted to prove His love."

"There was no way they could farm or raise cattle in the desert."

"There were too many people to feed the normal way."

"All they knew how to do was make bricks."

I honed in on the answer about God proving His love by reminding them of Jesus feeding large crowds of people with small amounts of food.

"Yeah, the little boy shared his lunch and Jesus multiplied it to feed thousands," several of them shouted at once.

We talked about how often God wants to remind us of how much He loves us and wants to provide for our needs in creative ways.

"Do you think some of them were still ungrateful?" I asked. "Do you think they got bored having the same thing to eat every day for forty years?"

Anna had a story about wanting to eat donuts instead of healthy food. Her wise mother told her she had to eat donuts and only donuts for a full day. At first it sounded like fun but it didn't take long before she felt really sick. It made her appreciate the healthy food served at meal times.

Trying to change the subject from donuts, I asked, "What would it be like for us if food fell from the sky?"

Jake replied, "I'd be happy if donuts rained on me!"

To eliminate the donut conversation (because we didn't have any), I showed them a children's book called *Cloudy With a Chance of Meatballs*.[122] Although it was new to me, every one of the BodishBabes knew it well and loved it. I read it aloud while we looked at the great illustrations.

It would have been an easy segué to make spaghetti and meatballs for supper, but since we had just had pasta and *Bolognese* sauce two days before, I opted for grilled pizza that night. We would be taking a field trip and wouldn't have a lot of time for food prep when we got back.

For dessert, however, we would make Manna Cookies.[123] There was a chorus of cheers!

Before our lunch and rest time, I had another assignment for them that had been mentioned on the first day: we were going to plan and open a restaurant!

I gave each child a page with questions to answer.
1. What kind of people (customers) are we trying to please in our restaurant?

---

[122] *Cloudy With a Chance of Meatballs*, Judy Barrett, author; Ronald Barrett, illustrator, Atheneum Books for Young Readers, 1978.

[123] See recipe in Appendix, C"amp Mimi Eats."

2. Do we want a theme?
3. What will we name it?
4. Do we want a logo?
5. What will be on our menu?
6. What is the most important thing we need to do in our restaurant?

Everyone began to talk at once as they voiced their ideas. I narrowed the discussion to one topic at a time.

The "customers" who were going to eat our food were going to be their parents and older siblings. We had to serve something they would like. That was non-negotiable.

Everyone wanted to have a theme and they had suggestions like "Beach Party," "Pizza Place," "Crab Claw Cave," and "Pasta Palace." They obviously were incorporating restaurant names into their themes.

"Let's start with choosing a menu. That might give us an idea of what we will name it," I suggested.

After much animated discussion, they decided that the best thing to serve would be things they already knew how to make. I agreed!

"Aren't we going to be cooking something every day at Camp Mimi?" Sophie asked.

"Yes, we are."

"Then let's wait until the last few days to decide what we'll serve, but let's make it all our favorites."

Her idea was unanimous so now it was time to determine a name for our unique establishment. Here are some of their suggested names: "FillR↑," "BodishBabe Café," "God's Glorious Grill," "Crayola Café," and "JACES," which incorporated all their initials. However, they finally decided on "Divine Diner."

Sophie volunteered to draw a logo for our restaurant which we would print on the menus for each of our guests. They were all ready to bolt from the table to get started.

"Before you go," I reminded them, "there's one more item. What is the most important thing we need to do in our restaurant?"

"Eat!" they yelled.

I told them that my priority was to make sure that everything we cooked tasted really good with lots of flavor. Unless it was tasty, our guests would not enjoy it. They agreed, and volunteered to taste test everything to give their stamps of approval.

They spontaneously decided that it was important to have entertainment at our restaurant and that all seven of us would participate.

During rest time there was a lot of planning and giggling going on, but they were left to the entertainment portion of the grand opening without any supervision or input from us. Papa and I were told that we would have roles but they didn't need help yet.

After a reasonable period of what was supposed to be rest time, we gathered the children in the car for our afternoon field trip. They assumed we were going to another grocery store and were trying to guess which one.

On the way, I gave each of them a handout about *Le Cordon Bleu*, one of the most respected names in culinary education. Originating in Paris in 1895, the cooking schools teach classic French techniques by professional chefs.

Le Cordon Bleu means "The Blue Ribbon" in French and is aptly named since being awarded a blue ribbon is a universal symbol for achieving the highest degree of excellence when people compete for prizes.

Each year, more than 20,000 people from 70 countries attend *Le Cordon Bleu* cooking schools throughout the world. Julia Child, Bobby Flay, Mario Batali, Giada de Laurentiis, and Jamie Oliver are some of their more notable graduates. The children were familiar with these famous chefs because they watch cooking channels on TV.

They also were impressed to learn that I had attended a short course at *Le Cordon Bleu* school in London.

"Really? What did you learn to cook?"

I explained that our long, involved lesson demonstrated how to totally debone a whole chicken and then reassemble it with veal stuffing to look like a chicken again. When it was roasted, you could slice totally through the chicken to serve beautiful boneless slices.

"Can we have that tonight?" Jake asked.

I gave him "the look." They had no way of knowing the precision and time it took to make something that complicated. I have made the dish only once since my foray into French cooking schools and that was more than enough. Hours of work, only to have it devoured in minutes!

About the time we finished our discussion of *Le Cordon Bleu*, we drove into the parking lot at True Midtown Kitchen and, looking official in our white chef's coats, knocked on the front door of the restaurant in spite of its "Closed" sign in the window.

Midtown Kitchen,[124] owned by the well-respected culinary True family had been at this location for three years. Previously, the historic building had long housed The Bakery Cafe, a popular eating establishment specializing in southern cuisine and seafood for many years.

Built in 1900, the building was originally designed to house The Smith Bakery and the interior architecture of brick arches and interesting industrial hardware revealed its history. Conlee and I had enjoyed many

---

[124] True Midtown Kitchen is now closed.

wonderful meals and parties in this place over the years.

He and I had a late lunch date at the Midtown Kitchen several months earlier. We already had begun planning our culinary Camp Mimi, talking about what activities the children might enjoy.

On a whim, I explained our concept to the manager and asked about bringing the children on a field trip to get a tour of his kitchen, learn about ordering food, see the prepping stations, and learn how to wait tables. He was extremely enthusiastic and suggested we come one afternoon when the restaurant was closed to the public between three and five o'clock. He gave me his business card and asked me to call the week before to confirm our appointment.

About four months later I did just that, only to find out that the very congenial manager was no longer with them and no one seemed to know anything about our arrangement. I spoke to the new manager, Richard True, who was obviously not very enthusiastic about having five children bombard his establishment while they were closed. He was rather formal and distant on the phone, but when I persisted, he reluctantly agreed and we set a time to come.

His telephone demeanor continued as he opened the locked door of the restaurant for us. Richard seemed uncomfortable and ill at ease as we all gathered at the reception desk. Without greeting the children or asking about our project, he began a boring litany about the seating chart, the reservation book, and showed us the stack of menus.

I thought, "Oh no, this is not going to be fun." The children picked up on the tension and his disinterest and were becoming restless.

So, I boldly asked Richard, nearly interrupting his monologue. "Tell us something about YOU! How did you get into this business? What is your training and background?"

What we soon discovered was that Richard's passion was acting, not food. His brother, renowned Chef Wesley True, needed a manager for his newest restaurant in Mobile and offered Richard a better paying job than part-time acting in New York City.

When we asked about what plays and shows he performed in, his personality came alive. He regaled us with fascinating stories about his acting experiences and the children were spellbound, asking lots of questions. All of a sudden, this field trip took a right turn toward FUN!

The story that endeared Richard to all of us was about his audition for the role of Jesus in *Jesus Christ Superstar*. He was working as a waiter, looking for his big break.

On the morning before his afternoon audition he was nervous and trying to go over his memorized lines while he was waiting tables. He took an order ticket and, without looking, slammed it down on the spike that held the other orders. He did it with such force that the spike went right through his hand and he had to go to the emergency room at the hospital, nearly missing his audition.

"Did you get the part?" everyone wanted to know.

"Of course," Richard replied. "I took off my bandage and showed them the nail mark in my hand and they saw how dedicated I was to this role."

Richard, now in full acting mode, gave us the grand tour of the restaurant, including his enthusiastic information about how each chair of the tables was numbered according to a unique system. This insured that the waiters knew exactly which plate to give which guest with no mix-ups.

We saw the prep area where vegetables were cleaned and cut before the cooks took over. We marveled at the huge vat, as high as Jake's head, on a gas burner on the floor where stock was simmering. This would become the base for many of their dishes. We walked through the enormous cooler with food labeled and stacked in what appeared to be disarray. Once we were told their system, however, it all made sense.

The *pièce de resistance* was when Richard introduced us to the executive chef, John, and asked if we wanted to watch him make their signature dish, shrimp and grits. There was an enthusiastic chorus of, "Yes!"

Chef John complimented the children for the professional way they looked and their behavior. He asked if they knew such basic things as *mirepoix* and *mise en place*. They were delighted to tell him what they were and he was impressed, showing us how he employed both.

He and his *sous chef* made us a healthy portion of shrimp and grits so fast that it was finished almost before they began. The secret was having everything ready. All he had to do was assemble the prepped ingredients. This is the beauty of *mise en place*.

We hoped that we might be able to have a small taste of his masterpiece, but never expected that Richard would seat us out in the dining room at the center table, which he had set with silverware, napkins and goblets of water. Each of us was served a small plate portion of the most delicious shrimp and grits we ever had.

Just when we were preparing to thank Richard and Chef John for the fabulous tour and meal, the chef came out with a dessert of brownie and ice cream sundaes for each of us! What a treat!

Richard refused to let us pay for our food and the tour, but when he cleared the table he discovered that Papa had left a hefty tip.

This outing was one of our Camp Mimi highlights. I took numerous pictures at the restaurant that the children included in a thank you letter to Richard. They described their favorite parts of the tour as well as a group picture of all of us with a beaming Richard in the center, taken by Papa.

We had such a stimulating afternoon and, due to the delicious food Richard fed us, we were not very hungry. However, the children were inspired to cook something in our kitchen after being exposed to a commercial kitchen. We made two very easy things: pizza dough[125] and Manna Cookies.[126] Both had scripted recipes for the children to follow and neither took very long. The pizza dough was covered in plastic wrap to rest and the cookies went in the oven.

While I watched the cookies and quickly assembled little bowls of our favorite pizza toppings on a tray, everyone else got on swim suits and headed for the pool. Hearing their happy screams and laughter, I took the tray of condiments outside, along with a plate of warm cookies, and joined the fun

While the children worked up an appetite, it was an easy task to fire up the gas grill and roll out small, individual pizza rounds on the outside table. They chose their own toppings and Papa grilled them to perfection. Eating homemade pizza outside while dripping wet from the pool was one of our favorite meals. Some of us even ate *manna* cookies before pizza!

While the sun went down we played in the pool and watched for the first twinkling stars and fireflies. Too tired to do much other than shower and get to bed, we all agreed it had been a fabulous day.

DAY 5 – JACOB AND ESAU AND LENTIL STEW

Right after breakfast and before we gathered at the Camp Mimi table, Papa asked who wanted to go out to the end of the pier to check the crab traps. They all love this, squealing with delight when a big blue crab gets loose, as at least one always does.

Because crabs are so plentiful in Mobile Bay, we always had many plastic bags of crab meat in our freezer. The children weren't quite up to cleaning crabs yet, but were fascinated by the process. I have cleaned so many over the years that I could clean what is known as a "mess of crabs" very quickly. I decided to put together West Indies Salad for an appetizer before dinner.

West Indies Salad originated in Mobile in 1947. Bill Bayley, owner of Bayley's Restaurant on Dauphin Island Parkway near the Bay, was looking for a good recipe to make use of the abundance of crabmeat. His version of a crab *seviche* became a classic. It's very simple and quick to make but it needs to marinate for several hours for the flavors to develop.

In a bowl, you very lightly mix 1 pound lump crabmeat, ½ cup vegetable oil, ½ cup ice water (including some ice), 1/3 cup apple cider vinegar, 1 very finely chopped small onion, and salt and pepper. You want to be sure you don't break up the lumps of crab. That's it! Cover it with plastic wrap and refrigerate.

---

[125] See recipe in Appendix, "Camp Mimi Eats."

[126] Ibid.

A bit later than usual after our crabbing adventure, but with everyone finally in place, they wondered what we would study about that morning. My only hint was that it was about twins

"Edie and Anna?" Jake asked, his face looking disappointed. "I don't want to learn about them!"

"No, these are twin boys in the Bible. Do you know their names?"

No one could guess and when I told them about Jacob and Esau, they all said they knew the names but didn't know they were twins. So, we started with the basics.

With several coloring sheets before them, they chose the ones they preferred. Their selections included illustrations of Jacob making a pot of stew on an open fire, a large pot with all the ingredients for soup, and Esau dressed for hunting, as well as sheets of mazes to find the pot of stew in the center.

I began telling them the story of the most expensive bowl of soup. It cost one's whole inheritance.[127]

First, I asked them if they ever fought with their brothers and sisters. A rhetorical question if ever there was one! They were extremely honest.

The twins in our Bible story fought with one another even before they were born. Their mother, Rebekah, asked God why this war was going on inside her body.

God gave her a prophetic answer. "The two children inside you will become the fathers of two nations. Just like the two are fighting with each other now, the two nations will struggle with each other. One will be stronger than the other, and the older will serve the younger."

Papa and I told them the story of the birth of Edie and Anna. The children always love to hear stories about themselves.

Their parents and Caleb lived in a small town in New Mexico, at the time. The nearest hospital was in Roswell, a 45 minute drive away. They had to be well prepared during the last few months since twins often are born early.

Carrying twins is hard on a pregnant mama and their mother, Bev, was very small and thin. The extra weight she carried was awkward for her and she was frequently nauseous. The babies inside, however, did not fight with each other. They just moved and stretched most of the time and kept their mama uncomfortable.

As predicted, they were born early and Bev had to have a C-section. Papa and I were working outside in our yard in Mobile when we got the call from Ben, who sounded out of breath, excited and nervous all at the same

---

[127] Paraphrased story from Genesis 25:19-34

time.

"We're at the hospital and had twin girls! The oldest by one minute is doing fine but the youngest is having breathing problems. They have to fly her to Albuquerque to a Neonatal Intensive Care unit in the next few minutes. Bev has to stay here with Anna. Pray for Eden! I'm flying with her to Albuquerque."

We both picked up on Ben's concern and Papa said, "Do you want me to come?"

There was a break in Ben's voice, almost a sob, and he simply said, "Can you?"

Papa took the earliest flight available, leaving within hours. He spent the next twenty-four hours traversing the country via airplanes and rented cars to reach Albuquerque.

For the next several days he sat with Ben and Edie in the NIC unit. Although Edie was hooked up to many tubes and monitors, Ben held her tightly, next to his chest, nearly all the time. He fed her, changed her and seldom left her side to the extent that nurses asked his permission to check her periodically. When he left her for short periods, Papa took over. They both felt it important that she never feel alone or abandoned.

They said later that it was so sad to see other infants in distress in the large unit who seldom, if ever, had visitors. Only when the nurses occasionally held them did they receive any physical contact. The medical staff told Ben and Conlee that the babies who thrive best have the most hands-on affection.

Edie improved rapidly and after a week she was able to be taken back to Roswell to be reunited with her mama and twin sister. A photograph I cherish is the first one taken of the baby girls together again in one crib in the Roswell hospital. As soon as they sensed one another's presence, they immediately embraced and settled into a peaceful sleep.

I flew out to stay with the growing family for a few weeks after Bev's mother left. By then, the twins were on somewhat of a schedule in the family's new routine.

It was my first time to be around twins and it was fascinating, even though exhausting. They are identical and it was nearly impossible to tell one from the other, especially at first. It helped to always put pink on Anna and another color on Edie. The thing that impressed me most was that they slept fitfully when apart, yet very securely and peacefully when touching one another.

Edie and Anna loved hearing their story told and I detected a tear or two in Papa's eyes as he recalled the emotional experiences of their first few days.

The twin relationship between Jacob and Esau was far different from that of Edie and Anna. The boys looked nothing alike. The oldest one was all red and covered with hair. His parents named him Esau because, in Hebrew, it sounds like the word for "red."

The youngest one, Jacob, was born immediately afterwards, grabbing onto Esau's heel, as if to pull him back. Jacob, sounds like the Hebrew word for "heel."

As they grew up their personalities and interests were as different as their appearance. Esau became a very skilled hunter and loved the outdoor life. His elderly father, Isaac, favored Esau because he loved to eat the wild game his son brought back from his hunting trips.

Conversely, Jacob was quiet and preferred staying at home, learning to cook and other domestic tasks from his mother. Perhaps he was what we might call a "mama's boy."

The competitive nature of the twin boys is demonstrated through one of their fascinating family stories. All family stories reveal the nature of the individual family members. They should be told over and over again until they become legacies of one's history. Some stories, like the one about Edie and Anna, inspire courage, prayer, faith, love, and bravery. These are encouraging to those who come after.

Other stories, however, like this particular one about Jacob and Esau, are sad, disappointing, and perhaps even discouraging. But they, too, should be told and not hidden in the family archives as taboo subjects. They demonstrate the frailty and vulnerability to sin we all have, teaching us to avoid such pitfalls and learn the value of redemption.

The story of the twin brothers begins with Esau out for a hunting trip. He was gone for several days and, contrary to his usual success, he came home with nothing to eat. He knew his father would be disappointed and Esau was tired, hungry and out of sorts.

"I get that way, too, when I'm hungry," interrupted Jake.

I told them that was a Bodishbaugh family trait. All of them get somewhat irritable when they're hungry. I had to learn early on to keep my husband and children well fed to keep them happy and optimistic.

Esau was certainly irritable when he returned from his hunting trip and smelled the stew that Jacob had simmering on an open fire.

"Give me some of that red stuff! I'm starving," he demanded.

Jacob's conniving character is revealed in the story by his immediate response.

"Sure, I'll give you some of my stew – *if* you give me your birthright."

Every head came up from the coloring pages and most of them asked at the same time, "What's a birthright?"

In Biblical families the birthright was very important. It insured that the oldest son in a family would receive the double portion of his father's inheritance. In the case of Isaac's family, since there were two sons, Isaac's inheritance was divided into three portions. At his death, one portion would go to Jacob, the youngest son, and two portions would go to Esau, the oldest son.

Caleb immediately declared that he would have the double portion in his family. Of course, this provoked Jake to declare, "That's not fair!"

I suggested that our Jake's response was exactly what the biblical Jacob's must have been. Then I added, "But please do not act the same way as biblical Jacob! He had to go through many hardships in his life to find the peace that God wanted to give him as his eternal spiritual inheritance."

I explained that being the oldest son, having the birthright, and receiving a double portion of a family inheritance implied a double portion of responsibility as well. The oldest son was expected to provide for the needs of his widowed mother for the rest of her life as well as for any siblings who could not support themselves. The oldest son had the responsibility of maintaining whatever estate was left and managing all of the family affairs. The extra portion he inherited might not be such an adequate compensation for all that was required of him.

But Jacob and Esau didn't think about any of these details or facts of reality. They were only concerned about their own selfish desires. Jacob was jealous of Esau's status in the family and Esau was hungry. And so, Esau sold his birthright to his younger brother for the price of a bowl of stew.

The Bible tells us that Jacob's stew was made of red lentils. Next to bread, lentils were one of the most important dietary ingredients for the ancient Israelites. They are mentioned four times in the Bible.

You might suppose that the two sons forgot about the transaction they made in their youth over a bowl of stew. However, years later in the narrative, we see that their hasty agreement determined life-changing circumstances.

Much later, their father, Isaac, was very old, totally blind, and about to die. As a last request, he asked his favorite son, Esau, to go hunting and bring back some of the game he loved to eat. He wanted this to be his final dinner. He promised Esau that when he finished his delicious meal he would give his oldest son his paternal blessing of the birthright.

Esau left with his bow and arrows in search of the meat for the meal, expecting to return and receive his inheritance.

Meanwhile, Rebekah took her favorite son, Jacob, aside, revealing what was about to happen. She schemed with Jacob to trick her dying husband.

Her plan included having Jacob make one of his best recipes of roasted goat, using the skins from the animals as a hairy disguise so that Isaac would think Jacob was the bristly oldest son. Amazingly, their deceptive plan worked.

Jacob donned the hair costume, took his aromatic steaming bowl of goat stew to his father, and lied about being Esau. Isaac was suspicious because the voice sounded more like Jacob's. But when he reached out to grasp him to make sure, he touched the hairy covering which felt like Esau's skin.

Once again he asked, to be certain, "Are you my son, Esau?"

And once again Jacob lied, "Yes, I am."

After Isaac ate his meal, he asked his son to come for his blessing. Jacob, the imposter/deceiver received what was intended for the first born.

What a mess! Can you see the confusion that is about to happen when Esau returns? This is a classic example of a dysfunctional family. No one tells the truth and values are placed in all the wrong places.

From that day on, the brothers hated each other. Jacob had to run away to a distant relative and Esau was destined to be estranged from his family.

You would think that was the end of the story. But when we give up – even in the worst circumstances – we underestimate God and His resourcefulness to bring healing to what seems impossible.

After many years and numerous hardships and disappointments, God brought reconciliation to the brothers and healed a family that one day brought forth the Messiah, Jesus.

There are many more fascinating aspects to this story but the children received their lesson for the day. When I asked them what they learned from this story, they were all on board.

"Don't lie."

"Don't cheat."

"Enjoy what you have and who you are and don't try to be someone else."

"Don't be envious of what other people have."

"When you have children, don't have favorites."

I would say it was a good conclusion for our morning class. Now it was time to cook!

We were going to Bellingrath Gardens after rest time. They all looked forward to this favorite field trip, but we needed to start preparing our supper – even before lunch. We were making "Jacob and Esau's Red Lentil Stew."[128] We needed to assemble it early in the day to allow the flavors to infuse in a slow cooker all afternoon.

We took a break, had snacks, and washed hands. Then, with printed recipe scripts in hand, we began our *mise en place* with a *mirepoix*. It was so fun to see them now familiar with the French culinary terms they had never heard of a few days earlier.

Sophie chopped onions and garlic in the little food processor, putting them into the slow cooker.

Jake opened cans of chicken broth, red beans, and chick peas with the

---

[128] Recipe in Appendix, "Camp Mimi Eats."

electric can opener. Next to cracking eggs, this was his favorite job. He poured in the broth and Edie and Anna added the vegetables.

Caleb chopped carrots and celery when Sophie finished with the processor, stirring them into the pot.

Jake squeezed a lemon and poured the juice into the mixture.

Edie used the other small processor to chop a potato and then Anna chopped cilantro. These were all added as well.

Sophie drizzled olive oil and sprinkled spices before the last ingredient was added, dried red lentils. This made it authentically Middle-Eastern, something Jacob and Esau would have eaten.

The only ingredient biblical Jacob would not have used was lemon, but the acidity greatly enhances the flavor so we intentionally overlooked that detail.

Caleb stirred it all well and we set the cooker on low.

When we returned from our field trip a few hours later, the whole house smelled wonderful! Jake remarked that if it smelled that good no wonder Esau was willing to sell his birthright.

After everyone cleaned up, we gathered on the porch for our West Indies Salad served with crackers. It was such a hit that everyone wanted to have it on our restaurant menu.

Then, we all set about doing our assigned tasks for the night. Edie, Anna, and Jake set the table and decorated, while Caleb and Sophie helped me assemble Sophie's Chicken *Spiedini*.[129] She couldn't imagine having a Camp Mimi without it. Caleb's tastes had matured so much that he actually offered to eat the chicken and cheese cooked together. A milestone!

I had doubts about whether the children would like the lentil stew. To my knowledge, they had never had anything quite like it in taste or texture. But it became an instant favorite.

"We have to have this on our restaurant menu, too!" They all agreed unanimously.

A close third in must-haves for the menu was Sophie's *Spiedini*. She beamed.

A big part of our menu was decided. We needed to finalize it and then begin to shop for ingredients for Divine Diner's opening night which was only three days away.

DAY 6 – PASSOVER AND A SEDER MEAL

The children knew a bit about the traditional Jewish Passover Meal or *Seder*. We studied about it, planned our own, and celebrated one the year our Camp Mimi theme was "Journey to Israel." We all needed our

---

[129] Ibid.

memories refreshed, however, and our approach was slightly different this year. Because of our culinary theme, I wanted to focus on the particular foods at a *Seder* and what they represented.

We started first by looking at God's commandment to the Israelites about observing an annual meal as a commemoration for God's deliverance from slavery and bondage. It is interesting to note that in Exodus 12, He commanded them to observe the event *before* the deliverance actually occurred. How certain our God is that what He declares will surely take place!

He said, "It is a day you are to commemorate; for the generations to come you shall celebrate it as a festival to the Lord – a lasting ordinance."[130]

Passover is important for Christians to understand as well as Jews. It was the venue Jesus chose to explain His ultimate sacrifice, the Crucifixion, and to reveal what it would mean to His disciples. Every component of the Passover meal points us to a step toward the eternal deliverance that God put in motion thousands of years before the Last Supper.

I gave them coloring sheets of the food items traditionally required at a *Seder* meal. There are special *Seder* plates available with sections to hold each item. Some families use these every year because it is meaningful to have certain vessels that are only brought out for special holidays.

I asked the children what they can remember about special things we use only for holidays. They recalled a Thanksgiving platter to hold the big turkey, Christmas dishes that aren't used any other time, and even the Communion cup that isn't used for any other meal except for the Lord's Supper. All great memories!

In addition to our *Seder* plate, we have other items that are reserved only for this special occasion. A special pitcher and basin is used for the hand-washing ceremony, and a special linen towel we don't use for any other purpose is laid over Papa's arm for drying the hands. It was a loving gift from a friend and is embroidered, "Christ is the Head of our household; the unseen Guest at every meal; the silent Listener to every conversation."

Our communion cup, a gift while in Israel, serves as our chalice, and even the two memorial candles are placed in special holders we only use for Passover and *Shabbat*.

Although the children are with us infrequently, especially for such occasions as Passover or *Shabbat*, they remember where every required item is stored and delight in getting them out to prepare our celebrations. There is something very comforting about having familiar traditions and the meaningful symbols that bind them to our hearts.

We looked at each of the food items individually, talking about what they symbolize to Jews and how we look at them as Christians. Our own

---

[130] **Exodus 12:14**

spiritual experiences will uniquely define a symbolic system for us.

- **Cups of Wine**

    Four cups of wine are served at a *Seder* meal. Each has special significance. Wine is a universal symbol of joy and happiness, so its presence indicates that there is celebration coming at the end of a narrative of difficulty and heartache.

    ▶ The first cup is the *Kiddush*, the cup of blessing. It is sipped while we bless God, the King of the universe.

    ▶ The second cup represents the plagues. This is the favorite part for the children because they get to dip their finger into their "kids' wine" when each of the ten plagues is mentioned, yelling out the names of the plagues. The purple dots they make on their plates symbolize the extent of the punishment for disobeying God.

    ▶ The third cup is the cup of redemption. It comes after telling the punishments and points to our hope for the future. This is the cup Jesus referred to at The Last Supper when he said, "This cup is the New Covenant in My Blood, which is poured out for you."

    ▶ The fourth cup is the cup of praise. At the end of the meal hymns of praise are sung and toasts are made to celebrate the feast, "Next year in Jerusalem!"

- *Karpas* – **(parsley)** – The parsley reminds us of the hyssop branches the Israelites used to paint the blood of the first Passover lambs on the doorways of their houses. The shed blood of the lamb caused the Angel of Death to pass over their homes. The parsley is dipped into salt water.

- **Salt Water** – This reminds us of the tears shed by the Israelites because Pharaoh made them work so hard in Egypt, and even killed some of their baby boys. It also recalls the tears of those who are outside the protection of the Blood of the Lamb when they face death. For them, there is no deliverance.

- *Matzah* – **(bread)** – Flat, unleavened bread is served as a reminder that when the Israelites left Egypt, they did not have time for their bread dough to rise. They were told by God to be ready at a moment's notice to go with Him.

- *Moror* – **(bitter herbs)** – The bitterness of the herbs reminds us of how terrible life was for the Israelites when they were slaves in Egypt, and for us before our sins are forgiven. We typically use horseradish to startle our senses.

- *Haroset* – **(sweet paste)** – Made of fruit and nuts, this sweetness reminds us that even in their slavery, the Israelites had hope in God. It symbolizes the mortar the slaves used between the bricks as they worked for Pharaoh. Using *matzah*, each one makes a *haroset* sandwich to taste.

- *Z'roa* – **(lamb bone)** – This recalls the sacrificial lamb that each family was required to eat on the night of their deliverance. It points us to the Lamb of God, Jesus, who takes away our sins by His sacrifice.

- *Beytza* – **(egg)** – The roasted egg is a symbol of new life.

Now that we were familiar once again with the traditional items on the Passover table, we looked at the story of the Last Supper, opening our Bibles to the account of that night written by John (found in chapters 13-17). John didn't include as many details about the preparation for the feast as the other Gospel writers, but he did include the powerful prayers Jesus prayed, as well as their conversations around the table.

During the part of the meal when the host/father normally went around the table to allow each person to wash their hands, Jesus did something very different, typically something only a slave would do. He washed their feet. This was embarrassing to the disciples, and at first they didn't want Him to do it. Peter even asked Him not to. But Jesus explained, through His symbolic action, that it was what they should do to one another. They were to serve, not expect to be served.

During the taking of *Matzah* and dipping it in the *Moror*, Jesus said that the one to whom He gave His symbol of the bitterness of life was the one who would betray Him. He dipped the *Matzah* into the bitter herb and gave it to Judas. Judas then left in the middle of the meal.

As the rest of them ate their meal together, Jesus turned the conversation to what would happen later than night and after He would leave them. It had to be very confusing at the time for the disciples to have their well-known traditional remembrance of Passover turn into something so different.

The traditional prayer to bless God for the *Matzah* turned into, "Take and eat. This is My Body."

The traditional prayer to bless God for the wine turned into, "This is My blood of the New Covenant, which is poured out for many."

The traditional prayers that had been prayed for generations turned into prayers for all believers who would be comforted by the sending of Holy Spirit.

The final cup and blessing was followed by a traditional hymn and a walk to the Mount of Olives. Satisfied with a full meal and four cups of wine, the disciples could not stay awake. But Jesus prayed to His *Abba*, honestly asking that the cup of death that He knew was coming soon be taken away from Him. Ultimately, He cried out to His Father, "Yet not what I will, but what You will."

It is no wonder that the Last Supper is remembered forever in our hearts. Jesus showed that the traditions people accept their whole lives can be turned in an instant into something so profound that it changes history.

We talked about that for a few minutes, recalling seemingly "normal" events that transform us and our families because Jesus interrupts with His presence. I mentioned the night we had the unusual holy visitation in our home while engaging in the most normal activity.[131] This is a story they love for us to tell over and over.

Edie told about a normal morning driving with the carpool to school when she saw Jesus by the side of the road. She never thought of Him the same after that because it was so intensely personal.

Caleb told about praying so hard for a baby brother after he had twin sisters. When Jake was born, Caleb knew that Jesus had answered his prayers. This was more than a new child in the family to him. For Caleb, Jake's life meant a personal encounter with Jesus.

I told the children that we would use our information about the Passover Meal and decorate our table for such a celebration that evening. The set-up and decorating team was Sophie, Edie and Anna. Jake and Caleb had assignments as sous-chefs.

But first, we were going on an afternoon trip to the Animal Preserve! Yea! Another Camp Mimi favorite, traditional field trip. We were all about tradition that day.

After a very hot afternoon, looking for our favorite rescue animals and finding many that were new to us, we returned home, ready for a swim and a rest. I got a rest, too, because supper was going to be easy. A chocolate cake and a chicken and rice casserole from the freezer were brought out to thaw and the makings of a salad were in the refrigerator. We all got a break from the kitchen that night.

Before we set up our Passover table (our large coffee table in the living room with pillows around on the floor), we gathered at the Camp Mimi table to complete our plans for the opening of Divine Diner. We finalized the menu and made a shopping list. Then the children presented their script for the entertainment. It was brilliant and needed only a little tweaking. We practiced several times until we were exhausted from laughing.

---

[131] <u>The Journey to Wholeness in Christ</u>, Signa Bodishbaugh, Journey Press, 1997, pp 34-38.

Our Passover Meal was beautifully and lovingly prepared. The filled *Seder* plate was placed in the center of the table, the candles arranged, the water basin and towel at the side, the wine goblets in place, the carafes of real wine and "kids' wine" (grape juice) on an adjoining table, the casserole warming in the oven, and the programs for a *Seder* meal[132] that we used several years ago on each one's plate. We were ready.

Barukh atah Adonai Eloheynu Melekh ha'olam

They knew the introductory words of blessing by heart because of numerous *Shabbat* meals which open with the same prayer, so they joined with Papa. Our chorus of very imperfect Hebrew but with loving, open hearts became the entrance into a night of history, remembrance and spiritual awareness.

DAY 7 – THE PRODIGAL SON AND THE FATTED CALF

We stayed up very late at our wonderful *Seder* meal the night before so we let everyone sleep in longer than usual. We all needed a slower start on our last day because we had been going at a very fast pace and rest times were becoming shorter as we went along.

Papa was in charge of breakfast so I could complete our certificates for that night's Awards Dinner. The BodishBabes were already talking about the traditional steak dinner and asked if I had the steaks yet and what kind they were. I was a bit evasive and they were insistent.

"Mimi, you are going to have steak, aren't you? It's tradition!"

"You *have* to have steak! We're tired of chicken."

Sophie, always the peacemaker, reasonably declared, "I know. We have to go to the grocery store to get the food for Divine Diner. We'll get the steaks then."

That satisfied everyone enough to gather for our last lesson at the Camp Mimi table for the year.

With lots of coloring pages, word searches and mazes, they got to work as I told them the story traditionally called, "The Prodigal Son."[133] A more apt title would be "A Loving Father and His Two Sons." The real star of the story is the father, not either of the sons. Both sons are ungrateful and have no idea how much their father loves them.

The Bible story is not necessarily true, but it could be. It is a parable, one of many illustrations that Jesus used to teach important life lessons.

---

[132] See Appendix, *Haggadah* for Passover

[133] Excerpted from Luke 15:11-32

This parable is intended to demonstrate the character of a loving, forgiving Father in heaven.

In the story, the younger son squanders the inheritance his father gives him and ends up in desperate circumstances. He is living worse than swine. He has nowhere else to go but back home, certain that his father will never forgive him and that he will be treated as one of the servants. He knows that he deserves it and shamefully returns home.

To his surprise, his father runs out to meet him, embraces him, and gives him symbolic gifts that show him to be a valued member of the family. The father immediately plans a big celebration dinner.

The older son has been under his father's protection all his life, dutifully doing what he is supposed to do, but never appreciating how much his father loves him. He is filled with jealousy, envy, and discontent. He doesn't even want to attend the party his father gives to celebrate the family reunion.

After telling the children the basic plot of the story, I then read the Bible passage from Luke. They were quiet when I finished.

Then I told them a modern version of the same story. This telling elicited much more emotional response.

"An ungrateful son decided to drop out of school and run away from home. Thinking he would be happier once he was away from the restrictions his parents put on him, he tried to make his way in a big city on his own. It didn't take long before he was tired, hungry, scared, and very lonely.

A pastor found the miserable boy begging on the sidewalk outside his church one day. He fed and clothed him and counseled him with some very good advice. 'Write your parents and tell them you are ready to come back home. Ask them to forgive you. I'll give you a train ticket to your home town.'

The boy wrote the following letter.

Dear Mom and Dad,

I am so sorry for leaving like I did. It took me a long time to realize what I have lost and how much you really did love me. I would like to come back home. I know I don't deserve your forgiveness but I will try to make it up to you.

A pastor gave me a train ticket and the train will take me right by our farm on the way to the local station. If you will allow me to come back home, please hang a white towel on the clothesline in our back yard. I will be able to see it from the train.

If it's there, I'll get off at the station.

If not, I'll know I shouldn't come back home.

The boy began the train ride, becoming more and more nervous as he got closer to his home town. His stomach was filled with butterflies and he was scared to look out the window to his right. Finally, he asked the man sitting next to him if he would look at the farm coming up just around the next curve. He described it to the man as having a white fence and a big red barn on the side.

'Just let me know if there's a white towel on the clothesline.' He gritted his teeth and closed his eyes.

The man nudged him, 'Son, you'd better open your eyes. Up ahead is that farm you described. But you need to look at this! I've never seen anything like it.'

The boy opened his eyes and couldn't believe it. There were white towels, sheets, and blankets on the clothesline, all along the fence, on top of the barn, and hanging in the trees.

He had come home and home was a place of love and forgiveness."

Each child loved this story so much that they wanted to draw pictures of the farm with all the white towels waving. What a symbol of God's love reaching out to us, no matter what we've done or where we've been!

I asked them if they remembered what the father in the Bible story served for the celebration dinner. They looked it up in their Bibles and then asked, "What's a fatted calf?"

I suggested that the father planned a celebratory steak dinner, just like we were going to have that night.

"Yea!"

Our field trip quest for the afternoon was going to be finding our "fatted calf." But they were in for some surprises.

We drove to a town across Mobile Bay, only about 30 minutes away. We had an appointment with Jim Shepler, the manager of the meat department at a new Winn-Dixie store in Daphne. This grocery store was one of Winn-Dixie's newest models, with specialty departments throughout.

Jim is the son-in-law of one of my dear friends, Judy Oschwald. I used her influence to talk him into giving our culinary school a tour of everything that goes into buying a steak for dinner. She went with us as our "official photographer."

On the drive to the store, I gave each child handouts about beef. We learned that "cow" is the name for adult female cattle, "heifer" for young females, "bull" for male cattle, and "calf" for all young cattle.

Jake immediately made the connection. "You mean the father in the story was going to kill a fat baby cow?"

"Well ... yes," I replied.

There was a rousing chorus of "Oooooooooo!" from the back seats.

We learned that cows do not have teeth on their upper jaws. They have four stomachs. They can smell something six miles away. They have almost 360 degrees of vision. They eat and drink about eight hours a day, consuming 95 pounds of food and 30 gallons of water. Their average weight is 1,400 pounds when full grown. They live to be about 25 years old.

Then I gave them handouts of a sectioned cow, colorfully showing the different cuts of meat that we were familiar with. We looked at the sirloin, rib, chuck, brisket, flank, and even the tongue. We were not so familiar with the sections called the clod, shin, and tail.

The children were all familiar with Captain Carbon stories from science classes in school. I was not. However, I found a story online of the little molecule, named Captain Carbon, traveling inside a cow that was about to become a steak for dinner.[134] For the rest of our short road trip to Winn-Dixie I read them the story and they were fascinated.

With Captain Carbon as our guide, we covered the cow's trip from the farm to the meat-packing plant, to the freezer, the meat cutter, the packaging, the refrigerated train trip, the grocery store, the shopping cart, the grill and the family table.

Sophie was the only one who had qualms even talking about raw meat. After we parked near the entrance of Winn-Dixie, we all straightened our chefs' jackets to enter the store. Sophie took a deep breath and said bravely, "Okay, let's get this over with!"

We greeted the manager at the front of the huge store and told him about our appointment with Jim in the meat department. He complimented us on our professional-looking appearance as a cooking school and told us to look around at the different sections of the store as he guided us to the back. We marched behind our leader, looking left and right at the different specialty areas within the store. It was a very unique lay-out.

Jim and his associates met us at the meat department. They were dressed as neatly in their white jackets as we were.

He welcomed us and asked what we had been studying all week. The children politely gave him the condensed version of our action-packed week.

"What would you like to do today?" he asked.

Jake blurted out, "We want to buy a fat calf for our celebration dinner!"

"Okay," Jim replied seriously. "We can make that happen!"

He gave each of us a special Winn-Dixie cap to wear, required when you go behind the counter. He took us all the way back to the loading dock, behind several swooshing heavy doors and freezing cold walk-in refrigerators. He said he would show us the route the steak takes when it

---

[134] Unfortunately, the website and story where this was located are no longer available.

first enters the door to the store.

He showed us how they received all of their meat uncut from refrigerated trucks. Huge chunks of meat hung from racks in the very cold rooms, some still sealed in plastic wrap, others open. He explained in great detail the different cuts of meat and where they had been on the cow. The handouts that had been in the children's hands just minutes ago now came to life.

Jim told us about the United States Department of Agriculture (USDA) and how they grade meats according to rigid standards. The grades given to meat become the language of the buyers to know what to order. Every beef carcass that has been approved by the USDA has a stamp on it. This insures that it has been handled safely and cleanly all along the way to the store and that you can take it home to eat without worrying about getting sick. A stamp also shows if it is rated *prime*, *choice*, or *select*, determined by the fat content or marbling of the meat.

After our very informative tour, we were freezing. It is hard to stay in the refrigerated rooms for very long at a time. The workers were dressed much warmer than we were. Before we left, however, Jim asked us what cut of steak we wanted.

I asked him, "What is your favorite cut? What would you take home for your family for a celebration dinner?"

Without any hesitation, he said, "A rib-eye for sure. It has the best marbling and flavor." He also told us that the rib-eye is known as the "butcher's cut," because they consider it the best one.

We said that's what we would have.

He went back to the refrigerated room and brought out a huge long cut of meat, telling us that was where the rib-eye steaks came from. He laid it down on a spotlessly clean table and asked how thick we wanted our steaks to be. Again, we asked for his expert advice. He recommended 1¼ inches thick.

He took a long knife and expertly cut us four huge steaks which would be plenty for our family, carefully weighed them and then wrapped them in butcher paper. He even gave us a discounted price!

We thanked Jim and his workers and proudly placed our steaks in a shopping cart, ready to get the rest of the items on our list.

Before leaving the meat department, we were greeted by the managers of the cheese shop, the bakery and the produce department, lined up waiting for us. All of them had been aware of our tour with Jim and they wanted to give us tours of their own areas as well.

And so our time in Winn-Dixie extended a couple of hours. We asked Jim to keep our cut steaks in his cooler while we explored other areas of the large food complex.

The lady in the cheese shop showed us a 150-pound wheel of *Parmigiano-*

Reggiano, the gold-standard cheese for Italian cooking (and my favorite). It is very expensive and is only made in the Parma region of Italy. She gave us samples from smaller pieces.

Then we tried cheeses from several other countries, each with a vivid description of where they originated and how they were formed. She invited us to choose any cheeses we saw and she would give us samples and descriptions. She was very knowledgeable.

By the time we left her area, we had tried dozens of cheeses, several olives, and were even given bottles of water.

Then the bakery lady took over, leading us to her area, taking us back where the big ovens were located. We all got to get our plastic-gloved hands in dough and formed little balls to become *boules,* the French term for bread rounds. She had some French bread just coming out of the oven, and while it was piping hot, she gave us healthy portions of a loaf. It was delicious and she made it even better by offering us butter to slather on our samples.

Finally, the produce man led us to a sample tray of some of their fruits. We tried kiwi, nectarine, passion fruit, grapes, strawberries and kumquats.

By now, full and exhausted, we retrieved our steaks, along with the other items we needed and headed home.

"I had no idea they would give us all that free food!" said Edie.

"Me either. I'm full," agreed Anna.

"I liked the cheeses best," said Jake.

"I liked the bread!" responded Caleb.

"I'm just glad he didn't give us raw meat samples!" sighed Sophie.

That night at our celebration/*Shabbat*/steak dinner we were all very thankful for our week together, our "Cordon Bleu" awards, many wonderful memories, and the best steak we had ever eaten.

OPENING NIGHT – DIVINE DINER

The big night finally arrived. Although the parents and older siblings, Alex and Macy, were excited about our restaurant, they had no idea how many hours of planning, preparation and final execution were involved in wha they were about to experience.

We packed the car with Divine Diner food in a huge cooler, reminiscent of my old catering days. We were excited to see the rest of the family when we gathered at the Destin beach house. The first thing everyone wanted to do was run to the ocean and feel the sand between our toes. We wouldn't work on our restaurant presentation until the next night.

Our biggest challenge was being in an unfamiliar kitchen and using what we could find to decorate and set a beautiful table. However, the children were quite resourceful and it didn't take long before they transformed an already lovely beach house into a dining extravaganza.

Seashells, coral, candles and flowers, along with all their notebooks and awards as centerpieces made the perfect background for Papa to serve as the *maitre d'* to seat each guest. At their places, each one found a printed menu showing what they could expect as the evening progressed.

The seven of us, wearing our chefs' coats, gathered in a row before our diners. I explained that there was a popular movement across the United States of "pop-up" restaurants. These are temporary, sometimes open only for one amazing meal, appearing in homes, factories, and shops. They are widely acclaimed by young chefs just getting started and by trendy food connoisseurs. Then came my scripted introduction, written by the children .

"Tonight is the grand opening of our pop-up restaurant, Divine Diner! So, relax … get comfortable … as we proudly present … your dinner!"

After that cue, each of us pulled a wooden spoon from our pockets and used them as batons as we sang the lyrics that Sophie and the others wrote to the tune of "Be Our Guest" from "Beauty and the Beast." It was totally plagiarized with thanks to songwriters Mitchell Hope and Marco Marinangeli.

ALL:	*Be our guest, be our guest*
	Put our service to the test
	We've been cooking long at Mimi's
JAKE:	*And we hope we did our best!*
ALL:	*Working hard, working long*
EDIE:	*Hope the recipe isn't wrong!*
ALL:	*Try our dishes, they're delicious*
PAPA:	*It's the truth, I did the dishes!*
ALL:	*We can sing, we can dance*
ANNA:	*But this isn't Paris, France!*
ALL:	*And dinner here is n e v e r s e c o n d b e s t …*
	Go on and take a seat …
SOPHIE:	*I really like the meat!*
ALL:	*Be our guest, be our guest*
MIMI:	*It's Divine Diner we suggest!*
ALL:	*Be our guest, be our guest* – ***B E O U R G U E S T!***

We ended with a drawn-out, cheesy, overly-exaggerated flourish, posing with the traditional lurch toward our audience, hand extended. We performed it without a hitch, except for Papa, who had to be prompted for his one line. We got a standing ovation.

Dinner was delicious and was enjoyed with gusto, each child telling details about the preparation, the reason behind each dish, and more than our guests wanted to know about all the ingredients.

After all was over, the dishes were done and the room was full of happy tummies and treasure chests of memories, the best part for me was when Ben and Matt, our two sweet adult sons, announced, "Tomorrow night we're taking this crew *out to eat* ! You deserve it!"

Divine Diner

A unique, once-in-a-lifetime dining experience

MENU

Appetizer—From the Bay
West Indies Salad

First Course– From the Bible
Jacob and Esau's Red Lentil Soup

Entrée– From Camp Mimi Favorites
Chicken Spiedini

Vegetables– From Family Favorites
Twice Baked Potatoes / Marinated Grilled Asparagus

Bread—From Shabbat
Challah

Dessert—From Our Love
Dark Chocolate Mousse with Manna

So whether you eat or drink or whatever you do, do it all for the glory of God!
1 Cor. 10:31

CAMP MIMI NINE

WEATHER

Most years I have been inspired by God with our themes for Camp Mimi. Sometimes Conlee and I prayed about what to do and, together, we came up with a subject. But this year's theme was totally Conlee's idea. He has always loved weather and looks everyday for the forecast, using a newspaper, website, or television.

Perhaps this is because he grew up with a father who was a pilot, always concerned about flying conditions. Conlee developed his father's interests and took his first solo flight when he was sixteen years old. It is easy to recognize pilots because they immediately look up in the sky when they hear a plane of any kind. People who love weather notice the sky, too, seeing things most of us ignore.

Conlee notices cloud formations, drops in humidity and temperature, the light, and even the way certain animals react to barometric pressure. I knew I would learn a lot when we began to prepare for this Camp Mimi several months out.

Searching online for books explaining weather and forecasting to children, I was pleased to find several great choices which I ordered and studied. At the end of Camp Mimi we gave the books to the children. One of our favorites was *The Kids' Book of Weather Forecasting* by meteorologist Mark Breen and Kathleen Friestad.[135] Because the children were getting older and had longer attention spans, we found we were able to delve into many more complex subjects than ever before.[136] It was both fun and a challenge, especially for me!

DAY 1 – WEATHER FACTS AND WEATHER STATION

The children arrived excited as usual, ready for The Big Reveal. Before I brought out the candle which identified our theme, I asked them a question, "What is the most talked about subject among most people?"

Conlee and I got so tickled at their answers that we almost fell off our chairs.

"Camp Mimi!" (That was very flattering, but also showed how limited Jake's world was).

"Food!" (Edie, with the metabolism of a bird, was always ready to eat).

"Horses!" (Anna's new passion was being revealed).

"Sex!" (The two almost-teenagers were definitely getting older!)

I brought out the candle with "Weather" on the label.

Their responses were, "Really?"

"Storms?"

"Hurricanes?"

"This will be a short Camp Mimi!"

Their expectations were not exceptionally high. We had our work cut out for us.

To begin our challenge, each child was presented with a brass name badge with their name and "Camp Mimi Meteorologist" engraved on it. I told them they would have to earn the right to deserve such a badge but they could wear them as reminders of our goal.

After reviewing the rules, singing the song, and getting organized, they decorated their new plastic boxes that would hold their treasures during the week. Their decorations were so much more artistic than when we first started this tradition several years ago. Some of them became works of art!

After their very concentrated artistic efforts were completed, they received their notebooks and we began our study for the morning.

Climate

"Do you know the word 'climate'?" I asked.

Jake thought it meant "climb it" but his older siblings corrected him.

---

[135] *The Kids' Book of Weather Forecasting*, Breen and Friestad, Ideals, 2008.

[136] As in "Fearfully and Wonderfully Made," this Camp Mimi was much more technical, involving experiments and math. The children were getting older and loved being stretched. Some of the lessons were difficult for the younger ones, but they persevered and were up to the challenge. I debated about including some of the specifics we covered, but decided *you* readers were up to the challenge, too!

"No, it's the same as 'weather,'" they said.

I refined their answer a bit, "Actually the climate describes a long-time average of weather, usually covering 30-100 years."

"That's older than you, Mimi!" exclaimed Jake. I thanked him profusely and told him I was somewhere in the middle of that number.

The Science of Meteorology

Weather typically describes what is happening in the atmosphere today. That is why it is such a current topic of conversation for most people, even among strangers.

"What is the weather today?" I asked. Everyone looked outside the wall of French doors to see a beautiful sunny morning.

"Sunny!" was the unanimous answer. This seemed easy.

"What is the forecast?" They automatically looked outside again, but didn't know how to answer. "Sunny?" Caleb guessed.

"How would you know it's not going to rain this afternoon?" I asked him. He wasn't sure.

This is why we have *meteorologists*, the big word on their name badges. A meteorologist is someone who studies the earth's atmosphere along with the weather. This title comes from the Greek word *meteoron* which means "thing in the heaven above." We practiced saying *meteorologist*. Of course, they were sure it must have something to do with meteors, too. After some off-the-track discussion of meteors, they came to the conclusion that meteors were one of the "things in the heaven above."

I gave them an assortment of coloring pages, depicting various weather conditions. They could choose the ones they liked best to work on during our lesson. Jake decided he wanted to draw his own picture of a meteor crashing to earth. Everyone else got busy coloring printed scenes of strong winds blowing down trees, snowy farmlands, sunny beaches, or rain outside one's window.

A weather forecaster, like the person you might see on a TV weather show, is not necessarily a meteorologist. You have to have a special degree from a college or university, completing your studies of this well-established science to earn the title of meteorologist or climatologist. You need to be good at science and math and be prepared to study hard for at least four years, taking such courses as computer sciences, calculus, physics and dynamics. Some jobs such as teaching, research, or management may require their meteorologists to have a master's degree in meteorology or atmospheric sciences and a doctoral degree as well.

The history of meteorology is interesting. At one time predicting the weather was considered witchcraft. This was because people were suspicious of the sciences. In 1542, England's King Henry VIII issued a Witchcraft Act, requiring the guilty to be punished by death. Included in the criteria for being a witch was predicting what the weather would be, identifying it as "going against the laws of God and nature."

Twenty years later, Queen Elizabeth I amended the act to be much more lenient toward the sciences and about what constituted witchcraft.

The natural curiosity of intelligent people prevailed over time and eventually those who studied the sciences became well-respected and encouraged to continue their education and experiments.

The effort to predict weather was one of the initial reasons for the development of computers. Meteorologists rely heavily on computers to accurately forecast weather a few days in advance. There are so many variables, however, like temperature, atmospheric pressure, moisture and wind, jet streams, ocean currents, land elevation, and clouds, that it is hard to be accurate much longer than that. For longer range forecasting, they use computer models with some degrees of accuracy.

Anna looked up from her coloring, "I don't know what most of those things are."

"You will by the end of the week!" I promised. "We'll have fun learning."

"Think of some people and places that really need meteorologists." They came up with some great examples.

"Airports." We talked about weather conditions that might shut down or delay flights.

"Schools." They all loved it when the TV or text alerts told them that school was closed for snow in the winter.

"Vacations." They wouldn't want to plan to go to the beach if there was a hurricane forecast.

"Builders." Papa mentioned that you wouldn't want to pour concrete on a job if it was going to rain.

"Ski resorts." Sophie's family recently had been on a ski trip and she knew how important it was to know if there would be plenty of snow.

"Farmers." I told them that my father farmed and he watched the weather constantly to know when to plant and when to harvest.

"TV and radio stations." Without knowing the weather they wouldn't have a show and no one would watch.

"Fishermen." Again, Papa spoke from experience. "Some fish don't bite if the weather conditions are not favorable."

"And you aren't supposed to go out in a boat if it's going to storm," added Jake.

"Shoppers." The girls were definitely the experts in this field. "You don't want to go shopping if it's going to rain, unless you go to the mall." They also admitted they liked to know about the weather to plan what to wear. "You don't want to show off your cute new shorts if it's going to be snowing."

I told them that meteorologists are a bit like pastors of a church.

"Is this a joke?" Caleb asked, skeptically.

"No joke," I responded. "People only see pastors preach or lead a service for about one hour once a week, but hours and hours of preparation go into the service that they don't see. A meteorologist on TV may have five minutes to give the weather forecast, but hours each day go into that forecast."

"Amen!" declared Papa, enthusiastically.

Satellites and Radar

I knew that Caleb would be interested in satellites and radar, so I mentioned a few facts about how they are used in meteorology. (I didn't tell him that my notes were about the extent of my knowledge on this subject).

Meteorologists rely heavily on weather satellites which are placed from 500 to about 22,000 miles up in orbit around the earth. That's about one-tenth of the way to the moon.

The first successful weather satellite was named TIROS-1, set in orbit in 1960. Its name stands for Television Infrared Observation Satellite. It changed weather forecasting forever. Today, there are many weather satellites in space, becoming more and more sophisticated in what they can detect.

Papa added some information about RADAR, which is also essential in accurate weather forecasting. RADAR is an acronym for Radio Detection and Ranging. He became familiar with RADAR in air defense artillery while serving in the Army. They used it to detect aircraft.

He told us that a specific type used to detect weather conditions is called Doppler RADAR, named for Christian Doppler, an Austrian scientist from the 1800s.

After the discovery of radio waves in 1887, about forty years after Doppler's death, his research helped scientists detect precipitation intensity, wind direction and speed, and provide estimates of hail size and rainfall amounts. Today, meteorologists who use Doppler RADAR can even measure how fast the drops of rain in a cloud are moving.

As suspected, Caleb was fascinated with all of this information, the rest of the children not so much. But they continued to concentrate on their coloring sheets.

"Where do you think it is hardest to forecast weather?" I asked.

Everyone had a guess. "The desert?" "The ocean?" "China?" "The North Pole?"

Finally, Caleb guessed correctly, "Near mountains."

Mountains get much stronger winds, more temperature changes, more clouds, more rain and snow, and more sudden thaws than anywhere else on earth. This makes accurate forecasting much more difficult. Since our house was at sea level, we felt we had a good chance to predict our weather with some simple tools.

The Farmer's Almanac

I gave each of the children a current copy of *The Farmer's Almanac*.[137] It has progressed a lot in looks and information since the first booklet was published during George Washington's first term as president of the United States.

As America's oldest, continuously-published periodical, it comes out annually in September. The original editor, Robert Thomas, had the successful vision of informing the public about astronomical events, such as the daily rising and setting times of the sun, the tide tables, and the weather forecast. He had a secret weather forecasting system that is locked away in a black tin box in the *Almanac* offices in Dublin, New Hampshire. He was amazingly accurate and edited the booklet for more than fifty years, until the day he died of old age.

An interesting story about *The Almanac's* popularity concerns a German spy who was apprehended by the FBI in New York City, in 1942. The spy had a copy of that year's *Almanac* in his coat pocket. It seems that the Germans were using its accurate weather forecasts to determine their military moves.

Current issues of the booklet feature weather, astronomy, gardening, recipes, and advice on numerous other subjects. Looking up the information for our particular day in our region, the children were especially interested to learn when the low tides would occur so they could scour the beach to see what items of interest may have washed up.

Although meteorologists don't give much credence to Thomas' secret formula, whatever it was, the book is still widely read by farmers today who plant and harvest their crops according to its predictions. My grandfather, who farmed as well as owned a hardware, feed and seed store, always had the current issue of *The Almanac* beside his bed. He read it every night to learn about what the weather would be the next day and the best predictions for when to plant crops.

The Law of Unintended Consequences

This term, popularized in the twentieth century, refers to outcomes of events that are quite different from the ones planned and foreseen. The unexpected results can sometimes be beneficial or can sometimes be disastrous. Caleb and Sophie were especially interested in what some of

---

[137] *Old Farmer's Almanac*, Yankee Publishing, Inc, 2016.

these consequences were.

"Are they always about weather?"

"No, they're about a variety of subjects."

"Like what?"

Knowing the older children had very inquisitive minds, I was prepared to give some examples. There were numerous accounts online, so I selected several that I thought the children would enjoy hearing about

For instance, when some state and local governments issued gun buy-back programs to decrease the number of guns in society, the number of guns on the street and gun-related crime actually increased. In 1999, the Oakland California Police Department bought guns in any condition from private citizens to get as many guns off the streets as possible. However, an independent institute discovered that people were selling their non-working guns, taking the money, and buying new guns.

"Why wouldn't the police think of that ahead of time?" asked Jake. This initiated an interesting conversation about guns that would have continued longer if I had not interrupted with another example of an unintended consequence.

During colonial rule in India, the British governor of Delhi, India, attempted to alleviate an infestation of cobras. He put a very lucrative bounty on the capture of the dangerous snakes. Instead of reducing the number of cobras, however, their numbers increased, because enterprising Indians started breeding cobras for profit.

Even Edie and Anna, who had been absorbed in their coloring pages, thought this was very enterprising of the snake breeders. However, they both declared emphatically, "I hate snakes!"

In 2008, Airbus decided to redesign its A380 airplane so that the engine noise level was greatly reduced, thinking that the quiet would be appreciated by the passengers. Instead, the plane's inside noises from lavatories, people coughing, sneezing, talking, crying babies, and noises from the galley, etc., caused passengers and crew to complain. The outside sound reduction remedies were recalled by Airbus.

For an example closer to home, we talked about the eggs we collected straight from our chicken coop. Occasionally some eggs had chicken poop on them, although not very often because we kept our nesting boxes filled with clean straw.

If you find dirty eggs, the natural instinct is to scrub them well so that you will have spotless eggs stored in the refrigerator. All commercial eggs sold in American grocery stores are required to be scrubbed in a bleaching solution. However, in doing so, much of the important protective covering from the eggs is removed and actually makes them more vulnerable for infection. Eggs that have been scrubbed must be refrigerated immediately and used sooner.

"So what do you do with the poop if you don't wash the dirty eggs?" Anna wanted to know.

"You wipe the eggs carefully with a paper towel, moistening it if you need to. Or you can use a sanding sponge. Just don't scrub them with water or any kind of cleaning solution."

One of the most relevant examples of the Law of Unintended Consequences was the ordinance banning texting and driving. If a police officer sees someone texting in a car, the driver is stopped and possibly ticketed. It sounds like a great solution to a serious driving hazard.

However, statistics show that texting accidents increased because, instead of texting with the phone on the top of the steering wheel where the driver could also view the road, drivers began to text with their phones in their laps, thereby causing more accidents.

There was so much discussion about these topics that we could have gone on all morning, but now, it was time to apply this law to weather. I told them about the Butterfly Effect, a name originally given to a symbolic example of a small, seemingly insignificant incident leading to something of major proportions.

A scientific question was posed: *Is it possible that a butterfly flapping its wings in the Amazon rain forest can set in motion a chain of events resulting in a major tornado in the Midwest weeks later?* Some people think such small actions form weather patterns. This is also known as the Chaos Theory.

Those who take such theories seriously have concern about the growing numbers of large scale wind farms, with turbines constantly turning to produce electricity. Will they change the patterns of our weather after years of use? This is something that scientists and weather-savvy people will debate for a long time.

Weather Proverbs and Traditions

Red sky at night, sailor's delight. Red sky at morning, sailors take warning. This is a very old, well-known saying that has proven to be an accurate forecast of the weather.

The reason that we see a red sunset is because the sun is low in the sky and its light passes through additional atmosphere. It is a beautiful phenomenon and is even enhanced if there is a region of high atmospheric pressure. We would talk about high and low pressures later. But for the present, we explained that high atmospheric pressure suppresses cloud formations and holds air contaminants near the earth. These "contaminants" scatter the colors of sunlight and cause the reddening effect in the west.

"Highs" usually bring good weather, so red skies in the evening indicate that fair weather probably is approaching from the west.

On the other hand, if the sky looks red in the eastern morning sky, the high pressure region has already passed through.

Jesus once referred to this ancient proverb. He lived by the Sea of Galilee and was often in boats on the water with His friends, many of whom were commercial fishermen. They lived with a constant awareness of the weather, much like people who work on or near the water still do.

Jesus said, *When evening comes, you say "It will be fair weather, for the sky is red," and in the morning, "Today it will be stormy, for the sky is red and overcast." You know how to interpret the appearance of the sky, but you cannot interpret the signs of the times.*[138]

A well-tested weather warning from the physiological realm is the increase of aches and pains in people's joints before a storm. This effect is associated with the barometric pressure. When the barometer falls before a storm, tiny bubbles of gas within the body may expand and exert a painful force against nerves. This is especially noticeable with bunions, arthritic joints, sensitive teeth, and headaches.

It is obvious that some animals have a keen sense of an approaching storm as well. Our dog, Ramsey, can tell up to an hour before it rains, even though it appears to be clear and sunny. She refuses to go outside and retreats under our bed. No amount of coaxing will get her to come out until the barometer rises again and the storm has passed. She is a more accurate predictor of rain at our house than the local forecaster.

Scientists have studied the behavior of groundhogs, caterpillars, ducks, fiddler crabs, birds, and fish, trying to learn their weather secrets. Air pressure affects their behavior markedly. No one has ever asked to study Ramsey, however.

Another popular proverb is: *Swallows fly high, clear blue sky. Swallows fly low, rain we shall know.* The children decided a better saying would be: *Ramsey at play, a beautiful day. Under the bed, rain instead.*

Because groundhogs react immediately to pressure changes, a national Groundhog Day was established for February 2 of every year to observe a groundhog's reactions to the weather as a prediction for spring.

This holiday was institutionalized in 1887, by the citizens of Punxsutawney, Pennsylvania, who adopted a town groundhog that they named Phil. Soon an elaborate ceremony was formed around the observation of Punxsutawney Phil at dawn every February 2. If it was sunny and the groundhog saw his shadow, it would indicate six more weeks of

---

[138] Matthew 16:1-3

winter weather. If it was cloudy when he came out of his burrow, it would indicate an early spring.

Phil, now known as "The National Groundhog Day Meteorologist," is the star of an annual summer Groundhog Picnic and Phil Phest, sponsored by the Punxsutawney Groundhog Club at Gobbler's Knob.

In reality, Phil's predictions are not very accurate. His average of being correct is only 39 percent.

The tradition of watching an animal on February 2 to predict the weather is also observed in France, where they watch bears come out of their caves, and in Germany, where farmers watch for badgers.

Why February 2? It began as a German Christian holiday called *Candlemas*. It commemorated the presentation of the infant Jesus being taken by His parents to the Temple for His dedication ceremony. At that time, an old, devout man named Simeon saw Jesus in the Temple and declared that the child would one day become a light for revelation to the Gentiles.[139]

The early church celebrated this event with a parade of people carrying candles. Thus: *Candlemas*. It was said, *"For as the sun shines on Candlemas day, so far will the snow swirl in May."* Many German immigrants settled in Pennsylvania, bringing the legend with them.

How groundhogs got involved? Who knows?

Each child received a coloring sheet of Punxsutawney Phil coming out of his burrow and a fun fact sheet, spoofing the famous little groundhog. It contained legendary information such as the following:

1. Punxsutawney Phil is the only true weather forecasting groundhog. All the others are imposters.
2. Punxsutawney Phil gets his longevity from drinking "groundhog punch" which is a secret recipe. At the Groundhog Picnic every summer, he takes one sip of the punch, which adds another seven years to his life.
3. When Phil makes his weather prediction every year, he only whispers to the Groundhog Club president in Groundhogese. His proclamation is then translated to the rest of the world.
4. He was named Phil for King Philip, a Native American chief who fought against American colonists in 1676.

Back Yard Weather Station

After Snack Time we started to put some of our newly-acquired weather knowledge to work. Each child was given a graph-lined sheet of

---

[139] Luke 2:32

paper with the heading: **Weather Log**. It was divided into the following categories:

**Date   General Weather Condition   Barometric Pressure
Temperature   Wind Direction   Wind Speed   Humidity
Precipitation   Clouds**

To collect the information for each category, our plan was to set up our own backyard weather station. Here is where Papa's knowledge and experience would be center stage.

Our weather station would include a **thermometer** to record temperature, a **rain gauge** to measure rainfall, a **weather vane** and **wind sock** to determine wind direction, a **barometer** to measure atmospheric pressure, an **anemometer** to measure wind speed, and a **hygrometer** to measure humidity. Each day the children would record their findings onto their Weather Logs.

Wind Sock

Our first task was to make a wind sock to show us the direction of the wind. The boys took a large bucket down to the beach, found a level spot, and filled it with sand. The girls made a colorful pennant from some old fabric and stapled it to the top of a discarded broom handle. They stuck the pole into the sand-filled bucket.

With Papa's compass, they determined north, south, east and west, and marked these with a wide marker on the sides of the bucket. The pole was tall enough so that they could observe the wind sock blowing in the breeze down on the beach while they were inside the house.

Barometer

The next project was to make a barometer. Papa explained that although air is light, it has mass and therefore does have some weight.

Barometers are somewhat like scales to measure the weight of the air, from sea level to the top of the atmosphere, about fifty miles up.

Barometers get their name from the Greek word *baros* which means "weight."

Obviously, if a bigger person steps on a scale to weigh, the reading is higher than when a small person weighs. In the same way, if the air is denser, the column of air above the barometer will be heavier and the reading will be higher. Less dense air will have a lower barometric pressure.

"But, what makes the air light or heavy?" Sophie wanted to know.

Papa tried to explain it without being too technical. "Let's say that you are in an area where the air pressure is high."

"That means it has more weight, right?" she asked.

"Yes, and it also means that the average temperature of that column of air is cold, even though it may not be cold on the ground."

Sophie thought about this for a few seconds and then asked, "So is low pressure air warmer?"

"The average temperature of the fifty-mile-high column of air is warmer, but it may not be warmer on the ground."

You could tell that Sophie was tempted to give up but, admirably, she persevered.

"But why do we need to know if the pressure is high or low?"

Papa kept it simple. "Because low atmospheric pressure tends to promote rain or snow. High pressure areas tend to produce fewer clouds and fairer weather. What kind of barometric pressure do you think you would have if you were in a hurricane?"

They all agreed, "Low pressure!"

Air pressure affects many things besides weather. For instance, the air pressure affects how high a cake will rise when baking. This is why temperatures, times, and proportions of leavening ingredients in recipes are different when people cook at high altitudes, where the air pressure is lower.

I asked the children some hypothetical questions to make sure they understood the concept of atmospheric pressure that was new to them.

"Let's suppose it's a beautiful sunny morning and we're planning a picnic for later in the day. You look at the barometer and notice that it is falling. Will it stay sunny?"

They were all quiet for a few minutes, thinking about how this applied to their new lesson. Finally Sophie blurted out, "We'd better plan to do something else!"

She was congratulated for her correct answer and Anna and Edie both said that they were about to say the same thing. I gave them another chance.

"You want to go to the park this afternoon. You check the barometer and it is a higher reading that it was yesterday. The barometric pressure is rising but it is cloudy. You are wondering if you will be able to go or if rain will ruin your plans."

They talked it through and everybody agreed, "Go to the park!"

Papa continued with information about atmospheric pressure. "Everyone walks around in about fifteen pounds of air pressure all the time and we are not aware of it. Air is held to the earth by gravity, just as we are."

He asked the children to put out their hands, palms up, imagining that a column of air about the size of a garden hose fifty miles high was pressing onto each hand.

"The weight of that amount of air is more than the weight of a bowling ball. Now, imagine several such columns on your hands. Each hand is feeling more than one hundred pounds of weight. The air pressure is not just pushing down from above, but from all sides and the bottom, too, equally in all directions. Amazingly, you aren't aware of it."

However, each child immediately felt their hands too heavy to hold them out any longer.

Then Papa asked them to put a hand over their mouth and make a tight seal by sucking the skin of their hand into their mouth. They were removing the air pressure from that part of the hand. The atmospheric pressure and the air from the other side of their hand pushed in with the equivalent weight of a bowling ball.

Each child had a plastic water bottle on the table left over from Snack Time. Those who had an empty bottle were asked to remove the top and put the small opening of the bottle into their mouth. They were told to suck the air out of the bottle and we watched their bottles collapse.

Without the air pressure inside the bottle, the outside pressure and its weight caused the bottle to implode. Air is heavy!

Those who still had water in their bottles were given a straw. They sucked up some water into the straw and, with a finger, blocked off the opening of the straw that had been in their mouth. The water stayed in the straw.

"Why?"

Caleb knew instantly. "Because the only place air pressure can get in the straw is from the bottom so it holds the water in the straw."

As soon as they removed their fingers, the air pressure from the top equalized what was in the straw and gravity took over, making the water fall out of the straw, and of course, all over the table. We had to pause for a clean-up. But it was only water.

I gave the children a sheet of paper with pictures of various types of barometers, from very simple ones to those that are more sophisticated. Papa explained the different pictures and how the barometers work.

The first known barometer was made by Evangelista Torricelli in 1643. He used a small glass bowl which he filled with mercury, inserting a glass straw vertically into the mercury. He called it a **weather glass.** He created a vacuum, much like we did with the straws in the water bottles, and sealed the open end. He observed that the atmospheric pressure on the surface of the mercury in the bowl forced the mercury up into the straw. He also noticed that as the weather changed, the level of the mercury in the glass straw varied.

Meteorologists who use **mercury barometers** report the barometric readings of so many inches. This is the height the air pushes mercury up a tube in this kind of barometer.

Scientists later developed **aneroid barometers.** This device has a round dial like a clock and does not use liquid of any kind. Rather, it contains small cells (or capsules) stacked together and held in place by a strong spring. Tiny changes in the external air pressure cause the cells to expand or contract. The movement drives mechanical levers so that the smallest movements are amplified and displayed on the face of the barometer.

This is the kind of barometer that is common in homes, small boats and planes, and is also frequently used in meteorology. In fact we had a large outdoor clock on our back porch that included a small aneroid barometer.

We made two barometers for our weather station, both of them very simple to put together, using common objects. First, Jake put about two inches of water into a clear glass measuring cup with a little pouring spout and Edie added some food coloring. She chose purple.

Then Caleb took an empty, clear plastic water bottle, removed the label and set it upside down in the cup, with the opening below the purple water line, but not touching the bottom. We had to make sure our cup and bottle were the right diameters to suspend the bottle.

On the side of the cup, Sophie marked the level of the water that was in the bottle.

Our second barometer used a jar with a balloon stretched tightly over the opening. We secured it with a rubber band. On the top of the balloon we taped a thin, wooden skewer, with most of it hanging off one side. Anna drew scaled markings on the face of a manila file folder which would stand vertically when partially opened. Her scale consisted of a vertical line divided into quarter inch increments. Edie placed the folder near the end of the skewer so that any movement up or down could be charted.

The job of our aspiring meteorologists was to check their barometers every day to note the water level in the bottle and the vertical movement of the end of the skewer.

Higher air pressure pushed the water down in the plastic cup, allowing it to rise in the bottle. If there was an approaching storm, the air pressure dropped, causing the water level to rise in the plastic cup and fall in the bottle.

Similarly, rising atmospheric pressure would depress the surface of the balloon, causing the free end of the skewer to rise. Lower air pressure would allow the balloon surface to rise, causing the free end of the skewer to drop.

We would attempt to chart any patterns that developed, plus we would observe Ramsey.

Thermometer

The outside clock on our porch also included a thermometer. Therefore finding the temperature every day was easy. It would be recorded on the Weather Logs. Papa told them that the temperature is determined by how fast the air molecules move around. When they speed up, the temperature increases.

Rain Gauge

The simplest way for us to measure precipitation was to place a straight-sided glass measuring cup with clearly marked increments out in the open. If we got any rain at all, we would record the amount on the Weather Log.

Hygrometer

A hygrometer measures the humidity which is the amount of water vapor in the air at a given time. One of the most common ways to see the effects of high humidity is to look at human hair. When hair is damp it makes curly hair more curly and straight hair straighter. Hair can absorb moisture from the air and become two percent longer or two percent curlier.

All the girls had stories about bad hair days, most of them complaining that their hair became unmanageable and limp on rainy days. My hair has just the opposite effect. It becomes much frizzier when the air is damp

Now we knew that the reason for the changes was because each hair strand absorbed so much moisture from the air. This fact is so dependable that we used hair in our homemade hygrometer to determine the humidity.

Each of the girls contributed a long hair. This was not a huge sacrifice because each one had a full head of very long hair. Their hair had become a joke in the family because when Sophie would come to visit when she was little I had a very hard time getting out the tangles each morning. (Remember, I only raised boys).

She would cry and I would get impatient. I mentioned that my grandmother used to tell me that morning hair looked like rats' nests. But this old family proverb only make her cry harder. Finally, one summer, with her permission, I cut her hair. She and I both loved it but her mother, Margo, was pretty upset. Every summer after that, when Margo would send Sophie to Camp Mimi, her parting words were, "I love you! Don't let Mimi cut your hair!"

Edie and Anna now had long hair, too. However, when they were about three years old they decided to cut one another's hair. The best things I can say about their efforts are that no one got hurt and the styles were interesting. Somewhat like unconstructed, asymmetrical Sassoon haircuts from the '70s, they were odd but they had character. Even after a professional hairdresser attempted to give them some shape, they had awkward looking hair for many months. It did make morning brush-outs very simple, though.

Once the sacrificial hairs were collected, laid out on a white piece of paper, correctly labeled with the donors' names and compared for length, we were ready to roll.

With a mild solution of alcohol and water, the girls wiped each hair strand, using cotton balls. This was to remove any oils or hair conditioner so that moisture would permeate the strands more easily. Then we allowed them to dry completely while we set up our base.

Meanwhile, the boys, who so far had contributed nothing to this project except offers to extract the girls' hairs, were in charge of putting the base together. I had assembled everything they needed for this job in an old shoe box. There was a block of wood (a 2"x4" about 10" long), a thin piece of plastic (we used a plastic lid), a large nail, a small nail, a dime, a glue stick, some tape, a hammer, and some scissors.

Caleb made a triangle out of a 3x3" piece of flat, thin plastic. We told him to cut an isosceles triangle and he knew just what to do. Explaining it to his little brother, he measured and cut out a triangle with two sides of the same length. This became the pointer for our hygrometer.

Jake was excited to get the nails and a hammer. He was always ready to pound something. With the large nail, he made a hole in the middle of the short side of the plastic triangle. This was the base. Caleb taped the dime near the point of the triangle.

Using the small nail, Jake nailed through the large hole he had just made in the triangle, securing it loosely to the lower fourth of the block of wood. This allowed the plastic pointer to spin freely. He hammered the large nail into the wood block about six inches above the plastic pointer.

The final job was to attach the hair and we let the contributors do this. By this time they couldn't tell which hair came from which girl so they just chose one. Edie wrapped a hair strand around the top nail, gently stretching it down to the point of the triangle. Anna put a spot of glue on the pointer and Sophie pressed the hair into the glue, holding it for a few seconds to let it dry.

When we shifted the wooden block to stand vertically, the point of the triangle, weighted by the dime, pulled the strand of hair taut. The triangle pointed horizontally, suspended from the hair. With more moisture in the air, the hair expanded and lengthened, making the triangle pointer tip down.

When the air was dryer, the hair contracted, and the tip of the pointer rose.

Caleb carefully made marks on the block with a marker, showing the position of the pointer. We took it into the bathroom, closed the door and turned on a hot shower for a few minutes. There was a noticeable change in the pointer from the humidity in the room.

We placed it on a table on the covered back porch so that we could check any changes in the humidity during the day.

Anemometer

Their next prepared shoe box contained items to assemble a device to measure the wind. In the box they found five small paper cups, a hole punch, scissors, very sticky tape (we used masking tape), three thin wooden dowels, and an empty plastic water bottle.

Sophie, who declared that she loved to use hole punches, made a hole in the side of each of four paper cups, making sure each one was identical in placement. On the fifth cup, she made four holes spaced evenly around the rim. This fifth cup became the center of our anemometer.

Edie slid two of the wooden dowels through the holes in the center cup. They crossed in an "X" in the center.

Anna inserted the ends of the dowels into the holes of the other cups and Caleb taped them into place. He made sure that each cup faced in the same direction.

Jake used the last dowel to make a hole in the bottom of the center cup. He pushed it up until it met the "X" and Caleb taped it securely.

Finally, Jake set the center dowel into the empty water bottle.

We took it for a test drive on the riding lawn mower. Papa drove and the children took turns riding with him, holding the anemometer to see how increased wind speed caused the cups to turn faster. They tried counting how many rotations occurred in 60 seconds. To make it easier, Caleb marked one of the four cups with a red marker.

It takes a bit of math to accurately determine the approximate wind speed but Papa told them not to be intimidated. He talked them through the process. After they counted the number of revolutions the anemometer made in 60 seconds, we all went back to the Camp Mimi table. They measured the distance in inches from center to center of two cups on opposite sides of the anemometer. This gave them its diameter.

He told them to multiply the diameter by 3.14 to get the circumference of the anemometer.

"That's *pi*!" Caleb shouted.

"Pie?" Jake suddenly got more interested. When Caleb explained that it was an ancient math symbol, he looked disappointed.

Caleb and Sophie ran to get their phones which had calculators to do the multiplication. Papa chose to do it the old-fashioned way with pen and paper. They came up with the same number, but Papa was somewhat faster. They then divided the number they got by 12 to get the circumference in feet.

The younger children were quickly losing interest and went back to coloring pages, but the older two stuck with it.

The next step was to multiply the circumference by the revolutions per minute. This gave them the distance the anemometer would travel in a minute.

That result was multiplied by 60 to get the distance in feet per hour.

Finally, that number was divided by 5,280 to get the distance in miles per hour. Ta-da! They had the wind speed!

"Whew!" Sophie gasped as she fell back in her chair. "That was hard!"

The younger three wanted to know when they could ride the mower again.

Clouds

Finally, the old-fashioned reliable standby for weather prediction was put into play. We used our common sense. What do the clouds look like? What is their shape, their color and their placement?

We planned to study cloud formations on another day, but we made a special effort to start noticing how they change. On the coast, where we were, there were some amazing cloud formations. Once you start looking closely, you observe many varieties.

We had put in a full day of "weather work" by lunch time. Everyone was more than ready for swimming and relaxation. It was very hot outside and we had spent a lot of time in the heat working on our weather station.

After all of the day's readings were recorded, we just played in the water until everyone was ready for a rest in air conditioning!

Our late afternoon outing was our annual trip to Bellingrath Gardens. It was a good idea to go later in the day when it was slightly cooler. It was still very humid, however, and the children left the gardens with sweating bodies and red faces. As they thoroughly enjoyed icy cold bottles of water we had in a cooler in the car, they remarked that they bet the hygrometer's hair was really limp.

"Which way would the pointer go?" I asked.

They were unanimous in their answer,

"Down as far as possible!"

DAY 2 – ATMOSPHERE OF EARTH AND HEAVEN

The first thing the children wanted to do when they got up on our second day was to check the weather conditions so that they could fill in the blanks on their Weather Logs. Although they could see the wind sock from the house, everyone still wanted to go to the beach, even though they were still in pajamas. The weather check provided a great reason to do so.

After noting the wind direction, scouring the shore for any washed up treasures and throwing a stick in the water for the dog to retrieve for a while, all of the other weather station devices were duly observed and recorded. I watched from the house while making their breakfast.

Later, when we finally gathered at the Camp Mimi Table for our morning lesson I told them we were going to talk about atmosphere.

"That's air," declared Anna with authority.

"Yes, it's air and even more. First, let's talk about some facts of what air is. There are many gases in the air we breathe." I showed them the list:

Nitrogen (78%)
Oxygen (21%)
Argon (.93%)
Carbon Dioxide (.035%)

Other gases (.035%). Some of the other gases include Neon, Helium, Methane, Krypton, Hydrogen, Carbon Monoxide, Xenon, Ozone, and Radon.

Caleb immediately said, "I can't wait until I can take chemistry!"

"Think about how perfect God's plan is for our air. If there was any more oxygen in our air, spontaneous fires would break out worldwide. If there was any less we could not breathe. If the level of carbon dioxide was larger, the earth would be too warm. If it was any less, plants would starve. Do you remember that after God created it all, He blessed it and saw it was **good**?"[140]

Papa's response to that was, "The word **good** seems like an understatement!"

I continued on, "Now, let's look at some facts about our atmosphere."

I asked them to take a sharpened pencil and draw a circle about two inches in diameter on a piece of paper. It didn't have to be perfect.

Jake wanted it to be noted that he had sharpened all the colored pencils and placed them neatly in the little red buckets we used to contain selections at each end of the table. He loved to use the electric pencil sharpener and his efforts were impressive.

I told them that the circle on their paper represented the earth. The earth's atmosphere is technically a thin blanket of gas that surrounds it.

Ninety-nine percent of our air is within twenty-five miles of the earth's surface. The depth of our atmosphere is less than the thickness of the pencil line they drew. It is vital to life on earth but it is limited.

Then we looked at a desk globe of the earth. If the earth was that size, the thickness of the atmosphere would be thinner than the edge of a dime. All weather, including clouds, storms, and precipitation occur in that thickness.

Another example for them related to the column of air pressure we

---

[140] Genesis 1:9

talked about the day before. If you could drive in a car straight up in the sky for about one hour, you would travel about fifty miles. At that point the air would run out. You would be in space, out of the earth's atmosphere, where there is no weather.

There was a chorus of "Wow!" around the table.

I gave each of them a chart showing the different layers of the atmosphere. They practiced saying the big words used to describe each layer, and colored each one a different color.

The lowest layer is about six miles high and is called the **Troposphere.** This is where all our weather occurs (winds, clouds, rain, etc.). It also is the highway for airplanes.

The middle layer of atmosphere, between six and thirty miles high, is called the **Stratosphere.** This is where the ozone layer is. The word literally means "flat" or "visibly layered." The air is very thin in this layer.

Although we didn't go into much detail, I mentioned the next known layers. The **Mesosphere** goes up to sixty miles, the **Ionosphere** up to six hundred miles, and then the **Thermosphere** and the **Exosphere.**

While they were coloring, I shared with them some verses from the Bible, found in 2 Corinthians 12:2-4. They were written by Paul and many people believe he was referring to a personal experience.

He said, "I know a man in Christ who fourteen years ago was caught up to the third heaven. Whether it was in the body or out of the body I do not know—God knows. And I know that this man—whether in the body or apart from the body I do not know, but God knows—was caught up to paradise and heard inexpressible things, things that no one is permitted to tell."

The experience was so real to him that it changed his life. He didn't know if he really went there, if he had a vision from God, or if it was a dream. All he knew was that it seemed more real than life on earth and that he learned things so awesome that he could not repeat them.

"Can you imagine such a thing happening to you?" I asked.

Of course, none of them had any points of reference to Paul's experience, but all agreed that they would like to.

"If God was present with the amazing revelations Paul experienced in the third heaven, what is in the first and second heavens?"

They all agreed that the first heaven must be earth's atmosphere where air, clouds, wind and weather are present. After some discussion, they decided that the second heaven must be the region of outer space with sun, moon, stars and planets. This is the heaven that God created in Genesis.

The third heaven must then be above the earth, its atmosphere, and above outer space. This is the location of what the Bible refers to as God's throne and Paradise.

I read Ephesians 4:10 to them. It speaks of Jesus who descended to earth and then, after His resurrection, ascended back to heaven. "He who descended is the very one who ascended higher than all the heavens, in order to fill the whole universe."

My next question to the children was, "Now that we know a little bit about the atmosphere of earth, what do we know about the atmosphere of heaven, where God dwells?"

Most of the children thought you couldn't know anything about it until you die. However, I reminded them that Paul didn't die when he had his revelation. Also, the Bible tells us a lot about heaven. I mentioned a few verses that paint pictures for us.

Paul didn't have an adequate language to describe what he experienced in heaven. Heaven must be so far beyond the realm of anything we humans experience on earth that there are simply no words to describe it.

When Jesus tried to depict the Kingdom of God (or Heaven), He only used similes. He said it was like a treasure hidden in a field,[141] a landowner who hired workers in his vineyard,[142] a farmer who sowed good seed,[143] a mustard seed,[144] yeast used to make bread,[145] a merchant seeking pearls,[146] a cast net,[147] and many other examples. Together, all of His descriptions add different colors into a painting of the Kingdom of God. It seems that even Jesus could not use human language to adequately describe its magnificence.

John, too, had difficulty writing what God showed him about heaven. In the book of Revelation, he could only give snippets about the grandeur that is truly *other worldly* in an atmosphere where "God wipes away every tear, death is extinct, and no one mourns, cries, or is in pain anymore."[148]

John wrote about a river of life, flowing from God's throne, throughout the main street of the City of God. He described the tree of life growing there, causing us to wonder if it is the same one that was in the Garden of Eden. John saw that it continually bears fruit and that its leaves are for healing. He wrote that there is no darkness at all in heaven because the brilliant light of God overcomes it.[149]

John saw twelve gates around the City of God, each made of pearl. He said the street where the river of life flowed was made of transparent gold.[150]

---

[141] Matthew 13:44

[142] Matthew 20:1

[143] Matthew 13:24-53

[144] Matthew 13:31

[145] Matthew 13:33

[146] Matthew 13:45

[147] Matthew 13:47

[148] Revelation 21:4

[149] Revelation 22:1-5

That image is unusual since no one has ever seen gold like that. Perhaps that was the best way he could find to describe something totally beyond his scope of knowledge

He saw a huge wall around the City of God, built of a precious stone which he called jasper, and adorned with every other kind of precious jewel.

All three girls, who love jewelry, wanted to know what jasper was. Fortunately, I had looked this up because I knew that our modern name "jasper" for a stone denotes one that is very dull in color, either dark red, blue or green. It certainly is not that beautiful. I also remembered that one of the stones in the high priest's breastplate was jasper.

After reading several scholarly accounts of the origin of the word, I found out that most authorities agree that the ancient *jaspar* was such a rare and perfect stone, it could only be compared to a perfect diamond today, clear and brilliant.

We talked about the pictures this description evokes. It was said that Solomon's Temple was so brilliant that when pilgrims walked up to Jerusalem, they were nearly blinded by its beauty in the sunlight. Can't you imagine the blinding beauty of the New Jerusalem, the City of God, surrounded by a huge wall of crystal clear diamond? And, picture the twelve gates of pearl within its walls. Truly, it is beyond description!

We also know from Jesus' own description of Heaven, that there is a special place for every believer within the walls of the City. Jesus told us that He was going to Heaven to prepare just such a place. He described these places as rooms, chambers, mansions, dwelling places, or tabernacles, according to the translation you read.[151]

Perhaps He was speaking of a sense of belonging or of home for each believer, rather than a literal, individual house as we know it in this world? Perhaps He wanted us to know that each believer will become an intimate, unique part of God's family, belonging in a way we cannot now imagine?

Immersed in all the vivid images of Heaven, Anna asked, "Mimi, do you believe God is really sitting on a big throne in Heaven?"

God was using her imagination in a holy way and I affirmed to her that Psalm 103 says that God has established His throne in heaven.[152] But I also suggested that, instead of a big, ornate chair as we know it, the description of God's throne from David, the psalmist, might be a word picture to tell us that God reigns over all.

Our discussion was a great way to convey to the children that imagery and symbols speak to our hearts far more than mere words describing

---

[150] Revelation 21:21-25

[151] John 14:2

[152] Psalm 103:19

something. The wisdom of God in giving us such powerful symbols of a place and life we have yet to experience make living in our present life rich with anticipation for what is yet to come.

This discussion was never intended to be as lengthy as it turned out to be. We were surprised at how interested the children were about the third Heaven and life after death for believers.

I played a CD for them called "Heaven – The City of God."[153] It is a recording Kirk Dearman and I made using the words of scripture to describe Heaven as it is revealed to us biblically. Kirk, our "Journey to Wholeness" conference worship leader for many years, inserted the beautiful background music. All of the children put down their crayons and listened very attentively. They were quiet at the end.

Finally, Sophie asked, "Have you ever known anyone who has seen Heaven like Paul or John?"

Actually, we knew a woman years ago who had been declared dead during open heart surgery. After a few minutes she was resuscitated and had vivid memories of an experience she had no words to relate. Much like Paul, she could only say that it was beyond description. Her life was dramatically changed after that experience. She burst into tears every time she attempted to talk about what she experienced, and her focus on what mattered in this life turned from daily cares to things of eternal value.

Within the last year Conlee and I had read *Heaven is for Real*,[154] the true story of a three year old boy named Colton Burpo. Written by his father, Pastor Todd Burpo, the account tells of Colton's near death experience when his appendix ruptured after a misdiagnosis.

Gradually, Colton was able to articulate some of the experiences he had while he was so near death. He knew accurate details of relatives who had died before he was born and related intimate conversations he had with them in Heaven.

The child was also able to recall precisely where his father had been and what he had been doing while Colton was undergoing emergency surgery. As if watching events from an out of body experience, he glimpsed things only hinted about in scripture and knew enough details to prove they were true.

Each of the children was so fascinated with this account that we began reading the book about Colton's experience aloud each night before bedtime. It was an opportunity to discuss the weighty subject of death and dying with children in a perfectly appropriate way that increased faith and

---

[153] "Heaven – The City of God," Signa Bodishbaugh, music by Kirk Dearman, mastered by Dave Chatel, www.JTWIC.org, 2000.

[154] *Heaven is For Real*, Todd Burpo, Sonja Burpo, Colton Burpo, Lynn Vincent, Thomas Nelson Publisher, 2011.

eliminated fear.

I shared several other written testimonies of people's visions of being in Heaven and coming back to earth. However, no story touched the children's hearts like that of Colton Burpo.

DAY 3 – WIND AND HOLY SPIRIT

After checking our home weather station and recording the readings, everyone was settled in at the Camp Mimi table for our next aspect of weather. Today it was all about wind.

Conlee and I have gone through several hurricanes on the Gulf coast. They are terrifying experiences, physically draining both in preparation and cleanup, and can be life-threatening. We have been forced to evacuate our home many times, not knowing what we would find when we returned.

The children's most vivid experience with severe wind was the **Squall** which came up so suddenly at a previous Camp Mimi. They all began to talk at once, animatedly recalling every detail of the storm, the large limbs down, blocking the driveway, the heavy planters turned over and broken, the pool filled with outdoor furniture and beach umbrellas, and all of their inflatable pool toys blown away somewhere, never to be found again. It was short-lived but violent.

I explained that wind is air in motion. It moves from higher to lower pressure regions, much like water flowing downhill. When we have constant or steady air pressure, the wind diminishes.

"What makes the air pressure change?" Caleb wanted to know.

The pressure differences result from uneven heating of the earth by the sun. Most of the sun's radiation is absorbed near the middle of the earth.

Caleb knew instantly, "That's the equator!"

The air then moves both north and south. Along the way, the air is deflected in different directions and to different altitudes. While it moves, it distributes moisture across the face of the earth. It stirs the earth's atmosphere. Without the wind, severe hot and cold spots would persist at different locations.

Wind is usually described by the direction it blows from. A "west wind" blows from west to east.

We had a weather vane on the cupola on our barn's roof. It was a large brass heron, wings outspread. Unfortunately, it was old and didn't move freely as it should. But we went out and looked at it and I commented that most farmers have working weather vanes somewhere on their farms so they will know if a wind might bring dry air or moisture.

We'd already talked about the violent sudden winds called squalls. However, in some places a squall can bring unexpected snow as well as the rain we had experienced in our squall.

For a little trivia, I told them that the windiest location on earth was

Mount Washington in New Hampshire. That was surprising to all of us. One of the most astounding facts happening at that location was recorded on April 12, 1934. Winds roared there at 188 miles per hour for five minutes, then gusted to 231 miles per hour for five minutes. To put that in perspective, the strongest hurricane winds recorded anywhere were 200 miles per hour.

High winds do not necessarily make a hurricane more deadly. The largest losses of life during hurricanes are from storm surges and flooding. We looked at the international icon for a hurricane. It, unfortunately, is a symbol that brings terrible memories to anyone who has watched the little spinning circle with two blades barreling towards their own location on the weather map.

"Have you ever heard of a **Jet Stream**?" I asked the children.

"Oh, it's the smoke tail behind jet planes!" one of our more exuberant campers answered.

"That's a good guess, but that is actually called a "con-trail" and it is warm water vapor that comes from an aircraft engine that mixes with the cold air in the sky. It's full name means "condensation trail."

The jet stream is a ribbon-shaped river of air, several miles high and hundreds of miles wide. It moves from west to east in wavy patterns at speeds of 50-300 miles per hour.

It was first discovered by bomber pilots during the 1940s. When American pilots flew westward toward targets in Japan, they accidently entered into the jet stream and found it was hard to make good time flying. They were literally "swimming upstream" against the wind. They found that these "highways" of moving air completely circle the earth.

Pilots now avoid these channels of wind when flying west and often go with them when flying east. Flights from California to New York take an hour less than the east to west route because of this wind current. The jet stream roughly divides cold air from the warmer air masses. It can move weather patterns and storms along like a leaf.

The next weather term we introduced was one you hear a lot on the TV weather news. It's called a **Front.** This is a huge chunk of air mass with special characteristics. A front contains air that is different from the air it is moving into.

"Do you remember what it smells like when we have a lot of shrimp or crab shells in the garbage sack for a few days?"

"Eewww!" Everyone had a vivid memory of this disgusting odor.

If you keep the garbage sack tightly sealed outside in the garbage can it doesn't bother you before the garbage truck hauls it away. But if you open that sack in the house, it doesn't take long before the whole house smells bad. The smell wafts everywhere.

A front is like opening up some foreign air into your air. It can be unexpectedly warm or cold, but when it moves in you know it! You might hear the terms "warm front," "cold front," "stationary front," or "occluded front" (where warm and cold airs meet).

Next, we talked about some special kinds of winds. Our first one was the **Santa Ana Winds.** These are warm, dry winds associated with mountainous areas. As warmer air is forced up the windward side of a mountain range it cools and loses its moisture. Then, when it descends on the down-slope side of the mountain range, it warms up and increases in speed to as much as 125 miles per hour.

In the Rocky Mountains they call this wind a "Chinook." It is also known as a "snow-eater wind," because it melts and evaporates any snow in its path. It can dry out vegetation, fan brush and forest fires, scorch leaves and corn on its stalks, and even bake apples on their trees. There are records of this wind overturning trucks in California, and derailing trains in Montana.

While the children were discussing such winds among themselves, I turned in my Bible to Jeremiah 4:11 and asked Edie to read the prophecy from God.

"A scorching wind from the barren heights in the desert blows toward My people, but not to winnow or cleanse; a wind too strong for that comes from Me."

Jeremiah was prophesying a judgment on people who had rebelled against God. I reminded them that it might not be a literal wind that God would send but something in their lives that was just as destructive to get their attention so that they would turn back to God.

"It sounds like a Santa Ana wind to me," proclaimed Sophie.

God used the same imagery for another prophecy He gave to Ezekiel. I read to them Ezekiel 19:10-14, telling them to look for the symbols of such a destructive wind in the prophet's words intended to get the hearer's attention.

"Your mother was like a vine in your vineyard planted by the water; it was fruitful and full of branches because of abundant water. Its branches were strong, fit for a ruler's scepter. It towered high above the thick foliage conspicuous for its height and for its many branches. But it was uprooted in fury and thrown to the ground. The east wind made it shrivel, it was stripped of its fruit; its strong branches withered and fire consumed them. Now it is planted in the desert, in a dry and thirsty land. Fire spread from one of its main branches and consumed its fruit. No strong branch is left on it fit for a ruler's scepter."

We talked about how sad it was that something so beautiful and fruitful could be ruined by disobedience to God. The imagery of such a fierce, burning wind consuming something with such potential was sobering indeed. The final verse summed up the sentiment: "This is a lament and is to be used as a lament."

I explained to them that a lament was something that caused a person to be very sorrowful, sad, and full of grief for something of value that they had lost.

God has and will use forces of nature to speak to our hearts about the things He values most.

Next, I introduced **El Niño.** They all blurted out, "The boy!" Spanish classes in school took credit for this knowledge.

El Niño refers to an unusual ocean current that begins to flow eastward in the Pacific Ocean every two to six years. Moving along the equator, the winds cause the water to flow opposite its usual current. When this happens, it brings the most disruptive influence on world weather patterns. It brings unusually warm water to Peru, along the west coast of South America.

Because it often occurs around Christmas, the Spanish name refers to the Christ child.

The El Niño phenomenon affects weather patterns around the world in harmful ways. It is possible for the sea level to rise a foot more than normal and for coastal waters to increase in temperature by as much as fifteen degrees, upsetting commercial fishing, and causing temporary economic disasters for such countries as Peru and Ecuador.

Severe rain and windstorms occur in other South American countries, too. Bird populations disappear. Droughts and wildfires occur in Australia, along with flooding in Louisiana and massive amounts of rain in southern California. This shows how one small component of the environment can have global results.

Our last weather term for the morning was **Derecho**, a new term for all of us. We had word search pages and mazes to illustrate this weather condition.

The name is derived from a Spanish word that means "straight." Derechos are strong, straight-lined, huge storms that can have treacherous results. They can cause hurricane-force winds, tornadoes, severe thunderstorms and flash floods. They usually occur in summer with straight-line winds up to 100 miles per hour.

We had talked about some deadly and terrifying types of wind, so I suggested that we make a list of some of the more refreshing benefits of wind. The suggestions that came forth painted more positive images to take with us into Snack Time.

Flying kites. Wind chimes. Birds soaring. Wind mills. Pin wheels. Hot air balloons. Flags flying. Sail boats. Cool breeze. Ocean waves.

After snacks and a fun time running around outside, we settled in for the spiritual application to wind. I began with this statement, "Wind is like Holy Spirit." [155]

Jake wanted to make sure he was on board, "Like Father, Son, and Holy Spirit?"

"Exactly! Let's talk about why Spirit and wind go together."

In both Hebrew and Greek the words for *Spirit* also mean "breath" or "wind." We already talked about wind being moving air, and air being essential for human life. It is easy to make the connection of Holy Spirit being the presence of God in our midst, essential for spiritual life.

Wind has no material shape or visible form. It is invisible. We cannot see the source or destination, but we are aware of its presence. It is a mysterious unseen force, mostly known for its effects.

We see trees swaying, boats sailing, or balloons flying high. These same descriptions could be given of Holy Spirit's presence in the world. He is unseen but the results of His presence produce tangible fruit such as transformation, encouragement, profound lessons, and life-changing attitudes.

Wind is also powerful. It cannot be stopped or controlled by people. Its force is often under estimated. Holy Spirit, too, is not subject to human control. What people may consider impossible can become a reality under the power of Holy Spirit.

There are many varieties of wind. It can be a gentle, soft, refreshing breeze. It can also be a forceful hurricane, taking large objects down in its path.

Holy Spirit, too, works in many ways. He may bring God's love to a hurting child, healing love to a desperately ill person, or deliverance from the effects of evil to another.

In the Bible we see various kinds of Holy Spirit action. Lydia, a gentle woman in Thyatira, was a dealer of purple cloth. She heard Paul preach and Holy Spirit lovingly opened her heart to respond to his message.[156]

In the same area and near the same time, Holy Spirit responded to the prayers and praises of Paul and Silas while they were in prison. God sent His Holy Spirit with a violent earthquake that shook the foundations of the prison, causing the jailer to receive a transformed and believing heart.[157]

---

[155] I use to not use the article "the" when speaking of Holy Spirit. It is a reminder to me that He is a Person of the Trinity and not an object.

[156] Acts 16:14-15

I gave each child a sheet of paper with six pictures on it. They identified each one: fire, oil, wind, water, cloud, and a dove. These are the six primary symbolic ways God describes Holy Spirit to us in the Bible. Like attempting to describe the Kingdom of God, it is impossible to describe who Holy Spirit is in a few words. We need word pictures and similes.

Since the time that Noah landed on dry ground after the great flood, the **dove** has been a symbol of purity, peace and promise. Holy Spirit is frequently portrayed in pictures as a descending dove, coming to us from Heaven.

God uses the images of **fire** often to demonstrate His presence and power. There was a burning bush, a pillar of fire in the wilderness, the fire of the altar to consume the sacrifices, descriptions of "words like fire" to give importance to prophetic messages that changed hearts, tongues of fire at Pentecost, a baptism of Holy Spirit and fire, descriptions of consuming fires of hell for the unrepentant, and even the awesome words, "My God is a consuming fire."[158]

Oil has been used since biblical times to anoint kings and priests as a symbol of receiving authority. It has also been used for anointing the sick, believing that the presence of God is contained in the action and accompanying prayers.

To anoint with oil literally means to rub the oil into a person or object until the two become one. If we use the symbol of Holy Spirit with anointing oil, we are receiving God's presence incorporated into the fabric of our lives for His purposes.

Many references to Holy Spirit as **water** are in the Bible. Both Holy Spirit and water are cleansing and refreshing. Jesus is known as Living Water. We are symbolically washed from sin in baptismal waters. The Word of God washes us clean like water. In the City of God, the Spirit's presence is symbolized by the River of Life and the Crystal Sea flowing from the throne of God.

Besides the pillar of fire by night in the wilderness, God's presence was also denoted by the pillar of **cloud** by day. The cloud symbolizes the place where God dwells, also known as the holy cloud of His presence. A term from rabbinic writings describing this cloud is *shekinah*, which means "dwelling place." It is often associated with God's glory. Although the word is not found in the Bible, the *shekinah cloud of glory* is a description of Holy Spirit's power that many Christians use.

And finally, we find the description of God's presence moving in our midst as **wind.** A mighty wind blew at Mount Sinai as God gave Moses the Ten Commandments. The same mighty wind blew at Pentecost as Holy

---

[157] Acts 16:25-34

[158] Hebrews 12:29

Spirit entered the hearts of the believers gathered in the Upper Room. The prophet, Elijah, was taken up from earth into Heaven by the same kind of holy wind.

When we combine many biblical descriptions of Holy Spirit, we are inundated with a mountain of verbs. He is never described as passive. He is always moving, responding to the word of the Father. I showed the children a small list of action verbs taken from Bible verses about Holy Spirit. We read them together.

Holy Spirit *creates, conceives, births, renews, resurrects, revives, heals, empowers, speaks, pours, anoints, baptizes, delivers, counsels, convicts, convinces, teaches, overcomes, lifts, carries, sends, declares, controls, leads, directs, ordains, summons, sanctifies, prophesies, prays, fills, rejoices* – among many other actions!

We looked at the first mention of Holy Spirit in the Bible in Genesis 1:2. He was "brooding" or "hovering" over the waters during creation.

Brooding is a word commonly associated with chickens. When a chicken is "broody" she steadfastly focuses on the eggs she has laid, constantly sitting on them to keep them warm as life grows within them.

However, she is not passively sitting in a nest, she is continually moving and turning the eggs so that the chicks inside will develop properly. If they are not kept in motion, they will not hatch.

What an awesome picture of Holy Spirit, so focused on the creative work of the Father to bring the world as we know it into existence, that He was in motion (like a wind) to make sure that God's desire would bear fruit!

We talked about how sometimes Holy Spirit keeps our lives in motion, even when we would prefer to do nothing. Yet, the ways He continually moves us onward ensures that we will be fruitful and never stagnant.

We also looked at the final mention of Holy Spirit in the Bible. Revelation 22 gives us the beautiful imagery of Holy Spirit as the ever-flowing river of life, clear as crystal, streaming from the throne of God. In Heaven, He is still in motion, still conveying the presence of God, still bearing fruit.

In between Genesis and Revelation are numerous accounts of the work of Holy Spirit. He conceived the Word made flesh, Jesus. He empowered the ministry of Jesus. He raised Jesus from the dead. He breathed the Word of God into prophets and apostles who wrote the sacred texts of scripture. He filled the hearts of believers. He fills our hearts today!

As we ended our lesson on Holy Spirit like a wind, Conlee and I prayed for the children the same way we pray for all those who attend our Journey conferences. We asked them to place a hand on their heart. Then they declared aloud, "Jesus lives in me!" We said this several times, letting the miracle of salvation sink in.

Then we asked them to raise the other hand toward Heaven, declaring, "I am connected to the Father by Jesus in my heart!"

Finally, we all declared, "Holy Spirit binds us together!"

As they maintained this posture, I explained that this is the great mystery that was hidden for ages and generations, but is now available to us.[159] Theologically, it is called *incarnation*. It means "Christ in me, the hope of glory!"

A tangible presence of the Holy came over all of us as we proclaimed the ancient truth. Holy Spirit continues to honor God's word and purpose every time we remember and declare the reality of our eternal relationship.

That night we all watched a local TV weather meteorologist, Jason Smith, on Fox 10 News (WALA), to see the way he pointed out the highs and lows and gave details of the upcoming weather with terms we had been discussing.

The girls all thought he was so "cute" and were glad the forecast was for fair weather in the upcoming days of Camp Mimi. After supper we continued our reading aloud of *Heaven is For Real*.

DAY 4 – VARIETIES OF WEATHER

After the children checked their weather stations and recorded the day's readings, we attempted to cover as many different kinds of weather as we could in one morning. They happily took stacks of coloring sheets, beginning with those relating to **Temperature.**

Our simple explanation of temperature was that it is a measure of the amount of motion of molecules. If an object – including air – is warm, its molecules move vigorously. They have more energy. When they increase their motion they also tend to spread out. This is called "thermal expansion." It is the basis of most thermometers. As mercury or another liquid expands and climbs up a thermometer tube, we can measure how warm it is.

The Italian scientist, Galileo, developed one of the earliest thermometers in 1593. He also was the first person to show that air has weight by inventing a device called a *thermoscope*, which measured the pressure of the atmosphere on water.

We had already talked about his student, Evangelista Torricelli, who substituted mercury for the water and made the first barometer.

"What is the freezing point?" was my next question.

Everyone but Jake knew the answer. We assured him that he, too, would be learning it in school soon.

Not only did they call out the freezing point in both *Fahrenheit* and *Celsius* (32°F and 0°C), they also knew the boiling point (212°F or 100°C).

Next was a harder question for Caleb and Sophie. "At which point do

---

[159] Colossians 1:26-27

both of the scales give the exact same reading?" To my surprise, they knew the answer: -40°F = -40°C. Above this point, the Fahrenheit temperature is always greater than the Celsius value.

"Why do we have two standards?" I asked.

None of them knew the answer to this one, so I shared my research notes.

Anders Celsius (1701-1744), a Swedish astronomer, developed the temperature scale at which fresh water freezes at 0°C and boils at 100°C. This scale is also called *Centigrade* and is used by most countries in the world.

The Fahrenheit standard is still commonly used in the United States because the metric system, upon which Celsius is based, is not commonly used. In 1714, Gabriel Fahrenheit, a Polish scientist, made the first mercury thermometer using the measurement scale of 32°F for freezing fresh water and 212°F for boiling water.

Papa interjected with the formulas for converting one standard to another. To convert degrees C to degrees F: multiply the temperature in C by 9; divide the answer by 5; and add 32.

To convert degrees F to degrees C: subtract 32 from the temperature in F; multiply by 5; and divide by 9.

Caleb immediately checked the outside temperature from the porch thermometer and set about converting to Celsius. Sophie took a break. The other children continued coloring.

Everyone was more interested in an old method of coming close to the actual temperature if you don't have a thermometer. Count the number of times a cricket chirps in a 14-second period; add 40. For instance, if a cricket chirps 20 times in 14 seconds, the temperature should be close to 60°F. The number in Fahrenheit will be amazingly accurate most of the time.

Another fun animal fact about temperature is that ants crawl faster as the temperature increases.

The highest temperature ever recorded in North America was in Death Valley, California on July 10, 1913. It was 134°F or 57°C! The highest world's record was in the Sahara Desert of North Africa in 1922: 136°F or 58°C!

I gave them a fun fact sheet about temperature and we discussed some of the items they were most interested in.

- The surface of the sun is about 11,000°F and 6000°C, while its interior is millions of degrees.
- The warmest sea on earth, the Red Sea, averages 95°F and 35°C.
- The most comfortable room temperature averages 72°F and 22°C.

- The ideal temperature for storing milk and perishable food is 40°F and 4.5°C.
- The water in the Arctic averages 30°F and -1°C. However, it never freezes because of the salt content.
- The daytime temperature on Mars averages -22°F and -5.5°C.

"When and where was the hottest you have ever been?"

Their answers ranged from playing baseball in the summer to running a race to constructing the outdoor Tabernacle at Camp Mimi one summer.

"When and where was the coldest?"

They animatedly talked about sledding, playing in the snow, and having no power during an ice storm.

"Do you know what **Frostbite** is?"

They guessed getting red skin when you get too cold and getting numb from the cold. Their guesses were both correct.

They all remembered times when their noses, ears, fingers or toes became numb. Since the bloodstream is composed of 90 percent water, ice crystals can actually form during prolonged extreme cold temperatures. When this happens, the water in the blood can also expand and destroy cells and damage skin tissue. The best way to treat frostbite is by gentle warming.

Animals are not affected by frostbite because of their insulated coverings of fur, fat or feathers. Birds have no blood flow in their feet so they can stand on ice for long periods of time. Turtles, frogs, and fish develop an antifreeze additive for their blood. Animals also have rapid heartbeats which help them stay warm.

I gave them a sheet of paper with pictures of several animals and a human and had them fill in the blanks of what their normal heart-beats per minute are.

Walrus:	40
Human resting:	70
Rabbit:	200
Duck:	240
Cardinal:	400
Mouse:	400
Shrew:	800

"Which creature is least likely to have frostbite?"
It was unanimous: "The shrew!"

Before we finished discussing temperature we used a term often heard on the TV weather news: **Wind Chill Factor.** This tells us how much colder the air feels when the wind is blowing. We don't notice cold temperature as much if the air is calm. This is because there is a thin layer of warmed air next to our exposed skin. It provides a measure of insulation.

When there is a breeze, the air layer is removed and replaced by colder air. Wind chill does not affect the reading on the thermometer.

When it was Snack Time, Jake, easily influenced by the subject matter, actually asked, "Can we have some hot chocolate?" Since the outside temperature was near 80°F or 26.5°C, he settled for chocolate milk.

The children wondered aloud what they might learn about **Rain.** Rain means you get wet, right? What more was there to know? We approached a familiar subject with some details that surprised them.

Precipitation is the all-encompassing word that describes any moisture that falls to the ground. Rain was only the first of many words we explored for the rest of the morning. On a blank sheet of paper, I asked the children to draw three circles, one large and two smaller ones attached like Mickey Mouse ears. This is a simple demonstration of a water molecule.

The larger face is the oxygen and the two ears are the hydrogen. Billions of these "heads" are in the smallest drop of water. A droplet forms when many water molecules stick to tiny "condensation nuclei" such as volcanic dust, smoke, pollen, or salt grains within a cloud.

The droplets grow larger and larger and fall through the cloud, sweeping up other moisture droplets, until they are heavy enough to leave the cloud and fall to the ground without evaporating completely.

Raindrops are limited in size because they disintegrate when they exceed about a quarter-inch. The surface tension of water is just right to prevent the drops from growing too large. Can you imagine rain drops the size of bowling balls or pianos?

A raindrop is the perfect size to disperse light into the rainbow colors. I read them the account of the rainbow appearing in the sky when God made a covenant with Noah after saving him and his family from the great flood.

"I have set My rainbow in the clouds, and it will be the sign of the covenant between Me and the earth."[160] The word for "rainbow" literally means a "battle bow."

God goes on to tell Noah, "Never again will the waters become a flood to destroy all life. Whenever the rainbow appears in the clouds, I will see it and remember the everlasting covenant between God and all living creatures of every kind on the earth,"[161]

Truly, He is saying that He has set His battle weapon (the flood) aside.

---

[160] Genesis 9:13

[161] Genesis 9:14-15

Whenever you see the rainbow, you should be reminded that God promises to always love and protect us, not destroy or desert us.

I told the children about a pastor's sermon I heard when I was a very young Christian. He said that so many people thought it would be effective if God re-arranged the stars to form the words in our language, "I AM GOD."

However spectacular it would be at first, eventually people would get used to the words and ignore them. Is this what we have done with the sign of the rainbow, symbolized by the light refracting through the raindrops?

"Have you ever heard the expression, 'It's raining cats and dogs?'"

Everyone had heard it and knew it meant a downpour, but didn't know the origin of the saying. It was a fun diversion to explore where it came from.

There are no definitive explanations for the saying which goes back to the 1700s in England. One of the most logical reasons for the odd saying describes heavy rains flooding the filthy streets of eighteenth century English towns, causing debris, including dead animals, to be carried along with the rushing waters.

The saying was publicized in a satire written by Jonathan Swift in 1738.[162] One of his characters feared that that it would "rain cats and dogs."

A true fact that happened in London in 1984, was that it actually rained live flounders. A waterspout lifted the fish out of the Thames and dropped them several miles away. In the same manner, it also rained frogs in England, in 1844.

One of the studies we had at Camp Mimi Culinary School was the lesson about manna dropping like rain in the desert. Everyone remembered that lesson and the Manna Cookies we made.

There is also such a thing as acid rain in which droplets combine with chemicals in the air. This can damage plants, fish, stone monuments, and many other things. It can also cause respiratory problems.

"Here's a challenge! Can you name five kinds of precipitation?"

Everyone immediately shouted out **Rain**! After a pause, other examples came quickly.

"Snow! Hail! Frost! Sleet! Fog! Mist! Dew! Clouds!"

Jake wanted to know what **dew** was so we took a moment to explain. Dew forms when the ground surface becomes cool during the night hours and condenses the moisture from the air that touches it. Dew can only form if there is no wind and few clouds. That gives rise to a saying, "Dew on the grass; rain will never come to pass."

---

[162] "Complete Collection of Genteel and Ingenious Conversation," Jonathan Swift, 1738.

A heavy cloud cover keeps the heat from rising into the atmosphere, so the air is never cool enough to produce dew (the dewpoint temperature).

In reality, I think Jake only wanted to know what dew looked like. It reminded me of the story of a little boy who wanted to know where he came from. His parents took a deep breath and launched into a long story of the "birds and the bees." Totally confused, the little boy finally said, "Tommy said he was from Chicago. I just wanted to know where I was from."

I shared with them a time when dew was used as a sign from God in the Bible. Found in Judges 6, the story rings true for many of us. Gideon had a visitation from an angel, bearing a message to him from God. At the time of the visitation, Gideon was cowering in a winepress, hiding from his enemies.

When the angel said, "The Lord is with you, mighty warrior," Gideon thought the message telling him to rise up and defeat his enemy was delivered to the wrong man. He questioned the Lord's wisdom, making all sorts of excuses for himself and his people. The only identity Gideon had of himself and his family was that of weakness.

Finally, Gideon asked the Lord to give him a sign that the message was really from God. He brought an offering to the Lord and was astounded to watch it be consumed by fire. God then told Gideon to tear down his family's idols and altars to other gods. Afraid to do so in the daytime, Gideon tore them down at night. After an investigation, he was identified as the culprit and faced death. It looked like he would die for daring to obey the Lord.

However, Gideon did not count on a mighty infilling of God's Holy Spirit. God empowered the once cowardly man who had a death sentence on his head to rise up and fight against the enemy, leading many others to join him.

Still, Gideon wanted to make sure he was hearing God correctly. He made another request of the Lord. "Look, I will place a wool fleece on the threshing floor. If there is dew only on the fleece and all the ground is dry, then I will know that You will save Israel by my hand, as You have said."

The next day, Gideon took the fleece from the dry ground, wrung it out, and found the dew had filled a bowl. Still, Gideon was unsure.

Again, he asked the Lord to make it clear. "This time make the fleece dry and the ground covered with dew." The next morning only the fleece was dry and the ground was covered with dew.

Gideon went on to defeat the Midianites, a mighty enemy of his people, by continually listening to God's directions and trusting that whatever He said would be the right thing to do.

The children loved this story and, after I told it to them, they wanted to read it in their children's Bible.

I mentioned that **hail** sent from God determined the outcome of a battle, led by Joshua, between the Israelites and their enemy, the Amorites.

The story in Joshua 10 tells us that when victory looked impossible to the Israelites, God confused the enemy and sent a fierce hail storm, killing more of the enemy from hail than from the swords of the Israelites.

Hail is formed when storm clouds are at a high, cold altitude and ice crystals are present, even if the ground below is warm. The ice crystals are carried downward within a cloud by gravity, and then back upward by strong wind updrafts. As they move up and down in the cloud, they become coated with multiple layers of ice. Eventually, they fall to earth. If you break open a hailstone, you will see many layers inside, much like a small onion.

The largest recorded hailstorm in recent times was in Bangladesh in 1986. One hail stone was measured at six inches across and weighed two-and-a-quarter pounds!

Conlee and I were traveling by car on an interstate highway a few years ago when an unexpected hail storm occurred. Along with all the other motorists, we pulled to the side of the highway until it passed.

The large hail stones pelted our car for almost fifteen minutes, leaving dozens of golf ball-sized indentations. Fortunately, we were driving a rental car and were insured. We showed the children pictures of our incident, along with more severe pictures of ruined crops, broken windshields, and hail the size of baseballs.

Papa told them five stories about how weather has determined the outcomes of some very important turning points in history. I gave each of them a fact sheet with pictures of the various events.

The first was that of the rescue of Noah and his family from the great flood, found in Genesis 6-9. God wiped the earth clean from the evil that prevailed at the time.

Second, we talked about Jonah, found in Jonah 1-4. A storm and a miraculous rescue of the prophet, Jonah, saved a city called Nineveh. The children were familiar with these stories. We had read and studied them before.

The last three examples were new to them and they listened attentively as they colored their weather-related pages.

In 1588, a Spanish fleet of 130 ships set sail for England, to invade the country and overthrow Queen Elizabeth I. Their intention was to put a stop to the Tudor establishment of Protestantism in England, and establish Spanish reign on the English throne.

After some naval opposition in the English Channel, the Spaniards attempted to regroup for a further, decisive attack when severe storms in the North Atlantic took them by surprise.

Many of their vessels were wrecked, 5,000 men died, and more than a third of the fleet failed to return to Spain.

"What would have been the results of this military invasion if the severe storms had not interfered?"

After some discussion, the best answer came from Sophie, "We probably would speak Spanish instead of English!"

On Christmas night in 1776, General George Washington was facing certain defeat for his ragtag American army. Military intelligence discovered that the Hessians, fighting with the British, were planning to cross the Delaware River for a full attack on Washington's troops as soon as it was frozen over and they could move. The weather was terrible and everyone knew that the solid freeze would come soon.

Washington's men were under-nourished, poorly dressed, mentally fatigued, and ready to quit and return to their homes. They were outnumbered by the British and their allies and morale was at an all-time low. Their only hope was to make a surprise attack on the Hessian camp, in spite of the deplorable weather conditions. The risky plan would either prove to be highly successful or extremely foolish.

Washington ordered each man in his army to prepare three days' worth of food and fresh flints for their muskets. As soon as it was dark, they began the treacherous ordeal. They were ordered to be as quiet as possible, walking eight abreast toward the river. As they walked, the weather got progressively worse, turning from drizzle to rain to sleet and snow. One soldier said it was blowing as hard as a hurricane.

Going in shifts, the soldiers, artillery, and the horses were transported in boats across the river, dodging large pieces of floating ice. Twelve hours later, the first American troops surprised the Hessians, overtaking the unsuspecting army, killing 22, wounding 98, and capturing 1000 prisoners.

Although two other difficult crossings were required to defeat the British, this first courageous act, defying the weather, decided the outcome.

Finally, Papa told them about the 1940 evacuation of British troops from Dunkirk, France. The children were fascinated with history and asked lots of questions as the story unfolded. All war stories are difficult to simplify because there are so many complicated components for each significant event. We tried to keep the World War II story of the miracle of Dunkirk related to weather, even though there were many fascinating details we had to omit.

After Axis forces had won many battles in France, about 330,000 Allied soldiers were trapped on the beaches of the English Channel near Dunkirk. The stranded and cornered British and French troops were looking at certain destruction by the German air force and ground troops.

Although Great Britain wanted to do everything in their power to rescue the trapped Allied soldiers, they knew that their Royal Air Force was incapable of fending off the powerful Germans. Any rescue ships they sent to Dunkirk would be blown out of the water. It was an impossible situation for the Allies.

Britain's Prime Minister, Winston Churchill, urged all British citizens to do whatever they could to join in the rescue attempt by bringing personal watercraft of all kinds across the Channel to evacuate Allied troops from destruction. The British people responded with enthusiasm. Even with their willingness to participate, it still could have been a blood bath if the Nazi bombers had taken them out.

At just the right time, a heavy mist and fog descended, grounding the Nazi planes and providing cover for the Allied soldiers to be evacuated. As water taxis, pleasure boats, ferries, fishing boats, life boats, and merchant marine craft formed a makeshift flotilla, thousands of Allied troops waded out into the unusually calm waters of the English Channel to be evacuated from certain destruction. Many of them waited for hours in waist deep water to get into the next available rescue boat, but the cloud of protection held until almost all were evacuated.

War stories always inspire the boys to re-enact their own imaginary battles, so it seemed wise to take their energy to the pool. Even as they all played together, references to our lessons were heard in animated conversations, when they weren't swimming underwater for surprise attacks.

"You can't see me because of the cloud cover!

"No, you can't see me because of the bad storm!"

Our afternoon activities focused on crafts. It was just too hot outside to do much else, even to go to one of our favorite field trip locations.

To think "cold," we focused on **snow.** With lots of white computer paper and some simple instructions about folding and cutting, they busied themselves making dozens of snowflakes, each unique.

I told them that the shape of real snowflakes is determined by the temperature at the time they are formed, the wind current, the humidity, and nearby snowflakes. The familiar six-pointed star shape occurs when cloud temperatures are between 3°F or 10°C. Each snowflake consists of tiny ice crystals, with trillions of water molecules inside. No two are alike on the outside or the inside.

While they worked on Project Snowflake, I asked, "What are some uses for snow?"

The number one answer was, "No school!"

Some of the answers they did not consider were:

(1) Slow, measured supplies of water to reservoirs, as opposed to rainwater which can be carried away as surface runoff and erosion.

(2) Snow provides insulation for the ground during cold weather. Nighttime temperatures are often 20° warmer beneath a layer of snow. Snow can protect small animals like mice that form tunnels under the snow.

(3) Snow purifies the air by capturing floating dust particles and other contaminants.

(4) Snowflakes show the creative glory of God.

They unanimously decided that their beautiful snowflakes would become the centerpiece for our evening meal.

We told them about our trips to Rothenburg ob der Tauber, Germany, where the featured dessert of the region is called a *Schneeball*, which means "snowball" in German. Every bakery window in the town displays varieties of this specialty.

You can find *Schneeballen* pastries with marzipan, chocolate, coconut, coffee, nuts, and just about anything else you can dream up. They are large round balls of shortbread pastry, fried, dipped in flavorings, and then covered in powdered sugar.

Of course, the children were enthusiastic about trying to make some. The process is quite involved. I showed them some amazing videos of professionals making them in Germany. Dough is rolled, cut in strips, arranged in an intricate pattern around a stick, and then deep-fried before being dipped and dusted.

It was a messy job, and ours were not nearly as good as the ones in Germany. But we had fun and everyone got a sugar fix.

The last weather topic of the afternoon was one they all wanted to know about: **lightning.** Lightning is both fascinating and frightening.

I told them about an incident when I was a child in the kitchen with my mother. On a rainy day, she was standing at the sink, washing an aluminum coffee pot. A lightning bolt came through the window, hit the coffee pot with a large blue burst of flame, bounced off the ceiling, leaving a large black spot, and ricocheted around the room.

Because the coffee pot had a wooden handle, my mother was protected from the electricity and was not injured. Terrified, she dropped the pot and screamed. I vividly remember the entire scenario. The ceiling and several places on the wallpaper around the kitchen and the dining area had to be repaired.

"What happened when the lightning hit my mother's coffee pot?" I asked.

No one was sure but knew it had something to do with electricity. Papa gave a simple scientific explanation.

Lightning begins with a separation of positive and negative electrical charges in a thunder cloud. Water droplets inside the cloud move up and down because of updrafts and gravity. They collide with each other and with ice crystals. Sometimes the sparks from the friction jump between clouds and sometimes they move up and down to the ground.

"Do you know what it is like when you walk across a carpet and become charged with static electricity?"

Everyone could relate to this!

Benjamin Franklin, in about 1752, discovered the same thing as he experimented with metal and electricity during a thunderstorm. He took a key, tied it to a kite string, and flew the kite while he saw lightning during a storm. He felt sparks jump from the key to his hand.

My mother always said that everything growing outside always "greened up" during a lightning storm. I wasn't sure what that meant when I was a child, but now I know that lightning produces nitrogen (the third most abundant element in the human body), which is a necessary element for plants to be healthy.

Tall trees attract lightning for the nitrogen. An old saying is, "Beware the oak; it draws the stroke." Trees have a high moisture content so they can conduct the surge of electricity.

The temperature of the air near an actual lightning bolt heats up to over 20,000°F and 11,093°C. This explains the burned places on the walls of my childhood kitchen. Because of the extreme heat, you can see lightning from as far as fifty miles away, even though you may not hear any thunder.

A particularly interesting lightning phenomenon is **St. Elmo's Fire.** This is a visible glow that sometimes appears at night on objects that are charged with electricity. It may crackle and often looks green or blue. Sometimes it is seen on sharp edges of aircraft. The name comes from one of the Italian patron saints of sailors (also known as Erasmus).

We took a break to walk outside to look at two trees on our property that had been hit by lightning. One of the large oaks had a huge black scar on its side where lightning had hit and burned a hole inside the tree. It eventually needed to be removed because it was rotting from the inside.

Another tree was cut off from half-way down, due to a lightning strike. It, too, would have to be removed.

Since every topic led to a story, we had to tell them about the one-armed man who was our tree-trimmer. An amazing man, he told us about losing an arm in an accident. However, he was unstoppable in his tree-trimming business. He could climb a tree faster than you would believe with only one arm and two good feet, attaching ropes to guide the tree's fall when they were cut down. The professional precision of a huge tree going down is quite impressive!

Lightning rods are sometimes used on the highest points of houses and buildings to deflect lightning current. They are connected by wire cable to metal stakes driven into the ground. If electrons surge from a thundercloud into a house, they will take the path of least resistance from the lightning rod down through the cable into the ground. The house will be spared.

If a house without lightning rods is struck, the charge often follows water pipes or wiring into the ground. It may burn out circuits or shock someone in contact with water or an electric appliance.

Lightning often starts fires. Buildings with steel frameworks are usually safe during lightning because the metal provides a safe electrical passage into the ground.

A car is also safe because its metallic outer body protects the occupants and the tires help insulate the vehicle. Electricians usually wear rubber-soled shoes for this same reason. We have a friend who put rubber-soled shoes under the four legs of her baby's crib just to be careful!

In 1769, in Brescia, Italy, the religious authorities declared that it was impossible that God would strike a church with lightning. They refused to mount lightning rods on the church steeples. Instead, they stored gun powder in churches, thinking it would be safe.

A steeple was struck and 3000 people died in the massive explosion which leveled the city. What is the moral of this story? Perhaps, it is not to take God for granted!

We followed up this lesson with lots of word search pages, fact sheets, and crossword puzzles on the subject. Here is one of our fun puzzles:

Add the number of:
- Days in two years _____
- Sheets of paper in a ream _____
- Pennies in $10 _____
- Cookies in 20 dozen _____
- Toes on three people _____

This sum equals the total number of lightning strikes estimated in western Washington state during one day![163]

After an afternoon of play and excursion, we watched the evening weather forecast on TV, shared a wonderful dinner, finished reading our book aloud, and played some games.

---

[163] July, 2008

DAY 5 – DROUGHT AND THE MEDIA

All week our mornings had been full of lessons and projects. During the afternoons we had enjoyed familiar field trips to places such as Bellingrath Gardens, the Animal Preserve, the Naval Air Museum, and water sports.

Our last day together would be a day of surprises for the children. They knew we would observe *Shabbat* at night since it was Friday, but other than that, there were no hints.

After checking the weather stations and recording the readings, the children wanted to know what aspect of weather we were going to study. I gave them fact and picture sheets about **drought.**

Explaining that a drought is a prolonged period of hot, dry weather with much less rain than normal, I pointed to the pictures on their pages. We looked at dry, cracked ground in several places in the world that have experienced severe drought. Some of them showed crops dried up and even dead cattle where there had once been lush pastures.

One of the pictures was of the Jesus Boat we had discussed before. It is a first-century fishing boat discovered on the bottom of the Sea of Galilee after a drought drastically lowered the water level.

I also included a painting of the prophet, Elijah, praying for rain after a severe drought in Israel. Some believers in Yahweh became so desperate that they turned away from God and began to worship pagan gods and engage in their despicable practices.

We read the account in 1 Kings 17-18. We told the children about being on Mount Carmel several times, the traditional site of the showdown between Elijah and God and the prophets of Baal. Elijah was so certain that God would answer his prayers to overcome the pagan gods and end the drought that he risked everything – and he was right!

While Elijah fervently prayed for rain, seven different times he told his servant to go look in the sky for rain clouds. Finally, his servant reported, "A cloud as small as a man's hand is rising from the sea."[164]

Thousands of years later, Conlee and I stood on the same spot, holding our hands in the air to demonstrate how small that first cloud looked to Elijah's weather spotter. The very small promise of God's provision turned into a dark sky, growing clouds, wind, and heavy rain. The drought was broken.

There are many references to droughts in the Bible, almost always connected to God's judgment when His people turned away from Him and trusted in other gods. Throughout the world, sometimes many months or even years go by without sufficient rain. People who live in arid climates are very aware of the destructive nature of such times.

Another time when we were in Israel, there had been a drought for

---

[164] 1 Kings 18:41

several months. Everywhere we went, people asked us to pray for rain.

While we were near the Sea of Galilee one day, God answered their prayers and it began to rain so hard that waterfalls gushed over dry rocks.

The celebration of the people was equal to a national holiday. Cars lined the roads near such waterfalls so that people could take pictures of the rains, some taking "selfies," while others lined up their children (or even the family dogs) for photographs to record God's answer to their prayers.

There was singing, laughing, and celebration everywhere we went.

The longest drought we know about was in Atacama, Chile, and it lasted 400 years! It is hard to imagine that there was almost no rain at all from 1570-1971. The lack of rainfall is mostly due to its location between two mountain ranges that prevent moisture coming from either the Atlantic or Pacific oceans.

No doubt, one of the most poignant droughts in modern history is the nearly ten year period in the United States, called the Dust Bowl or the Dirty Thirties. From 1934, to around 1940, the deadly combination of drought, bad farming practices, economic depression, and greed caused one of the worst national disasters.

When I asked the children if they had ever heard of the Dust Bowl, their first ideas were football games, comparing it to all the play-off "bowl games." Knowing that pictures are worth a thousand words to describe an event, I gave them pages of black and white photographs taken in the 1930s by the well-known American documentary photographer, Dorothea Lange.

The still photos are riveting. Besides the unbelievable pictures of the land – desiccated and cracked – and the massive clouds of dirt covering the landscapes, the desolation and emptiness that Lange captured in the faces of the men, women, and children are haunting.

The children looked at the pictures, asking, "Are these real?"

I gave them some facts about the horrible event. A fruitful area, called The Great Plains of the United States, included the states Oklahoma, Texas, Colorado, New Mexico, and Kansas. At one time, it was home to the Plains Indians and countless buffalo.

The land which had frequent droughts, was thickly covered with buffalo grass, a vegetation well-adapted to the harsh climate. Buffalo grass has five-foot-long roots that go deep into the earth for moisture. They keep the moisture level at a depth of one foot, preventing erosion of the soil even though constant winds sweep across the land.

In the late 1800s and early 1900s, land was cheap in these areas, and there was a growing need for wheat to sell to Western Europe because of World War I. Farmers purchased machinery to plow up the buffalo grass and plant wheat. After the war, the demand for wheat and its price diminished but farmers still needed to pay for the tractors they had purchased on credit. On top of this, the Great Depression hit the country about the same time as a severe drought began in the Great Plains. It was a triple whammy.

Desperate to survive, farmers plowed and re-plowed the land, sometimes working all night, trying to get in as many wheat crops as possible. Despite their efforts, many of them lost their homes, farms, farm machinery, and livestock because they could not pay their mortgages.

During this frantic period of poor farming practices, the layers of soil constantly blew away under the harsh winds. There was no moisture or grass to hold the land and the results were deadly. No crops could grow, the winds produced large dust storms that were as large as one mile high and two-hundred miles wide. Livestock suffocated.

The dust storms were called "black blizzards," and many thought it was surely the end of the world. Birds flew south, dark clouds blotted out the sunlight, and there was static electricity on anything metal the people touched. Even a special sticky tape that was sold to seal windows and doors of the modest homes could not keep several inches of dust from seeping in daily.

There were infestations of jack rabbits and locusts. People suffered from skin and eye infections because of the constant bombardment of dust and sand, as well as from respiratory diseases, pneumonia, and small pox.

Many died, especially children and the elderly.

We planned to show the children a short preview of the very well done video documentary, *The Dust Bowl*, by Ken Burns,[165] but once they started watching it, they were mesmerized. They wanted to watch the whole thing, originally produced in two sessions.

The documentary is narrated by Ken Burns and features ten people who survived the Dust Bowl in the 1930s. Between their personal testimonies and the pictures and videos collected from the time, the story comes alive in such a poignant way that all of us were moved to tears watching it.

Not wanting to leave such a depressing subject without hope, I asked them some questions.

"What does God's Word say about caring for the land?"

I pointed them to Exodus 23:10-11 and Anna wanted to read the scripture. "For six years you are to sow your fields and harvest the crops, but during the seventh year let the land lie unplowed and unused."

The children made the connection immediately. "The farmers during the Dust Bowl never let the land rest. They wore it out!"

Then I asked, "What would you say to someone who asked how a loving God would allow such a thing to happen to people?"

Their answers were brilliant!

"He already told them how to farm and they didn't obey."

---

[165] *The Dust Bowl*, directed by Ken Burns, Public Broadcasting System, 2012

"They were greedy and just wanted to make more and more money selling wheat."

"They didn't trust God and didn't listen to Him."

We were all so caught up in the story that we even skipped Snack Time – a Camp Mimi first! After lunch and a swim, everyone rested because we had a surprise field trip planned for 3:00.

I had everyone get cleaned up and wear their brass meteorologist badges. They also were told to bring along their Camp Mimi Weather Notebooks.

They were more than surprised when we pulled up to the portico at the beautiful WALA Fox 10 studios. They posed for a picture at the large front door and I was surprised at how nervous they became before we entered.

For the last few days we had all watched the TV weather forecast with meteorologist Jason Smith before dinner.

What we hadn't told them was that Jason is the son of Conlee's former ministry colleague and that we have known him since he was in high school. When I contacted him weeks prior about the possibility of giving the children a tour of the weather set, he was more than delighted. The father of five young children, he is especially good at imparting information in ways they can understand.

When Jason walked out into the large lobby of the TV station to greet us, I thought the children were going to faint. To them, it was like meeting a movie star.

He greeted each of them by name, looked at their notebooks and weather charts, asked questions about what they had been studying and whether they wanted to see the TV set and meet some of the people who make the weather show happen every night. There was a resounding, "YES!"

First, he led us through a large room where familiar WALA news anchors and reporters had their desks. Everyone greeted us warmly and welcomed us to their world.

After going through mazes of hallways and through heavy doors, we arrived at the central broadcasting room. Although it was huge, it was divided into small sets for the different shows they shoot daily. We walked past the very ornate news anchors' desk, a fancy kitchen set, a living room set for interviews, and other assorted areas.

At one corner was the elaborate, STORMTRACKER desk, familiar to everyone who watched the FOX 10 weather show. After a short tour of the rest of the studio, Jason stood behind the weather desk, just as he did on TV, and explained how the show was filmed. He talked about the many computers he used to determine the forecast, the weather models for storms, and the number of people it took to produce each segment.

Jason then called in a camera man and gave each of the children a chance to stand in front of the green screen to give a weather forecast on TV. Watching yourself on TV screens on both sides and in front of you, and, at the same time, pointing to an invisible map is much harder than it looks, but each child tried and sort of got the hang of it.

Jason had a video prepared for them to take home of their premier weather show.

Finally, he spent a long period of time telling them about how he prepared for his job every day, as well as how he chose his university studies to become a meteorologist. They asked lots of questions and he was incredibly patient and generous with his time. After about an hour he had to leave to prepare for the evening show and we thanked him profusely as we left.

All the way home the children kept saying, "That was so cool!" Everyone but Caleb decided they wanted a job in television.

After returning home, we enjoyed a wonderful evening beginning with watching Jason on the FOX 10 weather show, putting the finishing touches on our *Shabbat* steak dinner, decorating the table, having a treasure hunt that the girls orchestrated to find our silverware for dinner, observing *Shabbat*, having our traditional awards ceremony, and giving thanks.

The lingering images of the Dust Bowl prompted each of the children to ask God to help them preserve and protect the beautiful earth He placed us on, to not abuse it, and to learn His ways to keep our environment healthy for future generations.

What began as a doubtful theme for Camp Mimi, ended as a rousing success. Although we never got to subjects such as tornadoes, hurricanes, earthquakes, or floods, we covered more subjects than I ever thought possible, especially considering some of the obstacles we had to overcome.

Thankfully, on the last day, we were able to laugh about many of the disasters that occurred during our week together.

First, the septic tank overflowed, backing up sewage into the shower. We were not able to flush the toilets or bathe inside until an expert came to our rescue. This lasted for two days. The children were good sports about "camping out" and living primitively during this ordeal.

Perhaps a highlight of this disgusting ordeal was that the sewage clean-out man was the father of the girl who played Ariel at Disney World. That made him somewhat of a celebrity in their eyes.

Then Caleb had severe diarrhea for two days, fortunately after the sewage repair. This was followed by Sophie throwing up for more than a day. I felt a bit more like Nurse Mimi than the Camp Mimi director.

Although things were trying at times, everyone was able to laugh a lot and we survived!

The ending of a traditional Passover meal, which we had observed several times, always declares, "Next year in Jerusalem!"

Our personal parting words for *Shabbat* were, "Next year at Camp Mimi!" It was a good thing we did not declare, "Next year in Mobile!" because God had other plans.

CAMP MIMI TEN

BODISHBABES IN BIBLE TIMES

We had some huge changes occur between Camp Mimi Nine and Camp Mimi Ten.

For several years in Mobile, we had endured severe hurricanes which made us increasingly ready to move from our house on the water. Besides the constant maintenance of water-front living, the stress of evacuations, clean-up, and repairs were adding up financially and emotionally.

Because of this, a few years before, Conlee and I purchased several acres of beautiful, wooded, undeveloped property across the bay, intending to build a home in the country. We had house plans completed and had contacted a builder. All we needed to do was sell our bay house and make the move.

Unfortunately, homes on Mobile Bay were not selling very well. People were still nervous about the cycle of bad storms we had for several years, and it was nearly impossible to get new insurance on water-front property.

Three years before, we listed our house with a realtor and waited, but no one ever came to look. Eventually, we cancelled our listing and prayed earnestly about what to do.

The previous summer, about a month before Weather Camp Mimi, Conlee and I were in church, listing to our pastor's message on Holy Spirit anointing. He asked us all to stand, place our hands on our ears as a symbolic gesture, and receive an anointing to hear God's voice. The moment I did this, I "heard" God say to me, *"Move to Fayetteville!"*

It was such a deep and powerful impression going all through me that I did not doubt at all that it was a life-changing message. At the end of the service, our pastor had a prophetic word for the whole congregation, "You are going to have a major breakthrough by the end of the year." I wrote it in my prayer journal.

Fayetteville, Arkansas, is where Conlee and I went to university, fell in love, dated, and lived for the first year of our marriage. After he served briefly in the Army and worked for a construction company in Little Rock for a few years, we moved back to Fayetteville, where he started his own mechanical construction business.

It was in Fayetteville, that we met Jesus in an astounding way, and it was in Fayetteville, that we began to grow spiritually and had our lives changed for eternity.

From Fayetteville, we heard the call to go to seminary and from Fayetteville, we moved from our dream home and eventually ended up in Mobile, Alabama, for the next twenty-five years in full-time ministry.

Two of our three grown sons lived in Fayetteville, and seven of our eight grandchildren were there. Conlee had retired from full-time pastoral ministry in Mobile, three years earlier, so God's timing for a move was perfect!

The property we had purchased in the woods sold quickly and only one obstacle remained before we could move. We still had our lovely bay cottage and no one wanted to buy it. The sale of our house was essential for us to make the move that God was directing.

Sometimes it is necessary to put personal words from God (like *Move to Fayetteville!)* on the "back burner," knowing that in His time His word will be fruitful. We kept listening to God, ready to respond when He directed, but not forcing anything to happen.

During this time, a meaningful scripture to me was from Joshua 3:3-4. "Follow the Ark of the Covenant *(the Presence of God)*. Then you will know which way to go, since you have never been this way before." Staying close to God is always vital, but it was especially important to us during our waiting period.

Also, during the waiting, I had a vivid dream one night in which I saw our bedroom completely empty. It left such a lasting impression that I knew it was a promise from God about moving out of the house.

In November, we had a totally unplanned encounter with a woman at church. She was a very spiritually sensitive person whom we had known for years, and she was also a realtor.

Before the service began, I casually told her that God was prompting us to move and we needed to sell our house. We didn't want to list it but would like for her to be aware of its availability if she knew of someone looking for a home on the bay. She immediately asked if she could look at it. We scheduled a quick tour for the next day, which lasted more than an hour!

She prayed over every room in our house, sometimes prophetically, declaring that God was preparing our home for the right family just as surely as He was leading us to Arkansas. When she left, the whole atmosphere in our home was charged with God's presence.

A week before Christmas, Conlee and I went to Fayetteville, to spend the holidays with our children and grandchildren. While we were there, we received a text from our realtor friend that she wanted to show our house to someone. We gave her permission, told her how to enter the house, and didn't think anything more about it since our time was filled with family and Christmas preparations.

After Christmas, Conlee and I remarked that since the year was nearly over, the word from our pastor about a breakthrough before the end of the year must have been for someone else in the congregation. It surely hadn't happened to us.

In Fayetteville, our whole family was up late on New Year's Eve, enjoying a great meal, celebrating, and awaiting the coming of a new year.

Close to 11:00 p.m., Conlee received a phone call from the realtor in Mobile. The couple who had looked at the house wanted to make an offer.

This was the first offer we had! After some negotiating on the price, a signed contract was faxed to our son's house for us. We signed it and faxed it back. The time it came to pass? ***11:51 p.m.!***

God's word is faithful, often coming in surprising ways. Not until we looked at the signatures of the buyers on the contract, did we realize that we knew the couple who bought our home. They are strong Christians who are known for their deep faith and their commitment to invite the presence of God into any situation. They have continued to use the lovely cottage on the bay for God's purposes, having prayer and praise gatherings and giving Him glory in all they do.

Our realtor friend assured us that the spiritual investment we made into that home over the years was continuing to bear fruit in the lives of people we would never meet.

We shared all these details of our story with the BodishBabes because it is now a part of our family history. It honors God and demonstrates that He is involved in every detail of our lives. The story of our move to Fayetteville, is part of our legacy to them. It lets them know that we can trust His word and depend on Him, even when circumstances seem impossible. His ways often surprise us but they are always best for us – more than we know.

The children's reaction to our move was mixed. They were excited that we would be living in Fayetteville, near them, seeing them as much as we wanted. However, they were attached to the bay house and the years of loving memories that had accumulated in their hearts from being there.

One of their first questions to us was, "Where will we have Camp Mimi?" I assured them that God would provide a home for us and we would continue with whatever God directed. At the time, I did not realize this year would be our last official Camp Mimi, but as we came to an end, it was clear and right for all.

DAY 1-VILLAGE LIFE IN BIBLE TIMES - CLOTHING

We thought that being in the same town as the children would make it much easier to arrange a week for everyone to attend Camp Mimi, but it probably demanded the most complicated coordination yet. All of the children had so many activities going on, plus many friends and diversions close by. Our plans to defuse the inevitable interruptions were to take several out of town excursions.

The ground rules for this year included no contact with family or friends during the week, packing a bag just as if you were going to Mobile, and only using electronic devices during designated times. Everyone agreed and gathered with enthusiasm, in spite of a bit of confusion. One of their first questions was, "Are we still going to have field trips?" We assured everyone that we certainly would.

The large, glass-topped Camp Mimi table was the same one we had always used, although in new surroundings. Just sitting around it at their usual places gave us all some continuity.

We began with familiar traditions: the Camp Mimi Song, the rules (somewhat amended), and the Camp Mimi Candle with The Big Reveal.

When they saw "BodishBabes in Bible Times" as the theme on the candle, the screams of "We're going to Israel!" were deafening.

I told them that it wasn't the first time they had wrongly assumed an international trip. The year we had "Israel" as the Camp Mimi theme, they thought the same thing. We sincerely told them that if we could afford to, it would be our delight to take each one to the Holy Land. Instead, we were going to pretend we lived there during the first century, at the time of Jesus.

After they settled down, they decorated their boxes on which I had already painted their names in Hebrew, and they received their notebooks.

We explained that we were going to "put ourselves" into a typical Galilean village, much like Nazareth or Capernaum, or one of the other small places where Jesus lived and ministered. We would study seven major aspects of Israeli village life and even make a model of what our village looked like. On the last morning, we would invite the parents and older siblings to brunch and share with them what they had learned and made.

Everyone seemed content with this plan and began to express specific interests in the areas I presented to them.

"We will study the **clothing** people wore, the **family** structure and traditions, the **food** they ate and how they prepared it, the **houses** they lived in and how they were built, the **work** the people did, and the two main areas of spirituality: **studying** the Torah in the synagogue and **worshiping** in the Temple."

Sophie, by now a young teen-age *fashionista*, immediately honed in on the clothing. "Mimi, do you think they had fashion designers in Jesus' time?"

I admitted I had never considered such a thing, but suggested that if she wanted to, she could be in charge of designing and making everyone a costume that would be appropriate to the era we were studying. She started sketching right away.

Since this subject was already in motion, we began our first morning with coloring sheets and lessons about **clothing.** We started with what the priests wore and I gave them pictures of the detailed descriptions of their clothing from the Bible, along with word search pages about what each item represented.

They were somewhat familiar with this, but it had been several years since we studied the Tabernacle and the high priest and his garments. However, they immediately recalled the *ephod* they had made for Papa to wear when he represented the high priest at our backyard Tabernacle. They also vividly remembered how hot it was on that day when we constructed it.

The Torah provides specific details of what the priests wore when ministering in the Temple. They were required to wear white underpants made of linen which reached from the waist to the knees.[166] These were covered by a long white tunic, made of pure linen, from the neck to the feet. It was tied with a girdle (a belt of some kind), and had sleeves reaching to the wrists.

The high priest's tunic was similarly made but it was embroidered.[167] The High Priest also wore a blue robe over his white tunic. The hem of the robe was adorned with tassels, bells, and embroidered pomegranates. His sash (or girdle) was made of linen, decorated with elaborate embroidery in blue, purple and scarlet.[168]

The *ephod*, inset with twelve precious stones and the names of the tribes of Israel, was worn over the robe, attached to two golden shoulder brooches inset with sardonyx stones. On his head, he wore a turban, wound so that it formed a broad, flat-topped covering. On the front of the turban was a gold plate inscribed with the words, "Holiness unto YHWH." The other priests' turbans were shaped more like cones.

---

[166] Exodus 28:42

[167] Exodus 28:39-40

[168] Exodus 28:39, 39:29

Because God's second commandment[169] forbade paintings or sculptures of the human figure, it is difficult to be exact about what Jewish clothing looked like. This commandment was because the pagans made physical representations of their gods, reducing them to human proportions and worshiping their stone or wooden idols. God has always wanted His people to worship the Creator alone, not a part of creation.

Some of the earliest paintings of Jews come from a synagogue in Syria, made around 250 AD. However, by this time Jews had begun to dress like the Romans. The men had no beards and the women were bareheaded.

The best source we have of what clothing looked like in Jesus' time comes from tunics and other clothing found in caves in En Gedi. Similar fabrics and clothing were also found at Masada, dating from 70 AD. Archeologists discovered sandals, braided hair for women, leather drawstring purses for men, and long tunics for women, made to be tied at the waist with a girdle. Most of their tunics were sleeveless.

Women always covered their heads with a veil when praying or prophesying. This symbolized being covered by the presence of God. At other times a simple band or scarf held back their hair.

Typical sandals for men and women were made of leather with enclosed heels. They were fastened to the ankle by a thong that passed between the first and second toes. In contrast, Roman shoes covered the whole foot. Jews wore sandals to protect their feet from burning sand and from dampness. Usually, sandals were not worn in the house or in the sanctuary. However, to walk about outside without sandals indicated great poverty, slavery, or mourning.

A man normally wore a knee-length, wool tunic with half-sleeves. It was held at the waist by a rope or belt. He also might wear an over-robe or mantle with tassels on four corners of the hem. This was for protection from sun and storms.

His cloak was also used to carry things such as bread dough and kneading bowls, as described during the Passover in Exodus 12:34. Sometimes his mantle had decorative bands of contrasting fabric from the shoulder to the hem. It was made very simply from a large rectangular piece of rough, heavy woolen material, sewn together so that the front was unstitched and two openings were left for the arms. When a man worked outside, he usually took off this outer garment.

A woman wore a similar tunic and robe, which was longer and concealed her figure. She might use brighter colors and a finer fabric for her garment. She also wore a shawl that served at times as a head covering. Other than for a bride, a woman did not veil her face. The present custom

---

[169] Exodus 20:4-6

in the Middle East for women to cover their faces originates with Islam, not Judaism.

Sophie took notes and made drawings as we continued to learn about first century fashion.

Both men and women wore jewelry, made from gold, silver, jewels, colored glass, and pearls. These might include nose rings, toe rings, arm bracelets, brooches, rings, or earrings.

What did the average person look like? Probably somewhat different from the well-known paintings of Jesus and His disciples. They were very short. The average height for a man was about five feet tall. That was close to the size of Caleb and Sophie.

Men usually wore beards and shoulder-length hair, secured with bands of cloth. Women's hair was simple and long, bound with beads or cloth.

Because the climate was very hard on people's skin, they cared for it with olive oil, probably oiling their hair as well. They also used other essential oils to prevent parasites such as lice.

While Sophie continued her designs for each of the children, the rest of them colored pages of people from the Bible, noting the kind of clothing they wore. I gave them a short Bible study about clothing while their hands were busy.

"Who designed the first clothing?"

"God!" said the overwhelming majority, with one vote for Eve.

The Bible gives us the definitive answer by telling us that "The Lord God made garments of skin for Adam and his wife and clothed them."[170]

God gave the prophet Ezekiel a metaphorical description of His deep love for Israel and the people of the Land. God's picture shows how beautiful Israel was in His heart.

"I clothed you with an embroidered dress and put leather sandals on you. I dressed you in fine linen and covered you with costly garments. I adorned you with jewelry: I put bracelets on your arms and a necklace around your neck, and I put a ring on your nose, earrings on your ears and a beautiful crown on your head. So you were adorned with gold and silver; your clothes were of fine linen and costly fabric and embroidered cloth."[171]

The verses that follow are heart-breaking because they describe how Israel did not appreciate God's love and, in spite of all He did for her, turned to other gods.

"Why would Israel do that?" Edie asked.

This led to an interesting discussion, taking us away from our subject of clothing, but one of those "take advantage of the moment" times you sometimes have with children.

---

[170] Genesis 3:21

[171] Ezekiel 16:10-13

"Unfortunately, Edie, it's human nature to do what Israel did until God changes our hearts. Let's think about some of the things your parents give you and do for you because they love you so much. But all of us have times when we forget how much we are loved and we act like we deserve to have beautiful things and even demand more."

It got very quiet around the table. I didn't want this to feel like a lecture but more like a discussion.

I made it less personal. "What would have happened if Israel had been grateful to God for what He gave her? What if she had thanked Him and told Him how much she loved and appreciated Him?"

There were several ideas.

"He probably would have given her more."

"She would have been happier and wouldn't want to go to other gods."

One of their comments returned us to the personal connection, "I like it when people thank me for giving them stuff and doing things for them."

We talked for a few minutes about how gratitude makes us feel closer to someone, while ungratefulness produces distance in relationships. I reminded them that at the first Camp Mimi, God prompted us to use the scripture about Jesus healing ten lepers from their disease. Only one of them was grateful and came back to thank Jesus and worship Him. That one man received a wholeness that the other nine did not. All ten of the men left with healed skin. The grateful man left with a healed heart as well.[172]

"I don't think I was there for that Camp Mimi!" Jake bemoaned.

"Jake, you weren't the only one who missed it because it was only Sophie and Caleb that first year. You were just a newborn baby."

Jake gave his big brother a knowing look. "That's why I wasn't there!"

"I want to show you a very special article of Jewish clothing. It's called a *tallit*."

I carefully removed from its covering a Jewish prayer shawl we purchased in Jerusalem. It is beautifully made of white wool and embroidered with blue and silver silk. As we unfolded it, the children were amazingly reverent.

"Can we touch it?"

I suggested they wash their hands first and then each one would be allowed to have Papa place it over their heads just as a Jewish man would wear it for prayer. After each one had experienced the covering, we talked about the symbols of the rectangular piece of fabric that means so much to Jews.

The word *tallit* does not occur in the Torah, but the word means "to cover over." The covering that God wanted His people to wear included five requirements:

---

[172] Luke 17:11-19

1. The fringes must be on the border of your garment.[173]
2. The fringes must be on the four corners of the garment.[174]
3. The fringes must have at least one ribbon of royal blue or purple.[175]
4. The garment and fringes are not of "divers kinds" (no linen and wool woven together).[176]
5. When you look on the fringes you are to remember God's commandments to obey them.[177]

To illustrate the last requirement of remembering God's commandments, our *tallit* has symbols of the ten commandments and the following blessing embroidered in Hebrew on the neck piece: *Blessed are You our Lord God, King of the Universe who sanctifies us with his commandments and gave us the commandment of the tzitzit.*

"What is that word?" the children wanted to know.

It's a fun word to say. Try *zeet-zeet* and you will come close. We all tried it.

The *tzitzit* are the tassels and they are the whole point of wearing the garment. There are 613 knots on the tassels to remind the wearer of the 613 commandments given by God in Torah.

There's an interesting story about King Saul, the first king of Israel. Out of jealousy and fear, he wanted to kill David, the one whom God had ordained to be the next king. One time David was hiding in a cave at En Gedi to escape Saul's wrath when Saul went to the opening of that exact cave to relieve himself.

"Really? That's in the Bible?"

(There were lots of grade school/middle school comments, of course).

Saul was very vulnerable and David could easily have killed him, but David only cut off the tassels of Saul's garment.[178] This act spoke volumes about the character of David. Rather than take Saul's life, David removed the outward symbol of God's authority over the man.

Originally, the blue or purple tassels were only worn by people of nobility. In the New Testament we read about the garment with the *tzitzit* as being something everyone wore. Jesus referred to the extreme lengths of the *tzitzit* that some men displayed, perhaps trying to show others that they were more spiritual.[179]

---

[173] Numbers 15:38

[174] Deuteronomy 22:12

[175] Ibid., Numbers 15:38

[176] Deuteronomy 22:11

[177] Numbers 15:39-41

[178] 1 Samuel 24:1-7

"Does that mean they were show-offs?"

"Exactly. What do you think Jesus thought about show-offs?"

"I don't think He thought it was a good idea."

Good answer.

"Did Jesus wear one of those tassel things?" Anna asked.

Before I answered this great question, I told them that originally the *tallit* was an outer garment with tassels. Then it became worn as an inner garment, with the tassels showing. This is because God commanded that one "look upon" the tassels.[180]

Today, it is more of a shawl used specifically for prayer, although some modern Jews wear smaller ones under their suit coats. Also, today the *tallit* is only worn by men, and most Jews are buried in their prayer shawl. In Bible times, they were worn by women as well.

Some of the traditions that have been established about the wearing of the *tallit* are interesting.

- The minimum size for a *tallit* is that which can clothe a small child who is able to walk.
- During the first century, a Jewish father wrapped his son in his own *tallit* to take him to the school master for the first time. It symbolized that the child was wrapped in prayer.
- The blessing that is embroidered on our *tallit* is the one that is said before putting it on your head. However if you use a borrowed *tallit* you are not supposed to say the blessing.
- Many Jews pray with the *tallit* only covering their shoulders, not their heads.
- At synagogue, when the Torah scroll is carried in a procession down the aisle, men touch it with the fringes of their *tallit*.
- Most men kiss their *tallit* before wearing it.

We all thought this last tradition was interesting because Conlee always kissed his clerical stole when putting it on at the beginning of a service. We asked him why.

"It was not a tradition that was taught or learned, but something more intuitive for me. I did it to physically remind myself that I was acting as a priest/pastor under the authority of God."

And finally, here's a tradition that has developed in modern times. Men are not to wear their *tallit* into a restroom. In Israel, there are generally hooks outside the door for them. There also are specific rules about what to

---

[179] Matthew 23:5

[180] Numbers 15:39

do if you need to use the restroom while praying.

"Going back to your question, Anna, about whether Jesus wore a *tallit*, do you remember the story about the woman who had been bleeding for twelve years? What does it say she did to get healed?"

"She touched the hem of His garment."[181]

"Let's think about what that might mean. Suppose she grabbed on to one of the tassels? What would that signify?"

They thought about that for a minute.

"She knew He had the power to heal her? That was His authority?"

Wow! I have never heard an adult come to that conclusion. Most think she was only trying to get His attention. To think that she recognized His authority and held on to the utmost symbol of that authority gives even more depth to an already amazing story.

Another account says that people crowded around Jesus, begging to let them touch the edges of his cloak, and all who touched Him were healed.[182]

"Do you think everyone recognized this symbol of His authority or that they had heard about the bleeding woman who was healed in this way?"

We all agreed that we don't know for sure, but that the tassels symbolized something very important. The children then wanted to more closely examine the tassels on our *tallit*.

As they looked at the intricately woven tassels, I read them a scripture from Malachi 4:2. "The prophet said that 'those who revere the Lord, the sun of righteousness will rise with healing in its wings.' Is he saying that the sun will have wings? That would be an odd thing to say. However, if he declares that God's *name* is brilliant and powerful like the sun, and contains healing, where is the healing located?"

When the children looked at the scripture in their Bibles, they shouted out, "In wings!"

"If you knew Hebrew, you would realize that the word translated 'wings' can also mean something else. It can also mean 'a skirt, or corner of a garment.' With that in mind, what could the prophet Malachi be saying?"

They read it carefully as if trying to figure out a puzzle. Finally, the light bulbs ignited.

"It means that you can get healed if you touch the tassels of Jesus' *tallit*!"

I pointed out that there is no healing power in the *tzitzit* themselves, but in the authority of the name of God to which they point. It is important to make that distinction.

Finally, we concluded our study of prayer shawls with pictures of a *tallit* and the Israeli flag side by side. The similarity is obvious because the flag, adopted in 1948, was patterned after the *tallit*.

---

[181] Matthew 9:20

[182] Mark 6:56

By now Sophie was definitely ready to design and construct some biblical clothing for everyone. The other children were ready for Snack Time, so everyone got busy.

I had stacks of cotton fabric in various colors, collected at local thrift shops. For only one dollar, it was possible to purchase a king-size sheet and I accumulated several of them. They were washed and folded, ready for our "first-century designer" to work her magic.

Each child picked out two favorite colors from the stack and patiently let Sophie measure them and start cutting the fabrics. I had a sewing machine ready if needed but the pieces of fabric were so large, some simple cutting and tying did the trick. She even made garments for Papa and me.

By the time we were all decked out in our finest Capernaum-style fashions, not only did the BodishBabes pose for numerous pictures, but they wanted to go as a group to walk the neighborhood. They were disappointed that a TV camera crew did not meet up with them and feature them on the nightly news but they had fun and wanted to keep on the outfits at dinner.

DAY 2 – VILLAGE LIFE IN BIBLE TIMES – FOOD AND FAMILY

When the children got dressed, they put on their biblical costumes, thus giving all of us a headstart for the day. Having breakfast in first century attire gave an ordinary meal a festive quality. We had pancakes which, with a stretch of the imagination, could have resembled a typical flatbread cooked over an open fire.

As we began our lesson for the day, I handed the children several fact sheets and coloring pages about families in a Galilean village. Some of them showed Jewish brides and bridal processions in a village, others portrayed different aged people sharing a meal or working together in a field or garden. They picked the pages they wanted and began to color.

For reference, I showed them a map of Israel as I gave a brief history lesson. In 63 BC, the Roman general Pompey captured Jerusalem, the capital, and took charge over the whole nation of Israel. The children found Jerusalem on the map.

By the time Jesus was born it was considered normal to have Romans ruling over the people. The land was divided into three distinct areas: Galilee in the north, Samaria in the middle, and Judea in the south. The children identified these areas on the map.

While they continued to color, I told them a little about each section. **Galilee** was around the Sea of Galilee and was more rural, with small villages and fishermen and shepherds. We would talk more about Galilee later.

Samaria had an interesting history. At one time, in 722 BC, Samaria was the capital of Israel. The Assyrians captured it and deported many of the most influential, talented, and wealthy Jews from Samaria, to other parts of the Assyrian Empire. They could more easily manage those who were left behind – who were the very poorest.

The Assyrians soon realized that the nation was falling apart without capable leadership, so they brought non-Jews from other parts of their empire to live in Samaria, and govern the people. The people they imported were pagans who brought influences from other lands.

Again, the Assyrian leaders saw problems among the people – who had been bombarded with strange beliefs – so they tried another tactic. They brought a prominent Jewish priest, who had been exiled, back to Samaria.

However, by that time, many of the newcomers had intermarried with the remaining Israelites. Their descendants became known as Samaritans, not Israelites. Jews looked upon them as "half-breeds," a derogatory term indicating the combination of Jewish and pagan practices in their families.

By the time Jesus came, the Samaritans were despised because they were considered "impure." They worshiped God but they were not considered to be true Jews. The Samaritans even built their own temple.

"Where have you heard about Samaritans in the Bible?"

The familiar story of the Good Samaritan came as a quick answer.

"Why was it so remarkable in that parable that it was a Samaritan who helped the injured man on the road?"

"Oh, because the Jews were supposed to hate them!"

"The Jews probably didn't think Samaritans would do good deeds."

Great answers! Jesus' parable shows us that our prejudices keep us from seeing good in other people. I also reminded them that the one grateful leper whom Jesus healed was a Samaritan. And the woman at the well was in Samaria. These accounts show us how much Jesus loves all people and wants all people to be reconciled to Him.

We moved on to the third distinct area of the Land, **Judea.** This was the area around Jerusalem, the capital, and the location of the Temple.

Whenever one talked about going to Jerusalem, it was always "up," regardless of the direction used to get there. This is because Jerusalem was considered the center of all things, as well as being higher than its surroundings.

All over Israel, Jews were forced to pay taxes to Rome, which of course they resented.

"Remember when Joseph and Mary went to Bethlehem where their baby, Jesus, was born? They were going there to pay their taxes to the Romans."

Some of the Jews worked for the Romans as tax collectors and they were hated by other Jews. It was a job that paid well but alienated you from your countrymen.

"One of Jesus' disciples was a former tax collector. Do you know who it was?"

There were several guesses but no one guessed that it was Matthew.

Jesus called him from his tax collector's booth to follow Him.[183] Jesus also did something unheard of for a Jew: He went to Matthew's house for dinner, where they were joined by other tax collectors. The religious authorities were highly critical of these actions, especially by someone who was known as a rabbi or favored teacher. Jesus was undaunted by their criticisms and also went to the home of another tax collector in Jericho, that of Zacchaeus. He, too, became a follower of Jesus.

Jesus often surprised the religious Jews with His statements as well as His actions. For instance, Roman law stated that a Roman soldier could force anybody to carry his equipment for one mile. When Jesus told His disciples, "If somebody forces you to go one mile, go two miles with him,"[184] they were astonished.

Most first-century Jews in Israel, were looking for their Messiah to be a king to free them from the Romans. This sentiment caused much confusion when Jesus, whom many believed to be Messiah, established a spiritual kingdom rather than an earthly monarchy.

In spite of the resentment toward the Romans, many good things happened in Israel, during the Roman rule. For long periods of time there was peace among all the different countries in the Roman Empire.

The Romans established a structured government everywhere they reigned. They built networks of roads for safe and easy travel throughout their empire. This was important because ordinary people walked everywhere unless they were fortunate enough to have a donkey. Because horses were expensive, not many people owned them.

The common language throughout the Roman Empire was Greek, so many Jews learned this language and used it specifically for legal documents. They also knew Hebrew and Aramaic, the language most used among the common people.

Ironically, the Romans never realized that the improvements they introduced to Israel, especially the roads and the common language, would help spread the Gospel around the known world.

Rome conquered Spain, Germany, North Africa, Asia Minor, and Syria, as well as Israel. These became the beginnings of evangelism.

---

[183] Matthew 9:9

[184] Matthew 5:41

To put our studies into action, I suggested, "Let's imagine that we are an ordinary family, living in the Galilee area, near where Jesus grew up and ministered. Let's talk about what our life would have been like. Then after lunch, we're going to construct a model of such a village and include any of the details that you find interesting."

Everyone was on board, especially when Papa brought out a large piece of plywood that nearly covered the Camp Mimi table. It became the foundation for our Galilean village.

In Israel, during the first century, there was no real middle class. People were either very rich or very poor. The very poorest people often were the childless widows. With few jobs for women, without a son to support her, and without a daughter's family with whom she could live, a childless widow was likely to be destitute. Jesus had a lot to say about being compassionate and generous toward widows. In our model, we would represent poor people.

The home was of the utmost importance for every family. In one's home, weddings were held, children were born, and people died. Besides the synagogue, there was no other common meeting place.

"Let's talk about what our home is like for our Galilean family."

The children easily got into their "let's pretend" mode.

"We can either live in a house made of stones or mud bricks. If we live near the Sea of Galilee, with its rocky beaches, stones will be plentiful. If we live inland, we will have to form and bake bricks from mud.'

The vote was unanimous, "We want to live near the Sea of Galilee."

Our house is divided into two parts: the part nearest the only door has a beaten dirt floor. In winter, any animals we own live there. The other part is on a raised platform and that is where we live. If we have a little more money, we can have an upper room.

We also have a flat roof, which is very important. Up there, we dry fruit and grains, and even grow some vegetables in planters. When it's hot, we sleep and eat up there.

Because the houses in our village are all so close together, we can see and hear everything going on with our neighbors – and so can they!

Jesus said, "Be on your guard against the yeast of the Pharisees, which is hypocrisy. There is nothing concealed that will not be disclosed, or hidden that will not be made known. What you have said in the dark will be heard in the daylight, and what you have whispered in the ear in the inner rooms will be proclaimed from the roofs."[185]

This statement made His listeners aware of how important it was to guard their words, lest everyone in the village learn about it.

---

[185] Luke 12:1-3

Since there is no privacy, either in the home or in the village, modesty is very important to everyone. It is strongly encouraged and enforced.

The custom is to wash the dust from our feet before we enter the platform area of the house. When we enter the living area we always go barefoot. This is to keep everything as clean as possible.

Because we are poor, we have very little furniture. Our bed is just a mat or mattress full of wool or straw, which we lay out on the platform at night and roll up out of the way during the day. When it's cold, the whole family sleeps together, covered with goat's hair blankets.

Chairs are a great luxury. We usually sit on stools, which are easy to make. Even proper tables are expensive so we eat on a straw mat on the floor. If we were rich, we would have comfortable furniture, with proper beds made of wood, and fine woolen blankets and pillows.

Our house is lit by oil lamps, almost exactly like the clay lamps we use for *Shabbat* and *Passover*. They are filled with olive oil and placed in little niches in the stone walls. Our one small window, set high in the wall, allows very little light inside.

Our constant need is to provide food and water for our family. It is vital that we live near a well. The women and girls usually are responsible for supplying their homes with water.

Here's how our typical day begins. Just as the sun comes up, everyone pitches in to do the household chores. The wife and daughters go to the village well first thing in the early morning and again in the evening. They carry pitchers on their heads and shoulders. Sometimes they carry a leather portable bucket with a rope attached to let down into the water. If larger quantities of water are needed for special purposes, the men and boys assist by filling large sheep or goat skins from the well.

After bringing water to the house, anyone not working outside begins kitchen chores. Grain is ground, bread is baked, goats are milked, cheese and curds are made. Oil lamps are filled with olive oil and the wicks are trimmed. Fruit and vegetable gardens are tended, weeded and watered. Chickens are fed and eggs are gathered. And on it goes …

Typically the family eats only two meals a day. Those who spend the daylight hours farming, shepherding, or fishing carry a meal with them to be eaten at midmorning or noon. Supper is a more leisurely meal for everyone and is more substantial. It might consist of vegetables, eggs, cheese, bread, butter, nuts, fruit, milk, and occasionally chicken. Wine is usually reserved for feast days.

When the weather is warm, all the cooking is done in or on a portable clay oven outside the house. When it's cold outside, we bring the oven into the outer room. This helps heat the house but also fills all the rooms with smoke and cooking odors because there is no chimney.

Other than bread, most foods are boiled or stewed in a big clay pot. A good cook makes use of salt, onions, garlic, mint, dill, cumin, coriander, and mustard for seasoning. We grow these on the roof or in a common garden in the village.

We don't own plates or silverware. The only dishes we have are our cooking pots and we eat out of those, using bread as a utensil as well as a staple at each meal. If we have meat, we eat it with our fingers.

"That sounds fun," both boys agreed.

We looked at an example of this eating custom described at the Last Supper. Jesus told his disciples during the Passover meal, "The one who has dipped his hand into the bowl with Me will betray Me."[186]

We follow a customary ritual of washing our hands before and after meals. The father pours water from a pitcher over everyone's hands into a basin. Immediately, the water is thrown out. Wealthy people have servants to do this, so it is interesting to see that the father takes the role of a servant for his family.

If we entertain a large number of guests, such as a wedding, a lot of water is needed to observe this ritual washing. Some of the water pots in the home are quite large. When Jesus performed His first miracle at the wedding in Cana, there were "six stone water jars, the kind used by the Jews for ceremonial washing, each holding from twenty to thirty gallons."[187]

Jesus had the servants fill the pots with water to the brim. That is a lot of water!

When the servants drew water from the pots, the water had turned into wine – His first recorded miracle. That is also a lot of wine!

A wedding in the family is as elaborate as one can afford. If possible, the celebration lasts one week. The preparations are expected to be lavish and hospitable to honor the bride and groom, as well as the guests. This may be why Mary urged her son, Jesus, to do something about the shortage of wine at the wedding in Cana.

Weddings are full of tradition. It is important to marry someone from your own tribe. Mary and Joseph were both of the tribe of Benjamin.

The betrothal is formal and binding. It is ceremoniously held in the home of the bride, with her consent to the marriage. Her father gives his blessing, and the family witnesses the bride and groom sign a contract, which declares what they will give to one another in the marriage.

At this time, the groom gives his bride something of value as a gift and as a pledge of his love and commitment. It may be some time, even years, before the actual wedding. Until then, the bride remains living in her father's house, even though she is considered married right from the betrothal.

---

[186] Matthew 26:23, Mark 14:20

[187] John 2:6

The actual wedding is a huge event, both in the family and in the whole village. Special preparations are exciting for the bride. She goes through a ceremonial bathing, perfuming, and anointing by the other women. They also help her with the intricate layers of clothes and adornments. She is treated as a queen on this special day, seated on a special chair or bench, crowned with a wreath, and carried through the village, accompanied by many people singing and dancing. Rabbis and students interrupt their studies to join the celebration. Gifts are tossed to the couple, wine and oil are poured before their path, and torches are lit at night for the continuing procession.

The procession ends up at the groom's father's house. After the ceremony under the *chuppah* or canopy, the party begins and may last for a week. There are continual blessings, feasting, singing, all called "gladdening the bride and groom."

Weddings are traditionally held on Tuesdays to bring extra blessings to the couple. This is because in creation, God gave a blessing of "good" two times on the third day.[188] The couples feel that Tuesday is a doubly good day for their wedding.

As Conlee and I were walking toward the Western Wall in Jerusalem one day on a Tuesday morning we were surprised to get caught up in a wedding procession heading along the same path. They included us as if we were members of the family, encouraging us to dance, sing, skip, and join them in blessing the bride and groom.

Some of the people in the procession played flutes and tambourines. A dancing violinist, his *tzitzit* flying, played and whirled down the steps. They even passed a velvet bag to us, which we learned was to receive coins for the newly married couple. We threw in a few *shekels* as a blessing and were blessed ourselves with great joy, the intention of the ceremony.

After that experience, I received a deeper insight into Jesus' parable, comparing the Kingdom of Heaven with a wedding banquet given by a king for his son.[189] The unbridled joy we experienced in Jerusalem with an unknown couple pales in comparison to the joy we will experience one day with God face-to-face.

Returning to our first-century biblical family, we explored what happens after our family's evening meal.

We might gather on the roof to visit with one another and have Torah study, a nightly tradition that the father leads. Not only does the father serve as a servant to his family, but also as a teacher. Both parents teach the

---

[188] Genesis 1:10,12

[189] Matthew 22:1-14

children Bible verses at a very young age. Grandparents, too, have a big role in teaching Torah and taking a child to school.

Children memorize verses from the Torah (the first five books of the Bible) and learn Bible stories. When the boys are six years old they go to a school master in the synagogue where they are taught further. For the first four years of school, they learn only Torah, as well as reading and writing Hebrew. For the next seven years they study other books of the Bible and rabbinical writings. After the age of twelve, many boys quit school to work with the family. At this age he is considered to be a man.

Girls are taught at home, but seldom go to school to learn to read or write. By adolescence, most girls are married. Once married, she assumes many of the duties her mother has modeled. She grinds flour, bakes, launders, cooks, nurses her children, makes beds, spins wool, provides hospitality and lodging for travelers, and is in charge of giving alms to those in need.

When a man marries he is expected to provide food, clothing, and shoes for his family, as well as money for his wife's personal expenses. If he is called by God or inclined to study Torah or travel with a rabbi (as Jesus' married disciples did), he is required to come home to his wife at least every thirty days.

When a child is born, there is a celebration, observed by planting a tree – typically, a cedar tree for a son and an acacia tree for a daughter.

Baby boys are circumcised when eight days old by a rabbi, trained in such surgery. This is accompanied by a big celebration with blessings galore heaped upon the child. Here is a passage from the Talmud, describing the different stages of a boy's life.

"A minor who is no longer dependent on his mother is obliged by the commandment to sit in a booth;[190] if he can wave it, he is obliged to take a palm branch; if he can wrap it around himself, he is obliged to wear a prayer shawl; if he can care for them, his father should buy phylacteries[191] for him; if he can talk, his father should teach him the *shema*[192] and Torah and the sacred language;[193] if he knows how to slaughter animals, his slaughtering is kosher;[194] if he can keep his body clean, he may eat pure foods; if he can keep his hands clean, one may eat pure food from them; if he can eat a piece of meat the size of an olive, one may slaughter a paschal lamb for

---

[190] Indicates participation in the Feast of Tabernacles.

[191] Two small black leather cubes containing a piece of parchment inscribed with verses from Torah. One is attached with straps to the left arm and the other to the forehead during weekday morning prayers by Jewish men.

[192] Deuteronomy 6:4-9, 11:13-21, Numbers 15:37-41 are a vital part of morning and evening Jewish prayer.

[193] Hebrew

[194] The required method according to Jewish dietary laws

him."[195]

At age thirteen, a boy is permitted to serve as a leader in the synagogue by praying and performing other functions. By age twenty, he can become a judge.

When a person dies, there is great respect for the body. First, it is very important to continue to treat a person until everyone assures that he or she is dead.

When death is ascertained, some of the requirements for caring for a body after death are unquestioned. You must close the body's eyes, keep the body cool, and rinse and anoint the body with oil. The hair must be trimmed before burial, except for an unmarried girl. She is buried with her hair long.

All openings on the body are wrapped tightly with cloths and spices. Lighted candles are placed at the body's head and feet. The body must be buried immediately because it is considered disrespectful to leave a corpse unburied throughout the night for any reason.

Tradition requires hiring at least one paid keening woman and two pipers for even the poorest Jew. They accompany the procession of carrying the body for burial, stopping at intervals along the way to play the pipes, wail, and clap their hands.[196] At each interval, people who knew the deceased can give a eulogy. Those who carry the body are barefoot as a sign of mourning. People always stand still, stopping their work when a funeral procession passes.[197]

Burial places are always outside the village, in caves or under large rocks. Bodies are never covered with dirt but with rocks.[198] If they must be buried in a field, large markers are erected so they will not be plowed.

Another way of identifying a burial rock or cave is whitewashing the stones so that the grave is easily identified and will not be desecrated or moved. Jesus used this illustration once when pointing out the hypocrisy of some of the Pharisees.

"You are like whitewashed tombs, which look beautiful on the outside but on the inside are full of dead men's bones and everything unclean."[199]

After the funeral, even more customs are observed. Mourning lasts for

---

[195] *The Jewish People in the First Century, Volume 2*, S. Safrai and M. Stern, Fortress Press, Philadelphia, 1987, pp 771-772.

[196] Why this was done is uncertain. Perhaps to assure that each person received a proper mourning period, even if there were few or none to participate with genuine emotion. The act places a value on each life.

[197] In certain parts of our country today it is the custom to pull your car over to the side of the road and stop when a funeral procession goes by. In fewer areas, people still get out of their cars and bow their heads in respect.

[198] In Israel today, you see mourners place rocks on tombs of loved ones, rather than flowers.

[199] Matthew 23:27b

seven days, with mourners sitting barefoot on the ground or low benches with their heads covered. They are forbidden to work, wash, anoint themselves, or even study Torah. When people come to visit the family, they bring food and wine. Whenever ten men are present, blessings are given.

On the third day, everyone is required to visit the burial site to check the body. A traditional legend is that once a man was found alive on the third day and lived another twenty-five years. This custom is to verify that the person is really dead.[200] After several months, the bones are collected and placed in an ossuary or bone box.

Bedtime comes early in the first century because everyone has worked hard all day and because our house becomes quite dark after sundown. At daybreak, we start all over again. It is easy to see why feast days and the weekly *Shabbat* are so special and anticipated.

The children were already planning what they wanted their model village to look like. After lunch, we moved the big board upstairs to a room I call the Fun Room, our upstairs, over-the-garage, bonus room designated for crafts and exercise equipment. Papa put the board on a table in the middle of the room so that everyone had access to it, and the children checked out all the materials I had assembled for them to use in their project.

They enjoyed unloading a box filled with modeling clay in most colors, poster paints, paint brushes, colored markers, and an inexpensive hand-cranked pasta machine made for flattening clay.

Their enthusiasm quickly turned to confusion as each one had his or her own ideas and tried to talk over everyone else. Finally, Sophie, the perpetual organizer, had a suggestion that we all liked.

"Let's divide the board into five equal areas and each one of us take a section for whatever part of the village we want to make."

After the four corners were marked off with a center section of equal size, Jake immediately claimed the middle because he was interested in making the village well and knew that it should be centrally located.

Anna was a close second to claim one of the sections for animals. She decided on sheep.

Edie wanted to make a field of wheat and Caleb wanted his part to be the synagogue.

That left Sophie who wanted to make the houses and outdoor ovens.

My suggestion was that they start designing their village on graph paper, marking off spaces for each item to get good ideas of the sizes they needed to make everything look proportional and harmonious.

For the next several hours there was a happy buzz of busyness and not

---

[200] After Jesus was in the tomb for three days, He proved to everyone that He was indeed alive!

one cross word because no one was competing. The original design was modified somewhat as they went along and began to get more and more intricate. For a while I was worried that they might be attempting to do something far more complicated than possible, but my worries were unfounded. What began to take shape was creative, symbolic, and beautifully executed.

Each one painted the undercoat color of their section. Jake added texture with glue, sand and small gravel. Sophie added dirt for floors. Anna added grass for her sheep and Edie added straw. Caleb stuck with white paint for his synagogue.

Then the details began to take shape. The well was constructed from small stones stuck in clay, with a bucket and some clay jars beside it. Sheep were formed with clay squeezed through a garlic press. Most were white but Anna included one black one. Standing sheaves of wheat in rows were formed by weaving thin spaghetti strands of clay. Foundations of homes took shape, close together, some very modest with only one room, and some with two. Pillars of the synagogue were formed, with benches along the sides.

When it came time to clean up for supper, they were reluctant to leave their project. I assured them that they would have time to complete their details later. It was nice to have a spot to leave the mess and close the door until another day.

At supper that night Papa and I made an announcement.

"Tomorrow, we need you to be up by 7:00, showered, dressed, and have your bed made. You will need to pack a small carry-on bag or backpack with a complete change of clothes, a light rain jacket, and everything you need for an overnight. Wear comfortable walking shoes and bring a cap."

There was an explosion of questions.

"Where are we going?"

"What are we going to do?"

"I hate surprises."

"Please give us a hint."

Long after they went to bed, we could hear them all talking upstairs, sharing all sorts of ideas about what they thought the surprise trip was about.

DAY 3 – VILLAGE LIFE AND HOUSING

We had no trouble getting everyone up, fed, packed up, and in the car by 8:30. In fact, they impatiently urged us to hurry. And they didn't even know where they were going!

We told them that we had about an hour's drive and would use the time in the car for our morning lesson. Therefore, no electronic devices were allowed in the car. There was the expected chorus of groans but everyone complied.

Our mini-van was convenient for our number of passengers. Edie and Anna took the windows in the back, with Jake between them. Sophie and Caleb had the two middle seats. Papa drove and I negotiated the lesson from the front passenger seat. It was a bit awkward, but it worked.

Everyone got facts and picture sheets to start. They illustrated the foundations of homes in Capernaum the way the sites look today.

Papa and I told the children about walking through these foundations, imagining what they looked like when they were actual stone houses. They are unbelievably close to one another, within a very short stroll to the synagogue on one side and the village well on the other. A stone wall protected the village from a well-traveled road that went from Jerusalem to Damascus.

Today, a large protective glass structure, octagonal and modern in design, is built on concrete stilts over the largest home's foundation. It serves as a shrine and church because the home below is thought to be that of Simon Peter. If so, it shows that he was wealthier than most, due to the fact that he owned a fleet of fishing boats and perhaps employed many of the other villagers.

Many people who visit this amazing archeological dig at Capernaum complain about the modern structure that stands out in a disturbing way. However, had it not been constructed we would not be able to see the details that have been preserved. Through the glass floor inside the church one can look down on the ancient foundation.

Capernaum is located on the north side of the Sea of Galilee. Its name in Hebrew literally means "Nahum's village." Known as a fishing village since the second century BC, at one time it had a population of 1,500, counting those who lived around the village in the countryside.

Jesus lived here, with His disciple Peter, during most of His ministry. It was the hometown of many of His disciples, as well as Simon the tax collector. Jesus taught in the synagogue here and healed many people. Among them were a demonized man, Simon Peter's mother-in-law, the servant of a Roman centurion, and the paralytic man who was lowered through a roof by his friends.

Referring to their pictures of the foundations, I explained that some of the larger homes were known as "insula," which refers to several houses built around a common courtyard. The courtyard contained an oven which all the families used. Some of the homes had grinding stones as well. Each home had an exterior staircase to get to either the second story or the roof.

The foundation of the synagogue in Capernaum that you walk through today is from the fourth century. Although it was built on top of the one that existed at the time of Jesus, the footprint is thought to be the same as the original. It was built of large, white limestone blocks, taken from the hills west of Capernaum.

"Yes!" Caleb congratulated himself on insisting that his clay synagogue be all white.

The synagogue was built higher than the houses with two staircases leading up to the prayer hall from a courtyard. The whole synagogue was paved with large, thick slabs of smoothed limestone.

The decorations were typically Jewish. In Capernaum, a seven-branched menorah with a ram's horn and an incense shovel is carved on one of the pillars. On a door lintel is a depiction of a chariot carrying the Ark of the Covenant. There are also motifs of palm fronds, clusters of grapes and pomegranates.

Some partial inscriptions were found on the columns that remain. One says in Greek, "Herod son of Mo[ni]mos and Justus his son together with (his) children erected this column."

Another column found in the courtyard was inscribed in Aramaic, "Halfu son of Zebida the son of Yohanan made this column. May he be blessed."

Apparently donors liked to get recognition in public for their contributions even in the first century.

I gave the children some pencils and word search pages about Capernaum, but our road was getting very curvy and everyone decided that working on something in the car during the last few miles of our trip was not a good idea. Instead, the guessing game continued about what we had in store.

In less than an hour we arrived at our first destination, Eureka Springs, Arkansas. It is a fascinating town in the Ozark Mountains, known as the "Little Switzerland of America." We had been many times to the quaint Victorian town with its winding streets, steep steps, no traffic lights, and gingerbread houses built on the sides of hills, with their entrances on several streets and levels. It is a town full of artists and creativity. However, this time we did not head toward the heart of the town, but turned east to another destination.

After driving off the main road for a few minutes, we stopped in front of a large imposing edifice, built to look like the Temple in Jerusalem. We were at The Holy Land Tour and the site of The Great Passion Play.

Most of the comments from the back of the car were reduced to, "Wow!"

The view was especially impressive when you stood right at the arched entrance. Everyone piled out while Papa went to park the car. The day was overcast so we all grabbed our rain jackets. We had some mist at one point but it never actually got us wet. The weather was an unexpected blessing for us because we saw very few other visitors the whole day. It was as though we went to the Holy Land on a private tour.

While we were waiting for Papa to meet up with us, Edie called everyone together to tell us something in a hushed voice.

"See that guy across the road getting out of his car? He looks just like Jesus. He really does look like Jesus did when I saw Him that time going to school. Except my Jesus had on a blue robe."

We all looked and saw a very nice looking young man with a full dark beard locking his car in the employees' parking lot. He was wearing jeans and a plaid shirt. And yes, there really was something very sweet and honest about him, the way he moved, walked, and politely greeted another employee.

Perhaps there was something holy about being at this place. By the time Papa returned, the young man had disappeared and Edie immediately told him that he had missed seeing Jesus. What do you say to something like that?

Our day consisted of three reserved activities. We were scheduled for a one hour tour of the Tabernacle at 10:00. At noon, we were set to tour the Holy Land, and we had tickets for a performance of The Great Passion Play at 8:00 pm.

I had spent a lot of time online making reservations for the tours, performance and accommodations afterwards. I discovered that the size of our family qualified us for a group rate for all three events which made it much more affordable. No doubt, we all were all about to become immersed in the Bible in an unprecedented, experiential way.

Our Tabernacle guide appeared and he was delightful. An older, bearded man in a motorized wheelchair, he had served as a Jewish rabbi until he found his Messiah and became a Christian believer. We were surprised to learn that we were the only ones there for his morning tour and pleased that he gave us two full hours of teaching, touring, and personal revelation.

The rabbi (as he invited us to address him) took us first to a little shelter outside the tent to sit on wooden benches while he gave us an overview of the biblical Tabernacle.

He seemed surprised that the children were as knowledgeable as they were about what the Tabernacle was, what was in it, and how the worshipers made sacrifices. He received animated answers to every question he asked. We told him about Camp Mimi and the whole week we spent just studying the Tabernacle a few years earlier. He was very interested in our experience. I think our being such an attentive group was the reason he spent an extra hour with us.

The Tabernacle part of the Holy Land Tour is reconstructed exactly according to the specifications that God gave Moses in the Bible. The Tabernacle we had constructed on our back lawn in Mobile, had looked much larger because we did not have the tent sides or enclosed spaces for the Holy Place and the Holy of Holies. The open spaces we had to work with gave a distorted sense of the intimacy of the actual dimensions.

Our pace was slow and deliberate as we went through each station of the order of worship. This was partly because of the rabbi's limited mobility but also because of his intense reverence for the topic. At each stop along the way, he explained how everything led to the coming of Messiah and His sacrifice for us. His love for Jesus was obvious.

As we entered the large tent, we found ourselves in the open space called the courtyard. The most imposing structure in this area was the high altar. A ramp built of stones led up to a square box where the sacrifices were burned. Horns stuck out on each corner of the altar. The children climbed up the ramp and looked in as the rabbi told them that it was a place of death. Something had to die for each person's sins. Even as he said this, we heard thunder in the distance. It was as if God was emphasizing this important truth.

Next he led Papa and the boys to the laver. A bronze basin for washing one's hands before performing the sacrifices, it is a powerful symbol of cleansing of the heart as well as the body. This was something all the men did when they came to worship. The rabbi had our three men join him in a circle around the basin. He instructed them to hold their hands out, palms up, and follow his lead.

Slowly pouring water over one hand and then the other, they all participated in the ancient ritual, saying together,

"I wash my hands. I wash my heart. I wash my mind.
I wash my hands. I wash my heart. I wash my mind.
I wash my hands. I wash my heart. I wash my mind."

The girls and I watched reverently. It felt as though we had left a tour and entered into an ageless ceremony preparing us for something important.

When we moved inside the tented rooms containing the large menorah, the incense, and the table of showbread, it was fascinating and beautiful, as was our peek into the Holy of Holies with the Ark of the Covenant.

However, a special presence of God was over all of us when Conlee, Caleb, Jake, and the rabbi washed in the laver. It was one of those moments you never forget.

After our tour, we retrieved a cooler from our car containing a picnic lunch. It was cool for a summer day and we ate outside on a picnic table, enjoying our surroundings. It was a pastoral setting on top of a mountain with people walking around in biblical dress. All we needed were our own costumes, which we did not bring with us.

Next, it was time for the Holy Land Tour. We entered through the big arched opening and were immediately transported to the first century.

Everything we saw reflected our lessons at Camp Mimi over the previous two days. Crude fences and shelters held donkeys, goats and sheep. Shepherds and goatherds, dressed in costumes exactly like the ones Caleb and Jake had worn the day before, tended the animals and invited us in to pet them. We watched as they milked the goats. Anna, our animal lover, asked them how she could get to be a shepherd there.

We also saw some camels kept behind low rock enclosures. People in biblical villages would have seen camels frequently carrying wares on the trade routes.

A major Roman road called the *Via Maris* was only three miles from Capernaum. An offshoot of the trade route went right through Capernaum. This important road came up from Egypt, went along the coast of the Sinai peninsula into Israel, up to Mount Carmel, then eastward along the Jezreel Valley to the western shore of the Sea of Galilee. From there it crossed the Jordan River and went to Damascus and on to Mesopotamia. This was the main transportation and trade route in Jesus' time.

The camel herder told us that, although camels are very well-suited for long trips of transporting goods, they are not very sweet-tempered and demand a lot of respect. They smelled terrible.

Next, we walked a little further up the road and discovered some typical village homes, much like the ones Sophie was making for our project. We walked through them, noticing the clay oven outside and the place for livestock in the front room. We observed the small, high window and the niches in the interior rock walls for the clay oil lamps. Jake was especially interested in the oven and decided he was going to make a community one near his well.

Before we walked on down the hill to get on a small bus that would take us further into the mountains for the rest of the tour, we paused to sit on benches where an older man portrayed Moses, telling us what it was like to receive the Ten Commandments from God. He graciously allowed me to take a picture of him with the children.

The little bus took our family on a circuitous route, up and down hills and around mountains, until we were sufficiently disoriented and believed we were indeed, in another land, another time, and another culture. The bus disappeared after we got off at our destination and we were directed where to walk to see other areas. We were assured the bus would be waiting for us at the next location to take us to another seemingly remote location. It was a very effective way to transport us from one biblical event to another over some rough terrain.

Our first stop was at a typical first-century home. We were greeted at the door by Miriam, representing a first-century Jewish wife, who told us about her family and her life in a small village in Galilee. The things she shared were exactly what we needed to more accurately complete our clay village.

Miriam showed us how she brought water from the well to pour into the large jars on the raised platform inside, cooked on the oven outside, and took the oven into the outer room of the house in colder weather.

She demonstrated how the bed rolls were stored against the wall during the day and placed around the floor at night for sleeping. She filled clay lamps with oil and trimmed the wicks.

She told us what she would prepare for her family when they returned for supper. In spite of all the hard work, she convinced us that she was incredibly blessed and very happy.

Next, Miriam pointed the way for us to walk down to the Sea of Galilee.

We followed the trail and discovered a lake with a man in biblical dress, sitting beside his boat, mending a fishing net. He welcomed us and said he was Simon, whom Jesus had renamed Peter.

He told us how he first met Jesus and how it changed his life. Inviting the children to ask him questions, he explained about fishing techniques, what kind of fish he caught, and how hard it was to make a living at this kind of work. He said it was what his family had always done and he loved it. In spite of the thrill of catching fish, he said it was even more exciting to be a fisher of men.

As Peter told us about the time he was with the other disciples in his boat in the middle of the Sea and saw Jesus walking on the water, Jake yelled out, "It's Jesus!"

We all looked at where he was pointing and in the distance, near the far side of the lake, you could see the gleaming white robes of Jesus, walking on the water.

"That's just what it looked like," said Peter. "We all were afraid it was a ghost. We'd never seen anything like it. But Jesus identified Himself and told us not to be afraid. As soon as He said that, I wanted more than anything to join Him. I said, 'If it's really You, tell me to come where You are.' When He said, 'Come,' I couldn't wait to get into the water – and I did it! I really walked on water, just like you see Him now."

The man portraying Jesus stopped on the water, stretched out his hands, and in a booming voice, said, "Come."

At this invitation, Jake looked at me and asked, "Can I really?" He was ready to rush into the water.

Peter must have been prepared for such a response and indeed seemed to relish responding to it. He told us how the waves got really high while he was walking on the water and then he quit looking at Jesus and started looking at his precarious situation and nearly drowned. Jesus pulled him back into the boat and encouraged him to keep having faith. He told Jake that if he had faith and believed, Jesus would come to him.

About that time, the actor walked around some rocks right towards us. Edie nearly exploded, "It's Jesus! It's the guy we saw in the parking lot!"

He probably was the most perfect person imaginable for the role. There was a gentleness and sincerity that accompanied the young man's appearance that made us know that someone who truly loved God was in our midst. He loved hearing the story of how they saw him get out of his car that morning.

In our brief conversation, we learned how much it meant to him to play the role of Jesus at the Holy Land Tour and also at the Passion Play. When we told him we would be there that night he said that being in the play brought him closer to God at every performance.

Before we were instructed to walk on to the next venue, he asked about each of the children, their names, ages, and where they lived. He seemed genuinely interested. Then he asked if he could pray for them. He gently laid his hands on each one and prayed a prayer of blessing over them. They soaked it up. We all did.

He gave us directions to walk around a bend in the road for our next experience.

Waving goodbye to Jesus, we soon found a stone house with one side completely open so we could view the interior. Two women, dressed authentically, were busy preparing a meal. They invited us closer to show us what they were doing.

They told us that we were in the upper room of a house belonging to a friend of Jesus. They would be sharing their Passover Meal with Jesus that night and they were making the preparations. They asked the children if they knew what Passover was and the children remembered some of their favorite highlights, delighting the two women.

"We like to scream out the plagues and find the hidden *Afikomen* for a prize."

The women pointed out the very low, simple wooden table with cushions on the floor. The table was in the shape of a "U." There were crude pottery cups and bowls and little else, except for some fruit in the middle of the table.

One of the women asked, "Where do you think is the place of honor at the table? When you think you know, go and sit in that spot."

The children all ran to sit as close as possible to the middle of the center section. I was waiting until they got situated and then took a place on the far side of the table so I could take some pictures of them from an out-of-the-way position.

To my surprise the woman told the children, "Your grandmother picked the place of honor. It is always the place furthest away from the door. The lowest place of honor is right by the door."

Perhaps it is because of our impressions from Leonardo da Vinci's "The Last Supper" painting, but most Christians will automatically think of the same spot the children did.

She also had them practice "reclining at table," by leaning their left shoulder on the table with their legs stretched out straight behind them. This is how a woman was able to anoint Jesus' feet while he was reclining at a meal[201] without crawling under the table. Perhaps she thought no one else would notice. It also explains how His disciple John reclined at Jesus' breast in a very natural way that was not awkward.[202]

Before we left, she reviewed Jesus' establishing the symbol of the New Covenant by taking the bread as His body and the cup as His blood at such a Passover meal. She encouraged us to remember that when we take communion next time.

The bus came to take us to a last place where we could walk through some caves similar to burial places and some sites of pastures and fields where wheat was grown. It was hard to believe that we had been totally immersed in biblical culture for four hours. We were ready to rest.

Online I had reserved what I thought would be the perfect place for our overnight stay. On a reservation site we had used many times, I found a log cabin available very near the Holy Land Tour and Passion Play. It was situated in the woods, had enough beds for everyone, as well as a little kitchen where we could prepare our supper and breakfast the next morning. The pictures looked very cozy and welcoming.

While driving to Eureka Springs that morning I received a text from the owner apologizing for overbooking and telling me that, unfortunately, the log cabin would not be available. She had found something "even better" for us at the same price. However, it was in the heart of Eureka Springs.

Even using the GPS, it took a long time for us to locate our new accommodation. It was hidden between two homes with large fences, across the street from a church, on a very winding street, and the back part of the house hung off the side of the steep hill.

The children ran in first to inspect the house and before I could get to the door, they all ran back out, "Oh, Mimi and Papa, it's weird. Do we have to stay here?"

It *was* weird, in layout, décor, and location – but what choice did we have? It was already 5:00. We needed to feed the children and go back to the Passion Play, which started at 8:00. I had hoped everyone would get a rest first. It didn't look like that was going to happen.

---

[201] Luke 7:36-38

[202] John 13:23

After looking around inside, we assigned the girls the downstairs apartment of the house, which could only be entered by some steep steps outside. The boys got the couch in the upstairs living room which made into a bed and Papa and I had the upstairs bedroom. We prayed over our surroundings and decided to make the best of it.

In the cooler I had individually wrapped frozen chicken hand pies,[203] a favorite meal for excursions. So the first thing I did was turn on the upstairs oven. There was no oven downstairs. I thought I would be able to put the pies in the oven as soon as we got the car unpacked and that we would have supper in about twenty minutes. We had a plan.

It didn't take long for us to realize that the oven did not work. Fifteen minutes later it was as cold as when I turned it on. Time for Plan B. The natives were getting restless.

"Let's all go get ice cream!" (How's that for a plan?)

My suggestion was met with a lot of loud enthusiasm.

"Really???"

"Before supper?"

"Yes!"

Plan B was for Conlee to take the children for ice cream while I located a restaurant to get take-out for supper. We were a few steps from the main street of town and I knew from past trips to Eureka Springs that there were lots of ice cream parlors and little restaurants. This should be a cinch.

Conlee discovered that the two ice cream parlors on the main street closed at 5:00 so they headed on down the hill to find a third. While they were on their ice cream safari, I was unsuccessfully trying to find a restaurant.

The only eating establishment open was a biker bar with a large sign in the window stating, "No Underage Allowed." It looked like they might have bar food though. Maybe I could find something that would work.

I walked inside the dark room and was enveloped in a suffocating haze of cigarette smoke. It was one of those surreal moments when everything came to a halt. Each person in the crowded room stopped their conversations, turned toward the door, and stared at me. They weren't used to seeing a middle-aged woman with no tattoos in a large straw hat walk into their domain.

I mustered all my bravado and went right up to the bar, squeezing in between two huge mountains of black leather and chains, who turned out to be Shorty and Tiny. (It's true!)

"What can I get you, doll?" smirked the bartender, a tiny well-inked woman, also in black leather.

I took a deep breath. "I have five hungry grandchildren in a rented

---

[203] See Camp Mimi Eats

house around the corner and I need something for their supper before we go to the Passion Play tonight."

Everyone in the bar was listening to my request and suddenly I became the center of attention with suggestions coming from every bar stool and table.

"Them poppers are good, but they're probably too hot for kids."

"Try the nachos. They're my favorite."

"How 'bout them chili dogs?"

It seemed there was no written menu but all the regulars knew what was served. I decided on several orders of nachos, some with chicken and some with beef.

"You sit right here, little lady, and I'll find Arnie to make em for you. We don't have a kitchen here and he'll have to go to the hotel up the street. They don't have a restaurant anymore but we use their kitchen."

She got on her phone, trying to locate Arnie, and demanded that I sit at the bar.

"You boys move on over and let her have a seat. Mind your manners."

The two leather mountains managed to separate and I sat between them, realizing that the two of them had been using three stools. The one on my right yelled at the bartender, "Bring her a beer while she's waiting."

"Oh no, that's okay," I protested. "How long is this going to take?"

"You never know with Arnie. Anyhows, I don't talk to no one who won't drink with me."

I assumed this was an invitation for conversation.

Tish, the bartender, put a cold, long-necked bottle of beer in front of me and Tiny actually clinked bottles with me, "Down the hatch." By now we were all on a first name basis.

I had a sudden revelation of why there are mirrors behind all bars. It is the only acceptable way to look at someone sitting beside you.

"Tish is my ol' lady." It took me a minute to realize that he meant the bartender was his girlfriend.

"Oh, she is?" That was my sole response that led to the next fifteen minutes of learning about how Tish and Tiny met, his three exes, the kinds of bikes he's had, and how Shorty, the mountain on the other side of me, "don't say much."

Finally, a large sack filled with Styrofoam boxes of nachos appeared as Arnie walked in the front door, presumably from the hotel kitchen up the street. Everyone greeted him with gusto.

I paid the bill, left a sizeable tip, and thanked Tish, Tiny, and silent Shorty for taking good care of me.

With his elbows still on the bar and without making any eye contact, Tiny gave me his warm version of goodbye, "Y'all enjoy that Jesus play, ya hear? It's a good story. It'll make ya feel good."

I waved to the small audience of bikers as I left the bar. There were several responses from some of the table customers who had eavesdropped.

"Have fun tonight."

"Enjoy them nachos."

"Love on them grandkids."

"Come back sometime."

On the sidewalk outside, I was relieved to deeply breathe in some fresh air, but realized I had been in a place filled with its own kind of love and belonging.

At supper in the weird house, we all agreed that the nachos were the best we had ever eaten. I told the family the whole story while we ate and my favorite response to The Biker Bar Adventure was, "That Arnie sure can cook!"

Tiny was right. The Jesus story *does* make you feel good. The Passion Play, performed in a huge outdoor amphitheater, is one of several in the United States, on a par with the well-known performance in Oberammergau, Germany. The cast of characters, the action, the animals, and the hilly terrain of the set, all beautifully portray the most powerful story in the world. And we were especially blessed because we had personally met Jesus!

DAY 4 – TORAH STUDY AND SURPRISES

In spite of the girls' insistence that they never went to sleep in their odd downstairs apartment, everyone seemed rested and ready to go the next morning. We had the ingredients in our cooler to prepare a simple breakfast. Then we packed and loaded the car, presumably to return home.

While Papa drove, I began our mobile, morning Camp Mimi lesson on one of the most important areas of life to a first-century Jew – Torah study.

The first subjects most of us studied in school were reading, writing, numbers, and how to color inside the lines. However, in ancient Israel, the object of school was foremost to learn Torah.[204] But study was considered more than learning facts; it was an act of worship. To know the word of God was to honor Him and sacrifice your time to Him.

All first-century Jews had a holy obligation, not only to know God's word, but to apply it to their life. Also, when studying Torah, each person had an obligation to then teach others.

Can you imagine the after-supper conversations in a typical Jewish

---

[204] Torah is the first five books of the Bible, sometimes known as The Books of Moses. Studying Torah may also include study of the law and commandments of God.

home? The father calls everyone together for teaching and prayer. He encourages the children who attend school to share what they learned that day. Their education then benefits the whole family.

Besides the teachings received in the home, everyone heard readings and expositions of Torah at synagogue. Also, every annual festival (of which there were many during a year) revolved around a portion of Torah. Memorization of the Word of God was encouraged and practiced.

In Israel, the most effective way for children to memorize Torah was to repeat aloud what they heard or read. This method was considered the only way to overcome the danger of forgetting.

Until people had access to the written word, they relied on the amazingly accurate method of oral tradition. By continually repeating a story verbatim, mistakes and additions would quickly be spotted and corrected by the listeners. Minds were sharper and their memories were more reliable when people had to listen closely to absorb facts and truths.

When people began to read, it became harder to remember the exact words and accurate memories faded. This is why speaking aloud and repeating passages over and over made remembering accurate details much easier.

I asked the children if they ever studied this way. Not one of them admitted to repeating facts aloud in order to memorize. Today, it is not the normal method used to help children absorb information. Instead, many of them memorize for a test and then quickly forget. In the first century, much of the Torah was memorized by repetition of the verses and chanting them aloud.

The duty of every Jewish father was to teach his son Torah and a craft. Although very wise of the father, this was not just to provide for his son's future. Hard, productive work was considered to be a high calling. This is reflected in the Hebrew language in which there is no word for "leisure" as there is in Greek. The Jews did not consider leisure time to be godly.

Preparing one's son for future work was so important that some rabbis even permitted a father to negotiate arrangements for his son's apprenticeship and Torah education on a Sabbath. These arrangements were not considered work but acts of worship.

The love of God and Torah study were impressed upon children before they could walk or talk. On the doorpost of every home a *mezuzah* was affixed. This was a small metal or stone case which contained a folded piece of parchment on which two passages of scripture were written.[205] These scriptures reminded each person who entered or left their home of the attitudes of the heart that please God.

From the time a baby was carried in and out of the home in a parent's

---

[205] Deuteronomy 6:4-9 and 11:13-21

arms, the child would become used to seeing them reverently touch the case, kiss the finger that touched it, and hear them speak a benediction.

One verse frequently spoken upon every entry and exit was "The Lord will watch over your coming and going both now and evermore."[206]

Deep impressions of God's love and protection were formed in the heart of the smallest child, as well as reinforced by family prayers and study, weekly *Shabbat*, and the family participation in the many festivals honoring God throughout the year.

Parents took the commandment from God about child-rearing very seriously. "Train a child in the way he should go, and when he is old he will not turn from it."[207]

Besides learning Torah and memorizing scripture, children learned stories about heroes in the Bible, just as children do today in Sunday School.

I handed the children in the back of the car sheets of paper with pictures and questions and places to fill in the blanks. Each one received a pencil and we began our lesson of the hero for the day, Jonah.

"Aren't we going to get carsick if we do this?" Sophie wanted to know. She remembered the curvy mountain roads from yesterday.

"We're going home a different way," I assured her, bending the truth a little bit.

"What do you remember about the story of Jonah?"

Jonah had been one of the heroes we studied at a previous Camp Mimi, so they knew the basic story. There were shouts of "big fish," "ran away from God," "a worm ate his shelter," "was in the belly of a fish," and other points of the story that made an impression on them.

I read them excerpts about Jonah from *The Journey to Wholeness in Christ*,[208] a book I wrote describing Bible characters who learned lessons from God about becoming whole in every way. For Jonah, it was about hearing and obeying God's voice.

Some of the questions about Jonah on the children's pages were:

> Who was told to go to Nineveh to preach?
> Why did Nineveh need a prophet?
> Why did the prophet want to run away from God's call?
> Where did he run?
> Where was he during the storm?
> Why did sailors throw him overboard?

---

[206] Psalm 121:8

[207] Proverbs 22:6

[208] *The Journey to Wholeness in Christ*, Signa Bodishbaugh, Baker (Chosen) Books/Journey Press, 1997, pp 191-216.

Everyone was getting into the discussion about what Jonah did and why he ran from God when suddenly Anna cried out from the back of the car, "We're going the wrong way!"

She pointed out a big green sign on the side of the road, "Welcome to Missouri."

There were choruses of "Papa! You went the wrong way! We need to turn around."

It was obviously time for the next surprise to be revealed. Instead of heading south toward home we were going north. We were on our way to Branson, Missouri, to have lunch at one of our favorite hamburger places and then to see a matinee performance of a play about Jonah. There had been an ulterior motive in my choice of which Bible hero to study that morning.

The study quickly came to an end as the excitement built in the car about what our day would be like. They wanted to know every detail and couldn't believe they had been fooled.

We were able to take our time having a fun lunch at a popular place in Branson and arrived at the Sight and Sound Theater[209] just in time for the afternoon performance. With the story of Jonah fresh in our minds from our morning lesson, we especially loved seeing it come alive on stage as a musical. The sets and special effects, especially that of the huge fish consuming the hero, stirred all of our senses.

During the intermission while everyone stood to take a break, I noticed a man roaming the aisles, greeting people and thanking them for coming. The way he was dressed revealed that he definitely was not a native of Branson, Missouri. Wearing a dapper linen jacket and ascot and sporting an avant-garde hair style, he looked interesting, so I walked nearer and overheard that he was the general director of the play. Home-based at the other Sight and Sound Theater in Pennsylvania, he was in Branson, for just a few of the performances of *Jonah*.

I introduced myself, telling him that Conlee and I had our grandchildren with us and a brief version about our study of Bible times at Camp Mimi. He wanted to meet the children and, very animatedly, told us about how they prepare for their biblical musical productions.

"The whole production staff prays first about which story to present. Then for months we pray about how to make it come alive onstage. Every person involved is committed to one objective in all we do – to make the Bible real to our audience."

He shook our hands as the lights dimmed and the play was about to resume. As he left us, his parting words were, "The best is yet to come."

---

[209] Sight and Sound Theaters, Branson, MO and Lancaster, PA.

And he was so right! Even more spectacular than the ship in the storm and the big fish swallowing Jonah, was the scene when the Ninevites confessed their sins, repented, and were converted to believers in Yahweh.

I had never thought about the story from the viewpoint of the pagans. They heard Jonah's message about God, believed what he said, and had a change of heart so sincere and deep that their whole city was converted. In the play, this was one of the most powerful scenes I have ever witnessed on stage.

The transition from hard-hearted evil, to cynicism, to ridicule, to pondering the message was profoundly presented. God's Holy Spirit worked on one person at a time, revealing truth, changing hearts, and humbling the people until an evil nation received forgiveness and turned to God.

It was hard to believe this was accomplished as a musical but when the "Ninevites" exited the stage, down the center aisles among the audience, the anointing of Holy Spirit was upon each performer. Many of them were weeping as were many of us in the audience.

On the way home, after the outstanding performance, everyone in the car was still excited about what we had just witnessed. We all shared our favorite parts over and over. The children's enthusiasm helped the power of the play linger in our hearts, making the two hour drive home seem short.[210]

We arrived home around 7:00 p.m., tired and hungry. Oh, no! What was I going to feed everyone? Edie had the perfect solution.

"What about those chicken hand pies[211] we didn't get to eat last night?" Perfect!

After the car was unloaded, everyone scattered until supper was ready. Jake was the first one back downstairs and went to the kitchen sink to wash his hands. My heart soared as I observed him carefully pouring water over first one hand, then the other, saying three times, "I wash my hands. I wash my heart. I wash my mind."

When we sat together to eat our well-traveled meal, Caleb gave a divine perspective to our field trip, "God had a plan for us when that weird house oven didn't work and you had to go to the biker bar. These chicken pies are good."

DAY 5- FOOD, WORK AND WORSHIP

The children were ready to get back to work on their clay village project, wanting to add new details after touring the Holy Land. Before they went

---

[210] Perhaps you have guessed that this is when the children begged me to write this book and we began to remember the details of past years' Camp Mimi experiences.

[211] Recipe in Appendix, "Camp Mimi Eats."

upstairs to work on it, we gathered one last time at the Camp Mimi table with coloring and fact sheets about our last three subjects.

"What was the main food of ordinary people in Israel?"

They had no trouble answering this. It was prominent in everything we witnessed on our field trip. Everyone yelled out the answer together, "Bread!"

Caleb might have answered with the most enthusiasm since, even though his appetite for a variety of foods had increased considerably, his favorite food was still bread.

We now appreciated the effort it took to have bread for a meal. The farmer planted the grain (most likely wheat or barley), tended it, gathered it, and threshed it. The women ground the grain into flour using millstones. The girls brought water from the well. The women mixed the flour and water, with perhaps a bit of salt, into a simple dough, kneaded it to release the gluten, and then cooked it on the hot surface of their clay oven. The flatbread served as a staple and also as a utensil to eat other foods.

Bread was so important to each person that Jesus taught His disciples to pray, "Give us today our daily bread."[212] He also referred to Himself as "the bread of life."[213] What a relevant example to the people of His day to convey the message that His presence sustains every person in every way.

In a garden or on a rooftop, a family grew vegetables such as beans, cucumbers, garlic, leeks, onions and lentils. These could be used in stews, salads, or soups. They might also grow herbs such as cumin, fennel, dill, coriander, marjoram, mint, thyme, and mustard seed. Salt, too, was always available.

Fruits such as figs, pomegranates, grapes and olives were used for many purposes. They could be eaten fresh or dried and they could be crushed for wine or oil. And of course, near the Sea of Galilee, fish were plentiful.

With goats, sheep and chickens, the people could also enjoy milk, butter, cheese, curds, yogurt, and eggs.

We had a simple fill-in-the-blanks Bible Times Food Quiz that was fun to do together. Lots of questions were asked around the table about food.

"How was food stored if they couldn't eat it all at once?"

"They either dried or fermented certain foods."

"Did they eat desserts?"

"Foods were sweetened with fruit or honey."

"If you lived in Bible times what food would you prefer?"

"Bread!"

"Butter!"

"Bread *and* butter!"

---

[212] Matthew 6:11

[213] John 6:35

"Cheese!"

Of course, after spending so much time on this subject, everyone was ready for a snack.

After a break, we were on to the last area of community life in our village – worship. Worship was a common denominator for every Jewish village. Ideally, each person got to go to the Temple in Jerusalem once a year to worship. But to go once in your life was almost a requirement. The Temple was the center of worship in Israel. At the Temple, thousands of priests were employed on a rotating basis. Sacrifices were made and morning and evening prayer services were held.

In village life, the synagogue was the center of worship. There were no priests and no sacrifices in synagogues. Each synagogue was run by an elected committee, with a leader called "the synagogue ruler"[214] and his staff.

The *Shabbat* services began with prayers recited by one man standing in front of the Torah Ark, the cupboard containing the Torah scrolls. The reader stood on the *bema*, a raised platform in front of the people. Each man present put on his *tallit* and joined in the prayers.

After the prayers, the ruler took one of the scrolls from the Ark and gave it to the first of seven appointed readers. The texts were read in a prescribed order so that the whole Torah Law would be read within a set period of time. The text was in Hebrew. When the reader finished, he sat down in a chair called the Moses Seat and gave a sermon about the text. He may have spoken in Aramaic which is what many of the local people spoke.

Any Jewish man of age was qualified to read the Torah and preach. He was asked by the ruler of the synagogue.

When Jesus returned to Nazareth after His temptation in the wilderness, he went to the village synagogue and stood on the *bema* to read the designated scripture for the day. The scroll of Isaiah was handed to Him by the ruler. He unrolled it and read from Isaiah 61:1-2. Then He rolled up the scroll, gave it back to the ruler, and sat down in the Moses Seat. The eyes of everyone in the synagogue were fixed on Him as He proclaimed His succinct but mind-blowing sermon, "Today this scripture is fulfilled in your hearing."[215]

At the end of a service the alms and offerings were collected at the door as the people left.

---

[214] Luke 18:18-23

[215] Luke 4:14-21

We moved on to the next study for the morning – the professions that village men pursued. Near the Sea of Galilee, fishing was a big industry.

Some archeologists believe that Peter and his family had a fleet of fishing boats and a big business of salting, drying and exporting fish. Perhaps this was a business that helped support Jesus' ministry.

Many ordinary citizens were farmers, shepherds, and goatherds. And of course, skilled craftsmen included potters, tanners, makers of wine and olive presses, and weavers. In rural areas, most of these crafts were accomplished at home.

Another common area of work was what we typically call carpentry. It is documented that Jesus was the "son of a carpenter."[216] Many people assume that this was a trade in which He was trained by Joseph.

Because there are so few forests near the Galilee, and because we know that few ordinary people owned wooden furniture, many historians believe that the word[217] translated "carpenter" may also refer to stone masons. Without distorting scripture, it is possible that Jesus worked chiseling or carving stone or perhaps, even with mosaics.

The larger city of Sepphoris, a center of trade in the Galilee, was within walking distance of the much smaller village of Nazareth, which probably never had more than 450 people. In Sepphoris, archeologists have discovered the foundations of many frescoed and tiled rooms with intricate mosaic floors and private *mikveot*, the Jewish ritual baths, which proves that prosperous Jews lived there as well as Romans.

One of the discoveries in Sepphoris, reveals a magnificent Roman villa with what is considered the most beautiful mosaic of the third century on the floor of the banquet hall. Conlee and I once stood on site at this place for almost an hour, marveling at the intricacies of its execution. One of the female faces in the mosaic has been dubbed "the Mona Lisa of the Galilee."

It is highly unlikely that Jesus ever worked on any project depicting the human body in any form of art because of the second commandment about not making images of creatures. However, it is known that other beautiful mosaics in Sepphoris, date from the time of Jesus.

Therefore, it is possible that He walked to this nearby center of artistic endeavors six days a week to work in stone in some manner. Jesus and His disciples frequently used illustrations about stone masons to teach.[218]

At this point, I intended to introduce a fun project for the children, using mosaics. I had been saving broken plates and cups for quite a while and had a big box full of the colorful pieces. Conlee purchased five

---

[216] Matthew 11:55

[217] *Tekton* in Greek, a skilled craftsman referring to a carpenter, designer, construction engineer, stone mason, or architect.

[218] Luke 20:17, Acts 4:11, Luke 20:18, Romans 9:33, 1 Peter 2:4-5

concrete squares at the lawn and garden store. Our plan was to let the children set the pottery pieces in mortar on the concrete to make artistic stepping stones for the garden.

However, the children wanted to work on their clay village, so we scrapped the mosaics for another time. It was always necessary to be flexible!

After lunch, everyone worked diligently on the village. Jake perfected the common area around his well, with covered fruit and vegetable stands, and fish drying on a rack. In one corner he constructed the oven he liked so much, copied from the ones he studied on the Holy Land Tour. He even included a woman baking, and a person drawing water from the well, with water flowing from the bucket.

Anna made a simple stone shelter for her fluffy sheep, added grass for the pasture, and decided to add a small enclosed vineyard, detailed with tiny grapes on the staked vines.

Caleb's synagogue was centered with a *bema*, the elevated podium where the Torah was read, a Torah scroll, and the Seat of Moses, where the teacher for the Torah lesson sat. He included a worshiper, praising God with raised hands. Columns and benches around the sides completed the simple furnishings.

Sophie's houses were placed close together, one larger than the others. In some she had the sleeping mats spread out on the floor and in others she rolled them up to provide more living space. There were water jugs in the corners and the wealthiest homeowner had an oven inside the house. One home contained a simple loom because Sophie decided it housed a weaver.

Edie's farm area showed ripe grain growing, along with men harvesting the crop. She fashioned the kind of primitive tools they used for cutting the stalks and plowing, and included a collection place to gather the sheaves.

Together, they all worked on a grinding wheel at the edge of the community, along with some date palms.

When they finished, it was a true work of art. Amid many words of caution from everyone, Caleb and Papa carefully carried the village downstairs where it became the centerpiece for our celebration dinner and awards ceremony. We all dressed in our biblical finest as we enjoyed our *Shabbat* prayers and steak dinner.

Parents and older siblings were invited to come for brunch at ten o'clock the next morning. While the children packed their belongings and neatened the upstairs rooms, I put a breakfast casserole in the oven. By the time our guests arrived, we were all dressed one last time in our biblical clothing and ready to share every detail of our week's adventures.

It was so much fun to watch each child take a turn telling about which part of the village they had made and what it meant. They all had "back stories" to every detail.

Two hours later, everyone left and Papa and I looked at each other and laughed.

"We did it again!"

To be honest, sometimes during the middle of a Camp Mimi week, it seemed doubtful.

After ten years of Camp Mimi goodbyes, I knew it would be our last.

CAMP MIMI

EPILOGUE

Conlee and I were in a *SchlossHotel* in Germany for a few days' rest after leading a "Journey to Wholeness" conference. Surrounded by twelfth-century history and architecture, our room was up high in a cozy turret, overlooking the boat traffic on the Rhine. In the hallway outside our room stood a full set of knight's armor, which unnerved me every time we went in or out. Meals were served in a medieval hall and, because there were few other guests, it was very quiet and private.

We were there in the middle of November, almost four months since Camp Mimi Ten. It was off-season, which made our beautiful accommodations much more affordable, and with fewer guests.

We had arrived at our castle thankful and still enjoying the afterglow of Holy Spirit presence from the conference, but we were physically tired and looking forward to relaxing in a very refreshing environment.

I took my sketch book and watercolors downstairs to enjoy a few hours of uninterrupted alone time in the dining hall before the staff set up for dinner. Concentrating on the way the shadows turned to purple on the walls of the neighboring castle, and attempting to mix that unique hue, I suddenly heard from God.

It was unexpected but not unfamiliar. I have learned how to recognize the way He speaks to me. His "voice" comes to me as an impression deep inside and doesn't last long. In spite of its brevity, it is so unique and so powerful that I can't "un-hear" it.

Sometimes when He speaks to me it is like a large download of details conveyed in a single simple impression. This was one of those holy occasions. And this is what I wrote in my journal.

You pour yourself out to many people in different lands, most of whom you will never see again. You teach and minister to them the principles of wholeness that have changed your life and you see miracles in the lives of others. Yet, do not neglect those closest to you.

The years of Camp Mimi are over but the years of your relationship with your grandchildren are not. Do not neglect sharing the same principles with them that you share with others. Those closest to you will not receive these truths by osmosis. Be deliberate.

I began to see a single scene in picture form of exactly how this would happen. Sometimes, in ministry situations, God gives me a visual of what He wants to do. If I pay attention to it, it always happens.

Once, He showed me all the participants at a conference standing in a huddle up front and when they did, He began to do miracles among them, healing many. All I had to do at that conference was wait until He told me it was time. When I invited everyone to come forward, they all did, but it didn't seem right.

I remembered in the image He gave me that the people were all crowded, everyone touching. When the participants responded to my encouragement to come even closer so that they had to touch one another, something ignited in the Spirit world. Like a current of electricity, healing broke out from one to another. It happened exactly like He promised!

In the castle that afternoon, He showed me a picture of all the BodishBabes gathered at our house, all of us dressed up, around the Christmas tree. Somehow this picture melded together with the word from Him and when I shared it with Conlee, we prayed about it.

Out of that prayer, a plan developed.

On December 1, I sent the following text to all the BodishBabes (by far the most effective method of communication with their age group):

First Ever Dress-Up Camp Mimi Christmas Party
18 December, 6:00 PM
If even one of you can't make this date, we'll reschedule!
Love,
Mimi and Papa

We started getting responses right away.
I'll be there.
Works for me.
Are we dressing nice or is it casual?
Dress up!
Will do!
Have a test the next day, might have to leave early.
Sounds fun!

Everyone arrived looking beautiful. Our special dinner was a throw-back to the '70s when our sons were young. They used to love fondue dinners for special occasions. I had to go to some thrift stores to find cheap vintage fondue sets but my mission was accomplished.

I prepared chicken and beef cubes as well as vegetables to cook in boiling pots of oil at each end of the table. We even had chocolate fondue for dessert with all sorts of things to dip in the melted goodness. The dinner was a hit because none of them had ever done it before. They also enjoyed hearing stories about how their daddies had loved the same thing.

After dinner it was time to implement what God had illustrated for me in the German castle. We left the table and gathered by the Christmas tree. I explained to them the words I received from God about sharing with those dearest to us the principles that change lives.

I shared with them the simple prayer I always pray with people at our conferences:

Lord Jesus,
Speak to my heart.
Change my life.
Make me whole.

I explained that this simple prayer is so powerful because, when we ask Him to speak, His words bring life and they always change us, leading us to wholeness. Therefore, learning how to recognize His voice will be one of the most important things we ever do.

Conlee and I shared a few stories about some people who have told us that hearing what God said changed their life.

One man, who was headed for a disaster, told me, "I was ready to divorce my wife and leave my children because I found myself in an impossible situation, blaming my wife for the terrible marriage we had. When I finally took the time to be quiet and listen to God, He showed me what *I* was doing, about the sin in *my* life, and invited me to confess and receive His forgiveness. When I did, it changed my life and my marriage and the lives of my children. *What if I hadn't been listening?*"

The last question was left hanging. *What happens if we don't listen?*

After a moment, Conlee gave a wrapped gift to each child. There is always a child-like anticipation of opening a gift, no matter how old you are.

"Can I open it now?"

"Please do!"

They all unwrapped their gifts, each finding a different colored leather-bound journal. Their names were embossed in gold. On the opening page of each journal I had written the above prayer, both in English and in German, reminding them of how I heard God's instruction while we were in Germany.

Herr Jesus,
Sprich zu meinem Herzen.
Verändere mein Leben.
Mach mich heil.

They were admiring their own journals and each others' and thanking us as I said, "Each of you gets a pen, too. We are going to take a few moments of silence and ask God to speak to our hearts, telling us something He wants us to know. You might just want to wait for whatever He wants to say. Or you might want to ask Him a question. Then I want you to write the impressions He gives you on the first page. This will become your Listening Prayer Journal where you always have a place to keep a record of the important things He tells you and also a place to go back and read the history of those revelations."

We all prayed the simple prayer out loud together and then we waited. At first it was a bit awkward, but they closed their eyes and listened. Then, slowly, they began to write. That was a beautiful sight, knowing that they were hearing His voice and putting what they heard in their own handwriting.

When everyone seemed finished, we asked if any of them wanted to share what they heard and then recorded in their journals. They all did and the revelations were profound, each one appropriate to that child and his or her present circumstances. They ranged from finding one's life partner (for a college graduate) to being nice to one's siblings (for an elementary student).

Then Papa said he would like to lay hands on each one and pray for them to receive an anointing to always be able to hear God's voice above all the other voices that vie for their attention.

As I participated in what happened next, I was overwhelmed, thinking of the afternoon in the German castle when God showed me the brief picture of this little group gathering around the Christmas tree. The choreography to make that happen took time, effort and much planning from everyone involved. However, when we choose to obey what God orchestrates we have no idea how He will use it.

As Papa prayed for them, one at a time, everyone else gathered around, praying as well. Almost immediately, Holy Spirit fell. Soon, we were all on the floor in a huddle, holding one another and everyone was sobbing. We were transformed. God answered our prayer. He changed us as we listened to Him.

About the time when I remembered that someone had a test the next day, I gave them permission to leave but no one wanted to go. Alex, the oldest, said, "We should all pray for Mimi and Papa, too."

They gathered around the two of us and prayed powerfully. It was such an unexpected blessing that Conlee and I were undone.

Obeying God brings fruit that we don't even know exists.

We will continue the Camp Mimi Dress-Up Christmas Party tradition until God tells us to do something else. Meanwhile, I want to be listening.

At the beginning of this book, I asked you to declare, "I am unique!" I hope as you read about what the Bodishbaugh family learned to do to share our passions with the children in our life, that you had some "ah-ha" moments of your own, thinking of things you would like to share with someone close to you. No one else will be able to share your passions like you will.

Go for it! You will be nervous for sure. It's probably an unknown experience. But everyone alive loves having undivided attention paid to them and they know when you are sharing something that is important to you. It is a gift that is never forgotten.

Who in your life gave you such a gift? Perhaps it was a grandparent, teacher, coach, or parent. Their generosity of spirit helped form who you are today.

Perhaps you never experienced such a blessing and your heart hurts as you think of what you missed. I cannot emphasize enough the return of blessings you will receive in your own life when you dare to give to others. It is never too late to accumulate blessings!

Will you write me[219] to let me know how you implemented the principles of Camp Mimi? I know there will be more creative ideas released than I could ever imagine as you let loose of your restraints and say, "I'm doing it!"

Your efforts will inspire others and generations after you will be blessed. Again I say to you, "Have fun!"

Signa (*Mimi*)

---

[219] Send emails to Signa@signabodishbaugh.com

APPENDIX

ORDER FOR *SHABBAT SHALOM* MEAL

SHABBAT SHALOM!
KIDDUSH
A service for Shabbat Eve

And it was evening and it was morning – the sixth day. And the heavens and earth were finished. And on the seventh day God rested from His work. And God blessed the seventh day and made it a special day, because He Himself rested from His work. *Genesis 2:2*

Remember the day, Shabbat, to set it apart for God. *Exodus 20:8*

Blessed are You, O Lord, our God, King of the universe, whose commandments make us holy. In Your love You gave us a Shabbat rest to remind us of Your creative work and our redemption from slavery. Your love also provides us with times of refreshment and recreation.

1. Lighting the Candles – *Hadlakat Haneyrot*

Light was the first thing God created. In saying, "Let there be light" *(Genesis 1:3)*, He set in motion this wondrous universe. As this day of Shabbat begins, we take pleasure in joining with others around the world to celebrate and enjoy the gift of rest and renewal that the Father has given us. We honor Him and we honor His commandment to enjoy Shabbat.

The Candles are lighted by the Mother and Daughters

Blessed are You, Lord our God, King of the universe, Who has made us holy through His commandments and commanded us to kindle the Shabbat light.

Barukh atah Adonai Eloheynu, melekh ha'olam, asher kid'shanu b'mitzvotav v'tzivanu l'hadlik neyr shel Shabbat.

Mother: May it be your will, Lord my God, to be gracious to me and to my husband and to my children and to all my family, crowning our home with Your divine presence dwelling among us. Make me worthy to raise and affirm learned children and grandchildren who will dazzle the world with knowledge of You and Your goodness, and ensure that the glow of our lives will never be diminished.
Amen.

2. The Blessings - *Birkhat*

Both parents lay their hands on their children's heads.

To the Sons:
God make you like Ephraim and Manasseh.
Yisimkha Elohim k'Efrayim ukhiM'nashe.

Father: Just before he dies, Jacob blesses his two grandsons, Ephraim and Menashe. He says they should become role models for the Jewish people in the future. On the day that Jacob blessed them, he said, "In time to come, the people of Israel will use you as a blessing. They will say, 'May God make you like Ephraim and Menashe.'" *Genesis 48:20*

Ephraim and Menashe did in fact become role models worthy of emulation. Unlike those before them, including Cain and Abel, Isaac and Ishmael, Jacob and Esau, and Joseph and his brothers, Ephraim and Menashe were not rivals. Rather, Ephraim and Menashe were brothers united by their drive to perform good deeds.

To the Daughters:
God make you like Sarah, Rebecca, Rachel and Leah.
Yisimeykh Elohim k'Sarah, Rivkah, Racheyl v'Ley'ah

Each of the matriarchs had qualities that qualified them to be role models. The matriarchs were strong and laudable women. They endured difficult home lives, hardships in marriage, infertility, abduction, envy from other women, and difficult children. Nevertheless, these righteous women, through their individual passion, their partnerships with the patriarchs and their loyalty to God, succeed to build a nation.

To Both: **The Priestly Blessing** *Birkat haCohanim*

The Lord bless you and keep you, the Lord make His face to shine upon you, and give you His peace.
Ye'varech'echa Adonay ve'yish'merecha.
Ya'ir Adonay panav eilecha viy-chuneka.
Yisa Adonay panav eilecha, ve'yasim lecha shalom.

Children may be given a small treat

The blessing of Husband to Wife:
Who can find a capable wife?
Her value is far beyond that of pearls.
Her husband trusts her from his heart,
And she will prove a great asset to him.
She works to bring him good, not harm,
All the days of her life. *Proverbs 31:10-12*

The wife may be given a small treat

3. The Washing of the Hands—*N'tilat Yadayim*

Father: **Blessed are You, O Lord our God, King of the Universe, Who has caused us to wash our hands before You, as a symbol of the cleansing You do in us. AMEN.**
Barukh atah Adonay, Eloheynu melekh ha'olam, asher kidshanu b'mitzvotav v'tzivanu al n'tilat yadayim. Amen.

The hands, above all else on the human body, symbolize the way we are connected to the world, through contact with others, work and gesture. This is a symbolic act of being set apart for God's purposes and enjoyment for Shabbat.

The father or son may pass around a pitcher, basin and towel, pouring water on each person's hands and praying for each person as they are washed.

Who may go up to the mountain of the Lord?
Who can stand in His holy place?
Those with clean hands and pure hearts,
Who don't lift up their soul to an idol
Or swear by what is false.
They will receive blessing from the Lord
And justice from God, Who saves them. *Psalm 24:3-5*

4. The Wine and Bread – *Kiddush v'Hamotzi*

The Kiddush Cup
The father or son raises the cup of wine – the Kiddush cup – the symbol of rest and rejoicing, saying:
> **Blessed are You, O Lord our God, King of the universe, Creator of the fruit of the vine. AMEN.**
> *Barukh atah Adonay, Eloheynu melekh ha'olam, borey p'ri hagafen. Amen.*

The Kiddush cup (cup of blessing) is passed in silence around the table to each person as the father reads.

I am the vine and you are the branches. Those who stay united with Me, and I with them, are the ones who bear much fruit; because apart from Me you can bear nothing. This is how the Father is glorified – in your bearing much fruit. This is how you will prove to be My *talmidim* (disciples). John 15:5,8

The Challah
The father or son uncovers the Challah. There are two loaves, symbolic of the double portion of Manna that God provided for Shabbat in the wilderness. He raises the bread, the symbol of work and sustenance.

> **Blessed are You, O Lord our God, King of the universe, Who brings forth food from the earth. AMEN**
> *Barukh atah Adonay Eloheynu melekh ha'olam, ha'motzi lechem min ha'aretz. Amen.*

The Challah, a symbol of a human being's hands and of all food, is passed around the table, each person breaking off a large piece. It is not cut. A knife too closely resembles an instrument of war and swords are to be beaten into plowshares. The pieces of bread are sprinkled with salt and eaten. They may be dipped into condiments on the table such as olive oil or hummus.

This is an opportunity to thank God for the gift of meaningful work and to pray for those without work and without bread.

5. The Meal – *HaMazon*
L'Hayim!

6. After the Meal – *Birkat HaMazon*
Three blessings are said. They may be led by the father, son, or any of the family or guests, with everyone adding personal prayers.

First Blessing – *Birkat Hazan*
Bless God for providing food. Give thanks for God's goodness to all mankind.

Second Blessing – *Birkat Ha'arets*
Bless God for the land He has given us, our physical home and spiritual home, present and eternal.

Third Blessing – *Boneh Yerushalayim*
Pray for the *Shalom* (wholeness) of Jerusalem and the continued blessings of God for our future.

7. Psalm 126 – A Song of Ascents

The words were sung by worshipers as they climbed the Temple steps to worship Yahweh.

When the Lord brought back the captives to Zion, we were like men who dreamed.
Our mouths were filled with laughter, our tongues with songs of joy.
Then it was said among the nations, "The Lord has done great things for them."
The Lord *has* done great things for us, and we are filled with joy.
Restore our fortunes, O Lord, bring back all the captives, like streams in the Negev.
Those who sow in tears will reap with songs of joy.
He who goes out weeping, carrying seed to sow, will return with songs of joy, carrying sheaves with him.

SHABBAT SHALOM!

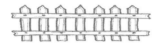

HAGGADAH FOR PASSOVER
Celebration of a Family *Seder* Meal

PASSOVER

Passover is the great Jewish feast of redemption and liberation, the memorial of the Israelites' deliverance from their bondage in Egypt. The word "Passover" means "deliverance," since in the story of the Exodus, Yahweh "passed over the houses of the children of Israel in Egypt. *(Exodus 12:27)*

Passover is also known as The Feast of Unleavened Bread, since in their haste to flee Egypt, "the people carried off their dough, still unleavened." *(Exodus 12:34)*

The lamb offered at each Pascal meal recalls the first Passover sacrifice, whose blood protected the Israelites from the avenging angel of Yahweh. *(Exodus 12:21-33)*

Passover is a festival of great joy, which reveals how God "led us from captivity to freedom, from sadness to joy, from mourning to fasting, from servitude to redemption, darkness to brilliant light." *(Mishnah, Pesachim 10:5)*

THE *SEDER* MEAL

The ritual meal which commemorates the events of the Exodus is called the *Seder* ("order" in Hebrew). The primary aim of the *Seder* is to transmit to future generations the story of the Exodus, the central event in Jewish history.

As a family shares a meal they symbolize their faith in the future and their thanksgiving for the past. As Christians, we are able to not only observe this meal but fully enter in as we make the connections with the Last *Seder* that Jesus celebrated with His disciples on the night of His betrayal, and our own Jewish roots which provided the context for Holy Eucharist.

Introduction

Leader: This night is the most important of all Jewish feasts. It is celebrated each year by God's people to help them remember how God protected them from the plagues that were sent by God upon Egypt, and how He delivered them from being slaves to Pharaoh so that they might be the holy people of God.

As we gather tonight to celebrate this ancient tradition in the presence of our loved ones, let us remember that we are rejoicing with the whole house of Israel, both young and old. This feast links us with the past because it has been handed down from generation to generation.

Jesus celebrated this feast every year of His earthly life with His family and friends. He did so for the same reason we do tonight: so that the story becomes our own! At His last Passover He gave it new meaning!

The story we will celebrate tonight is the powerful story of God's protection, redemption and freedom that so many of us have experienced through our Messiah Jesus. God is the same yesterday, today, and forever. Alleluia!

ALL: God is the same yesterday, today, and forever. Alleluia!

1. *Lighting the Festival Lights* (Mother)
Barukh atah Adonai Eloheinu, Melech ha'olam, Asher kid'shanu b'mitzvotav v'tzivanu l'hadlik ner shel Yom Tov.

Mother: Blessed are You, O Lord our God, King of the universe, Who brings light out of darkness, and Who has made us holy through Your Word, and Whom we honor with these lights tonight. **AMEN.**
(The mother lights two candles and fans their light to all at table).

2. *Kiddush – The Cup of Holiness* – *the first cup of wine*

Leader: Each cup of wine that we share in the *Seder* has a special meaning. The first cup (the *Kiddush*) is the Cup of Sanctification or Holiness. There will be four cups of wine during the meal. Pour only a small portion at a time because each cup will be consumed. The cups recall the four terms in the Exodus story which describe God's action in rescuing the Israelites from slavery:

I brought out   *(I bring you out)*
I saved   *(I save you)*
I delivered   *(I deliver you)*

I blessed   *(I bless* you)
We drink each of them in thanksgiving.
(The father stands and pours wine or grape juice for each person at the table. Everyone raises his glass together for the prayer).

Barukh atah Adonai Eloheynu, Melech ha'olam b'ray p'ri hagafen.

Father : Blessed are You, O Lord our God, King of the universe, Who created the fruit of the vine. **AMEN.**

Leader: Blessed are You, O Lord our God, King of the universe, Who has chosen us from among all peoples and made us holy through Your Word. For in Your love You have given us times for gladness, rejoicing, and festivals. You have given us this feast of unleavened bread as a celebration of the freedom You give us and in memory of our departure from slavery.

Blessed are You, O Lord our God, Who has kept us alive and made us holy, and You have brought us safely to this day of rejoicing. **AMEN.**
(All drink from the first cup, the Cup of Sanctification or Holiness, a reminder of being brought out of slavery and made holy unto God).

3. The Washing of the Hands
Leader: Blessed are You, O Lord our God, King of the universe, Who has caused us to wash our hands before You, as a symbol of the cleansing You do in us. **AMEN.**

(The father pours water over his own hands, then goes to each person with a pitcher, basin and towel, pouring water on each person's hands).

The hands, above all else on the human body, symbolize the way we are connected to the world, through contact with others, work, and gesture. This is a symbolic act of being set apart for God's purposes and enjoyment of His blessings.

4. The Karpas – The Parsley
(The father holds up the Seder Plate).
Leader: On the *Seder* Plate are sprigs of parsley. This reminds us of the hyssop branches that the Israelites used to apply the blood of the sacrificial lamb on the door posts of their homes. The blood brought life. Without the blood, there was death.

There is also a bowl of salt water, reminding us of the tears of sorrow that are shed when one is in slavery.

Take a piece of parsley and dip it in the salt water and eat it to remember. This pass it around the table.

Barukh atah Adonai Eloheynu, Melech ha'olam, boreh p'ri ha'adamah.

Father: Blessed are You, O Lord our God, King of the universe, Who brings forth fruit from the earth. **AMEN.**

Leader: "See, winter is past, the rains are over and gone. The flowers appear on the earth. The season of glad songs has come." *(Song of Songs 2:10-12)*

5. *The Breaking of the Matzah*

Leader: There is a covered plate of *Matzah* on the table. The father stands and lifts the covering to reveal the three pieces of *Matzah*. Remove the *middle* piece. It is called the *Afikomen*. It means "dessert.

This is the Bread of Affliction which Israel ate in the land of Egypt. It is a symbol of days of slavery and pain. Let all who are hungry come and eat. Let all who are in need come and celebrate the Passover.

Father: *(breaks the Afikomen overhead in two pieces)*
Our Passover is sacrificed for us.
ALL: Therefore let us keep the feast.

Leader: Bring one of the broken pieces of the *Afikomen* to me. Hide the other piece between the two whole pieces of *Matzah*. Pass the *Matzah* around the table so that each person can break off two pieces to put on his/her plate.

6. *The Four Questions*

Leader: The youngest person at the table will ask the following questions to those gathered.

Youngest:
    Why is this night different from all other nights?
    Why on this night do we only eat *Matzah*?
    Why on this night do we eat bitter herbs?
    Why on this night do we eat with special ceremony?

Leader: God commanded that parents tell their children the story of the Passover so that they will always remember how His character is to reach out to those who call out to Him and He rescues them from their misery. He loves to bring His children into freedom. Each of the foods we eat tonight reminds us of the story of freedom.

(The father passes around the Seder Plate so that each person may take just a little bit of each food, except for the bone, for his/her plate. All will wait to eat together).

The bitter herbs are called ***Maror.*** They symbolize the bitterness of the sufferings and the tears the Israelites shed in Egypt. In the Bible it says, "The Egyptians forced the children of Israel into slavery and made their lives unbearable with hard labor, work with clay and bricks, all kinds of work in the fields; they forced on them every kind of labor." It was all for a harsh master and they were not blessed. Let us taste the bitterness.

*(Everyone tastes the **Maror**).*

The ***Haroset*** is sweet and thick. It symbolizes the mixture of clay and straw the Israelites used to make bricks. It is a reminder of the hard labor they were forced to do in Egypt. Yet, there is a sweetness to it because even in the most difficult times there is always hope when we believe and trust God.

Take two pieces of *Matzah* and put some *Haroset* between them. It is like eating the mortar between the bricks.

(Everyone tastes the Matzah and Haroset).

The ***Beytza*** is the egg that symbolizes new life. The eldest sons in Egypt were given new life when the Angel of Death passed over. God provides a way for us to have new life when we are covered by the Blood of the Lamb, Messiah. Eat a bite of the egg and give thanks for new life.

(Everyone tastes the Beytza).

The ***Zeroah*** is the bone from a lamb, reminding us that while all the firstborn children of the Egyptians died, the children of the Hebrews were protected by the blood of the lamb that they spread over their doors. The Lamb of God provides eternal life.

(Everyone gives thanks for the Lamb of God).

7. ***The Cup of Judgment which leads to Salvation*** – *the second cup of wine*

Leader: The father pours the second cup of wine for each person. Do not drink it yet.

God sent Moses to Pharaoh to set God's people free. Pharaoh said, "No!" So God sent judgment upon all the Egyptians so that the promise of deliverance could be accomplished. The judgment was in the form of ten plagues. As we remember them, we will dip a finger into our wine and then touch our plate with it as a symbol of God's awesome power to save. Say after me, very slowly, the name of each plague as we "paint" it on our plate.

Blood – Frogs – Lice – Wild beasts – Pestilence –
Boils – Hail – Locusts – Darkness – Death of the firstborn

It is our joy and our duty to thank, praise, glorify, exalt, honor, bless, extol, and adore Him Who performed all these miracles for us and for those who have gone before us. He brought us all from slavery to freedom, from anguish to rejoicing, from mourning to fasting, from darkness to light, from bondage to redemption. Let us sing a new song to Him. Alleluia!

(Everyone recite Psalm 114 or sing a song of praise).

All lift the second cup of Salvation.
Barukh atah Adonai Eloheynu, Melekh ha'olam, b'ray p'ri hagafen.

Father : Blessed are You, O Lord our God, King of the universe, Who redeemed us and our forefathers, and brought us here tonight to celebrate Your presence.

Blessed are You, O Lord, Who has redeemed Israel.

Blessed are You, O Lord our God, King of the universe, Who created the fruit of the vine. **AMEN.**

Leader: Let us all drink of the Cup of Salvation together.

(Everyone drinks the second cup).

8. *The Testimony*

(There will be one or two brief testimonies of coming out from a slavery to sin and into freedom and salvation in Messiah Jesus. These may be spontaneous or planned ahead).

9. *The Cup of Deliverance* – *the third cup of wine*

(The father pours everyone the third cup of wine and prays).

Barukh atah Adonai Eloheinu, Melech ha'olam b'ray p'ri hagafen.

Father: Blessed are You, O Lord our God, King of the universe, Who created the fruit of the vine. **AMEN.**

Leader: Deliverance comes from the Lord. May Your blessings of deliverance be upon Your people. You, O Lord, will always be our hiding place. You will surround us with songs of deliverance. **AMEN.**

10. The Meal

Leader: Indeed our Passover Lamb, Messiah, has been sacrificed for us. So let us celebrate The Feast, not with the old leaven of malice and wickedness, but with the unleavened bread of sincerity and truth. **AMEN.**
ALL: L'Hayim!

(The third cup of wine is enjoyed with the meal. The meal is served and enjoyed with music and laughter. At the end of the meal, the children search for the hidden Afikomen. It is brought to the Leader and redeemed for a prize).

11. The Cup of Blessing – *the fourth cup of wine*

(The father pours everyone the fourth cup of wine).

Leader: For many hundreds of years this final cup of the *Seder* was the Cup of Elijah, filled and waiting for the prophet to reappear. It was believed and hoped that he would come as Messiah to God's people, bringing them holiness, salvation, and deliverance, the cups of which we drank tonight.

However, on the night of Jesus' last *Seder* meal with His disciples, He took this final cup at the end of the meal and said something they did not expect: a surprise from God.

This cup is the New Covenant in My Blood which is poured out for many.

No longer do we have to await Elijah, but we celebrate Jesus, the Messiah of God, Who has come to take away the sins of the world, to make us holy, to bring us God's salvation, to deliver us from sin, and to bless us.

In the words of St. Paul, (I Corinthians 10:16), "The cup of blessing which we bless, is it not a sharing in the Blood of Christ?"

Barukh atah Adonai Eloheynu, Melech ha'olam b'ray p'ri hagafen.

Father: Blessed are You, O Lord our God, King of the universe, Who created the fruit of the vine. **AMEN.**

Leader: Let us all stand and raise our Cup of Blessing to God Who has sent our Messiah.
 The All-Merciful!
 He shall reign over us forever and ever.
 The All-Merciful!
 He shall be blessed in heaven and on earth.
 The All-Merciful!
 He shall be praised through all generations.

The All-Merciful!
He shall be glorified among us and honored forever.
The All-Merciful!
He shall break the yoke off our neck and lead us to our land.
The All-Merciful!
He shall send abundant blessing on our house of prayer and our home.
The All-Merciful!
He has sent Jesus, our Messiah, Who brings us Good News.
The All-Merciful!
He shall bless those present and those on our hearts.
The All-Merciful!
He shall make us worthy of the Days of Messiah and the life of the world to come.
May the Lord, the Maker of Shalom, give Shalom to each of us and to the Land of Israel.
AMEN.

(Everyone drinks the fourth cup, the Cup of Blessing).

Leader: L'Hayim!

ALL: L'Hayim! Next year in Jerusalem!

THE CAMP MIMI SONG

"It's Camp Mimi time; it's Camp Mimi time.
We're all here and we're sitting in a line.
It's Camp Mimi time; it's Camp Mimi time.
We're waiting for Mimi to give us the sign.
(Girls) We're all here.
(Boys) We're all here.
(Girls) We're all here.
(Boys) We're all here.
We're all here and we're sitting in a line.
We're waiting for Mimi to give us the sign.
We're all here; it's Camp Mimi time!"

CAMP MIMI EATS

Favorite Camp Mimi Recipes

This is not intended to be a professional cookbook. Please note that these recipes are not tested by professional cooks in professional kitchens. In some cases they don't even have specific measurements. They are recipes that taste good to us and that our children love. Most of them have been taken from cookbooks I can no longer locate. They have been tweaked and doctored up to please our family, as I'm sure your own favorite recipes have too.

The recipes are given in the order they were mentioned in the book.

If I use some ingredients you don't like, feel free to improvise until it tastes just right to you. The number one rule in my home kitchen is: There are no rules.

Cooking should be fun and expressive of your personality. Experiment and get everyone involved. And my repetitive advice is always: "Have fun!"

SOPHIE'S CHICKEN SPIEDINI

In Italian, "spiedini" typically means something skewered. We adapted this to bake in the oven to simplify the cooking process, however you could take all the ingredients and make a marinade for the chicken and put them on rosemary skewers to grill. Just use less bread crumbs and more olive oil.

It's a perfect meal to cook while you begin Shabbat.

You'll need about 4 good-sized boneless, skinless chicken breasts for this. If they're already frozen, only let them partially thaw. If not frozen, stick them in the freezer for about 8 minutes. Then slice them horizontally to make them thinner.

Now, have fun pounding them flat with a meat mallet or the bottom of a heavy glass. Salt and pepper each one.

In a bowl, mix together:
- 1 cup seasoned bread crumbs
- ½ cup grated *Parmigiano Reggiano*[220] cheese
- ½ cup extra virgin olive oil (or more to make moist, not soaked)
- ¼ cup finely chopped onion
- ¼ cup fresh chopped parsley
- 2 cloves fresh chopped garlic

Lay out a pounded slice of the chicken and place a dollop of the breadcrumb mixture on it. Spread and press it down with your fingers. Then add a slice of Swiss or Provolone cheese and a slice of prosciutto ham and more Parmesan, if you have any left, in the center and roll it up. You may have to secure with a toothpick.

Line them up in a greased baking dish and place a bay leaf *between* each *Spiedini*. If you have any mixture left over, just spread it on top.

Cover with foil and bake at 325°F for 60 minutes.

Then uncover and bake at 300° for 10 minutes.

Serves 8.

SCHNITZEL MIT SPÄTZLE

In Germany, Schnitzel is any kind of meat (we used pork tenderloin) coated in breadcrumbs and fried. Spätzle is a German type of egg noodle that is fun to make if you have the time. You also can buy them frozen and, with a good sauce, it is the perfect accompaniment to the Schnitzel.

This Spätzle recipe was based on one developed by Tyler Florence.

SPÄTZLE
(SPAY-zlee)

Combine:
- 1 cup flour
- 1 teaspoon salt
- ½ teaspoon ground pepper

Into the flour mixture, add:
- 2 eggs

---

[220] This is the best Parmesan cheese. If you can afford it, use it. You can also substitute Romano or Pecorino. It's also best to grate your own. Don't use the powdery kind in the can!

¼ cup milk

Mix this together until it is thick and smooth. Then let it rest for 10 or 15 minutes. (This is a good time to prepare the meat).

Bring about 3 quarts of well-salted water to a boil in a large pot. Then reduce it to a simmer. Here comes the fun part:

Take a colander (or you can also use a slotted spoon) and, with a spatula, push the dough through the holes into the simmering water. Do it in batches so they don't get crowded. Stir them gently so they don't stick together. They only need to cook for 3-4 minutes. They're done when they float to the top. Then take them out, rinse in cold water to stop the cooking, and let them rest until you're almost ready to eat.

Right before you serve them, melt 3 Tablespoons of butter in a skillet and toss the *spätzle* to warm them up and give them a little color.

They're really good with some chopped chives and salt and pepper added.

SCHNITZEL

The Schnitzel is pretty easy too. We used a pork tenderloin that we sliced into 1-inch pieces and pounded thin. Each slice was seasoned with salt and pepper, and then dipped into flour, beaten egg and bread crumbs, in that order. The children loved doing this.

Brown the meat in a skillet in a little bit of olive oil or bacon fat. It doesn't take long, maybe 2-3 minutes on each side. Set the meat aside while you make the sauce.

When you finish cooking the meat you will have brown bits in the bottom of your skillet which are perfect for making the sauce. You can add mushrooms, onions, herbs, or whatever you like.

Melt about 4 Tablespoons of butter into the hot skillet where you browned the meat and mix in 4 Tablespoons of flour. Cook this for a couple of minutes, then slowly whisk in 3 cups of hot beef stock, stirring until it thickens. It will take about 5 minutes and you need to stir it constantly. Season it to your taste with salt and pepper.

Put the cooked cutlets into this luscious sauce and let them warm up for a minute or two.

Serve with the hot buttered *Spätzle*.

TORTILLAS

It's really easy to buy tortillas at the grocery store. But, if you've never tried this, you have no idea how good homemade tortillas taste and how easy they are to make. The only reason I buy tortillas anymore is to cut them into triangles and deep fry them into corn chips. I'm going to give you recipes for both flour and corn tortillas, but using masa and making corn tortillas is the most authentic.

My recipe for Flour Tortillas is adapted from one by Ree Drummond.

FLOUR TORTILLAS

Combine:
    2 ½ cups flour
    2 ½ teaspoons baking powder
    1 teaspoon salt
Add:
    ½ cup of lard or shortening and cut into flour mixture until it looks like coarse crumbs.

Slowly pour in 1 cup hot water, stirring and then gently kneading until it forms a ball and is less sticky. Cover and let it rest for at least an hour. Roll into balls about the size of ping-pong balls, cover and let rest 20-30 minutes.

When you're ready to cook the tortillas, heat a cast iron skillet or griddle to high heat. Flatten the balls between plastic wrap in a tortilla press. If you don't have a press you can roll them out until they are very thin. If you are going to make tortillas very often, it definitely is worth the small investment to buy a cast iron press.

Throw them on the hot griddle. If they burn immediately, turn down the heat. You have to experiment with a couple to get the heat just right. They only cook for 20-30 seconds on each side. Keep them warm in a towel or wrapped in foil if you're going to serve them right away. If not, let them cool and store in a tight container to heat later in the microwave or oven.

CORN TORTILLAS

Making Corn Tortillas is even easier and these are the ones I usually make.

To 2 cups of corn tortilla flour *(masa)*, add about 1¾ cups of warm water and a teaspoon of salt. Mix this with your hands until it is the consistency of play dough. You may need to keep adjusting the amounts of *masa* and water to reach this goal, but these proportions work for me. This dough will dry out quickly so when you are not using it, be sure to cover it well.

Make small balls and use your tortilla press to flatten the balls between plastic wrap. [Jake is an expert at this!]

Cook on a hot griddle *(comal)* for only 30 seconds on one side. Flip and cook about 1 minute on the other side. Then flip again for another 10 seconds. The tortillas should puff slightly in places and take on a bit of color like freckles.

Delicioso!

POSOLE
(po-SOH-lay)

Posole *means "hominy" in Spanish. Hominy is dried corn that is soaked in a mild solution of lye, lime, or wood ash. When ground, this becomes* masa. Posole *is a typical soup/stew from Mexico and is often served at celebrations like weddings, birthdays, baptisms, New Year's Day, and, of course, Cinco de Mayo. However, most people are not familiar with either hominy or* Posole. *Try it with your homemade tortillas for a fun, south-of-the-border family meal. There are lots of variations of this recipe using green or red sauce, beef or pork, but this one with pork is the one we like. I also included a slow-cooker method with pork if you're going to be gone all day. It's* delicioso, *too!*

Get about a 2-pound pork loin or boneless pork shoulder to serve 6-8 people. Then rub a spice mix all over the pork. I use equal mixtures of:

Cumin, garlic powder, and smoked paprika.

Sprinkle with salt and pepper.

Line a baking pan with foil and place the pork, covered with sliced onions. Pour ½ cup of water in the pan and cover tightly with foil. Roast at 275°F until the meat is very tender. It will take about 5-6 hours. Then let the pork rest until it cools.

Shred the pork into bite-sized pieces. Then skim the fat from the juices left in the pan.

All this can be done ahead! I have gotten to this point and frozen everything until I needed it. Now, to make it *Posole!*

Heat some oil in a large pot and sauté chopped onion until translucent. This takes about 5 minutes.

Add minced garlic and cook another 2 minutes. Don't let it burn! Then, stir in

    6 cups chicken broth

    1 28-oz can undrained pinto beans

    1 28-oz can drained white hominy

    1 28-oz can of diced tomatoes

    1 Tablespoon oregano

    2 teaspoons cumin

Add as much heat as you like with ground chiles of your choice. I like anchos, but you can leave this out if you don't want the heat.

Bring this all to a boil and then reduce to a simmer for about 30 minutes.

Finally, add the shredded pork to the *posole* and let it simmer, uncovered for another 30 minutes. Season with salt and pepper to your taste.

When you serve it, garnish with traditional toppings chosen from the following: shredded cabbage, shredded cheese, cilantro, lime wedges, sliced radishes, and avocado. Don't forget your warm, homemade tortillas!

If you are going to be busy all day but still want to enjoy the same tasty flavors, try the slow cooker method.

Cut your pork loin or boneless pork shoulder into 1-inch cubes. (You can also do this with chicken). Place it in the slow cooker.

Add:
- 2 cans chicken broth
- 1 can beef broth
- 1 can drained hominy

For seasoning, add
- 2 cans enchilada sauce
- 1 diced onion
- ¼ cup chopped cilantro
- 4 cloves minced garlic
- 2 teaspoons dried Mexican oregano
- 2 Tablespoons of cumin
- ½ teaspoon of salt .

Mix all together well and cook on high setting for 4-5 hours or on low setting for 6-7 hours.

If you like more heat, add some dried chiles. Serve with the garnishes mentioned above. And don't forget the tortillas!

CAPRESE SALAD
(Alex's favorite)

This couldn't be simpler for an elegant summer salad. It's positively imperative to have fresh, ripe tomatoes. There are many ways to arrange everything artistically on a serving platter which totally disguises how easy it is to put it together.

Slice perfect tomatoes and arrange on a plate.
In between each tomato, put a slice of fresh mozzarella cheese.
Tuck fresh basil leaves between each slice.
Salt and pepper everything.
Drizzle with a good olive oil.

Then, for the final delicious touch, drizzle with reduced balsamic vinegar.

Buon Appetito!

GRILLED PIZZA

This takes ordinary pizza to a new level. Everyone loves to make their own so it's a fun party activity as well as the meal. Make the pizza dough up to 3 days before. It keeps well in the refrigerator if covered tightly. The recipe makes enough for 4 small pizzas. It doubles, triples, and quadruples easily. The key to making this fun and not work is to have all your topping ingredients prepped in little bowls beside your grill.

The Dough

Mix together:
- 2 envelopes active dry yeast (2 ¼ teaspoons = 1 envelope)
- ½ teaspoon warm water
- ½ teaspoon sugar

Cover and let bloom (activate) for 30 minutes.

To the yeast mix, add:
- 3 cups unbleached white flour
- 1 teaspoon salt
- 3 Tablespoons olive oil
- 5-7 Tablespoons water

When it comes together, knead until it forms a smooth ball. Dust with flour, cover, and let rise 1 hour.

You can make this up to three days ahead and keep in a tightly sealed container in the refrigerator. When ready to use, form the dough into baseball-sized balls. Place on parchment paper and cover for 1 hour. Then roll out as thin as possible on floured board and place on hot grill over direct heat, cooking for 2-3 minutes. Brush with olive oil and flip over onto a board or tray next to the grill.

Put your favorite toppings on the grilled side. Place pizza back on grill over indirect heat, with cover closed until all cheese is melted and it is sufficiently cooked through, slightly charred on the edges (about 3 minutes).

When you get the hang of it, you can start another pizza over the direct heat while the first one finishes on the indirect side.

Our favorite toppings include pizza sauce (without spreading it all the way to the edges), cheeses, salamis, sautéed onion, sautéed mushrooms, cooked sausage, sliced jalapeños, and a drizzle of olive oil.

If you're adventurous you can add squash, eggplant, artichokes, an egg, or any kinds of meats. You're only limited by your imagination and taste buds. Keep whatever ingredients you choose to 3 or 4 at the most. The thicker the toppings, the harder it is to get the crust crunchy.

CHALLAH
(HA-la)

Challah *is a traditional Jewish braided egg bread eaten on Shabbat and other Jewish holidays. It is delicious with the addition of fruit, but since we usually serve it during a meal, we omit the sweet ingredients.*

In a large bowl, combine
¼ cup of lukewarm water
1 envelope of dry activated yeast (2 ¼ teaspoons)
1 teaspoon sugar
Let it bloom (activate) for 10 minutes. It should look foamy.

In another bowl, mix together
1¼ cup lukewarm water
1 egg
3 egg yolks
1/3 cup honey
2 Tablespoons oil
2 teaspoons salt
Whisk this into the yeast mixture.

Add 4 ½ - 6 cups unbleached white flour, a little at a time, stirring until you have to use your hands to knead the dough. Add only enough flour until it feels pliable and smooth.

Place the dough in an oiled bowl, turning the dough over until all sides are coated. Cover with a clean, damp kitchen towel for 1 hour.

Punch the dough down to remove all air pockets, cover and let it rise for 1 more hour.

Punch dough down again and divide into two equal portions.

Braid the *challah* by dividing each portion into three equal portions and, laying them on a floured board, rolling each one into a long strand, as long as you want your loaf to be. Then, laying the three strands side by side, braid them as you would braid girls' hair, tucking in the ends. Place each braided loaf on a parchment covered baking sheet.

Brush each loaf with an egg wash made with 1 egg beaten with 1 Tablespoon water and ½ teaspoon salt. Reserve the left-over egg wash.

Let the braids rise 30-45 minutes.

Have your oven preheated to 350°F. Bake for 20 minutes. Then remove the braids from the oven, brush again with the remaining egg wash, turn the baking sheets around, and bake 20 minutes longer – a total of 40 minutes.

During the second time in the oven you can sprinkle the tops with sesame seeds, a traditional topping. Our children didn't care for the seeds.

If, during the baking time, the *challah* looks too brown, cover it with foil and continue baking, removing the foil for the last 2 minutes.

You know it's done when you tap it and hear a hollow sound (the "*challah*" sound). Let them cool on a wire rack.

Your whole house will smell wonderful! Shabbat Shalom!

PITA

It is believed that people have been making pita bread since 2500 BC. You will enter into ancient history when you tackle this fun kitchen project. You also can cook pita on the outdoor grill, on a stovetop comal, or over an open camp fire. It's like magic to watch the dough rounds puff up, and even more fun to fill the hollow shells with something yummy!

This makes 8 pitas.

Put 1 teaspoon of activated dry yeast into ¼ cup lukewarm water. Stir it until it looks creamy. Add ½ Tablespoon olive oil, ½ Tablespoon honey, and ¾ cup warm water. Whisk until all is combined.

Gradually mix in 2 ½ cups unbleached flour. It will form a rough dough. Cover the bowl and let it rest for 20 minutes.

Put the dough on a floured board and sprinkle with 1 teaspoon salt.

Knead for about 10 minutes till the dough is smooth and springy.

Put into a large bowl with room for the dough to triple in size. Cover and let rise 1 hour.

On the floured board, divide the dough into 8 pieces and make balls. Cover with a kitchen towel for 30 minutes.

If you're really in a hurry, just go ahead and roll them out. There will be little difference. This 30 minute period is when I preheat my oven to 500°F with a baking or pizza stone heating up. You want it really hot to bake properly.

Roll each ball into a flat disc, about 6 inches in diameter and 3/8 inch thick. If you are going to stack them, flour each one lightly.

Place the discs directly on a hot baking stone in the preheated 500°F oven for about 5 minutes. You might want to turn the pita over half way through cooking but it isn't necessary.

If you grill your pita outside, preheat the grill to high and place each disc directly on the grill. Close the lid for 2 minutes. Turn over with tongs when they have puffed. Cook on the other side until done, about 2-3 minutes more.

LATKES
(LOT-keys)

Latkes are potato pancakes that must be fried in oil when served at Hanukkah. This is because of the miracle of the supply of oil for the Menorah in the Jewish Temple.

It's important to use a starchy potato (like a russet or baking potato) to get the best results. The potatoes and onions should be grated, either with a hand grater, or, with a food processor to make it easier. Remove as much liquid as possible from the grated vegetables. The most effective way is to put them in a clean kitchen towel and squeeze out all the liquid you can.

Traditionally, latkes were fried in olive oil, but peanut oil is a good substitute. Many Jewish cooks add some schmaltz (rendered chicken fat) to the oil for flavor. Schmaltz is full of cholesterol but is tasty.

If you're not trying to cook kosher, you can start with frozen hash browns in a package. Just make sure they are thawed and well-drained.

12 russet potatoes, grated
3 medium onions, grated
4 eggs, beaten lightly
5 Tablespoons matzah meal (or bread crumbs or flour)
3 teaspoons salt
1 teaspoon pepper

Form individual pancakes by hand and carefully slide into the ¾ inch deep hot oil in a heavy skillet. Leave room between pancakes.

When browned on one side, carefully turn and cook until brown on the other and the edges are crisp. Remove with a spatula and drain on paper towels. Serve immediately or keep warm in a hot oven.

Traditionally, latkes are served with applesauce.

BOLOGNESE SAUCE

This is my adaptation of two of the most famous Bolognese sauces in the culinary world: those of chefs Alice Waters and Marcella Hazan. They have left us great culinary legacies for every kitchen.

Mix together :
1 onion, diced

1 celery stalk, diced
1 carrot, diced
2 garlic cloves, diced
(This is called the soffritto in Italian or mirepoix in French).

Cook 4 strips of bacon in a large Dutch oven until crisp and remove to paper towels.

Cook the *soffritto* in the bacon drippings until tender, about 10 minutes.

While the vegetables are cooking, brown 1 pound of ground meat (can be a combination of beef and pork) in a separate skillet. Drain, if necessary, and return meat to skillet. Season well with salt and pepper..

Add 1 cup dry white wine to the meat and let the alcohol cook out, scraping any bits from the bottom of the skillet.

Add meat to the tender vegetables along with
> 1 can diced tomatoes
> 1 teaspoon dried thyme
> 1 teaspoon dried sage
> 1 bay leaf
> Pinch of dried red pepper flakes
> 1 teaspoon salt.

Stir well, then add
> ½ cups milk
> 2 cups beef broth

Let simmer, uncovered, for at least 3 hours. If it gets dry, you can add a little water.

The flavors are even better if made a few days before and reheated. Perfect for a hearty pasta with sprinklings of grated Parmesan and chopped parsley.

PASTA

All children love pasta and love to make it even more. If you are going to make it at home you need a pasta machine. You just can't roll it thin enough by hand. There are attachments for electric mixers but we use the hand-crank version.

On a clean counter, make a volcano looking pile of 3 cups of unbleached flour. Make an indentation in the middle and pour in 3 cracked eggs, 3 Tablespoons of olive oil, and 1 Tablespoon salt.

Begin mixing it all together with a fork, using a bench scraper to gather in the sides. When it's partially mixed, ditch the fork and use your hands. Knead it until it reaches the proverbial "smooth as a baby's bottom" stage. Form it into a ball and let it rest for 30 minutes.

Divide into portions and roll out in your pasta machine, following the machine's instructions, going as thin as you desire.

From this stage, you can cut the pasta any size you like from very narrow *vermicelli* to very wide *pappardelle*, which is ideal for the Bolognese Sauce.

Cook the pasta in heavily salted water at the rolling boil stage for only about 2 minutes. Fresh pasta cooks very quickly. Drain and serve. Do not rinse.

If you are going to put it in a sauce it will continue to cook. If you serve it buttered as a side dish, you may want to cook it an extra minute.

ROASTED CHICKEN

This is the scripted version we gave the BodishBabes to teach them the basics of a classic roasted chicken. Each one had a part and the result was as professional as any I have ever eaten. I suggest cooking two chickens at a time and using left-overs for other recipes such as Chicken-Rice Casserole or Chicken Salad.

The Ingredients:
- 1 whole chicken, 2½ -4 pounds
- Salt and pepper
- 1 lemon
- 4-5 thyme sprigs (and other herbs of your choice)
- 2 Tablespoons olive oil
- 4 Tablespoons softened butter

Preheat oven to 375°F.

JAKE: Pull packet out of inside the chicken and wash the chicken thoroughly.
ANNA: Zest the lemon.
SOPHIE: Cut lemon in half and place inside chicken. Salt inside chicken.
EDIE: Put thyme sprigs inside chicken, along whatever other herbs you desire. (*Rosemary, sage, basil, chives, etc. are all tasty*).
CALEB: Tie up legs and wings with kitchen twine.
SOPHIE: Salt and pepper outside of chicken.
ANNA: Rub outside of chicken with olive oil.

Roast in pan with rack for 60-65 minutes until the meat thermometer reaches 160°F in the thickest part of the thigh and the juices run clear.

Remove from oven, cover with foil, and allow to rest before cutting. This will raise the internal temperature to 165°F, which is safe to eat.

EDIE:	Mix soft butter and lemon zest together with a small amount of salt. Spread the lemon-butter on the warm cut chicken.

EVE'S APPLE CRUMBLE

This is another scripted recipe from Camp Mimi Culinary School. We have made it numerous times since and it is always a favorite.

Here's what you need:
- 1 ½ pounds apples
- 1 Tablespoon orange marmalade
- 1 orange
- ½ teaspoon cinnamon
- ½ cup flour
- 4 Tablespoons butter
- ¼ cup oats
- ¼ cup brown sugar
- Extra butter

JAKE:	Preheat oven to 375°F. Grease a pie plate with some butter.
CALEB:	Peel and core the apples.
SOPHIE:	Assist Caleb peeling and coring apples.
PAPA:	Cut the apples into slices.
JAKE:	Put the apple slices in a saucepan.
ANNA:	Zest the orange. Squeeze the juice onto the apple slices.
EDIE:	Add marmalade and cinnamon to the apples. Stir. Cook gently on low heat until apples are soft.
JAKE:	Spoon the apples evenly into the pie plate and set aside.
CALEB:	Measure flour into a mixing bowl and whisk in orange zest.
SOPHIE:	Add 4 Tablespoons butter to the flour and mix with your fingers until it looks like fine bread crumbs.
EDIE:	Add oats to bowl.
ANNA:	Add brown sugar to bowl.
JAKE:	Stir well to make the topping.
CALEB:	Sprinkle the topping evenly over the apples.
SOPHIE:	Put several dots of butter over topping.

Bake for 30-35 minutes until the topping is golden brown. Serve warm with ice cream.

MANNA COOKIES

This is a simple sugar cookie recipe with the additions of two biblical ingredients for Manna, honey and coriander. There are lots of things you can do with these cookies. Dip them in chocolate, crumble on ice cream, layer in trifle, decorate with icing or candies, – or just eat them!

3 eggs
1 cup unbleached flour
½ teaspoon ground coriander
1 cup honey
1/8 teaspoon salt
½ teaspoon vanilla

Preheat oven to 350°F.
Beat eggs, honey, and vanilla.
Sift together flour, salt, and coriander. Mix all together.
Spread thinly on well-buttered baking sheet.
Bake 10-15 minutes.
Cool and cut into squares.

JACOB AND ESAU'S RED LENTIL STEW

I wouldn't sell my birthright for this but it is really good! Perfect for a hearty meal in cold weather. This is the Camp Mimi script for cooking it as a team. The children used a small electric processor to chop the vegetables. You can simmer it on the stove all day or place all ingredients in a slow cooker set for 4-5 hours on high or 6-7 hours on low. Stir occasionally.

Here's what you need:
2 onions, chopped
2 cloves garlic, minced
8 cups chicken broth
1 ½ cups red lentils
1 can beans (use what you have or what you like – red beans, pinto beans, etc.)
1 can chick peas (garbanzo beans)
1 small can diced tomatoes
½ cup diced carrots
½ cup chopped celery
2 Tablespoons lemon juice
1 large potato, diced

Fresh cilantro, chopped
Ground cumin
1 Tablespoon olive oil
Spices to taste (salt, pepper, cayenne, etc.)

SOPHIE:	Chop onions and garlic. Place in pot.
JAKE:	Add chicken broth to pot.
EDIE:	Add beans to pot.
ANNA:	Add chick peas to pot.
CALEB:	Chop carrots and celery. Place in pot.
JAKE:	Add lemon juice to pot.
EDIE:	Chop potato. Place in pot.
ANNA:	Chop cilantro. Place in pot.
SOPHIE:	Add olive oil and spices to pot.
CALEB:	Add red lentils to pot and stir everything together.

Cook all day. When done, you can puree until smooth with an immersion blender or serve as is.

CHICKEN HAND PIES

This is a great travel food. You can make these, wrap them individually, unbaked in foil, and then freeze. Or you can make and bake, and then freeze. Either way, they are delicious and a BodishBabe favorite.

Make a chicken pot pie filling, put some in delicious little pie crusts, and then bake. Here is a filling I make along with my all-time favorite pastry recipe. I can make this with my eyes closed and it's always perfect.

The filling recipe doubles well. I recommend making two batches of dough rather than doubling one batch.

The Pastry:
Mix together:

    2 cups unbleached flour
    ½ teaspoon baking powder
    ½ teaspoon salt

Cut in:

    ¾ cup vegetable shortening (it should look like fine bread crumbs)

Add:

    ½ cup iced water

The key is: **Do Not Overmix!**

Form into a disc, wrap in plastic wrap, and refrigerate until ready to roll out.

The Chicken Filling:
Melt 2-4 Tablespoon butter in large skillet.
Add
    ½ onion, diced
    1 carrot, diced
    1 stalk celery, diced
    Salt and pepper
Cook until softened, about 10 minutes.
Add:
    1 clove garlic, minced
    1 teaspoon Italian seasoning
Cook for 1 minute, stirring.
Add:
    4 Tablespoons flour
Cook for about 2 minutes, until raw flour taste is gone
Deglaze pan with:
    ½ cup white wine
Whisk in:
    1 cup chicken broth
    1 teaspoon Dijon mustard
    1 teaspoon Worcestershire
Add:
    ½ cups frozen green peas
    1½ cups diced, cooked chicken breast
Simmer until thickened into a gravy. Adjust seasonings. Remove from heat.

Roll out pastry as if for pie crust and cut into rounds, using a large cookie cutter, drinking glass, or even soup bowl as a template. Spoon some of the chicken mixture onto one half of each round, fold over and crimp with a fork to seal.

Brush with egg wash (1 egg with splash of water) on tops of each.

Make a small slit on top to vent.

Bake at 375°F until golden brown, about 30 minutes. Let cool at least 10 minutes before eating.

ACKNOWLEDGEMENTS

I am so grateful for all my friends who begged me to write the story of our Camp Mimi adventures, and who affirmed this project when Conlee and I were just flying by the seats of our pants, one year after another.

Many thanks to The Writers of the Roundtable of Fayetteville, Arkansas (a loving critique group). I am also indebted to Joy Hilley, Deborah Parrott, and others who made significant contributions to seeing this book come to life.

I couldn't have done it without Alex, my oldest granddaughter, whose talents provided the beautiful cover and immense technical advice.

And consistently Conlee has been by my side, reading through the manuscript numerous times, often out loud! Proof-reading took far longer than necessary because he and I would get side-tracked with sweet memories along the way.

Of course, my love and constant gratitude to our beloved BodishBabes. It was all for you!

ABOUT THE AUTHOR

Signa's passion for living life to the fullest is reflected in her varied interests. Painting, cooking, gardening, decorating, writing, the Bible, and teaching are some of the arts she explores and shares with others.

She has lived with the love of her life (Conlee) for nearly sixty years. They share their own facsimile of an Italian villa in northwest Arkansas, with two black Labs.

Contact her at Signa@SignaBodishbaugh.com

Made in the USA
San Bernardino, CA
11 January 2018